Software Testing

Principles and Practices

Srinivasan Desikan
Director of Quality Assurance,
Agile Software Enterprise, Pvt. Ltd.
Bangalore, India

Gopalaswamy Ramesh
Consultant and Adjunct Professor,
International Institute of Information Technology,
Bangalore, India

PEARSON
Education

Editor in Chief: **Prof H N Mahabala**

Titles under the series include

- Software Maintainence
  Gopalaswamy Ramesh and *Ramesh Bhattiprolu*

- Software Testing – Principles & Practices
  Gopalaswamy Ramesh and *Srinivasan Desikan*

- Managing Global Software Projects
  Gopalaswamy Ramesh

- Mobile Computing – Technology Applications & Service Creation
  Asoke K Talukder and *Roopa Yavagal*

ISBN 81-7758-121-X

First Impression, 2006
Second Impression, 2006
Third Impression, 2006
Fourth Impression, 2007
Fifth Impression, 2007

Published by Dorling Kindersley (India) Pvt. Ltd., licensees of Pearson Education in South Asia.

Head Office: 482, F.I.E., Patparganj, Delhi 110 092, India.
Registered Office: 14 Local Shopping Centre, Panchsheel Park, New Delhi 110 017, India.

Laser typeset by Sigma Publishing Services, Chennai.

Printed in India by Baba Barkha Nath Printers.

*Parents and Teachers who taught me the basics of
life and science*
                            —Srinivasan Desikan

*To the millions of differently-abled children who are
wrongly labeled as "disabled" because of the
inappropriate testing practices of our society*
                            —Gopalaswamy Ramesh

Preface

The area of Software Testing has acquired wider horizon and significance. Customers demand defect-free products; regulatory authorities go into the nitty-gritties of the tests to which a piece of software is subjected, just as pharmaceutical companies are mandated to declare how they test the medicines before release. Most of the books available in the market cover theoretical aspects but very few address practical aspects. To prepare students for a career in testing and to be of value to practitioners, one needs to provide a pragmatic and practical view of testing, together with the right balance of people, process and technology. This forms the basis of the book *Software Testing—Principles and Practices*.

As the title indicates, the emphasis is on principles and practices. The material in this book has already been "Beta tested" by several universities in India such as Anna University in Chennai and International Institute of Information Technology, Bangalore (iiit-b). iiit-b is also adopting the book for its Center of Excellence in Software Engineering and for its M. Tech students. Some concepts in the book have already been presented to practitioners through international conferences and guest lectures by the authors of this book.

We have added chapters that focus on managing geographically distributed teams. This is especially relevant for multinational companies, where distributed teams in different continents work together in unison—developing, testing and delivering products to a global customer base. We have included emerging trends in testing like extreme testing, ad hoc testing and so on.

The contents of this book can be used by practitioners to understand the state-of-practice in the testing industry. The chapters on Metrics and Measurements, Test Planning, Test Management and Automation have been added to help the practitioners adopt these concepts at work. We have provided sufficient academic rigor to satisfy the contents of the syllabi of the various universities.

We would like to thank Ms. Gayathri Chandrasekar, Test manager at eFunds, Chennai for her contributions to some of the chapters in the book.

Srinivasan Desikan

Gopalaswamy Ramesh

Acknowledgements

My gratitude are due to all the previous organizations (Wipro, Novell and Talisma) I worked with, for the opportunities and infrastructure provided for me to learn the practical aspects of testing on the job. My thanks are due to the testing professionals across the globe for interacting with me and providing insights and information for developing this book. Last but not least, I would like to thank my wife, son and daughter for their sacrifices and support. I can be contacted at srinivasan.desikan@gmail.com.

Srinivasan Desikan

I want to thank Prof. Mahabala, my Guru, who has been a champion in software testing and has motivated me towards it. He has been a constant source of inspiration for me over the last twenty years. I also want to thank Department of Computer Science, Anna University and International Institute of Information Technology, Bangalore for enabling me to teach courses of Software Testing, which has been a source of learning. My special thanks are also due to Prof. Sadagopan, for the iiit-b Press initiative. Finally, I want to acknowledge the support of my family, without which I would not have been able to give the kind of effort that went in to making this book. I can be contacted at gopalaswamy_ramesh@yahoo.com.

Gopalaswamy Ramesh

Foreword

Software is becoming ubiquitous in today's world. Customers' expectations have increased dramatically and the old fate of resignation that "it is OK for software to fail, we will have to live with it" is simply no longer applicable. Software is expected to work, meeting customers' changing demands, first time and every time, consistently and predictably. Earlier, the software systems were used for back-office and non-critical operations of organizations. Now, more and more critical applications are implemented globally. This increased expectation for error-free functioning of software has increased the demand of quality output from software vendors. In turn, we have seen over the last decade, the focus has shifted from mere programming and development to a more holistic goal of producing software that works first time and all the time, thus increasing the focus on testing.

Testing, in particular, has attracted significant interest over the past decade. Consider the following which tell the whole story:

- ✠ the number of testing jobs has increased several-fold providing bright career opportunities;
- ✠ the compensation levels of testing functions are on the rise;
- ✠ testing has become a major opportunity for outsourcing;
- ✠ the number of conferences and similar events dedicated to testing has increased significantly over the last five years; and
- ✠ more and more professionals are considering software testing as a career.

The modus operandi of testing has also undergone a radical change, in keeping with the increased demand. Firstly, globalization is here to stay. Organizations today exploit the geographic time difference and global talent by distributing development and testing teams in different continents, working seamlessly together. In order to be successful in this new world order, an organization must master the art of working in geographically distributed teams. Secondly, testing has transformed from an ad hoc and haphazard hit-and-run attempt to a systematic, planned activity, complete with all processes and measured by scientific metrics. Thirdly, success in testing today requires careful exploitation of various technologies to meet product's time to market requirements. Test automation—automation of all parts of testing life cycle—has become a necessity and is no longer a luxury. Finally, people's aspirations in testing careers have also undergone a sea change—a successful organization should show career paths for the testing professionals and nurture their talent to ensure their longevity within the organization and within the testing profession.

This book has come in a timely fashion to address the needs of the practitioners and aspiring testing professionals and students. Both Ramesh and Srinivasan, have brought to life their forty years of combined practical experience. This book covers some of the aspects which are essential for the industry's success, but seldom touched upon by other books, such as:

- ✠ Balance between theory and practice: Most books, while trying to give theoretical rigor, try to oversimplify the real-life problems. The authors have consistently started from what exists in the real world and have provided the theoretical foundation to address the real life situations.

- ✠ Balance between people, process, and technology issues: Successful organizations work systematically, exploit technologies and leverage people. The authors have successfully resisted the temptation of only discussing "cool technology issues" at the expense of practicalities. As an example, you will find coverage of topics like automation (which is technology-intensive), people and organizational structures (which is people-centric) and test organization and reporting (which is process-focused).

- ✠ A solid exposure to foundations, from a practical viewpoint of the practitioners: The authors have covered all the different types of testing extensively. As an example, topics like Internationalization—which are considered esoteric—are discussed at length.

- ✠ This book is the first that I know which has recognized and articulated the importance of globalization and explicitly discussed the various global team structures possible and the issues thereof. This clearly demonstrates the authors experience of leading global software testing teams.

- ✠ This book covers some of the recognized methodologies for testing which have been accepted and presented in several international testing conferences throughout the world.

In addition to all of the above, the practical exercises given at the end of the chapters will expose the reader to the realities of testing. The authors' experience of teaching full semester courses on software testing is evident in various exercises. I am confident that with the advent of this book, such courses will spread to various colleges and universities, thereby formalizing software testing as a discipline and widening the net for developing more competent testing professionals.

I wish the book and the authors all success in their continuing endeavor to create an environment where software testing is considered a critical phase of any software development life cycle, careers in testing are valued significantly, and testing develops as an engineering discipline.

Vikram Shah

Vikram Shah is currently serving in the Board of Directors in Silver Software, IT-People and is an active member of BiTES (Board for IT education Standards by Karnataka government). Vikram mentors start-up Information Technology companies. Vikram Shah is an industry veteran with more than 30 years of experience and is currently serving as MD of Independent Technologies (INTEC). In the past he served as MD of several companies such as Mahindra British Telecom, Novell, Andiamo Software, and Talisma Software. Vikram did BS in Electronics from BITS, Pilani and MS in Computer Science from University of California, Berkeley.

Contents

Part I | Setting the Context

Part II | Types of Testing

3 White Box Testing   47

4 Black Box Testing   73

7   Performance Testing   169

8   Regression Testing   193

Part III   Select Topics in Specialized Testing

Part IV   People and Organizational Issues in Testing

14 Organization Structures for Testing Teams   320

Part V | Test Management and Automation

16	**Software Test Automation**	**387**

17	**Test Metrics and Measurements**	**420**

Part ONE

Setting the Context

This part of the book sets the context for the entire book. We start Chapter 1, *Principles of Testing*, by discussing the changes in the software scenario over the last few years and the demands that these changes make on software quality. We translate these demands into eleven basic principles which provide anchors to rest of the chapters. In Chapter 2, *Software Development Life Cycles*, we define key terms like verification, validation, quality assurance, and quality control, go into the details of the various life cycle models and the implication of these models on verification and validation activities. We also introduce the concepts of entry and exit criteria that will be necessary to understand the different phases of testing later in the book.

Principles of Testing

CHAPTER 1

In this chapter—

1.1   CONTEXT OF TESTING IN PRODUCING SOFTWARE

Almost everything we use today has an element of software in it. In the early days of evolution of software, the users of software formed a small number compared to the total strength of an organization. Today, in a typical workplace (and at home), just about everyone uses a computer and software. Administrative staff use office productivity software (replacing the typewriters of yesteryears). Accountants and finance people use spreadsheets and other financial packages to help them do much faster what they used to do with calculators (or even manually). Everyone in an organization and at home uses e-mail and the Internet for entertainment, education, communication, interaction, and for getting any information they want. In addition, of course, the "technical" people use programming languages, modeling tools, simulation tools, and database management systems for tasks that they were mostly executing manually a few years earlier.

> In god we trust, everything else we test

The above examples are just some instances where the use of software is "obvious" to the users. However, software is more ubiquitous and pervasive than seen in these examples. Software today is as common as electricity was in the early part of the last century. Almost every gadget and device we have at home and at work is embedded with a significant amount of software. Mobile phones, televisions, wrist watches, and refrigerators or any kitchen equipment all have embedded software.

Another interesting dimension is that software is being used now in mission critical situations where failure is simply unacceptable. There is no way one can suggest a solution of "please shutdown and reboot the system" for a software that is in someone's pacemaker! Almost every service we have taken for granted has software. Banks, air traffic controls, cars are all powered by software that simply cannot afford to fail. These systems have to run reliably, predictably, all the time, every time.

This pervasiveness, ubiquity, and mission criticality places certain demands on the way the software is developed and deployed.

First, an organization that develops any form of software product or service must put in every effort to drastically reduce and, preferably, eliminate any defects in each delivered product or service. Users are increasingly intolerant of the hit-and-miss approach that characterized software products. From the point of view of a software development organization also, it may not be economically viable to deliver products with defects. For instance, imagine finding a defect in the software embedded in a television after it is shipped to thousands of customers. How is it possible to send "patches" to these customers and ask them to "install the patch?" Thus, the only solution is to do it right the first time, before sending a product to the customer.

Second, defects are unlikely to remain latent for long. When the number of users was limited and the way they used the product was also predictable (and highly restricted), it was quite possible that there could be defects in the software product that would never get detected or uncovered for a very long time. However, with the number of users increasing, the chances of a defect going undetected are becoming increasingly slim. If a defect is present in the product, *someone* will hit upon it sooner than later.

Third, the nature of usage of a product or a service is becoming increasingly unpredictable. When bespoke software is developed for a specific function for a specific organization (for example, a payroll package), the nature of usage of the product can be predictable. For example, users can only exercise the specific functionality provided in the bespoke software. In addition, the developers of the software know the users, their business functions, and the user operations. On the other hand, consider a generic application hosted on the Internet. The developers of the application have no control over how someone will use the application. They may exercise untested functionality; they may have improper hardware or software environments; or they may not be fully trained on the application and thus simply use the product in an incorrect or unintended manner. Despite all this "mishandling," the product should work correctly.

Finally, the consequence and impact of every single defect needs analysis, especially for mission critical applications. It may be acceptable to say that 99.9% of defects are fixed in a product for a release, and only 0.1% defects are outstanding. It appears to be an excellent statistics to go ahead and release the product. However, if we map the 0.1% failure in mission critical applications, the data will look like this.

✠ A total of 10,000 incorrect surgery operations per week.
✠ Three airplane crashes every day.
✠ No electricity for five hours every week.

For sure, the above data is unacceptable for any individual, organization, or government. Providing a workaround, such as "In case of fire, wear this dress," or documenting a failure, such as "You may lose only body parts in case of a wrong airplane landing" would not be acceptable in cases of mission critical applications.

This book focuses on software testing. Traditionally, testing is defined as being narrowly confined to testing the program code. We would like to consider testing in a broader context as encompassing all activities that address the implications of producing quality products discussed above. Producing a software product entails several phases (such as requirements gathering, design, and coding) in addition to testing (in the traditional sense of the term). While testing is definitely one of the factors (and one of the phases) that contributes to a high quality product, it alone cannot *add* quality to a product. Proper interaction of testing with other phases is essential for a good product. These interactions and their impact are captured in the grid in Figure 1.1.

Figure 1.1

Relationship of effectiveness of testing to quality of other phases.

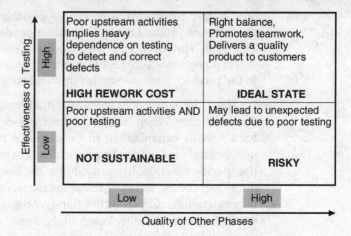

	Poor upstream activities Implies heavy dependence on testing to detect and correct defects **HIGH REWORK COST**	Right balance, Promotes teamwork, Delivers a quality product to customers **IDEAL STATE**
	Poor upstream activities AND poor testing **NOT SUSTAINABLE**	May lead to unexpected defects due to poor testing **RISKY**

Effectiveness of Testing (High / Low)

Quality of Other Phases (Low / High)

If the quality of the other phases is low and the effectiveness of testing is low (lower left-hand corner of the grid), the situation is not sustainable. The product will most likely go out of business very soon. Trying to compensate for poor quality in other phases with increased emphasis on the testing phase (upper left-hand corner of the grid) is likely to put high pressure on everyone as the defects get detected closer to the time the product is about to be released. Similarly, blindly believing other phases to be of high quality and having a poor testing phase (lower right-hand side of the grid) will lead to the risky situation of unforeseen defects being detected at the last minute. The ideal state of course is when high quality is present in all the phases including testing (upper right-hand corner of the grid). In this state, the customers feel the benefits of quality and this promotes better teamwork and success in an organization.

1.2   ABOUT THIS CHAPTER

In this chapter, we discuss some of the basic principles of testing. We believe that these principles are fundamental to the objective of testing, namely, to provide quality products to customers. These principles also form the motivation for the rest of the book. Thus this chapter acts as an anchor for the rest of the book.

The fundamental principles of testing are as follows.

1. The goal of testing is to find defects before customers find them out.

2. Exhaustive testing is not possible; program testing can only show the presence of defects, never their absence.

3. Testing applies all through the software life cycle and is not an end-of-cycle activity.

4. Understand the reason behind the test.

5. Test the tests first.

6. Tests develop immunity and have to be revised constantly.

7. Defects occur in convoys or clusters, and testing should focus on these convoys.

8. Testing encompasses defect prevention.

9. Testing is a fine balance of defect prevention and defect detection.

10. Intelligent and well-planned automation is key to realizing the benefits of testing.

11. Testing requires talented, committed people who believe in themselves and work in teams.

We will take up each of these principles in the subsequent sections. Where appropriate, we will illustrate the principle with a simple story from outside the arena of information technology to drive home the point.

1.3   THE INCOMPLETE CAR

Car Salesman: "The car is complete—you just need to paint it."

Eventually, whatever a software organization develops should meet the needs of the customer. Everything else is secondary. Testing is a means of making sure that the product meets the needs of the customer.

We would like to assign a broader meaning to the term "customer." It does not mean just *external* customers. There are also *internal* customers. For example, if a product is built using different components from different groups within an organization, the users of these different components should be considered customers, even if they are from the same organization. Having this customer perspective enhances the quality of all the activities including testing.

We can take the internal customer concept a step further where the development team considers the testing team as its internal customer. This way we can ensure that the product is built not only for usage requirements

Sales representative / Engineer: "This car has the best possible transmission and brake, and accelerates from 0 to 80 mph in under 20 seconds!"
Customer: "Well, that may be true, but unfortunately it accelerates (even faster) when I press the brake pedal!"

but also for testing requirements. This concept improves "testability" of the product and improves interactions between the development and testing teams.

We would like to urge the reader to retain these two perspectives—customer perspective and perspective of quality not being an add-on in the end, but built in every activity and component right from the beginning—throughout the book.

If our job is to give a complete car to the customer (and not ask the customers to paint the car) and if our intent is to make sure the car works as expected, without any (major) problems, then we should ensure that we catch and correct all the defects in the car ourselves. This is the fundamental objective of testing. Anything we do in testing, it behoves us to remember that.

> Testing should focus on finding defects before customers find them.

1.4   DIJKSTRA'S DOCTRINE

Consider a program that is supposed to accept a six-character code and ensure that the first character is numeric and rests of the characters are alphanumeric. How many combinations of input data should we test, if our goal is to test the program *exhaustively*?

The first character can be filled up in one of 10 ways (the digits 0–9). The second through sixth characters can each be filled up in 62 ways (digits 0–9, lower case letters a–z and capital letters A–Z). This means that we have a total of $10 \times (62^5)$ or 9,161,328,320 valid combinations of values to test. Assuming that each combination takes 10 seconds to test, testing all these valid combinations will take approximately 2,905 years!

Therefore, after 2,905 years, we may conclude that all valid inputs are accepted. But that is not the end of the story—what will happen to the program when we give *invalid* data? Continuing the above example, if we assume there are 10 punctuation characters, then we will have to spend a total of 44,176 years to test all the valid and invalid combinations of input data.

All this just to accept one field and test it exhaustively. Obviously, exhaustive testing of a real life program is *never* possible.

All the above mean that we can choose to execute only a subset of the tests. To be effective, we should choose a subset of tests that can uncover the maximum number of errors. We will discuss in Chapter 4, on Black Box Testing, and Chapter 3, on White Box Testing, some techniques such as equivalence partitioning, boundary value analysis, code path analysis, and so on which help in identifying subsets of test cases that have a higher likelihood of uncovering defects.

> Testing can only prove the presence of defects, never their absence.

Nevertheless, regardless of which subset of test cases we choose, we can never be 100% sure that there are no defects left out. But then, to extend an old cliché, nothing can be certain other than death and taxes, yet we live and do other things by judiciously managing the uncertainties.

1.5   A TEST IN TIME!

Defects in a product can come from any phase. There could have been errors while gathering initial requirements. If a wrong or incomplete requirement forms the basis for the design and development of a product, then that functionality can never be realized correctly in the eventual product. Similarly, when a product design—which forms the basis for the product development (*a la* coding)—is faulty, then the code that realizes the faulty design will also not meet the requirements. Thus, an essential condition should be that every phase of software development (requirements, design, coding, and so on) should catch and correct defects at that phase, without letting the defects seep to the next stage.

Let us look at the cost implications of letting defects seep through. If, during requirements capture, some requirements are erroneously captured and the error is not detected until the product is delivered to the customer, the organization incurs extra expenses for

✠   performing a wrong design based on the wrong requirements;

✠   transforming the wrong design into wrong code during the coding phase;

✠   testing to make sure the product complies with the (wrong) requirement; and

✠   releasing the product with the wrong functionality.

In Figure 1.2 the defects in requirements are shown in gray. The coloured figure is available on page 457. As you can see, these gray boxes are carried forward through three of the subsequent stages—design, coding, and testing.

Figure 1.2

How defects from early phases add to the costs.

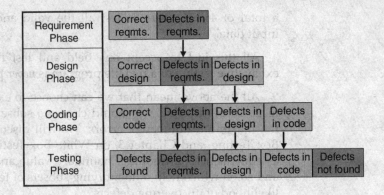

> The cost of building a product and the number of defects in it increase steeply with the number of defects allowed to seep into the later phases.

When this erroneous product reaches the customer after the testing phase, the customer may incur a potential downtime that can result in loss of productivity or business. This in turn would reflect as a loss of goodwill to the software product organization. On top of this loss of goodwill, the software product organization would have to redo all the steps listed above, in order to rectify the problem.

Similarly, when a defect is encountered during the design phase (though the requirements were captured correctly, depicted by yellow), the costs of all of the subsequent phases (coding, testing, and so on) have to be incurred multiple times. However, presumably, the costs would be lower than in the first case, where even the requirements were not captured properly. This is because the design errors (represented by yellow boxes) are carried forward only to the coding and testing phases. Similarly, a defect in the coding phase is carried forward to the testing phase (green boxes). Again, as fewer phases are affected by this defect (compared to requirements defects or design defects), we can expect that the cost of defects in coding should be less than the earlier defects. As can be inferred from the above discussion, the cost of a defect is compounded depending on the delay in detecting the defect.

Hence, smaller the lag time between defect injection (i.e., when the defect was introduced) and defect detection (i.e., when the defect was encountered and corrected), lesser are the unnecessary costs. Thus, it becomes essential

Figure 1.3

Compounding effect of defects on software costs.

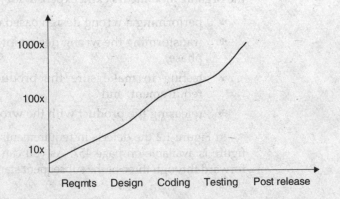

to catch the defects as early as possible. Industry data has reaffirmed these findings. While there is no consensus about the costs incurred due to delay in defect detection, a defect introduced during the requirement phase that makes it to the final release may cost as much as a thousand times the cost of detecting and correcting the defect during requirements gathering itself.

1.6   THE CAT AND THE SAINT

A saint sat meditating. A cat that was prowling around was disturbing his concentration. Hence he asked his disciples to tie the cat to a pillar while he meditated. This sequence of events became a daily routine. The tradition continued over the years with the saint's descendents and the cat's descendents. One day, there were no cats in the hermitage. The disciples got panicky and searched for a cat, saying, *"We need a cat. Only when we get a cat, can we tie it to a pillar and only after that can the saint start meditating!"*

Testing requires asking about and understanding what you are trying to test, knowing what the correct outcome is, and why you are performing any test. If we carry out tests without understanding why we are running them, we will end up in running inappropriate tests that do not address what the product should do. In fact, it may even turn out that the product is modified to make sure the tests are run successfully, even if the product does not meet the intended customer needs!

"Why one tests" is as important as "What to test" and "How to test."

Understanding the rationale of why we are testing certain functionality leads to different types of tests, which we will cover in Part II of the book. We do white box testing to check the various paths in the code and make sure they are exercised correctly. Knowing which code paths should be exercised for a given test enables making necessary changes to ensure that appropriate paths are covered. Knowing the external functionality of what the product should do, we design black box tests. Integration tests are used to make sure that the different components fit together. Internationalization testing is used to ensure that the product works with multiple languages found in different parts of the world. Regression testing is done to ensure that changes work as designed and do not have any unintended side-effects.

1.7   TEST THE TESTS FIRST!

An audiologist was testing a patient, telling her, "I want to test the range within which you can hear. I will ask you from various distances to tell me your name, and you should tell me your name. Please turn back and answer." The patient understood what needs to be done.

Doctor (from 30 feet): What is your name?
...

Doctor (from 20 feet): What is your name?
...

Doctor (from 10 feet): What is your name?
Patient: For the third time, let me repeat, my name is Sheela!

From the above example, it is clear that it is the audiologist who has a hearing problem, not the patient! Imagine if the doctor prescribed a treatment for the patient assuming that the latter could not hear at 20 feet and 30 feet.

Tests are also artifacts produced by human beings, much as programs and documents are. We cannot assume that the tests will be perfect either! It is important to make sure that the tests themselves are not faulty before we start using them. One way of making sure that the tests are tested is to document the inputs and expected outputs for a given test and have this description validated by an expert or get it counter-checked by some means outside the tests themselves. For example, by giving a known input value and separately tracing out the path to be followed by the program or the process, one can manually ascertain the output that should be obtained. By comparing this "known correct result" with the result produced by the product, the confidence level of the test and the product can be increased. The practices of reviews and inspection and meticulous test planning discussed in Chapter 3 and Chapter 15 provide means to test the test.

> Test the tests first—a defective test is more dangerous than a defective product!

1.8   THE PESTICIDE PARADOX

Defects are like pests; testing is like designing the right pesticides to catch and kill the pests; and the test cases that are written are like pesticides. Just like pests, defects develop immunity against test cases! As and when we write new test cases and uncover new defects in the product, other defects that were "hiding" underneath show up.

Every year, pests of various types attack fields and crops. Agriculture and crop experts find the right antidote to counter these pests and design pesticides with new and improved formulae. Interestingly, the pests get used to the new pesticides, develop immunity, and render the new pesticides ineffective. In subsequent years, the old pesticides have to be used to kill the pests which have not yet developed this immunity and new and improved formulae that can combat these tougher variants of pests have to be introduced. This combination of new and old pesticides could sometimes even hinder the effectiveness of the (working) old pesticide. Over time, the old pesticides become useless. Thus, there is a constant battle between pests and pesticides to get ahead of the other. Sometimes pesticides win, but in a number of cases, the pests do succeed to defy the latest pesticides. This battle results in a constant churning and evolution of the nature and composition of pesticides.

> Tests are like pesticides—you have to constantly revise their composition to tackle new pests (defects).

There are two possible ways to explain how products develop this "immunity" against test cases. One explanation is that the initial tests go a certain distance into the code and are stopped from proceeding further because of the defects they encounter. Once these defects are fixed, the tests proceed further, encounter newer parts of the code that have not been dealt with before, and uncover new defects. This takes a "white box" or a code approach to explain why new defects get unearthed with newer tests.

A second explanation for immunity is that when users (testers) start using (exercising) a product, the initial defects prevent them from using the full external functionality. As tests are run, defects are uncovered, and problems are fixed, users get to explore new functionality that has not been used before and this causes newer defects to be exposed. This "black box" view takes a functionality approach to explain the cause for this "more we test more defects come up" phenomenon.

An alternative way of looking at this problem is not that the defects develop immunity but the tests go deeper to further diagnose a problem and thus eventually "kill the defects." Unfortunately, given the complex nature of software and the interactions among multiple components, this final kill happens very rarely. Defects still survive the tests, haunt the customers, and cause untold havoc.

The need for constantly revising the tests to be run, with the intent of identifying new strains of the defects, will take us to test planning and different types of tests, especially regression tests. Regression tests acknowledge that new fixes (pesticides) can cause new "side-effects" (new strains of pests) and can also cause some older defects to appear. The challenge in designing and running regression tests centers around designing the right tests to combat new defects introduced by the immunity acquired by a program against old test cases. We will discuss regression tests in Chapter 8.

1.9   THE CONVOY AND THE RAGS

All of us experience traffic congestions. Typically, during these congestions, we will see a convoy effect. There will be stretches of roads with very heavy congestions, with vehicles looking like they are going in a convoy. This will be followed by a stretch of smooth sailing (rather, driving) until we encounter the next convoy.

Testing can only find a part of defects that exist in a cluster; fixing a defect may introduce another defect to the cluster.

Defects in a program also typically display this convoy phenomenon. They occur in clusters. Glenford Myers, in his seminal work on software testing [MYER-79], proposed that the *probability of the existence of more errors in a section of a program is proportional to the number of errors already found in that section*.

This may sound counter-intuitive, but can be logically reasoned out. A fix for one defect generally introduces some instability and necessitates another fix. All these fixes produce side-effects that eventually cause the convoy of defects in certain parts of the product.

From a test planning perspective, this means that if we find defects in a particular part of product, more—not less—effort should be spent on testing that part. This will increase the return on investments in testing as the purpose of testing is find the defects. This also means that whenever a product undergoes any change, these error-prone areas need to be tested as they may get affected. We will cover these aspects in Chapter 8, Regression Testing.

Figure 1.4

The number of defects yet to be found increases with the number of defects uncovered.

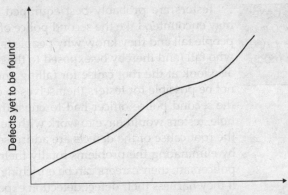

A fix for a defect is made around certain lines of code. This fix can produce side-effects around the same piece of code. This sets in spiraling changes to the program, all localized to certain select portions of the code. When we look at the code that got the fixes for the convoy of defects, it is likely to look like a piece of rag! Fixing a tear in one place in a shirt would most likely cause damage in another place. The only long-term solution in such a case is to throw away the shirt and create a new one. This amounts to a re-architecting the design and rewriting the code.

1.10   THE POLICEMEN ON THE BRIDGE

There was a wooden bridge on top of a river in a city. Whenever people walked over it to cross the river, they would fall down. To take care of this problem, the city appointed a strong policeman to stand under the bridge to save people who fall down. While this helped the problem to some extent, people continued to fall down the bridge. When the policeman moved to a different position, a new policeman was appointed to the job. During the first few days, instead of standing at the bottom of the bridge and saving the falling people, the new policeman worked with an engineer and fixed the hole on the bridge, which had not been noticed by the earlier policeman. People then stopped falling down the bridge and the new policeman did not have anyone to save. (This made his current job redundant and he moved on to do other things that yielded even better results for himself and the people...)

> Prevention is better than cure—you may be able to expand your horizon much farther.

Testers are probably best equipped to know the problems customers may encounter. Like the second police officer in the above story, they know people fall and they know why people fall. Rather than simply catch people who fall (and thereby be exposed to the risk of a missed catch), they should also look at the root cause for falling and advise preventive action. It may not be possible for testers themselves to carry out preventive action. Just as the second police officer had to enlist the help of an engineer to plug the hole, testers would have to work with development engineers to make sure the root cause of the defects are addressed. The testers should not feel that by eliminating the problems totally their jobs are at stake. Like the second policeman, their careers can be enriching and beneficial to the organization if they harness their defect detection experience and transform some of it to defect prevention initiatives.

Defect prevention is a part of a tester's job. A career as a tester can be enriching and rewarding, if we can balance defect prevention and defect detection activities. Some of these career path possibilities are encapsulated in a three-stage model in Chapter 13, Common People Issues. We will now visit the question of what is the right balance between defect prevention and defect detection.

1.11   THE ENDS OF THE PENDULUM

The eventual goal of any software organization is to ensure that the customers get products that are reasonably free of defects. There are two approaches to achieving this goal. One is to focus on defect detection and correction and the second is to focus on defect prevention. These are also called *quality control* focus and *quality assurance* focus.

Testing is traditionally considered as a quality control activity, with an emphasis on defect detection and correction. We would like to take a broader view of testing and believe that there are aspects of testing that are also defect prevention oriented. For example, one of the aspects of white box testing, discussed in Chapter 3, is static testing, that involves desk checking, code walkthroughs, code reviews, and inspection. Even though these are traditionally considered as "quality assurance" activities, planning for overall testing activities with an intent to deliver quality products to customers, cannot be done effectively unless we take a holistic view of what can be done using quality assurance and what can be done with quality control (or the traditional definition of testing).

Quality assurance is normally associated with process models such as CMM, CMMI, ISO 9001, and so on. Quality control, on the other hand, is associated with testing (that form the bulk of the discussions in this book). This has caused an unnatural dichotomy between these two functions. Unfortunately, organizations view these two functions as mutually exclusive, "either–or" choices. We have even heard statements such as "with good processes, testing becomes redundant" or "processes are mere overheads—we

Figure 1.5

Quality control and quality assurance as two methods to achieve quality.

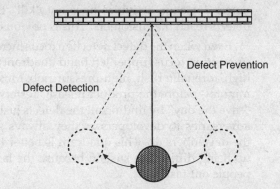

Defect Prevention

Defect Detection

can find out everything by testing." It is almost as if there are two schools of thought at either extremes of a pendulum—one rooting for defect prevention (quality assurance) focus and the other rooting for the defect detection (quality control) focus. It is also common to find an organization swinging from one extreme to another over time, like a pendulum (Figure 1.5).

Rather than view defect prevention and defect detection as mutually exclusive functions or ends of a pendulum, we believe it is worthwhile to view these two as supplementary activities, being done in the right mix. Figure 1.6 gives a defect prevention—defect detection grid, which views the two functions as two dimensions. The right mix of the two activities corresponds to choosing the right quadrant in this grid.

When the focus on defect prevention is low, the emphasis on the use of appropriate standards, reviews, and processes are very low. This acts as an ideal "breeding ground" for defects. Most of the effort in ensuring quality of a product is left in the hands of the testing and defect detection team. If the focus on defect detection is also low (represented by the lower left-hand quadrant), this is a bad state for an organization to be in. Lack of testing and

Figure 1.6

Relationship between defect detection focus and defect prevention focus.

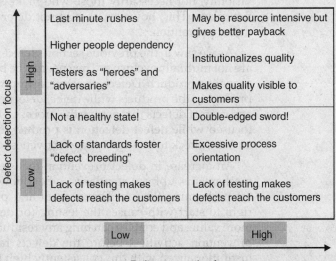

Defect detection focus	Low defect prevention focus	High defect prevention focus
High	Last minute rushes Higher people dependency Testers as "heroes" and "adversaries"	May be resource intensive but gives better payback Institutionalizes quality Makes quality visible to customers
Low	Not a healthy state! Lack of standards foster "defect breeding" Lack of testing makes defects reach the customers	Double-edged sword! Excessive process orientation Lack of testing makes defects reach the customers

Defect prevention focus

defect detection activities does not "kill" these defects in time; hence the defects reach the customers. This is obviously not a healthy state to be in.

Even when the defect detection focus increases, with continued low defect prevention focus (upper left hand quadrant), the testing functions become a high-adrenalin rush, high-pressure job. Most defects are detected in the last minute—before the product release. Testers thus become superheroes who "save the day" by finding all the defects just in time. They may also become adversaries to developers as they always seem to find problems in what the developers do. This quadrant is better than the previous one, but ends up being difficult to sustain because the last-minute adrenalin rush burns people out faster.

Three Chinese doctors were brothers. The youngest one was a surgeon and well known in all parts of the world. He could find tumors in the body and remove them. The middle one was a doctor who could find out disease in its early days and prescribe medicine to cure it. He was known only in the city they lived in. The eldest of the brothers was not known outside the house, but his brothers always took his advice because he was able to tell them how to prevent any illness before they cropped up. The eldest brother may not have been the most famous, but he was surely the most effective.

Preventing an illness is more effective than curing it. People who prevent defects usually do not get much attention. They are usually the unsung heroes of an organization. Those who put out the fires are the ones who get visibility, not necessarily those who make sure fires do not happen in the first place. This, however, should not deter the motivation of people from defect prevention.

As we saw in the previous section, defect prevention and defect detection are not mutually exclusive. They need to be balanced properly for producing a quality product. Defect prevention improves the quality of the process producing the products while defect detection and testing is needed to catch and correct defects that escape the process. Defect prevention is thus process focused while defect detection is product focused. Defect detection acts as an extra check to augment the effectiveness of defect prevention.

An increase in defect prevention focus enables putting in place review mechanisms, upfront standards to be followed, and documented processes for performing the job. This upfront and proactive focus on doing things right to start with causes the testing (or defect detection) function to add more value, and enables catching any residual defects (that escape the defect prevention activities) before the defects reach the customers. Quality is institutionalized with this consistently high focus on both defect prevention

Defect prevention and defect detection should supplement each other and not be considered as mutually exclusive.

and defect detection. An organization may have to allocate sufficient resources for sustaining a high level of both defect prevention and defect detection activities (upper right-hand quadrant in Figure 1.6).

However, an organization should be careful about not relying too much on defect prevention and reducing the focus on defect detection (lower right-hand quadrant in Figure 1.6). Such a high focus on defect prevention and low focus on defect detection would not create a feeling of comfort amongst the management on the quality of product released since there are likely to be minimal internal defects found. This feeling will give rise to introduction of new processes to improve the effectiveness of defect detection. Too much of processes and such defect prevention initiatives may end up being perceived as a bureaucratic exercise, not flexible or adaptable to different scenarios. While processes bring in discipline and reduce dependency on specific individuals, they—when not implemented in spirit—could also end up being double-edged swords, acting as a damper to people's drive and initiative. When an organization pays equally high emphasis to defect prevention and defect detection (upper right corner in the grid), it may appear that it is expensive but this investment is bound to have a rich payback by institutional quality internally and making the benefits visible externally to the customers.

An organization should choose the right place on each of these two—defect detection and defect prevention—dimensions and thus choose the right place in the grid. The relative emphasis to be placed on the two dimensions will vary with the type of product, closeness to the release date, and the resources available. Making a conscious choice of the balance by considering the various factors will enable an organization to produce better quality products. It is important for an organization not to over-emphasize one of these at the expense of the other, as the next section will show.

1.12   MEN IN BLACK

Pride in "test" will take care of the "rest!"

As we can see from all the above discussions, testing requires abundant talent in multiple dimensions. People in the testing profession should have a customer focus, understanding the implications from the customer's perspective. They should have adequate analytical skills to be able to choose the right subset of tests and be able to counter the pesticide paradox. They should think ahead in terms of defect prevention and yet be able to spot and rectify errors that crop up. Finally (as we will see in the next section), they must be able to perform automation functions.

Despite all these challenging technical and inter-personal skills required, testing still remains a not-much-sought-after function. There was an interesting experiment that was described by De Marco and Lister in their book, *Peopleware* [DEMA–1987]. The testing team was seeded with motivated people who were "free from cognitive dissonance that hampers developers when testing their own programs." The team was given an identity (by a black dress, amidst the traditionally dressed remainder of the organization) and tremendous importance. All this increased their pride in work and made their performance grow by leaps and bounds, "almost like magic." Long after the individual founding members left and were replaced by new people, the "Black Team" continued its existence and reputation.

The biggest bottleneck in taking up testing as a profession is the lack of self-belief. This lack of self-belief and apparent distrust of the existence of career options in testing makes people view the profession as a launching pad to do other software functions (notably, "development," a euphemism for coding). As a result, testers do not necessarily seek a career path in testing and develop skepticism towards the profession.

We have devoted an entire chapter in Part III of the book to career aspirations and other similar issues that people face. A part of the challenge that is faced is the context of globalization—the need to harness global resources to stay competitive. We address the organizational issues arising out of this in another chapter in Part III.

1.13   AUTOMATION SYNDROME

A farmer had to use water from a well which was located more than a mile away. Therefore, he employed 100 people to draw water from the well and water his fields. Each of those employed brought a pot of water a day but this was not sufficient. The crops failed.

Just before the next crop cycle, the farmer remembered the failures of the previous season. He thought about automation as a viable way to increase productivity and avoid such failures. He had heard about motorcycles as faster means of commuting (with the weight of water). Therefore, he got 50 motorcycles, laid off 50 of his workers and asked each rider to get two pots of water.Apparently, the correct reasoning was that thanks to improved productivity (that is, speed and convenience of a motorcycle), he needed fewer people. Unfortunately, he choose to use motorcycles just before his crop cycle started. Hence for the first few weeks, the workers were kept busy learning to use the motorcycle. In the process of learning to balance the motorcycles, the number of pots of water they could fetch fell. Added to this, since the num-

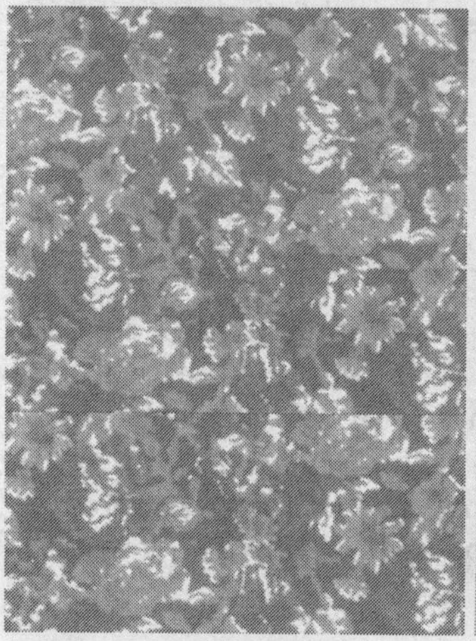

ber of workers was also lower, the productivity actually dropped. The crops failed again.

The next crop cycle came. Now all workers were laid off except one. The farmer bought a truck this time to fetch water. This time he realized the need for training and got his worker to learn driving. However, the road leading to the farm from the well was narrow and the truck did not help in bringing in the water. No portion of the crop could be saved this time also.

After these experiences the farmer said, "My life was better without automation!"

Failures outnumber successes in automation. Equal skills and focus are needed for automation as in product development.

If you go through the story closely there appear to be several reasons for the crop failures that are not to do with the automation intent at all. The frustration of the farmer should not be directed at automation but on the process followed for automation and the inappropriate choices made. In the second crop cycle, the reason for failure was lack of skills and in the third cycle it is due to improper tool implementation.

In the first crop cycle, the farmer laid off his workers immediately after the purchase of motorcycles and expected cost and time to come down. He repeated the same mistake for the third crop cycle. Automation does not yield results immediately.

The moral of the above story as it applies to testing is that automation requires careful planning, evaluation, and training. Automation may not produce immediate returns. An organization that expects immediate returns from automation may end up being disappointed and wrongly blame automation for their failures, instead of objectively looking at their level of preparedness for automation in terms of planning, evaluation, and training.

A large number of organizations fail in their automation initiatives and revert to manual testing. Unfortunately, they conclude—wrongly—that automation will never work.

Testing, by nature, involves repetitive work. Thus, it lends itself naturally to automation. However, automation is a double-edged sword. Some of the points that should be kept in mind while harping on automation are as follows.

- Know first why you want to automate and what you want to automate, before recommending automation for automation's sake.
- Evaluate multiple tools before choosing one as being most appropriate for your need.
- Try to choose tools to match your needs, rather than changing your needs to match the tool's capabilities.

❧   Train people first before expecting them to be productive.

❧   Do not expect overnight returns from automation.

1.14   PUTTING IT ALL TOGETHER

We have discussed several basic principles of testing in this chapter. These principles provide an anchor to the other chapters that we have in rest of the book. We have organized the book into five parts. The first part (which includes this chapter) is *Setting the Context*, which sets the context for the rest of the book. In the chapter that follows, we cover Software Development Life Cycle (SDLC) Models in the context of testing, verification and validation activities.

In Part II, *Types of Testing*, we cover the common types of testing. Chapters 3 through 10 cover white box testing, black box testing, integration testing, system and acceptance testing, performance testing, regression testing, internationalization testing, and ad hoc testing.

Part III, *Select Topics in Specialized Testing*, addresses two specific and somewhat esoteric testing topics—object oriented testing in Chapter 11 and usability and accessibility testing in Chapter 12.

Part IV, *People and Organizational Issues in Testing*, provides an oftignored perspective. Chapter 13 addresses the common people issues like misconceptions, career path concerns and so on. Chapter 14 address the different organizational structures in vogue to set up effective testing teams, especially in the context of globalization.

The final part, Part V, *Test Management and Automation*, addresses the process, management, and automation issues to ensure effective testing in an organization. Chapter 16 discusses test planning management and execution. This discusses various aspects of putting together a test plan, tracking a testing project and related issues. Chapter 17 goes into details of the benefits, challenges, and approaches in test automation—an area of emerging and increasing importance in the test community. The final chapter, Chapter 18, goes into details of what data are required to be captured and what analysis is to be performed for measuring effectiveness of testing, quality of a product and similar perspectives and how this information can be used to achieve quantifiable continuous improvement.

While we have provided the necessary theoretical foundation in different parts of the book, our emphasis throughout the book has been on the state of practice. This section should set the context for what the reader can expect in rest of the book.

REFERENCES

One of the early seminal works on testing is [MYER-79]. In particular, the example of trying to write test cases for verifying three numbers to be the sides of a valid triangle still remains one of the best ways to bring forth the principles of testing. [DEMA-87] provides several interesting perspectives of the entire software engineering discipline. The concept of black team has been illustrated in that work. The emphasis required for process and quality assurance methodologies and the balance to be struck between quality assurance and quality control are brought out in [HUMP-86]. Some of the universally applicable quality principles are discussed in the classics [CROS-80] and [DEMI-86]. [DIJK-72], a Turing Award lecture brings out the doctrine of program testing can never prove the absence of defects. [BEIZ-90] discusses the pesticide paradox.

PROBLEMS AND EXERCISES

1. We have talked about the pervasiveness of software as a reason why defects left in a product would get detected sooner than later. Assume that televisions with embedded software were able to download, install and self-correct patches over the cable network automatically and the TV manufacturer told you that this would just take five minutes every week "at no cost to you, the consumer." Would you agree? Give some reasons why this is not acceptable.

2. Your organization has been successful in developing a client-server application that is installed at several customer locations. You are changing the application to be a hosted, web-based application that anyone can use after a simple registration process. Outline some of the challenges that you should expect from a quality and testing perspective of the changed application.

3. The following were some of the statements made by people in a product development organization. Identify the fallacies if any in the statements and relate it to the principles discussed in this chapter.
   a. "The code for this product is generated automatically by a CASE tool – it is therefore defect – free."
   b. "We are certified according to the latest process models – we do not need testing."
   c. "We need to test the software with dot matrix printers because we have never released a product without testing with a dot matrix printer."

    d. "I have run all the tests that I have been running for the last two releases and I don't need to run any more tests."

    e. "This automation tool is being used by our competitors – hence we should also use the same tool."

4.   Assume that each defect in gathering requirements allowed to go to customers costs $10,000, and that the corresponding costs for design defects and coding defects are $1,000 and $100, respectively. Also, assume that current statistics indicate that on average ten new defects come from each of the phases. In addition, each phase also lets the defects from the previous phase seep through. What is the total cost of the defects under the current scenario? If you put a quality assurance process to catch 50% of the defects from each phase not to go to the next phase, what are the expected cost savings?

5.   You are to write a program that adds two two-digit integers. Can you test this program exhaustively? If so, how many test cases are required? Assuming that each test case can be executed and analyzed in one second, how long would it take for you to run all the tests?

6.   We argued that the number of defects left in a program is proportional to the number of defects detected. Give reasons why this argument looks counterintuitive. Also, give practical reasons why this phenomenon causes problems in testing.

Software Development Life Cycle Models

CHAPTER 2

In this chapter—

- ✓ Phases of software project
- ✓ Quality, quality assurance, and quality control
- ✓ Testing, verification, and validation
- ✓ Process model to represent different phases
- ✓ Life cycle models

2.1   PHASES OF SOFTWARE PROJECT

A software project is made up of a series of phases. Broadly, most software projects comprise the following phases.

- ✠ Requirements gathering and analysis
- ✠ Planning
- ✠ Design
- ✠ Development or coding
- ✠ Testing
- ✠ Deployment and maintenance

2.1.1   Requirements Gathering and Analysis

During requirements gathering, the specific requirements of the software to be built are gathered and documented. If the software is bespoke software, then there is a single customer who can give these requirements. If the product is a general-purpose software, then a product marketing team within the software product organization specifies the requirements by aggregating the requirements of multiple potential customers. In either case, it is important to ensure that the right requirements are captured at every stage. The requirements get documented in the form of a System Requirements Specification (SRS) document. This document acts as a bridge between the customer and the designers chartered to build the product.

2.1.2   Planning

The purpose of the planning phase is to come up with a schedule, the scope, and resource requirements for a release. A plan explains how the requirements will be met and by which time. It needs to take into account the requirements—what will be met and what will not be met—for the current release to decide on the scope for the project, look at resource availability, and to come out with set of milestones and release date for the project. The planning phase is applicable for both development and testing activities. At the end of this phase, both project plan and test plan documents are delivered.

2.1.3   Design

The purpose of the design phase is to figure out how to satisfy the requirements enumerated in the System Requirements Specification document. The design phase produces a representation that will be used by the following phase, the development phase. This representation should serve two purposes. First, from this representation, it should be possible to verify that all the requirements are satisfied. Second, this representation should give sufficient information for the development phase to proceed with the coding and implementation of the system. Design is usually split into two levels—high-level design and low-level or a detailed design. The design step produces the system design description (SDD) document that will be used by development teams to produce the programs that realize the design.

2.1.4 Development or Coding

Design acts as a blueprint for the actual coding to proceed. This development or coding phase comprises coding the programs in the chosen programming language. It produces the software that meets the requirements the design was meant to satisfy. In addition to programming, this phase also involves the creation of product documentation.

2.1.5 Testing

As the programs are coded (in the chosen programming language), they are also tested. In addition, after the coding is (deemed) complete, the product is subjected to testing. Testing is the process of exercising the software product in pre-defined ways to check if the behavior is the same as expected behavior. By testing the product, an organization identifies and removes as many defects as possible before shipping it out.

2.1.6 Deployment and Maintenance

Once a product is tested, it is given to the customers who deploy it in their environments. As the users start using the product in their environments, they may observe discrepancies between the actual behavior of the product and what they were given to expect (either by the marketing people or through the product documentation). Such discrepancies could end up as product defects, which need to be corrected. The product now enters the maintenance phase, wherein the product is maintained or changed to satisfy the changes that arise from customer expectations, environmental changes, etc. Maintenance is made up of *corrective maintenance* (for example, fixing customer-reported problems), *adaptive maintenance* (for example, making the software run on a new version of an operating system or database), and *preventive maintenance* (for example, changing the application program code to avoid a potential security hole in an operating system code).

2.2 QUALITY, QUALITY ASSURANCE, AND QUALITY CONTROL

A software product is designed to satisfy certain requirements of a given customer (or set of customers). How can we characterize this phrase—"satisfying requirements"? Requirements get translated into software features, each feature being designed to meet one or more of the

> Quality is meeting the requirements expected of the software, consistently and predictably.

requirements. For each such feature, the *expected behavior* is characterized by a set of *test cases*. Each test case is further characterized by

1. The environment under which the test case is to be executed;
2. Inputs that should be provided for that test case;
3. How these inputs should get processed;
4. What changes should be produced in the internal state or environment; and
5. What outputs should be produced.

The *actual behavior* of a given software for a given test case, under a given set of inputs, in a given environment, and in a given internal state is characterized by

1. How these inputs actually get processed;
2. What changes are actually produced in the internal state or environment; and
3. What outputs are actually produced.

If the actual behavior and the expected behavior are identical in all their characteristics, then that test case is said to be passed. If not, the given software is said to have a *defect* on that test case.

How do we increase the chances of a product meeting the requirements expected of it, consistently and predictably? There are two types of methods—quality control and quality assurance.

Quality control attempts to build a product, test it for expected behavior after it is built, and if the expected behavior is not the same as the actual behavior of the product, fixes the product as is necessary and rebuilds the product. This iteration is repeated till the expected behavior of the product matches the actual behavior for the scenarios tested. Thus quality control is defect-detection and defect-correction oriented, and works on the product rather than on the process.

Quality assurance, on the other hand, attempts defect prevention by concentrating on the process of producing the product rather than working on defect detection/correction after the product is built. For example, instead of producing and then testing a program code for proper behavior by exercising the built product, a quality assurance approach would be to first review the design before the product is built and correct the design errors in the first place. Similarly, to ensure the production of a better code, a quality assurance process may mandate coding standards to be followed by all programmers. As can be seen from the above examples, quality assurance normally tends to apply to all the products that use a process. Also, since quality assurance continues throughout the life of the product it is everybody's responsibility; hence it is a staff function. In contrast, the responsibility for quality control is usually localized to a quality control team. Table 2.1 summarizes the key distinctions between quality control and quality assurance.

Table 2.1. Difference between quality assurance and quality control.

Quality Assurance	Quality Control
Concentrates on the process of producing the products	Concentrates on specific products
Defect-prevention oriented	Defect-detection and correction oriented
Usually done throughout the life cycle	Usually done after the product is built
This is usually a staff function	This is usually a line function
Examples: reviews and audits	Examples: software testing at various levels

We will see more details of quality assurance methods such as reviews and audits in Chapter 3. But the focus of the rest of this book is on software testing, which is essentially a quality control activity. Let us discuss more about testing in the next section.

2.3   TESTING, VERIFICATION, AND VALIDATION

> Verification is the process of evaluating a system or component to determine whether the products of a given phase satisfy the conditions imposed at the start of that phase.

The narrow definition of the term "testing" is the phase that follows coding and precedes deployment. Testing is traditionally used to mean testing of the program code. However, coding is a downstream activity, as against requirements and design that occur much earlier in a project life cycle. Given that the objective of a software project is to minimize and prevent defects, testing of program code alone is not sufficient. As we saw in the last chapter, defects can creep in during any phase and these defects should be detected as close to the point of injection as possible and not wait till the testing of programs. Hence against this, if each phase is "tested" separately as and when the phase is completed (or, better still, as the phase is being executed), then defects can be detected early, thereby reducing the overall costs.

Timely testing increases the chances of a product or service meeting the customer's requirements. When a product is tested with appropriate and realistic tests that reflect typical usage patterns by the intended users, the chances of the product satisfying the customer's requirement is much higher. While testing does not guarantee zero defects, effective testing certainly increases the chances of customer acceptance of the software.

The purpose of testing is to uncover defects in the system (and to have someone fix the defects). Testing is done by a set of people within a software product (or service) organization whose goal and charter is to uncover the defects in the product before it reaches the customer (see Section 1.3). As we saw in the previous chapter, the purpose of testing is NOT to prove that the product has no defects. The purpose of software testing is to find defects in a software product. As we will see in the chapters on people and organizational issues (Chapters 13, 14), the reward systems and the organization structures should create and foster an environment that encourages this purpose of testing.

Testing is NOT meant to replace other ways of ensuring quality (like reviews). It is one of the methods to detect defects in a software product. There are other methods that achieve the same function. For example, we will see later that following well-defined processes and standards reduces the chances of defects creeping into a software. We will also discuss other methods like reviews and inspections, which actually attempt to prevent defects coming into the product. To be effective, testing should complement, supplement, and augment such quality assurance methods discussed in the previous section.

The idea of catching defects within each phase, without letting them reach the testing phase, leads us to define two more terms—verification and validation.

During the requirements gathering phase, the requirements are faithfully captured. The SRS document is the product of the requirements phase. To ensure that requirements are faithfully captured, the customer verifies this document. The design phase takes the SRS document as input and maps the requirements to a design that can drive the coding. The SDD document is the product of the design phase. The SDD is verified by the requirements team to ensure that the design faithfully reflects the SRS, which imposed the conditions at the beginning of the design phase.

Verification takes care of activities to focus on the question "*Are we building the product right*?" and validation takes care of a set of activities to address the question "*Are we building the right product*?"

To build the product right, certain activities/conditions/procedures are imposed at the beginning of the life cycle. These activities are considered "*proactive*" as their purpose is to prevent the defects before they take shape. The process activities carried out during various phases for each of the product releases can be termed as verification. Requirements review, design review, and code review are some examples of verification activities.

To build the right product, certain activities are carried out during various phases to validate whether the product is built as per specifications. These activities are considered "*reactive*" as their purpose is to find defects that affect the product and fix them as soon as they are introduced. Some examples of validation include unit testing performed to verify if the code logic works, integration testing performed to verify the design, and system testing performed to verify that the requirements are met.

To summarize, there are different terminologies that may stand for the same or similar concepts. For all practical purposes in this book, we can assume verification and quality assurance to be one and the same. Similarly quality control, validation, and testing mean the same.

2.4 PROCESS MODEL TO REPRESENT DIFFERENT PHASES

A process model is a way to represent any given phase of software development that effectively builds in the concepts of validation and verification to prevent and minimize the delay between defect injection and defect detection (and eventual correction). In this model, each phase of a software project is characterized by the following.

✠ Entry criteria, which specify when that phase can be started. Also included are the inputs for the phase.

✠ Tasks, or steps that need to be carried out in that phase, along with measurements that characterize the tasks.

✠ Verification, which specifies methods of checking that the tasks have been carried out correctly.

✠ Exit criteria, which stipulate the conditions under which one can consider the phase as done. Also included are the outputs for only the phase.

This model, known as the **Entry Task Verification eXit** or **ETVX** model, offers several advantages for effective verification and validation.

1. Clear entry criteria make sure that a given phase does not start prematurely.

2. The verification for each phase (or each activity in each phase) helps prevent defects, or at least, minimizes the time delay between defect injection and defect detection.

3. Documentation of the detailed tasks that comprise each phase reduces the ambiguity in interpretation of the instructions and thus minimizes the variations that can come from repeated executions of these tasks by different individuals.

4. Clear exit criteria provide a means of validation of the phase, after the phase is done but before handing over to the next phase.

An example of applying the ETVX model to the design phase is presented in Figure 2.1.

Figure 2.1
ETVX model applied to design.

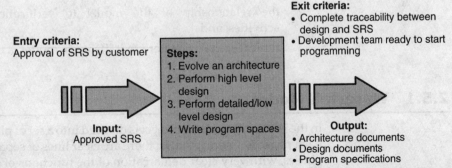

Entry criteria:
Approval of SRS by customer

Steps:
1. Evolve an architecture
2. Perform high level design
3. Perform detailed/low level design
4. Write program spaces

Input:
Approved SRS

Exit criteria:
• Complete traceability between design and SRS
• Development team ready to start programming

Output:
• Architecture documents
• Design documents
• Program specifications

2.5 LIFE CYCLE MODELS

The ETVX model characterizes a phase of a project. A Life Cycle model describes how the phases combine together to form a complete project or life cycle. Such a model is characterized by the following attributes.

The activities performed In any given software project, apart from the most common activities or phases—requirements gathering, design, development, testing, and maintenance—there could be other activities as well. Some of these activities could be technical activities (for example, porting) and some could be non-technical (for example, hiring).

The deliverables from each activity Each activity produces a set of deliverables, which are the end products of that activity. For example, the requirements gathering phase produces the SRS document, the design phase produces the SDD document, and so on.

Methods of validation of the deliverables The outputs produced by a given activity represent the goal to be satisfied by that activity. Hence it is necessary to have proper validation criteria for each output.

The sequence of activities The different activities work together in unison in a certain sequence of steps to achieve overall project goals. For example, the process of requirements gathering may involve steps such as interviews with customers, documentation of requirements, validation of documented requirements with customers, and freezing of requirements. These steps may be repeated as many times as needed to get the final frozen requirements.

Methods of verification of each activity, including the mechanism of communication amongst the activities The different activities interact with one another by means of communication methods. For example, when a defect is found in one activity and is traced back to the causes in an earlier activity, proper verification methods are needed to retrace steps from the point of defect to the cause of the defect.

We will now look at some of the common life cycle models that are used in software projects. For each model, we will look at:

1. a brief description of the model;
2. the relationship of the model to verification and validation activities; and
3. typical scenarios where that life cycle model is useful.

2.5.1 Waterfall Model

In the Waterfall model, a project is divided into a set of phases (or activities). Each phase is distinct, that is, there are clear lines of separation between the phases, with very clear demarcation of the functions of each of the phases.

A project starts with an initial phase, and upon completion of the phase, moves on to the next phase. On the completion of this phase, the project moves to the subsequent phase and so on. Thus the phases are strictly time sequenced.

We depict one example of a project in the Waterfall model in Figure 2.2. The project goes through a phase of requirements gathering. At the end of requirements gathering, a System Requirements Specification document is produced. This becomes the input to the design phase. During the design phase, a detailed design is produced in the form of a System Design Description. With the SDD as input, the project proceeds to the development or coding phase, wherein programmers develop the programs required to satisfy the design. Once the programmers complete their coding tasks, they hand the product to the testing team, who test the product before it is released.

If there is no problem in a given phase, then this method can work, going in one direction (like a waterfall). But what would happen if there are problems after going to a particular phase? For example, you go into the design phase and find that it is not possible to satisfy the requirements,

Figure 2.2

Waterfall model.

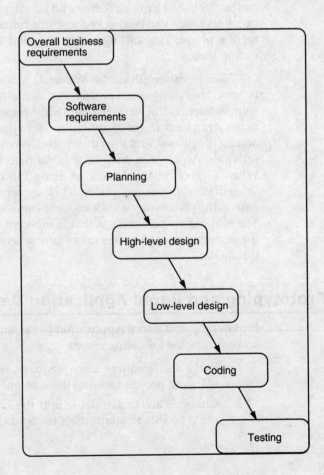

A Waterfall model is characterized by three attributes.

1. The project is divided into separate, distinct phases.

2. Each phase communicates to the next through pre-specified outputs.

3. When an error is detected, it is traced back to one previous phase at a time, until it gets resolved at some earlier phase.

going by the current design approach being used. What could be the possible causes and remedies? You may try an alternative design if possible and see if that can satisfy the requirements. If there are no alternative design approaches possible, then there must be feedback to the requirements phase to correct the requirements.

Let us take the example one step further. Suppose a design was created for a given set of requirements and the project passed on to the programming/development phase. At this point of time, it was found that it was not possible to develop the programs because of some limitations. What would you do? One approach would be to try out alternative strategies in the development phase so that the design could still be satisfied. Another possibility could be that there are flaws in design that cause conflicts during development and hence the design has to be revisited. When the design phase is revisited—like in the previous case—it may happen that the problem may have to be addressed in the requirements phase itself. So, a problem in one phase could potentially be traced back to *any* of the previous phases.

Since each phase has an output, the latter can be validated against a set of criteria. To increase the effectiveness, the completion criteria for each output can be published a priori. Before a phase starts, the completion criteria for the previous phase can be checked and this can act as a verification mechanism for the phase. This can minimize the kind of delays we discussed in the example above.

The main strength of the Waterfall Model is its simplicity. The model is very useful when a project can actually be divided into watertight compartments. But very few software projects can be divided thus. The major drawback in the Waterfall model arises from the delay in feedback among the phases, and thus the ineffectiveness of verification and validation activities. An error in one phase is not detected till at least the next phase. When a given phase detects an error, the communication is only to the immediately preceding phase. This sequential nature of communication among the phases can introduce inordinate delays in resolving the problem. The reduced responsiveness that is inherent in the model and the fact that the segregation of phases is unrealistic severely restricts the applicability of this model.

2.5.2   Prototyping and Rapid Application Development Models

Prototyping and Rapid Application Development (RAD) models recognize and address the following issues.

1.   Early and frequent user feedback will increase the chances of a software project meeting the customers' requirements.

2.   Changes are unavoidable and the software development process must be able to adapt itself to rapid changes.

> 1. A Prototyping model uses constant user interaction, early in the requirements gathering stage, to produce a prototype.
>
> 2. The proto-type is used to derive the system requirements specification and can be discarded after the SRS is built.
>
> 3. An appropriate life cycle model is chosen for building the actual product after the user accepts the SRS.

The Prototyping model comprises the following activities.

1. The software development organization interacts with customers to understand their requirements.

2. The software development organization produces a prototype to show how the eventual software system would look like. This prototype would have the models of how the input screens and output reports would look like, in addition to having some "empty can functionality" to demonstrate the workflow and processing logic.

3. The customer and the development organization review the prototype frequently so that the customer's feedback is taken very early in the cycle (that is, during the requirements gathering phase).

4. Based on the feedback and the prototype that is produced, the software development organization produces the System Requirements Specification document.

5. Once the SRS document is produced, the prototype can be discarded.

6. The SRS document is used as the basis for further design and development.

Thus, the prototype is simply used as a means of quickly gathering (the right) requirements. This model has built-in mechanisms for verification and validation of the requirements. As the prototype is being developed, the customer's frequent feedback acts as a validation mechanism. Once the SRS is produced, it acts as the verification mechanism for the design and subsequent steps. But the verification and validation activities of the subsequent phases are actually dictated by the life cycle model that is followed after the SRS is obtained.

This model is obviously advantageous when a customer can participate by giving feedback. This model is also useful in cases where the feedback can be easily quantified and incorporated, for example, determining user interface, predicting performance, and so on.

For a general-purpose product, which is meant for many customers, there is no single customer whose feedback can be taken as final. In these cases, a product manager in the marketing group of the product vendor usually plays the role of the eventual customer. Hence the applicability of this model is somewhat limited to general-purpose products. Furthermore, the prototype is used as a means of capturing requirements and is not necessarily meant to be used afterwards. Oftentimes, the prototype (or parts of the prototype) makes its way to becoming the product itself. This can have undesirable effects as the prototype usually employs several short cuts, unstructured methods, and tools to achieve a quick turnaround. Such short cuts are potential sources of defects in live environments and thus can place a heavy burden on maintenance and testing.

The Rapid Application Development model is a variation of the Prototyping Model. Like the Prototyping Model, the RAD Model relies on feedback and interaction by the customers to gather the initial requirements.

However, the Prototyping model differs from the RAD Model on two counts.

First, in the RAD Model, it is not a prototype that is built but the actual product itself. That is, the built application (prototype, in the previous model) is not discarded. Hence, it is named Rapid Application Development model.

Second, in order to ensure formalism in capturing the requirements and proper reflection of the requirements in the design and subsequent phases, a Computer Aided Software Engineering (CASE) tool is used throughout the life cycle, right from requirements gathering. Such CASE tools have

- methodologies to elicit requirements;
- repositories to store the gathered requirements and all downstream entities such as design objects; and
- mechanisms to automatically translate the requirements stored in the repositories to design and generate the code in the chosen programming environment.

The methodologies provided by a CASE tool can provide inbuilt means of verification and validation. For example, the tool may be able to automatically detect and resolve inconsistencies in data types or dependencies. Since the design (and, perhaps, even the program code) can be automatically generated from the requirements, the validation can be very complete, extending to all the downstream phases, unlike the Prototyping model.

This method can have wider applicability for even general-purpose products. The automatic generation of the design and programs produced by a CASE tool makes this model more attractive. The cost of such CASE tools is a factor that an organization would have to consider before deciding on the use of this model for a given project. In addition, CASE tools and this model is generally more suited for applications projects rather than systems type projects.

2.5.3 Spiral or Iterative Model

The Spiral or Iterative model follows a process in which the requirements gathering, design, coding, and testing are performed iteratively till all requirements are met. There is also a good amount of overlap among the activities of requirements gathering, design, coding, and testing following this model. What phase the product is in is difficult to conclude as each requirement can be at a different phase. The only conclusion that can be made is at what phase *each* of the requirements is in. If a defect is produced in any phase of a given requirement, it may cause that requirement to revisit an earlier phase. This model enables incremental development whereby the product evolves, with requirements getting added to it dynamically. This enables the product to be demonstrated, at any point of time, with the functionality available at that point of time. It also enables the "increments" to be sent to the customer for approval. The progress of the product can be

Table 2.2 Some product requirements and phases.

Requirements	Status/Phase currently in
Requirement-1	Coding
Requirement-2	Design
Requirement-3	Requirement
Requirement-4	Testing
Requirement-5	Released

Figure 2.3

Spiral model.

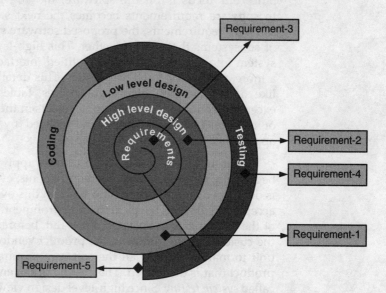

seen from the beginning of the project as the model delivers "increments" at regular intervals. Even though it will be very difficult to plan a release date following this model, it allows the progress to be tracked and the customer approvals to be obtained at regular intervals, thereby reducing the risk of finding major defects at a later point of time. Table 2.2 gives an example of phases for some of the requirements in the product.

Figure 2.3 (the coloured figure is available on page 457) depicts the Spiral model and the phases involved in the model, for the example on Table 2.2. As can be seen, each requirement is "spiraling outwards" through the different phases as the entire project evolves.

2.5.4 The V Model

The Waterfall Model viewed testing as a post-development (that is, post-coding) activity. The Spiral Model took this one step further and tried to break up the product into increments each of which can be tested separately. The V Model starts off being similar to the Waterfall Model in that it envisages product development to be made up of a number of phases or levels. However, the new perspective that the V Model brings in is that different types of testing apply at different levels. Thus, from a testing perspective, the type of tests that need to be done at each level vary significantly.

For instance, consider a typical product development activity represented as a Waterfall Model earlier in Figure 2.2. The system starts with the overall business requirements from the point of view of customers. These requirements cover hardware, software, and operational requirements. Since our focus is on the software, moving from overall requirements to software requirements becomes the next step. In order to realize the software requirements, the proposed software system is envisaged as a set of subsystems that work together. This high-level design (of breaking the system into subsystems with identified interfaces) then gets translated to a more detailed or low-level design. This detailed design goes into issues like data structures, algorithm choices, table layouts, processing logic, exception conditions, and so on. It results in the identification of a number of components, each component realized by program code written in appropriate programming languages.

Given these levels, what kind of tests apply in each of these levels? To begin with, for overall business requirements, eventually whatever software is developed should fit into and work in this overall context and should be accepted by the end users, in their environment. This testing, the final proof of the pudding, is *acceptance testing*. But, before the product is deployed in the customer's environment, the product vendor should test it as an entire unit to make sure that all the software requirements are satisfied by the product that is developed. This testing of the entire software system can be called *system testing*. Since high-level design views the system as being made up of interoperating and integrated (software) subsystems, the individual subsystems should be integrated and tested together before a full blown system test can be done. This testing of high-level design corresponds to *integration testing*. The components that are the outputs of the low-level design have to be tested independently before being integrated. Thus, the testing corresponding to the low-level design phase is *component testing*. Finally, since coding produces several program units, each of these smaller program units have to be tested independently before trying to combine them together to form components. This testing of the program units forms *unit testing*.

Figure 2.4 depicts the different types of testing that apply to each of the steps. For simplicity, we have not shown the planning phase as a separate entity since it is common for all testing phases. But, it is not possible to *execute* any of these tests until the product is actually built. In other words, the step called "testing" is now broken down into different sub-steps called acceptance testing, system testing, and so on as shown in Figure 2.4. So, it is still the case that all the testing *execution* related activities are done only at the end of the life cycle.

Figure 2.4

Phases of testing for different development phases.

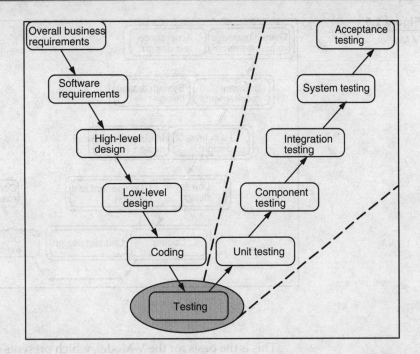

1. The V-model splits testing into two parts—design and execution.

2. Test design is done early, while test execution is done in the end.

3. There are different types of tests for each phase of life cycle.

Even though the execution of the tests cannot be done till the product is built, the *design* of tests can be carried out much earlier. In fact, if we look at the aspect of skill sets required for *designing* each type of tests, the people best suited to design each of these tests are those who are actually performing the function of creating the corresponding artifact. For example, the best people to articulate what the acceptance tests should be are the ones who formulate the overall business requirements (and, of course, the customers, where possible). Similarly, the people best equipped to design the integration tests are those who know how the system is broken into subsystems and what the interfaces between the subsystems are—that is, those who perform the high-level design. Again, the people doing development know the innards of the program code and thus are best equipped to *design* the unit tests.

Not only are the skill sets required for designing these different types of tests different, but also, there is no reason to defer the designing of the tests till the very end. As and when each activity on the left-hand side of the "V" is being carried out, the design of the corresponding type of tests can be carried out. By performing an early design of the tests and deferring only the test execution till the end, we achieve three important gains.

⌘ First, we achieve more parallelism and reduce the end-of-cycle time taken for testing.

⌘ Second, by designing tests for each activity upfront, we are building in better upfront validation, thus again reducing last-minute surprises.

⌘ Third, tests are designed by people with appropriate skill sets.

Figure 2.5

V Model.

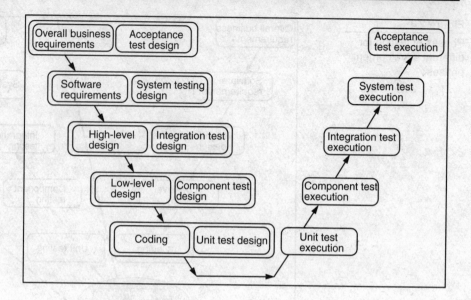

This is the basis for the V Model, which presents excellent advantages for verification and validation. As shown in Figure 2.5, for each type of test, we move the design of tests upstream, along with the actual activities and retain the test execution downstream, after the product is built.

2.5.5   Modified V Model

The V Model split the design and execution portion of the various types of tests and attached the test design portion to the corresponding earlier phases of the software life cycle.

An assumption made there was that even though the activity of test execution was split into execution of tests of different types, the execution cannot happen until the entire product is built. For a given product, the different units and components can be in different stages of evolution. For example, one unit could be still under development and thus be in the unit-testing phase whereas another unit could be ready for component testing while the component itself may not be ready for integration testing. There may be components that are ready (that is, component tested) for integration and being subjected to integration tests (along with other modules which are also ready for integration, provided those modules can be integrated). The V Model does not explicitly address this natural parallelism commonly found in product development.

In the modified V Model, this parallelism is exploited. When each unit or component or module is given explicit exit criteria to pass on to the subsequent stage, the units or components or modules that satisfy a given phase of testing move to the next phase of testing where possible, without

> 1. The modified V model recognizes that different parts of a product are in different stages of evolution.
> 2. Each part enters the appropriate testing phase (such as unit testing, component testing, and so on) when the appropriate entry criteria are met.

necessarily waiting for all the units or components or modules to move in unison from one phase of testing to another, as shown in Figure 2.6.

Just as the V Model introduced various *types* of testing, the modified V model introduces various *phases* of testing. A phase of testing has a one-to-one mapping to the types of testing, that is, there is a unit-testing phase, component-testing phase, and so on. Once a unit has completed the unit-testing phase, it becomes part of a component and enters the component-testing phase. It then moves to integration-testing phase and so on. Rather than view the product as going through different types of tests (as the V model does), the modified V Model views each part of the product to go through different phases of testing. These are actually two sides of the same coin and thus provide complimentary views. The main advantage the modified V model brings to the table is the recognition of the parallelism present in different parts of the product and assigning each part to the most appropriate phase of testing that is possible. In Figure 2.6, the columns of the table represents one side of V, and rows (which are test phases) represent the other side of V.

In Figure 2.6, notice that different phases of testing are done in parallel. While starting a phase of testing it is important to look at whether the product is ready for testing. It is determined by a set of *entry criteria*. The earliest possible quality to start the next phase of testing is denoted by entry criteria, and to start the next phase of testing the earlier phase need not have completed. The testing phases are also associated with a set of exit criteria to complete the test activities for each phase. They are determined by *exit criteria*. The entry and exit criteria for each of the phases ensure that right quality of product delivered for starting the test and right amount of testing is completed for the release. Even though it is indicated in the picture all of the test phases finish at the same time, practically it can have different time lines. The longest phase determines the release date.

In Figure 2.6, there are two additional activities that have not been discussed before. The coloured figure is available on page 458. These are "Component (1,2…) Complete" and "Components Complete"; these are not additional

Figure 2.6
Modified V Model.

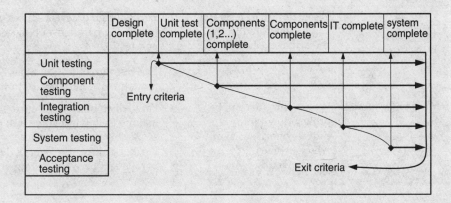

phases in a life cycle. They have been introduced just to denote that integration testing can start after two components have been completed, and when all components are integrated and tested, the next phase of testing, that is, system testing can start.

Table 2.3 Model applicability and relevance to verification and validation.

Models	Where Applicable	Relevant Verification and Validation (V & V) Issues
Waterfall	Where very clearly demarcated phases are present When deliverables of each phase can be frozen before proceeding to the next phase	Testing / V & V postponed by at least one phase Typically testing is among the most downstream activities Communication of error (and hence time for correction) can be high
Prototyping	Where we have a user (or a product manager) who can give feedback	Provides inbuilt feedback for the requirements Reuse of prototype (instead of throwing it away) can make verification and validation difficult and may produce undesirable effects
RAD	Where we have a user (or a product manager) who can give feedback When we have CASE and other modeling tools	Built-in feedback available beyond requirements also CASE tools can generate useful documentation that further enhances V & V
Spiral	Products evolving as increments Intermediate checking and correction is possible	Extends V & V to all increments Extends V & V to all phases (that is, those beyond requirements gathering as well) Enables the products to be demonstrated at any phase and enables frequent releases
V model	When design of tests can be separated from the actual execution	Early design of tests reduces overall delay by increasing parallelism between development and testing Early design of tests enables better and more timely validation of individual phases
Modified V model	When a product can be broken down into different parts, each of which evolves independently	Parallelism of V model further increased by making each part evolve independently Further reduces the overall delay by introducing parallelism between testing activities

2.5.6 Comparison of Various Life Cycle Models

As can be seen from the above discussion, each of the models has its advantages and disadvantages. Each of them has applicability in a specific scenario. Each of them also provides different issues, challenges, and opportunities for verification and validation. We summarize in Table 2.3 the salient points about applicability and relevance to verification and validation for each of the models.

REFERENCES

The Waterfall Model was initially covered in [ROYC-70]. The origins of the Prototyping Model come from [BROO-75]. The Spiral Model was originally proposed in [BOEH-88]. [GRAD-97] provides some variations to the Spiral Model. [RAME-2002], [PRES-97] and [HUMP-86] provide overviews to all the models.

PROBLEMS AND EXERCISES

1. Which SDLC model would be most suitable for each of the following scenarios?

   a. The product is a bespoke product for a specific customer, who is always available to give feedback.

   b. The same as above, except that we also have access to a CASE tool that generates program code automatically.

   c. A general purpose product, but with a very strong product marketing team who understand and articulate the overall customer requirements very well.

   d. A product that is made of a number of features that become available sequentially and incrementally.

2. Which of the following products would you say is of "high quality," based on the criteria we discussed in the book? Justify your answer.

   a. Three successive versions of the product had respectively 0, 79, and 21 defects reported.

   b. Three successive versions of the product had respectively 85, 90, and 79 defects reported.

3. List three or more challenges from the testing perspective for each of the following models:

   a. Spiral Model.

   b. V Model.

   c. Modified V Model.

4. What are some of the challenges that you should expect when moving from the V Model to the Modified V Model?

5. Figure 2.1 gave the ETVX Diagram for the design phase of a software project. Draw a similar ETVX Diagram for the coding phase.

6. In the book we have discussed the Spiral Model as being ideally suited for a product that evolves in increments. Discuss how the V Model is applicable for such an incrementally evolving product.

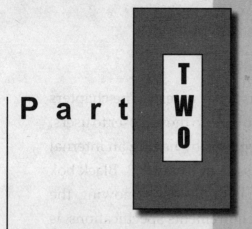

Part T W O

Types of Testing

This part of the book discusses various types of tests. The chapters progress from the types of tests closer to code to those closer to users. White box testing, which tests the programs by having an internal knowledge of program code, is discussed in Chapter 3. Black box testing, which tests the product behavior by only knowing the external behavior as dictated by the requirements specifications, is discussed in Chapter 4. As software gets developed in a modular fashion and the modules have to be integrated together, integration testing is covered in Chapter 5. System and acceptance testing, which tests a product completely from a user's perspective in environments similar to customer deployments, is discussed in Chapter 6. Performance testing, which tests the ability of the system to withstand typical and excessive work loads, is discussed in Chapter 7. Since software is always characterized by change and since changes should not break what is working already, regression testing becomes very important and is discussed in Chapter 8. As software has to be deployed in multiple languages across the world, internationalization testing, the topic of Chapter 9, comes into play. Finally, adhoc testing, in Chapter 10, addresses the methods of testing a product in typical unpredictable ways that end users may subject the product to.

White Box Testing

CHAPTER 3

In this chapter—

- ✓ What is white box testing?
- ✓ Static testing
- ✓ Structural testing
- ✓ Challenges in white box testing

3.1   WHAT IS WHITE BOX TESTING?

Every software product is realized by means of a program code. White box testing is a way of testing the external functionality of the code by examining and testing the program code that realizes the external functionality. This is also known as *clear box*, or *glass box* or *open box* testing.

White box testing takes into account the program code, code structure, and internal design flow. In contrast, black box testing, to be discussed in Chapter 4, does not look at the program code but looks at the product from an external perspective.

A number of defects come about because of incorrect translation of requirements and design into program code. Some other defects are created by programming errors and programming language idiosyncrasies. The different methods of white box testing discussed in this chapter can help reduce the delay between the injection of a defect in the program code and its detection. Furthermore, since the program code represents what the product actually does (rather than what the product is intended to do), testing by looking at the program code makes us get closer to what the product is actually doing.

As shown in Figure 3.1, white box testing is classified into "static" and "structural" testing. The corresponding coloured version of Figure 3.1 is available on page 458. We will look into the details of static testing in Section 3.2 and take up structural testing in Section 3.3.

Figure 3.1

Classification of white box testing.

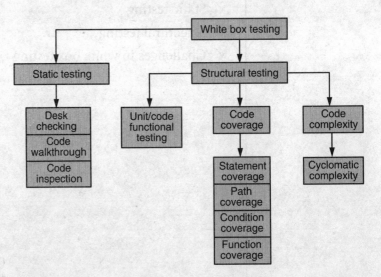

3.2   STATIC TESTING

Static testing is a type of testing which requires only the source code of the product, not the binaries or executables. Static testing does not involve executing the programs on computers but involves select people going through the code to find out whether

✠ the code works according to the functional requirement;

✠ the code has been written in accordance with the design developed earlier in the project life cycle;

✠ the code for any functionality has been missed out ;

✠ the code handles errors properly.

Static testing can be done by humans or with the help of specialized tools.

3.2.1 Static Testing by Humans

These methods rely on the principle of humans reading the program code to detect errors rather than computers executing the code to find errors. This process has several advantages.

1. Sometimes humans can find errors that computers cannot. For example, when there are two variables with similar names and the programmer used a "wrong" variable by mistake in an expression, the computer will not detect the error but execute the statement and produce incorrect results, whereas a human being can spot such an error.

2. By making multiple humans read and evaluate the program, we can get multiple perspectives and therefore have more problems identified upfront than a computer could.

3. A human evaluation of the code can compare it against the specifications or design and thus ensure that it does what is intended to do. This may not always be possible when a computer runs a test.

4. A human evaluation can detect many problems at one go and can even try to identify the root causes of the problems. More often than not, multiple problems can get fixed by attending to the same root cause. Typically, in a reactive testing, a test uncovers one problem (or, at best, a few problems) at a time. Often, such testing only reveals the symptoms rather than the root causes. Thus, the overall time required to fix all the problems can be reduced substantially by a human evaluation.

5. By making humans test the code before execution, computer resources can be saved. Of course, this comes at the expense of human resources.

6. A proactive method of testing like static testing minimizes the delay in identification of the problems. As we have seen in Chapter 1, the sooner a defect is identified and corrected, lesser is the cost of fixing the defect.

7. From a psychological point of view, finding defects later in the cycle (for example, after the code is compiled and the system is being put together) creates immense pressure on programmers. They have to fix defects with less time to spare. With this kind of pressure, there are higher chances of other defects creeping in.

There are multiple methods to achieve static testing by humans. They are (in the increasing order of formalism) as follows.

1. Desk checking of the code
2. Code walkthrough
3. Code review
4. Code inspection

Since static testing by humans is done before the code is compiled and executed, some of these methods can be viewed as process-oriented or defect prevention-oriented or quality assurance-oriented activities rather than pure testing activities. Especially as the methods become increasingly formal (for example, Fagan Inspection), these traditionally fall under the "process" domain. They find a place in formal process models such as ISO 9001, CMMI, and so on and are seldom treated as part of the "testing" domain. Nevertheless, as mentioned earlier in this book, we take a holistic view of "testing" as anything that furthers the quality of a product. These methods have been included in this chapter because they have visibility into the program code.

We will now look into each of these methods in more detail.

3.2.1.1 Desk checking   Normally done manually by the author of the code, desk checking is a method to verify the portions of the code for correctness. Such verification is done by comparing the code with the design or specifications to make sure that the code does what it is supposed to do and effectively. This is the desk checking that most programmers do before compiling and executing the code. Whenever errors are found, the author applies the corrections for errors on the spot. This method of catching and correcting errors is characterized by:

1. No structured method or formalism to ensure completeness and
2. No maintaining of a log or checklist.

In effect, this method relies completely on the author's thoroughness, diligence, and skills. There is no process or structure that guarantees or verifies the effectiveness of desk checking. This method is effective for correcting "obvious" coding errors but will not be effective in detecting errors that arise due to incorrect understanding of requirements or incomplete requirements. This is because developers (or, more precisely, programmers who are doing the desk checking) may not have the domain knowledge required to understand the requirements fully.

The main advantage offered by this method is that the programmer who knows the code and the programming language very well is well equipped to read and understand his or her own code. Also, since this is done by one individual, there are fewer scheduling and logistics overheads. Furthermore, the defects are detected and corrected with minimum time delay.

Some of the disadvantages of this method of testing are as follows.

1. A developer is not the best person to detect problems in his or her own code. He or she may be tunnel visioned and have blind spots to certain types of problems.

2. Developers generally prefer to write new code rather than do any form of testing! (We will see more details of this syndrome later in the section on challenges as well as when we discuss people issues in Chapter 13.)

3. This method is essentially person-dependent and informal and thus may not work consistently across all developers.

Owing to these disadvantages, the next two types of proactive methods are introduced. The basic principle of walkthroughs and formal inspections is to involve multiple people in the review process.

3.2.1.2 Code walkthrough

This method and formal inspection (described in the next section) are group-oriented methods. Walkthroughs are less formal than inspections. The line drawn in formalism between walkthroughs and inspections is very thin and varies from organization to organization. The advantage that walkthrough has over desk checking is that it brings multiple perspectives. In walkthroughs, a set of people look at the program code and raise questions for the author. The author explains the logic of the code, and answers the questions. If the author is unable to answer some questions, he or she then takes those questions and finds their answers. Completeness is limited to the area where questions are raised by the team.

3.2.1.3 Formal inspection

Code inspection—also called Fagan Inspection (named after the original formulator)—is a method, normally with a high degree of formalism. The focus of this method is to detect all faults, violations, and other side-effects. This method increases the number of defects detected by

1. demanding thorough preparation before an inspection/review;

2. enlisting multiple diverse views;

3. assigning specific roles to the multiple participants; and

4. going sequentially through the code in a structured manner.

A formal inspection should take place only when the author has made sure the code is ready for inspection by performing some basic desk checking and walkthroughs. When the code is in such a reasonable state of readiness, an inspection meeting is arranged. There are four roles in inspection. First is the *author* of the code. Second is a *moderator* who is expected to formally run the inspection according to the process. Third are the *inspectors*. These are the people who actually provides, review comments for the code. There are typically multiple inspectors. Finally, there is a *scribe*, who takes detailed notes during the inspection meeting and circulates them to the inspection team after the meeting.

The author or the moderator selects the review team. The chosen members have the skill sets to uncover as many defects as possible. In an introductory meeting, the inspectors get copies (These can be hard copies or soft copies) of the code to be inspected along with other supporting documents such as the design document, requirements document, and any documentation of applicable standards. The author also presents his or her perspective of what the program is intended to do along with any specific issues that he or she may want the inspection team to put extra focus on. The moderator informs the team about the date, time, and venue of the inspection meeting. The inspectors get adequate time to go through the documents and program and ascertain their compliance to the requirements, design, and standards.

The inspection team assembles at the agreed time for the inspection meeting (also called the *defect logging meeting*). The moderator takes the team sequentially through the program code, asking each inspector if there are any defects in that part of the code. If any of the inspectors raises a defect, then the inspection team deliberates on the defect and, when agreed that there is a defect, classifies it in two dimensions—*minor/major* and *systemic/mis-execution*. A mis-execution defect is one which, as the name suggests, happens because of an error or slip on the part of the author. It is unlikely to be repeated later, either in this work product or in other work products. An example of this is using a wrong variable in a statement. Systemic defects, on the other hand, can require correction at a different level. For example, an error such as using some machine-specific idiosyncrasies may have to removed by changing the coding standards. Similarly, minor defects are defects that may not substantially affect a program, whereas major defects need immediate attention.

A scribe formally documents the defects found in the inspection meeting and the author takes care of fixing these defects. In case the defects are severe, the team may optionally call for a review meeting to inspect the fixes to ensure that they address the problems. In any case, defects found through inspection need to be tracked till completion and someone in the team has to verify that the problems have been fixed properly.

3.2.1.4 Combining various methods
The methods discussed above are not mutually exclusive. They need to be used in a judicious combination to be effective in achieving the goal of finding defects early.

Formal inspections have been found very effective in catching defects early. Some of the challenges to watch out for in conducting formal inspections are as follows.

1. These are time consuming. Since the process calls for preparation as well as formal meetings, these can take time.

2. The logistics and scheduling can become an issue since multiple people are involved.

3. It is not always possible to go through every line of code, with several parameters and their combinations in mind to ensure the correctness of the logic, side-effects and appropriate error handling. It may also not be necessary to subject the entire code to formal inspection.

In order to overcome the above challenges, it is necessary to identify, during the planning stages, which parts of the code will be subject to formal inspections. Portions of code can be classified on the basis of their criticality or complexity as "high," "medium," and "low." High or medium complex critical code should be subject to formal inspections, while those classified as "low" can be subject to either walkthroughs or even desk checking.

Desk checking, walkthrough, review and inspection are not only used for code but can be used for all other deliverables in the project life cycle such as documents, binaries, and media.

3.2.2   Static Analysis Tools

The review and inspection mechanisms described above involve significant amount of manual work. There are several static analysis tools available in the market that can reduce the manual work and perform analysis of the code to find out errors such as those listed below.

1. whether there are unreachable codes (usage of GOTO statements sometimes creates this situation; there could be other reasons too)

2. variables declared but not used

3. mismatch in definition and assignment of values to variables

4. illegal or error prone typecasting of variables

5. use of non-portable or architecture-dependent programming constructs

6. memory allocated but not having corresponding statements for freeing them up memory

7. calculation of cyclomatic complexity (covered in the Section 3.3)

These static analysis tools can also be considered as an extension of compilers as they use the same concepts and implementation to locate errors. A good compiler is also a static analysis tool. For example, most C compilers provide different "levels" of code checking which will catch the various types of programming errors given above.

Some of the static analysis tools can also check compliance for coding standards as prescribed by standards such as POSIX. These tools can also check for consistency in coding guidelines (for example, naming conventions, allowed data types, permissible programming constructs, and so on).

While following any of the methods of human checking—desk checking, walkthroughs, or formal inspections—it is useful to have a code review checklist. Given below is checklist that covers some of the common issues. Every organization should develop its own code review checklist. The checklist should be kept current with new learning as they come about.

In a multi-product organization, the checklist may be at two levels—first, an organization-wide checklist that will include issues such as organizational coding standards, documentation standards, and so on; second, a product- or project-specific checklist that addresses issues specific to the product or project.

CODE REVIEW CHECKLIST

DATA ITEM DECLARATION RELATED

- Are the names of the variables meaningful?
- If the programming language allows mixed case names, are there variable names with confusing use of lower case letters and capital letters?
- Are the variables initialized?
- Are there similar sounding names (especially words in singular and plural)? [These could be possible causes of unintended errors.]
- Are all the common stru tures, constants, and flags to be used defined in a header file rather than in each file separately?

DATA USAGE RELATED

- Are values of right data types being assigned to the variables?
- Is the access of data from any standard files, repositories, or databases done through publicly sup- ported interfaces?
- If pointers are used, are they initialized properly?
- Are bounds to array subscripts and pointers properly checked?

- Has the usage of similar-looking operators (for example, = and == or & and && in C) checked?

CONTROL FLOW RELATED

- Are all the conditional paths reachable?

- Are all the individal conditions in a complex condition separately evaluated?

- If there is a nested IF statement, are the THEN and ELSE parts appropriately delimited?

- In the case of a multi-way branch like SWITCH / CASE statement, is a default clause provided? Are the breaks after each CASE appropriate?

- Is there any part of code that is unreachable?

- Are there any loops that will never execute?

- Are there any loops where the final condition will never be met and hence cause the program to go into an infinite loop?

- What is the level of nesting of the conditional statements? Can the code be simplified to reduce complexity?

STANDARDS RELATED

- Does the code follow the coding conventions of the organization?

- Does the code follow any coding conventions that are platform specific (for example, GUI calls specific to Windows or Swing)

STYLE RELATED

- Are unhealthy programming constructs (for example, global variables in C, ALTER statement in COBOL) being used in the program?

- Is there usage of specific idiosyncrasies of a particular machine architecture or a given version of an underlying product (for example, using "undocumented" features)?

- Is sufficient attention being paid to readability issues like indentation of code?

MISCELLANEOUS

- Have you checked for memory leaks (for example, memory acquired but not explicitly freed)?

DOCUMENTATION RELATED

- Is the code adequately documented, especially where the logic is complex or the section of code is critical for product functioning?
- Is appropriate change history documented?
- Are the interfaces and the parameters thereof properly documented?

3.3　STRUCTURAL TESTING

Structural testing takes into account the code, code structure, internal design, and how they are coded. The fundamental difference between structural testing and static testing is that in structural testing tests are actually run by the computer on the built product, whereas in static testing, the product is tested by humans using just the source code and not the executables or binaries.

Structural testing entails running the actual product against some pre-designed test cases to exercise as much of the code as possible or necessary. A given portion of the code is exercised if a test case causes the program to execute that portion of the code when running the test.

As discussed at the beginning of this chapter, structural testing can be further classified into unit/code functional testing, code coverage, and code complexity testing.

3.3.1　Unit/Code Functional Testing

This initial part of structural testing corresponds to some quick checks that a developer performs before subjecting the code to more extensive code coverage testing or code complexity testing. This can happen by several methods.

1. Initially, the developer can perform certain obvious tests, knowing the input variables and the corresponding expected output variables. This can be a quick test that checks out any obvious mistakes. By repeating these tests for multiple values of input variables, the confidence level of the developer to go to the next level

increases. This can even be done prior to formal reviews of static testing so that the review mechanism does not waste time catching obvious errors.

2. For modules with complex logic or conditions, the developer can build a "debug version" of the product by putting intermediate print statements and making sure the program is passing through the right loops and iterations the right number of times. It is important to remove the intermediate print statements after the defects are fixed.

3. Another approach to do the initial test is to run the product under a debugger or an Integrated Development Environment (IDE). These tools allow single stepping of instructions (allowing the developer to stop at the end of each instruction, view or modify the contents of variables, and so on), setting break points at any function or instruction, and viewing the various system parameters or program variable values.

All the above fall more under the "debugging" category of activities than under the "testing" category of activities. All the same, these are intimately related to the knowledge of code structure and hence we have included these under the "white box testing" head. This is consistent with our view that testing encompasses whatever it takes to detect and correct defects in a product.

3.3.2 Code Coverage Testing

Since a product is realized in terms of program code, if we can run test cases to exercise the different parts of the code, then that part of the product realized by the code gets tested. Code coverage testing involves designing and executing test cases and finding out the percentage of code that is covered by testing. The percentage of code covered by a test is found by adopting a technique called *instrumentation* of code. There are specialized tools available to achieve instrumentation. Instrumentation rebuilds the product, linking the product with a set of libraries provided by the tool vendors. This instrumented code can monitor and keep an audit of what portions of code are covered. The tools also allow reporting on the portions of the code that are covered frequently, so that the critical or most-often portions of code can be identified.

Code coverage testing is made up of the following types of coverage.

1. Statement coverage
2. Path coverage
3. Condition coverage
4. Function coverage

3.3.2.1 Statement coverage

Program constructs in most conventional programming languages can be classified as

1. Sequential control flow
2. Two-way decision statements like `if then else`
3. Multi-way decision statements like `Switch`
4. Loops like `while do`, `repeat until` and `for`

Object-oriented languages have all of the above and, in addition, a number of other constructs and concepts. We will take up issues pertaining to object oriented languages together in Chapter 11. We will confine our discussions here to conventional languages.

Statement coverage refers to writing test cases that execute each of the program statements. One can start with the assumption that more the code covered, the better is the testing of the functionality, as the code realizes the functionality. Based on this assumption, code coverage can be achieved by providing coverage to each of the above types of statements.

For a section of code that consists of statements that are sequentially executed (that is, with no conditional branches), test cases can be designed to run through from top to bottom. A test case that starts at the top would generally have to go through the full section till the bottom of the section. However, this may not always be true. First, if there are asynchronous exceptions that the code encounters (for example, a divide by zero), then, even if we start a test case at the beginning of a section, the test case may not cover all the statements in that section. Thus, even in the case of sequential statements, coverage for all statements may not be achieved. Second, a section of code may be entered from multiple points. Even though this points to not following structured programming guidelines, it is a common scenario in some of the earlier programming languages.

When we consider a two-way decision construct like the `if` statement, then to cover all the statements, we should also cover the `then` and `else` parts of the `if` statement. This means we should have, for each `if then else`, (at least) one test case to test the `Then` part and (at least) one test case to test the `else` part.

The multi-way decision construct such as a `Switch` statement can be reduced to multiple two-way `if` statements. Thus, to cover all possible `switch` cases, there would be multiple test cases. (We leave it as an exercise for the reader to develop this further.)

Loop constructs present more variations to take care of. A loop—in various forms such as `for`, `while`, `repeat`, and so on—is characterized by executing a set of statements repeatedly until or while certain conditions are met. A good percentage of the defects in programs come about because of loops that do not function properly. More often, loops fail in what are called "boundary conditions." One of the common looping errors is that the termination condition of the loop is not properly stated. In order to make sure that there is better statement coverage for statements within a loop, there should be test cases that

1. Skip the loop completely, so that the situation of the termination condition being true before starting the loop is tested.
2. Exercise the loop between once and the maximum number of times, to check all possible "normal" operations of the loop.
3. Try covering the loop, around the "boundary" of **n**—that is, just below **n**, **n**, and just above **n**.

> Statement Coverage = (Total statements exercised / Total number of executable statements in program) * 100

The statement coverage for a program, which is an indication of the percentage of statements actually executed in a set of tests, can be calculated by the formula given alongside in the margin.

It is clear from the above discussion that as the type of statement progresses from a simple sequential statement to if then else and through to loops, the number of test cases required to achieve statement coverage increases. Taking a cue from the Dijkstra's Doctrine in Chapter 1, just as exhaustive testing of all possible input data on a program is not possible, so also exhaustive coverage of all statements in a program will also be impossible for all practical purposes.

Even if we were to achieve a very high level of statement coverage, it does not mean that the program is defect-free. First, consider a hypothetical case when we achieved 100 percent code coverage. If the program implements wrong requirements and this wrongly implemented code is "fully tested," with 100 percent code coverage, it still is a wrong program and hence the 100 percent code coverage does not mean anything.

Next, consider the following program.

```
Total = 0; /* set total to zero */
if (code == "M") {
    stmt1;
    stmt2;
    Stmt3;
    stmt4;
    Stmt5;
    stmt6;
    Stmt7;
}
else percent = value/Total*100; /* divide by zero */
```

In the above program, when we test with code = "M," we will get 80 percent code coverage. But if the data distribution in the real world is such that 90 percent of the time, the value of code is not = "M," then, the program will fail 90 percent of the time (because of the divide by zero in the highlighted line). Thus, even with a code coverage of 80 percent, we are left with a defect that hits the users 90 percent of the time. Path coverage, discussed in Section 3.3.2.2, overcomes this problem.

Path Coverage =
(Total paths exercised/
Total number of paths
in program) * 100

3.3.2.2 Path coverage

In path coverage, we split a program into a number of distinct paths. A program (or a part of a program) can start from the beginning and take any of the paths to its completion.

Let us take an example of a date validation routine. The date is accepted as three fields mm, dd and yyyy. We have assumed that prior to entering this routine, the values are checked to be numeric. To simplify the discussion, we have assumed the existence of a function called leapyear which will return TRUE if the given year is a leap year. There is an array called DayofMonth which contains the number of days in each month. A simplified flow chart for this is given in Figure 3.2 below.

As can be seen from the figure, there are different paths that can be taken through the program. Each part of the path is shown in red. The coloured representation of Figure 3.2 is available on page 459. Some of the paths are

- ✠ A
- ✠ B-D-G
- ✠ B-D-H
- ✠ B-C-E-G
- ✠ B-C-E-H
- ✠ B-C-F-G
- ✠ B-C-F-H

Regardless of the number of statements in each of these paths, if we can execute these paths, then we would have covered most of the typical scenarios.

Figure 3.2

Flow chart for a date validation routine.

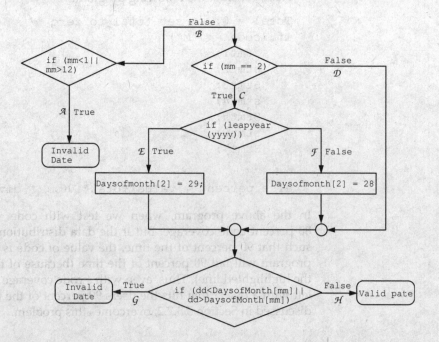

Path coverage provides a stronger condition of coverage than statement coverage as it relates to the various logical paths in the program rather than just program statements.

3.3.2.3 Condition coverage In the above example, even if we have covered all the paths possible, it would not mean that the program is fully tested. For example, we can make the program take the path A by giving a value less than 1 (for example, 0) to mm and find that we have covered the path A and the program has detected that the month is invalid. But, the program may still not be correctly testing for the other condition namely $mm > 12$. Furthermore, most compilers perform optimizations to minimize the number of Boolean operations and all the conditions may not get evaluated, even though the right path is chosen. For example, when there is an OR condition (as in the first IF statement above), once the first part of the IF (for example, $mm < 1$) is found to be true, the second part will not be evaluated at all as the overall value of the Boolean is TRUE. Similarly, when there is an AND condition in a Boolean expression, when the first condition evaluates to FALSE, the rest of the expression need not be evaluated at all.

For all these reasons, path testing may not be sufficient. It is necessary to have test cases that exercise each Boolean expression and have test cases test produce the TRUE as well as FALSE paths. Obviously, this will mean more test cases and the number of test cases will rise exponentially with the number of conditions and Boolean expressions. However, in reality, the situation may not be very bad as these conditions usually have some dependencies on one another.

> Condition Coverage = (Total decisions exercised / Total number of decisions in program) * 100

The condition coverage, as defined by the formula alongside in the margin gives an indication of the percentage of conditions covered by a set of test cases. Condition coverage is a much stronger criteria than path coverage, which in turn is a much stronger criteria than statement coverage.

3.3.2.4 Function coverage This is a new addition to structural testing to identify how many program functions (similar to functions in "C" language) are covered by test cases.

The requirements of a product are mapped into functions during the design phase and each of the functions form a logical unit. For example, in a database software, "inserting a row into the database" could be a function. Or, in a payroll application, "calculate tax" could be a function. Each function could, in turn, be implemented using other functions. While providing function coverage, test cases can be written so as to exercise each of the different functions in the code. The advantages that function coverage provides over the other types of coverage are as follows.

1. Functions are easier to identify in a program and hence it is easier to write test cases to provide function coverage.

2. Since functions are at a much higher level of abstraction than code, it is easier to achieve 100 percent function coverage than 100 percent coverage in any of the earlier methods.

3. Functions have a more logical mapping to requirements and hence can provide a more direct correlation to the test coverage of the product. In the next chapter, we will be discussing the requirements traceability matrix, which track a requirement through design, coding, and testing phases. Functions provide one means to achieve this traceability. Function coverage provides a way of testing this traceability.

4. Since functions are a means of realizing requirements, the importance of functions can be prioritized based on the importance of the requirements they realize. Thus, it would be easier to prioritize the functions for testing. This is not necessarily the case with the earlier methods of coverage.

5. Function coverage provides a natural transition to black box testing.

We can also measure how many times a given function is called. This will indicate which functions are used most often and hence these functions become the target of any performance testing and optimization. As an example, if in a networking software, we find that the function that assembles and disassembles the data packets is being used most often, it is appropriate to spend extra effort in improving the quality and performance of that function. Thus, function coverage can help in improving the performance as well as quality of the product.

> Function Coverage = (Total functions exercised / Total number of functions in program) * 100

3.3.2.5 Summary Code coverage testing involves "dynamic testing" methods of executing the product with pre-written test cases, and finding out how much of code has been covered. If a better coverage of a code is desired, several iterations of testing may be required. For each iteration, one has to go through the statistics and write a new set of test cases for covering portions of the code not covered by earlier test cases. To do this type of testing not only does one need to understand the code, logic but also need to understand how to write effective test cases that can cover good portions of the code. This type of testing can also be referred to as "gray box testing" as this uses the combination of "white box and black box methodologies" (white + black = gray) for effectiveness.

Thus, better code coverage is the result of better code flow understanding and writing effective test cases. Code coverage up to 40–50 percent is usually achievable. Code coverage of more than 80 percent requires enormous amount of effort and understanding of the code.

The multiple code coverage techniques we have discussed so far are not mutually exclusive. They supplement and augment one another. While statement coverage can provide a basic comfort factor, path, decision, and function coverage provide more confidence by exercising various logical paths and functions.

In the above discussion, we have looked at the use of code coverage testing for various functional requirements. There are also a few other uses for these methods.

Performance analysis and optimization   Code coverage tests can identify the areas of a code that are executed most frequently. Extra attention can then be paid to these sections of the code. If further performance improvement is no longer possible, then other strategies like caching can be considered. Code coverage testing provides information that is useful in making such performance-oriented decisions.

Resource usage analysis   White box testing, especially with instrumented code, is useful in identifying bottlenecks in resource usage. For example, if a particular resource like the RAM or network is perceived as a bottleneck, then instrumented code can help identify where the bottlenecks are and point towards possible solutions.

Checking of critical sections or concurrency related parts of code   Critical sections are those parts of a code that cannot have multiple processes executing at the same time. Coverage tests with instrumented code is one of the best means of identifying any violations of such concurrency constraints through critical sections.

Identifying memory leaks   Every piece of memory that is acquired or allocated by a process (for example, by `malloc` in C) should be explicitly released (for example, by `free` in C). If not, the acquired memory is "lost" and the amount of available memory decreases correspondingly. Over time, there would be no memory available for allocation to meet fresh memory requests and processes start failing for want of memory. The various white box testing methods can help identify memory leaks. Most debuggers or instrumented code can tally allocated and freed memory.

Dynamically generated code   White box testing can help identify security holes effectively, especially in a dynamically generated code. In instances where a piece of code is dynamically created and executed, the functionality of the generated code should be tested on the fly. For example, when using web services, there may be situations wherein certain parameters are accepted from the users and html/java code may be generated and passed on to a remote machine for execution. Since after the transaction or service is executed, the generated code ceases to exist, testing the generated code requires code knowledge. Hence, the various techniques of white box testing discussed in this chapter come in handy.

3.3.3   Code Complexity Testing

In previous sections, we saw the different types of coverage that can be provided to test a program. Two questions that come to mind while using these coverage are:

1.   Which of the paths are independent? If two paths are not independent, then we may be able to minimize the number of tests.

2.   Is there an upper bound on the number of tests that must be run to ensure that all the statements have been executed at least once?

Cyclomatic complexity is a metric that quantifies the complexity of a program and thus provides answers to the above questions.

A program is represented in the form of a *flow graph*. A flow graph consists of *nodes* and *edges*. In order to convert a standard flow chart into a flow graph to compute cyclomatic complexity, the following steps can be taken.

1. Identify the predicates or decision points (typically the Boolean conditions or conditional statements) in the program.

2. Ensure that the predicates are simple (that is, no and/or, and so on in each predicate). Figure 3.3 shows how to break up a condition having or into simple predicates. Similarly, if there are loop constructs, break the loop termination checks into simple predicates.

3. Combine all sequential statements into a single node. The reasoning here is that these statements all get executed, once started.

4. When a set of sequential statements are followed by a simple predicate (as simplified in (2) above), combine all the sequential statements and the predicate check into one node and have two edges emanating from this one node. Such nodes with two edges emanating from them are called *predicate nodes*.

5. Make sure that all the edges terminate at some node; add a node to represent all the sets of sequential statements at the end of the program.

We have illustrated the above transformation rules of a conventional flow chart to a flow diagram in Figure 3.4. We have color coded the different boxes (coloured figure on page 459) so that the reader can see the transformations more clearly. The flow chart elements of a given color on the left-hand side get mapped to flow graph elements of the corresponding nodes on the right-hand side.

Intuitively, a flow graph and the cyclomatic complexity provide indicators to the complexity of the logic flow in a program and to the number of independent paths in a program. The primary contributors to both the

Figure 3.3

Flow graph translation of an OR to a simple predicate.

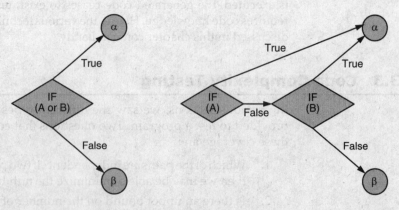

(a) A predicate with a Boolean OR   (b) An equivalent set of simple predicates

Figure 3.4

Converting a
conventional flow
chart to a flow graph.

Conventional flow chart   Flow diagram for calculating complexity

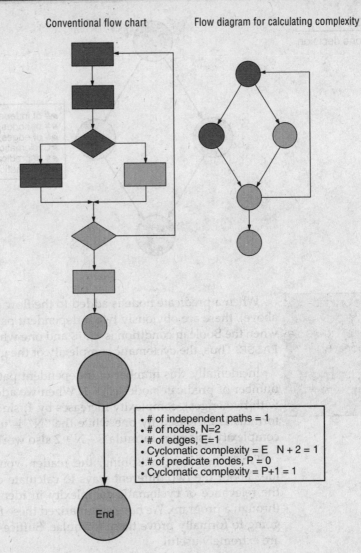

Figure 3.5

A hypothetical
program with no
decision node.

- # of independent paths = 1
- # of nodes, N=2
- # of edges, E=1
- Cyclomatic complexity = E   N + 2 = 1
- # of predicate nodes, P = 0
- Cyclomatic complexity = P+1 = 1

complexity and independent paths are the decision points in the program. Consider a hypothetical program with no decision points. The flow graph of such a program (shown in Figure 3.5 above) would have two nodes, one for the code and one for the termination node. Since all the sequential steps are combined into one node (the first node), there is only one edge, which connects the two nodes. This edge is the only independent path. Hence, for this flow graph, cyclomatic complexity is equal to one.

This graph has no predicate nodes because there are no decision points. Hence, the cyclomatic complexity is also equal to the number of predicate nodes (0) + 1.

Note that in this flow graph, the edges (E) = 1; nodes (N) = 2. The cyclomatic complexity is also equal to $1 = 1 + 2 - 2 = E - N + 2$.

Figure 3.6

Adding one decision
node.

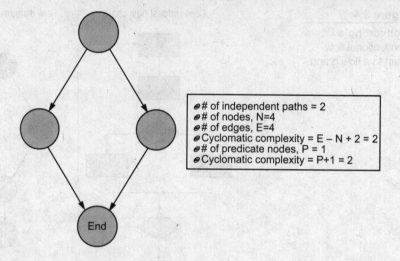

# of independent paths = 2
# of nodes, N=4
# of edges, E=4
Cyclomatic complexity = E – N + 2 = 2
# of predicate nodes, P = 1
Cyclomatic complexity = P+1 = 2

Cyclomatic
Complexity =
Number of Predicate
Nodes + 1

Cyclomatic
Complexity =
E – N + 2

When a predicate node is added to the flow graph (shown in Figure 3.6 above), there are obviously two independent paths, one following the path when the Boolean condition is TRUE and one when the Boolean condition is FALSE. Thus, the cyclomatic complexity of the graph is 2.

Incidentally, this number of independent paths, 2, is again equal to the number of predicate nodes (1) + 1. When we add a predicate node (a node with two edges), complexity increases by 1, since the "E" in the E – N + 2 formula is increased by one while the "N" is unchanged. As a result, the complexity using the formula E – N + 2 also works out to 2.

From the above reasoning, the reader would hopefully have got an idea about the two different ways to calculate cyclomatic complexity and the relevance of cyclomatic complexity in identifying independent paths through a program. We have summarized these formulae below. We are not going to formally prove these formulae. Suffice to say that these formulae are extremely useful.

The above two formulae provide an easy means to calculate cyclomatic complexity, given a flow graph. In fact the first formula can be used even without drawing the flow graph, by simply counting the number of the basic predicates. There are other formulations of cyclomatic complexity derived from the foundations of Graph Theory, which we have not covered here. The references given at the end can provide pointers for the interested reader.

Using the flow graph, an *independent path* can be defined as a path in the flow graph that has at least one edge that has not been traversed before in other paths. A set of independent paths that cover all the edges is a *basis set*. Once the basis set is formed, test cases should be written to execute all the paths in the basis set.

Table 3.1

Complexity	What it means
1–10	Well-written code, testability is high, cost/effort to maintain is low
10–20	Moderately complex, testability is medium, cost/effort to maintain is medium
20–40	Very complex, testability is low, cost/effort to maintain is high
>40	Not testable, any amount of money/effort to maintain may not be enough

3.3.3.1 Calculating and using cyclomatic complexity For small programs cyclomatic complexity can be calculated manually, but automated tools are essential as several thousands of lines of code are possible in each program in a project. It will be very difficult to manually create flow graphs for large programs. There are several tools that are available in the market which can compute cyclomatic complexity. But, we would like to caution that calculating the complexity of a module after it has been built and tested may be too late—it may not be possible to redesign a complex module after it has been tested. Thus some basic complexity checks must be performed on the modules before embarking upon the testing (or even coding) phase. This can become one of the items to check for in a code review. Based on the complexity number that emerges from using the tool, one can conclude what actions need to be taken for complexity measure using Table 3.1.

3.4 CHALLENGES IN WHITE BOX TESTING

White box testing requires a sound knowledge of the program code and the programming language. This means that the developers should get intimately involved in white box testing. Developers, in general, do not like to perform testing functions. This applies to structural testing as well as static testing methods such as reviews. In addition, because of the timeline pressures, the programmers may not "find time" for reviews (an euphemism for wanting to do more coding). We will revisit this myth of dichotomy between testing and development functions in the chapter on people issues (Chapter 13).

Human tendency of a developer being unable to find the defects in his or her code As we saw earlier, most of us have blind spots in detecting errors in our own products. Since white box testing involves programmers who write the code, it is quite possible that they may not be most effective in detecting defects in their own work products. An independent perspective could certainly help.

Fully tested code may not correspond to realistic scenarios Programmers generally do not have a full appreciation of the external (customer) perspective or the domain knowledge to visualize how a product will be deployed in realistic scenarios. This may mean that even after extensive testing, some of the common user scenarios may get left out and defects may creep in.

These challenges do not mean that white box testing is ineffective. But when white box testing is carried out and these challenges are addressed by other means of testing, there is a higher likelihood of more effective testing. Black box testing, to be discussed in the following chapter addresses some of these challenges.

REFERENCES

[MCCA-76] defined the Cyclomatic Complexity. The web reference [NIST-l] discusses code coverage and code complexity. [FAGA-86] covers the details of inspection. [PRES-97] provides a comprehensive coverage of all white box testing issues.

PROBLEMS AND EXERCISES

1. In the book, we discussed how to convert a Boolean **or** to simple predicates that can be used to derive the flow graph. Following similar technique, convert an expression like **if A and B** to a flow graph.

2. Given below is a simple C program to accept a set of inputs and calculate standard deviation. It has consciously been seeded with defects. If you were asked to perform white box testing on this program, identify some of the defects in the program. Also, list the methodology you used to identify these defects

CODE FOR CALCULATING STANDARD DEVIATION - PROBLEM 2 AND 3

```c
#include <stdio.h>
void main (argc, argv)
   {
     int no_numbers; /* The number of numbers for
which std dev is to be calculated */
     float mean, stdev; / * temporary variables */
     int i, total; /* temporary variables */
     int numbers[100]; /* the actual numbers */
     printf ("Please enter the number of numbers \n");
     scanf("%d", &no_numbers);
```

```
    /* First accept the numbers and calculate their
sum as we go along */
    for (i=0; i<no_numbers; i++)
      (
          scanf("%d", &numbers[i]);
          total+=numbers[i];
      }
    mean = total/no_numbers;
    /* now start calculating standard deviation */
    total = 0;
    for (i=0; i<no_numbers; i++)
      {
          total +=
                 ((mean - numbers[i]) * (mean -
numbers[i]))
      }
    stdev = total/no_numbers;
    printf ("The standard deviation is %d\n", stdev);
return (0);
  }
```

3. For the above program, draw the flow graph and hence calculate the cyclomatic complexity of the program.

4. Given below is a C program for deleting an element from a linked list. Suggest a set of test data to cover each and every statement of this program.

CODE FOR DELETING ELEMENTS FROM A DOUBLY LINKED LIST PROBLEMS 4 AND 5

```
/* definition of the list is assumed to be given by the
following structure:
  struct llist {
              int value;
              llist * next;
              llist * prev;
              }
  The caller is supposed to pass a pointer to the
start of the llist and the value to be deleted; There
is assumed to be at most one value to be deleted */

void delete_list (llist * list, int value_to_be_
deleted)
    {
      llist* temp;
  for (temp = list; temp != NULL, temp = temp->next)
```

```
    {
    if (temp → value == value_to_be_deleted)
        if (temp → prev ! = NULL)
                temp →prev →next = temp → next;
        if (temp → next ! = NULL)
                temp → next → prev = temp → prev;
        return (0);
        }
    return (1); /* value to be deleted is not found
at the end of search */
    }
```

5. In the example of the previous problem, even when the set of test data provides 100% statement coverage, show that there are still uncovered defects.

6. Given below are parts of the code segment actually written by two students for date validation. The two students used two different approaches as given in the code segments 6a and 6b. Which of these two would you think is easier from a white box testing perspective? Which of the techniques of white box testing discussed in this chapter would be most relevant to apply for 6a and which for 6b? How would you improve the effectiveness of the code in terms of susceptibility to defects in either case and ability to detect defects more easily?

CODE FOR DATE VALIDATION - PROBLEM 6 - SEGMENT 6a

```
int month_days [13]= {0, 31, 28, 31, 30, 31, 30, 31,
                    31,30, 31, 30, 31 };
valid = TRUE;
if (is_leap-year(yy))
    month_days [2] = 29;
if (mm < 1 !! mm > 12) valid = FALSE;
else
    if (day < 1 !! day> month(month_length[month])
        valid = FALSE;
    else if (year < 1)
        valid = FALSE;
return (VALID);
/* In the above, the function is_leap-year is defined
as follows */
int is_leap-year (int year)
  {
    int result;
    if ((year%4) != 0 ) result = FALSE;
    else (if (( year %400) == 0) result = TRUE;
```

```
         else if ((year %100) == 0) result = FALSE;
     return (result);
}
```

CODE FOR DATE VALIDATION – PROBLEM 6 – SEGMENT 6b

```
If (!(dd > 0 && dd < 32))
    printf ("enter a number between 1 and 32 only\n");
    return (1);
if ((mm=4) !! (mm==6) !! (mm==9) !! (mm==11)) && day> 30)
    {
        printf ("invalid date; maximum days should be 30");
        return (1);
    }
if ((1=(year%100!=0) && (year%4==0)!!(year%400==0)))
        &&        (day<=29))    !!
                                    (day < 29))

    {
        printf ("valid date \n");
        return (0);
    }
else
    {
        printf("invalid date\n");
        return (1);
    }
```

7. In Problem 6b, the test data presented in Table P1 was used to test the leap year part of the validation. Calculate the various coverage factors for this test data for the leap year part of the code.

Table P1   Values for testing segment 3B.

Value	Reason for choosing the value
29 Feb 2003	To check days> 28 for a non-1eap year
28 Feb 2003	To check 2003 not a leap year and day = 28 is valid
29 Feb 2000	Check the day limit for leap year
30 Feb 2000	Check the day limit for leap year
14 Feb 2000	To test day within day limit
29 Feb 1996	To check day = 29 is valid for leap year

8. Write a simple matrix multiplication program and try to take care of as many valid and invalid conditions as possible. Identify what test data would you use for testing program. Justify your answer.

9. A reentrant code is a piece of program that does not modify itself. In contrast, a non-reentrant code is a piece of program that modifies itself. Discuss the problems you will face from the white box testing perspective and from the point of view of ongoing maintenance of such a program.

10. Discuss the negative effects of the following constructs from a white box testing perspective:

   a. GOTO statements

   b. Global variables

11. Discuss the pros and cons of function coverage vis à vis other forms of coverage.

Black Box Testing

CHAPTER 4

In this chapter—

4.1   WHAT IS BLACK BOX TESTING?

> Black box testing is done without the knowledge of the internals of the system under test.

Black box testing involves looking at the specifications and does not require examining the code of a program. Black box testing is done from the customer's viewpoint. The test engineer engaged in black box testing only knows the set of inputs and expected outputs and is unaware of how those inputs are transformed into outputs by the software.

Black box tests are convenient to administer because they use the complete finished product and do not require any knowledge of its construction. Independent test laboratories can administer black box tests to ensure functionality and compatibility.

Let us take a lock and key. We do not know how the levers in the lock work, but we only know the set of inputs (the number of keys, specific sequence of using the keys and the direction of turn of each key) and the expected outcome (locking and unlocking). For example, if a key is turned clockwise it should unlock and if turned anticlockwise it should lock. To use the lock one need not understand how the levers inside the lock are constructed or how they work. However, it is essential to know the external functionality of the lock and key system. Some of the functionality that you need to know to use the lock are given below.

Functionality	What you need to know to use
Features of a lock	It is made of metal, *has a hole provision to lock,* has a facility to insert the key, and the keyhole ability to turn clockwise or anticlockwise.
Features of a key	It is made of metal and created to fit into a particular lock's keyhole.
Actions performed	Key inserted and turned clockwise to lock Key inserted and turned anticlockwise to unlock
States	Locked Unlocked
Inputs	Key turned clockwise or anticlockwise
Expected outcome	Locking Unlocking

With the above knowledge, you have meaningful ways to test a lock and key before you buy it, without the need to be an expert in the mechanics of *how* locks, keys, and levers work together. This concept is extended in black box testing for testing software.

Black box testing thus requires a functional knowledge of the product to be tested. It does not mandate the knowledge of the internal logic of the system nor does it mandate the knowledge of the programming language used to build the product. Our tests in the above example were focused towards testing the features of the product (lock and key), the different states, we already knew the expected outcome. You may check if the lock works with some other key (other than its own). You may also want to check with a hairpin or any thin piece of wire if the lock works. We shall see in further sections, in detail, about the different kinds of tests that can be performed in a given product.

4.2 WHY BLACK BOX TESTING

Black box testing helps in the overall functionality verification of the system under test.

Black box testing is done based on requirements It helps in identifying any incomplete, inconsistent requirement as well as any issues involved when the system is tested as a complete entity.

Black box testing addresses the stated requirements as well as implied requirements Not all the requirements are stated explicitly, but are deemed implicit. For example, inclusion of dates, page header, and footer may not be explicitly stated in the report generation requirements specification. However, these would need to be included while providing the product to the customer to enable better readability and usability.

Black box testing encompasses the end user perspectives Since we want to test the behavior of a product from an external perspective, end-user perspectives are an integral part of black box testing.

Black box testing handles valid and invalid inputs It is natural for users to make errors while using a product. Hence, it is not sufficient for black box testing to simply handle valid inputs. Testing from the end-user perspective includes testing for these error or invalid conditions. This ensures that the product behaves as expected in a valid situation and does not hang or crash when provided with an invalid input. These are called positive and negative test cases.

The tester may or may not know the technology or the internal logic of the product. However, knowing the technology and the system internals helps in constructing test cases specific to the error-prone areas.

Test scenarios can be generated as soon as the specifications are ready. Since requirements specifications are the major inputs for black box testing, test design can be started early in the cycle.

4.3 WHEN TO DO BLACK BOX TESTING?

Black box testing activities require involvement of the testing team from the beginning of the software project life cycle, regardless of the software development life cycle model chosen for the project.

Testers can get involved right from the requirements gathering and analysis phase for the system under test. Test scenarios and test data are prepared during the test construction phase of the test life cycle, when the software is in the design phase.

Once the code is ready and delivered for testing, test execution can be done. All the test scenarios developed during the construction phase are executed. Usually, a subset of these test scenarios is selected for regression testing.

4.4 HOW TO DO BLACK BOX TESTING?

Black box testing exploits specifications to generate test cases in a methodical way to avoid redundancy and to provide better coverage.

As we saw in Chapter 1, it is not possible to exhaustively test a product, however simple the product is. Since we are testing external functionality in black box testing, we need to arrive at a judicious set of tests that test as much of the external functionality as possible, uncovering as many defects as possible, in as short a time as possible. While this may look like a utopian wish list, the techniques we will discuss in this section facilitates this goal. This section deals with the various techniques to be used to generate test scenarios for effective black box testing.

The various techniques we will discuss are as follows.

1. Requirements based testing
2. Positive and negative testing
3. Boundary value analysis
4. Decision tables
5. Equivalence partitioning
6. State based testing
7. Compatibility testing
8. User documentation testing
9. Domain testing

4.4.1 Requirements Based Testing

Requirements testing deals with validating the requirements given in the Software Requirements Specification (SRS) of the software system.

As mentioned in earlier chapters, not all requirements are explicitly stated; some of the requirements are implied or implicit. Explicit requirements are stated and documented as part of the requirements specification. Implied or implicit requirements are those that are nor documented but assumed to be incorporated in the system.

The precondition for requirements testing is a detailed review of the requirements specification. Requirements review ensures that they are consistent, correct, complete, and testable. This process ensures that some implied requirements are converted and documented as explicit requirements, thereby bringing better clarity to requirements and making requirements based testing more effective.

Some organizations follow a variant of this method to bring more details into requirements. All explicit requirements (from the Systems Requirements Specifications) and implied requirements (inferred by the test team) are collected and documented as "Test Requirements Specification" (TRS). Requirements based testing can also be conducted based on such a TRS, as it captures the testers' perspective as well. However, for simplicity, we will consider SRS and TRS to be one and the same.

A requirements specification for the lock and key example explained earlier can be documented as given in Table 4.1.

Requirements (like the ones given above) are tracked by a *Requirements Traceability Matrix* (RTM). An RTM traces all the requirements from their

Table 4.1 Sample requirements specification for lock and key system.

S.No.	Requirements identifier	Description	Priority (High, med, low)
1	BR–01	Inserting the key numbered 123–456 and turning it clockwise should facilitate locking	H
2	BR–02	Inserting the key numbered 123–456 and turning it anticlockwise should facilitate unlocking	H
3	BR–03	Only key number 123–456 can be used to lock and unlock	H
4	BR–04	No other object can be used to lock	M
5	BR–05	No other object can be used to unlock	M
6	BR–06	The lock must not open even when it is hit with a heavy object	M
7	BR–07	The lock and key must be made of metal and must weigh approximately 150 grams	L
8	BR–08	Lock and unlock directions should be changeable for usability of left-handers	L

genesis through design, development, and testing. This matrix evolves through the life cycle of the project. To start with, each requirement is given a unique id along with a brief description. The *requirement identifier* and *description* can be taken from the Requirements Specification (above table) or any other available document that lists the requirements to be tested for the product. In the above table, the naming convention uses a prefix "BR" followed by a two-digit number. BR indicates the type of testing—"Black box-requirements testing." The two-digit numerals count the number of requirements. In systems that are more complex, an identifier representing a module and a running serial number within the module (for example, INV–01, AP–02, and so on) can identify a requirement. Each requirement is assigned a *requirement priority*, classified as high, medium or low. This not

Table 4.2 Sample Requirements Traceability Matrix.

Req. ID	Description	Priority (H,M,L)	Test conditions	Test case IDs	Phase of testing
BR–01	Inserting the key numbered 123–456 and turning it clockwise should facilitate locking	H	* Use key 123–456	Lock_001	Unit, Component
BR–02	Inserting the key numbered 123–456 and turning it anticlockwise should facilitate unlocking	H	* Use key 123–456	Lock_002	Unit, Component
BR–03	Only key number 123–456 can be used to lock and unlock	H	* Use key 123–456 to lock * Use key 123–456 to unlock	Lock_003 Lock_004	Component
BR–04	No other object can be used to lock	M	* Use key 789–001 * Use hairpin * Use screwdriver	Lock_005 Lock_006 Lock_007	Integration
BR–05	No other object can be used to unlock	M	* Use key 789–001 * Use hairpin * Use screwdriver	Lock_008 Lock_009 Lock_010	Integration
BR–06	The lock must not open even when it is hit with a heavy object	M	* Use stone to break the lock	Lock_011	System
BR–07	The lock and key must be made of metal and must weigh approximately 150 grams	L	* Use weighing machine	Lock_012	System
BR–08	Lock and unlock directions changed for usability of lefthanders	L			Not implemented

only enables prioritizing the resources for development of features but is also used to sequence and run tests. Tests for higher priority requirements will get precedence over tests for lower priority requirements. This ensures that the functionality that has the highest risk is tested earlier in the cycle. Defects reported by such testing can then be fixed as early as possible.

As we move further down in the life cycle of the product, and testing phases, the cross-reference between requirements and the subsequent phases is recorded in the RTM. In the example given here, we only list the mapping between requirements and testing; in a more complete RTM, there will be columns to reflect the mapping of requirements to design and code.

The *"test conditions"* column lists the different ways of testing the requirement. Test conditions can be arrived at using the techniques given in this chapter. Identification of all the test conditions gives a comfort feeling that we have not missed any scenario that could produce a defect in the end-user environment. These conditions can be grouped together to form a single test case. Alternatively, each test condition can be mapped to one test case.

The *"test case IDs"* column can be used to complete the mapping between test cases and the requirement. Test case IDs should follow naming conventions so as to enhance their usability. For example, in Table 4.2, test cases are serially numbered and prefixed with the name of the product. In a more complex product made up of multiple modules, a test case ID may be identified by a module code and a serial number.

Once the test case creation is completed, the RTM helps in identifying the relationship between the requirements and test cases. The following combinations are possible.

- ✠ One to one—For each requirement there is one test case (for example, BR–01)
- ✠ One to many—For each requirement there are many test cases (for example, BR–03)
- ✠ Many to one—A set of requirements can be tested by one test case (not represented in Table 4.2)
- ✠ Many to many—Many requirements can be tested by many test cases (these kind of test cases are normal with integration and system testing; however, an RTM is not meant for this purpose)
- ✠ One to none—The set of requirements can have no test cases. The test team can take a decision not to test a requirement due to non-implementation or the requirement being low priority (for example, BR–08)

A requirement is subjected to multiple phases of testing—unit, component, integration, and system testing. This reference to the *phase of testing* can be provided in a column in the Requirements Traceability Matrix. This column indicates when a requirement will be tested and at what phase of testing it needs to be considered for testing.

An RTM plays a valuable role in requirements based testing.

1. Regardless of the number of requirements, ideally each of the requirements has to be tested. When there are a large numbers of requirements, it would not be possible for someone to manually keep a track of the testing status of each requirement. The RTM provides a tool to track the testing status of each requirement, without missing any (key) requirements.

2. By prioritizing the requirements, the RTM enables testers to prioritize the test cases execution to catch defects in the high-priority area as early as possible. It is also used to find out whether there are adequate test cases for high-priority requirements and to reduce the number of test cases for low-priority requirements. In addition, if there is a crunch for time for testing, the prioritization enables selecting the right features to test.

3. Test conditions can be grouped to create test cases or can be represented as unique test cases. The list of test case(s) that address a particular requirement can be viewed from the RTM.

4. Test conditions/cases can be used as inputs to arrive at a size / effort / schedule estimation of tests.

The Requirements Traceability Matrix provides a wealth of information on various test metrics. Some of the metrics that can be collected or inferred from this matrix are as follows.

✠ Requirements addressed prioritywise—This metric helps in knowing the test coverage based on the requirements. Number of tests that is covered for high-priority requirement versus tests created for low-priority requirement.

✠ Number of test cases requirementwise—For each requirement, the total number of test cases created.

✠ Total number of test cases prepared—Total of all the test cases prepared for all requirements.

Once the test cases are executed, the test results can be used to collect metrics such as

✠ Total number of test cases (or requirements) passed—Once test execution is completed, the total passed test cases and what percent of requirements they correspond.

✠ Total number of test cases (or requirements) failed—Once test execution is completed, the total number of failed test cases and what percent of requirements they correspond.

✠ Total number of defects in requirements—List of defects reported for each requirement (defect density for requirements). This helps in doing an impact analysis of what requirements have more defects and how they will impact customers. A comparatively high-defect density in low-priority requirements is acceptable for a release. A high-defect density in high-priority requirement is considered a high-risk area, and may prevent a product release.

Table 4.3 Sample test execution data.

S.No.	Req. ID	Priority	Test cases	Total test cases	Test cases passed	Test cases failed	% Pass	No. of defects
1	BR–01	H	Lock_01	1	1	0	100	1
2	BR–02	H	Lock_02	1	1	0	100	1
3	BR–03	H	Lock_03, 04	2	1	1	50	3
4	BR–04	M	Lock_05, 06, 07	3	2	1	67	5
5	BR–05	M	Lock_08, 09, 10	3	3	0	100	1
6	BR–06	L	Lock_11	1	1	0	100	1
7	BR–07	L	Lock_12	1	1	0	100	0
8	BR–08	L		0	0	0	0	1
Total	**8**			**12**	**10**	**2**	**83**	**12**

✠ Number of requirements completed—Total number of requirements successfully completed without any defects. A more detailed coverage of what metrics to collect, how to plot and analyze them, etc are given in Chapter 17.

✠ Number of requirements pending—Number of requirements that are pending due to defects.

A more detailed coverage of what metrics to collect, how to plot and analyze them etc are given in Chapter 17.

To illustrate the metrics analysis, let us assume the test execution data as given in Table 4.3.

> Requirements based testing tests the product's compliance to the requirements specifications.

From the above table, the following observations can be made with respect to the requirements.

✠ 83 percent passed test cases correspond to 71 percent of requirements being met (five out of seven requirements met; one requirement not implemented). Similarly, from the failed test cases, outstanding defects affect 29 percent (= 100 – 71) of the requirements.

✠ There is a high-priority requirement, BR–03, which has failed. There are three corresponding defects that need to be looked into and some of them to be fixed and test case Lock_04 need to be executed again for meeting this requirement. Please note that not all the three defects may need to be fixed, as some of them could be cosmetic or low-impact defects.

✠ There is a medium-priority requirement, BR–04, has failed. Test case Lock_06 has to be re-executed after the defects (five of them) corresponding to this requirement are fixed.

✠ The requirement BR–08 is not met; however, this can be ignored for the release, even though there is a defect outstanding on this requirement, due to the low-priority nature of this requirement.

Figure 4.1

Graphical
representation of
test case results.

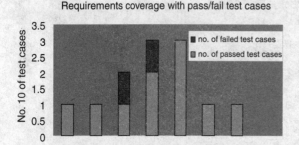

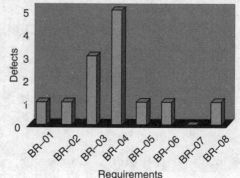

The metrics discussed can be expressed graphically. Such graphic representations convey a wealth of information in an intuitive way. For example, from the graphs given in Figure 4.1, (coloured figure available on page 460) it becomes obvious that the requirements BR–03 and BR–04 have test cases that have failed and hence need fixing.

4.4.2   Positive and Negative Testing

Positive testing tries to prove that a given product does what it is supposed to do. When a test case verifies the requirements of the product with a set of expected output, it is called positive test case. The purpose of positive testing is to prove that the product works as per specification and expectations. A product delivering an error *when it is expected to give an error*, is also a part of positive testing.

Positive testing can thus be said to check the product's behavior for positive and negative conditions as stated in the requirement.

For the lock and key example, a set of positive test cases are given below. (Please refer to Table 4.2 for requirements specifications.)

Let us take the first row in the below table. When the lock is in an unlocked state and you use key 123–456 and turn it clockwise, the expected outcome is to get it locked. During test execution, if the test results in locking, then the test is passed. This is an example of "positive test condition" for positive testing.

In the fifth row of the table, the lock is in locked state. Using a hairpin and turning it clockwise should not cause a change in state or cause any damage to the lock. On test execution, if there are no changes, then this positive test case is passed. This is an example of a "negative test condition" for positive testing.

Table 4.4 Example of positive test cases.

Req. no.	Input 1	Input 2	Current state	Expected output
BR–01	Key 123–456	Turn clockwise	Unlocked	Locked
BR–01	Key 123–456	Turn clockwise	Locked	No change
BR–02	Key 123–456	Turn anticlockwise	Unlocked	No change
BR–02	Key 123–456	Turn anticlockwise	Locked	Unlock
BR–04	Hairpin	Turn clockwise	Locked	No change

> Positive testing is done to verify the known test conditions and negative testing is done to break the product with unknowns.

Negative testing is done to show that the product does not fail when an unexpected input is given. The purpose of negative testing is to try and break the system. Negative testing covers scenarios for which the product is not designed and coded. In other words, the input values may not have been represented in the specification of the product. These test conditions can be termed as unknown conditions for the product as far as the specifications are concerned. But, at the end-user level, there are multiple scenarios that are encountered and that need to be taken care of by the product. It becomes even more important for the tester to know the negative situations that may occur at the end-user level so that the application can be tested and made foolproof. A negative test would be a product *not delivering an error when it should* or *delivering an error when it should not.*

Table 4.5 gives some of the negative test cases for the lock and key example.

Table 4.5 Negative test cases.

S. No.	Input 1	Input 2	Current state	Expected output
1	Some other lock's key	Turn clockwise	Lock	Lock
2	Some other lock's key	Turn anticlockwise	Unlock	Unlock
3	Thin piece of wire	Turn anticlockwise	Unlock	Unlock
4	Hit with a stone		Lock	Lock

In the above table, unlike what we have seen in positive testing, there are no requirement numbers. This is because negative testing focuses on test conditions that lie outside the specification. Since all the test conditions are outside the specification, they cannot be categorized as positive and negative test conditions. Some people consider all of them as *negative test conditions*, which is technically correct.

The difference between positive testing and negative testing is in their coverage. For positive testing if all documented requirements and test conditions are covered, then coverage can be considered to be 100 percent. If the specifications are very clear, then coverage can be achieved. In contrast there is no end to negative testing, and 100 percent coverage in negative testing is impractical. Negative testing requires a high degree of creativity among the testers to cover as many "unknowns" as possible to avoid failure at a customer site.

4.4.3 Boundary Value Analysis

As mentioned in the last section, conditions and boundaries are two major sources of defects in a software product. We will go into details of conditions in this section. Most of the defects in software products hover around *conditions* and *boundaries*. By conditions, we mean situations wherein, based on the values of various variables, certain actions would have to be taken. By boundaries, we mean "limits" of values of the various variables.

We will now explore boundary value analysis (BVA), a method useful for arriving at tests that are effective in catching defects that happen at boundaries. Boundary value analysis believes and extends the concept that the density of defect is more towards the boundaries.

To illustrate the concept of errors that happen at boundaries, let us consider a billing system that offers volume discounts to customers.

Most of us would be familiar with the concept of volume discounts when we buy goods —buy one packet of chips for $1.59 but three for $4. It becomes economical for the buyer to buy in bulk. From the seller's point of view also, it is economical to sell in bulk because the seller incurs less of storage and inventory costs and has a better cash flow. Let us consider a hypothetical store that sells certain commodities and offers different pricing for people buying in different quantities—that is, priced in different "slabs."

Number of units bought	Price per unit
First ten units (that is, from 1 to 10 units)	$5 .00
Next ten units (that is, from units 11 to 20 units)	$4.75
Next ten units (that is, from units 21 to 30 units)	$4.50
More than 30 units	$4.00

From the above table, it is clear that if we buy 5 units, we pay 5*5 = $25. If we buy 11 units, we pay 5*10 = $50 for the first ten units and $4.75 for the eleventh item. Similarly, if we buy 15 units, we will pay 10*5 + 5*4.75 = $73.75.

The question from a testing perspective for the above problem is what test data is likely to reveal the most number of defects in the program? Generally it has been found that most defects in situations such as this happen around the boundaries—for example, when buying 9, 10, 11, 19, 20, 21, 29, 30, 31, and similar number of items. While the reasons for this phenomenon is not entirely clear, some possible reasons are as follows.

✻ Programmers' tentativeness in using the right comparison operator, for example, whether to use the <= operator or < operator when trying to make comparisons.

✻ Confusion caused by the availability of multiple ways to implement loops and condition checking. For example, in a programming language like C, we have `for` loops, `while` loops and `repeat` loops. Each of these have different terminating conditions for the loop and this could cause some confusion in deciding which operator to use, thus skewing the defects around the boundary conditions.

✻ The requirements themselves may not be clearly understood, especially around the boundaries, thus causing even the correctly coded program to not perform the correct way.

In the above case, the tests that should be performed and the expected values of the output variable (the cost of the units ordered) are given in Table 4.6 below. This table only includes the positive test cases. Negative test cases

Table 4.6 Boundary values for the volumes discussed in the example.

Value to be tested	Why this value should be tested	Expected value of the output
1	The beginning of the first slab	$5.00
5	A value in the first slab, removed from the boundaries	$25.00
9	Just below the second slab or just at the end of the first slab	$45.00
10	The limit for the second slab	$50.00
11	Just above the first slab, just into the second slab	$54.75
16	A value in the second slab, removed from the boundaries	$28.50
19	Just below the third slab or just at the end of the second slab	$92.75
20	The limit for the third slab	$97.50
21	Just above the third slab, just into the third slab	$102.00
27	A value in the third slab, removed from the boundaries	$129.00
29	Just below the fourth slab or just at the end of the third slab	$138.00
30	The limit for the fourth slab	$142.50
31	Just above the fourth slab	$146.50
50	Well above the lower limit for the fourth slab	$182.50

like a non-numeric are not included here. The circled rows are the boundary values, which are more likely to uncover the defects than the rows that are not circled.

> Boundary value analysis is useful to generate test cases when the input (or output) data is made up of clearly identifiable boundaries or ranges.

Another instance where boundary value testing is extremely useful in uncovering defects is when there are internal limits placed on certain resources, variables, or data structures. Consider a database management system (or a file system) which caches the recently used data blocks in a shared memory area. Usually such a cached area is limited by a parameter that the user specifies at the time of starting up the system. Assume that the database is brought up specifying that the most recent 50 database buffers have to be cached. When these buffers are full and a 51st block needs to be cached, the least recently used buffer—the first buffer—needs to be released, after storing it in secondary memory. As you can observe, both the operations—inserting the new buffer as well as freeing up the first buffer—happen at the "boundaries."

As shown in Figure 4.2 below, there are four possible cases to be tested—first, when the buffers are completely empty (this may look like an oxymoron statement!); second, when inserting buffers, with buffers still free; third, inserting the last buffer, and finally, trying to insert when all buffers are full. It is likely that more defects are to be expected in the last two cases than the first two cases.

To summarize boundary value testing.

✠   Look for any kind of gradation or discontinuity in data values which affect computation—the discontinuities are the boundary values, which require thorough testing.

✠   Look for any internal limits such as limits on resources (as in the example of buffers given above). The behavior of the product at these limits should also be the subject of boundary value testing.

Figure 4.2

Various test cases of buffer management.

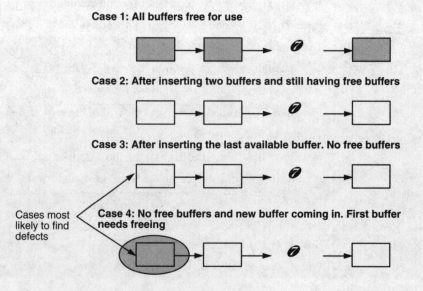

Case 1: All buffers free for use

Case 2: After inserting two buffers and still having free buffers

Case 3: After inserting the last available buffer. No free buffers

Cases most likely to find defects

Case 4: No free buffers and new buffer coming in. First buffer needs freeing

✠ Also include in the list of boundary values, documented limits on hardware resources. For example, if it is documented that a product will run with minimum 4MB of RAM, make sure you include test cases for the minimum RAM (4MB in this case).

✠ The examples given above discuss boundary conditions for input data—the same analysis needs to be done for output variables also.

Boundary value analysis discussed here in context of black box testing applies to white box testing also. Internal data structures like arrays, stacks, and queues need to be checked for boundary or limit conditions; when there are linked lists used as internal structures, the behavior of the list at the beginning and end have to be tested thoroughly.

Boundary values and decision tables help identify the test cases that are most likely to uncover defects. A generalization of both these concepts is the concept of *equivalence classes*, discussed later in this chapter.

4.4.4 Decision Tables

To illustrate the use of conditions (and decision tables) in testing, let us take a simple example of calculation of standard deduction on taxable income. The example is meant to illustrate the use of decision tables and not to be construed as tax advice or a realistic tax scenario in any specific country.

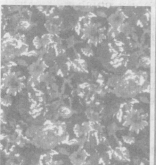

Most taxpayers have a choice of either taking a standard deduction or itemizing their deductions. The standard deduction is a dollar amount that reduces the amount of income on which you are taxed. It is a benefit that eliminates the need for many taxpayers to itemize actual deductions, such as medical expenses, charitable contributions, and taxes. The standard deduction is higher for taxpayers who are 65 or older or blind. If you have a choice, you should use the method that gives you the lower tax.

1. The first factor that determines the standard deduction is the filing status. The basic standard deduction for the various filing status are:

Single	$4,750
Married, filing a joint return	$9,500
Married, filing a separate return	$7,000

2. If a married couple is filing separate returns and one spouse is is not taking standard deduction, the other spouse also is not eligible for standard deduction.

3. An additional $1000 is allowed as standard deduction if either the filer is 65 years or older or the spouse is 65 years or older (the latter case applicable when the filing status is "Married" and filing "Joint").

4. An additional $1000 is allowed as standard deduction if either the filer is blind or the spouse is blind (the latter case applicable when the filing status is "Married" and filing "Joint").

From the above description, it is clear that the calculation of standard deduction depends on the following three factors.

1. Status of filing of the filer
2. Age of the filer
3. Whether the filer is blind or not

In addition, in certain cases, the following additional factors also come into play in calculating standard deduction.

1. Whether spouse has claimed standard deduction
2. Whether spouse is blind
3. Whether the spouse is more than 65 years old

A decision table lists the various decision variables, the conditions (or values) assumed by each of the decision variables, and the actions to take in each combination of conditions. The variables that contribute to the decision are listed as the columns of the table. The last column of the table is the action to be taken for the combination of values of the decision variables. In cases when the number of decision variables is many (say, more than five or six) and the number of distinct combinations of variables is few (say, four or five), the decision variables can be listed as rows (instead of columns) of the table. The decision table for the calculation of standard deduction is given in Table 4.7.

The reader would have noticed that there are a number of entries marked "−" in the decision table. The values of the appropriate decision variables in these cases do not affect the outcome of the decision. For example, the status of the spouse is relevant only when the filing status is "Married, filing separate return." Similarly, the age of spouse and whether spouse is blind or not comes into play only when the status is "Married, filing joint return." Such entries are called *don't cares* (sometimes represented by the Greek character *phi*, Φ). These don't cares significantly reduce the number of tests to be performed. For example, in case there were no don't cares, there would be eight cases for the status of "Single": four with status of spouse as

Table 4.7 Decision table for calculating standard deduction.

Status	Status of spouse	Age > 65? > 65?	Age of spouse	Blind? spouse	Spouse blind?	Standard deduction amount
Single	—	NO	—	NO	—	$4,750
Single	—	NO	—	YES	—	$5,750
Single	—	YES	—	NO	—	$5,750
Single	—	YES	—	YES	—	$6,750
Married, filing separate return	Claimed standard deduction	NO	—	NO	—	$7,000
Married, filing separate return	Claimed standard deduction	NO	—	YES	—	$8,000
Married, filing separate return	Claimed standard deduction	YES	—	NO	—	$8,000
Married, filing separate return	Claimed standard deduction	YES	—	YES	—	$9,000
Married, filing separate return	Did not claim standard deduction	—	—	—	—	$0
Married, filing joint return	—	NO	NO	NO	NO	$9,500
Married, filing joint return	—	YES	—	NO	NO	$10,500
Married, filing joint return	—	YES	—	YES	—	$11,500
Married, filing joint return	—	—	YES	NO	NO	$10,500
Married, filing joint return	—	—	YES	—	YES	$11,500

Note: *Strictly speaking, the columns of a decision table should all be Boolean variables. So, we should have named the first column as "Spouse Claimed Standard Deduction?" We have used the heading "Status of Spouse" for better clarity.*

claimed standard deduction and four with spouse status being not claiming standard deduction. Other than this one difference, there is no material change in the status of expected result of the standard deduction amount. We leave it as an exercise for the reader to enumerate the number of rows in the decision table, should we not allow don't cares and have to explicitly specify each case. There are formal tools like Karnaugh Maps which can be used to arrive at a minimal Boolean expression that represents the various Boolean conditions in a decision table. The references given at the end of this chapter discuss these tools and techniques.

Thus, decision tables act as invaluable tools for designing black box tests to examine the behavior of the product under various logical conditions of input variables. The steps in forming a decision table are as follows.

1. Identify the decision variables.

2. Identify the possible values of each of the decision variables.

3. Enumerate the combinations of the allowed values of each of the variables.

4. Identify the cases when values assumed by a variable (or by sets of variables) are immaterial for a given combination of other input variables. Represent such variables by the don't care symbol.

5. For each combination of values of decision variables (appropriately minimized with the don't care scenarios), list out the action or expected result.

6. Form a table, listing in each but the last column a decision variable. In the last column, list the action item for the combination of variables in that row (including don't cares, as appropriate).

> A decision table is useful when input and output data can be expressed as Boolean conditions (TRUE, FALSE, and DON'T CARE).

Once a decision table is formed, each row of the table acts as the specification for one test case. Identification of the decision variables makes these test cases extensive, if not exhaustive. Pruning the table by using don't cares minimizes the number of test cases. Thus, decision tables are usually effective in arriving at test cases in scenarios which depend on the values of the decision variables.

4.4.5   Equivalence Partitioning

Equivalence partitioning is a software testing technique that involves identifying a small set of representative input values that produce as many different output conditions as possible. This reduces the number of permutations and combinations of input, output values used for testing, thereby increasing the coverage and reducing the effort involved in testing.

The set of input values that generate one single expected output is called a *partition*. When the behavior of the software is the same for a set of values, then the set is termed as an *equivalance class* or a *partition*. In this case, one representative sample from each partition (also called the *member of the equivalance class*) is picked up for testing. One sample from the partition is enough for testing as the result of picking up some more values from the set will be the same and will not yield any additional defects. Since all the values produce equal and same output they are termed as equivalance partition.

Testing by this technique involves (a) identifying all partitions for the complete set of input, output values for a product and (b) picking up one member value from each partition for testing to maximize complete coverage.

From the results obtained for a member of an equivalence class or partition, this technique extrapolates the expected results for all the values in that partition. The advantage of using this technique is that we gain good coverage with a small number of test cases. For example, if there is a defect in one value in a partition, then it can be extrapolated to all the values of that particular partition. By using this technique, redundancy of tests is minimized by not repeating the same tests for multiple values in the same partition.

Let us consider the example below, of an insurance company that has the following premium rates based on the age group.

Life Insurance Premium Rates

A life insurance company has base premium of $0.50 for all ages. Based on the age group, an additional monthly premium has to be paid that is as listed in the table below. For example, a person aged 34 has to pay a premium = base premium + additional premium = $0.50 + $1.65 = $2.15.

Age group	Additional premium
Under 35	$1.65
35–59	$2.87
60+	$6.00

Based on the equivalence partitioning technique, the equivalence partitions that are based on age are given below:

✠ Below 35 years of age (valid input)

✠ Between 35 and 59 years of age (valid input)

✠ Above 60 years of age (valid input)

✠ Negative age (invalid input)

✠ Age as 0 (invalid input)

✠ Age as any three-digit number (valid input)

We need to pick up representative values from each of the above partitions. You may have observed that even though we have only a small table of *valid* values, the equivalence classes should also include samples of *invalid* inputs. This is required so that these invalid values do not cause unforeseen errors. You can see that the above cases include both positive and negative test input values.

The test cases for the example based on the equivalence partitions are given in Table 4.8. The *equivalence partitions table* has as columns:

✠ Partition definition

✠ Type of input (valid / invalid)

✠ Representative test data for that partition

✠ Expected results

Each row is taken as a single test case and is executed. For example, when a person's age is 48, row number 2 test case is applied and the expected result is a monthly premium of $3.37. Similarly, in case a person's age is given as a negative value, a warning message is displayed, informing the user about the invalid input.

The above example derived the equivalence classes using ranges of values. There are a few other ways to identify equivalence classes. For example, consider the set of real numbers. One way to divide this set is by

1. Prime numbers

2. Composite numbers

3. Numbers with decimal point

These three classes divide the set of numbers into three valid classes. In addition, to account for any input a user may give, we will have to add an invalid class—strings with alphanumeric characters. As in the previous case, we can construct an equivalence partitions table for this example as shown in Table 4.9.

Thus, like in the first example on life insurance premium, here also we have reduced a potentially infinite input data space to a finite one, without losing the effectiveness of testing. This is the power of using equivalence

Table 4.8 Equivalence classes for the life insurance premium example.

S.No.	Equivalence partitions	Type of input	Test data	Expected results
1.	Age below 35	Valid	26, 12	Monthly premium = $(0.50 + 1.65) = $2.15
2.	Age 35–59	Valid	37	Monthly premium = $(0.50 + 2.87) = $3.37
3.	Age above 60	Valid	65, 90	Monthly premium = $(0.50 + 6.0) = $6.5
4.	Negative age	Invalid	–23	Warning message—Invalid input
5.	Age as 0	Invalid	0	Warning message—Invalid input

Table 4.9 A sample equivalence partition for the set of real number.

S.No.	Equivalence partitions	Type of input	Test data
1.	Prime number	Valid	7, 29
2.	Composite (non-prime) number	Valid	444
3.	Numbers with decimal point	Valid	78.67,–85.91
4.	Non-numbers	Invalid	ABC23RTF

classes: choosing a minimal set of input values that are truly representative of the entire spectrum and uncovering a higher number of defects.

The steps to prepare an equivalence partitions table are as follows.

> Equivalence partitioning is useful to minimize the number of test cases when the input data can be divided into distinct sets, where the behavior or outcome of the product within each member of the set is the same.

✠ Choose criteria for doing the equivalence partitioning (range, list of values, and so on)

✠ Identify the valid equivalence classes based on the above criteria (number of ranges allowed values, and so on)

✠ Select a sample data from that partition

✠ Write the expected result based on the requirements given

✠ Identify special values, if any, and include them in the table

✠ Check to have expected results for all the cases prepared

✠ If the expected result is not clear for any particular test case, mark appropriately and escalate for corrective actions. If you cannot answer a question, or find an inappropriate answer, consider whether you want to record this issue on your log and clarify with the team that arbitrates/dictates the requirements.

4.4.6   State Based or Graph Based Testing

State or graph based testing is very useful in situations where

1. The product under test is a language processor (for example, a compiler), wherein the syntax of the language automatically lends itself to a state machine or a context free grammar represented by a railroad diagram.

2. Workflow modeling where, depending on the current state and appropriate combinations of input variables, specific workflows are carried out, resulting in new output and new state.

3. Dataflow modeling, where the system is modeled as a set of dataflow, leading from one state to another.

In the above (2) and (3) are somewhat similar. We will give one example for (1) and one example for (2).

Consider an application that is required to validate a number according to the following simple rules.

1. A number can start with an optional sign.
2. The optional sign can be followed by any number of digits.
3. The digits can be optionally followed by a decimal point, represented by a period.
4. If there is a decimal point, then there should be two digits after the decimal.
5. Any number—whether or not it has a decimal point, should be terminated by a blank.

The above rules can be represented in a state transition diagram as shown in Figure 4.3.

The state transition diagram can be converted to a state transition table (Table 4.10), which lists the current state, the inputs allowed in the current state, and for each such input, the next state.

Figure 4.3

An example of a state transition diagram.

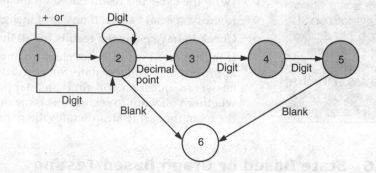

Table 4.10   State transition table for Figure 4.3.

Current state	Input	Next state
1	Digit	2
1	+	2
1	–	2
2	Digit	2
2	Blank	6
2	Decimal point	3
3	Digit	4
4	Digit	5
5	Blank	6

The above state transition table can be used to derive test cases to test valid and invalid numbers. Valid test cases can be generated by:

1. Start from the Start State (State #1 in the example).
2. Choose a path that leads to the next state (for example, +/–/digit to go from State 1 to State 2).
3. If you encounter an invalid input in a given state (for example, encountering an alphabetic character in State 2), generate an error condition test case.
4. Repeat the process till you reach the final state (State 6 in this example).

A general outline for using state based testing methods with respect to language processors is:

> Graph based testing methods are applicable to generate test cases for state machines such as language translators, workflows, transaction flows, and data flows.

1. Identify the grammar for the scenario. In the above example, we have represented the diagram as a state machine. In some cases, the scenario can be a context-free grammar, which may require a more sophisticated representation of a "state diagram."
2. Design test cases corresponding to each valid state-input combination.
3. Design test cases corresponding to the most common *invalid* combinations of state-input.

A second situation where graph based testing is useful is to represent a transaction or workflows. Consider a simple example of a leave application by an employee. A typical leave application process can be visualized as being made up of the following steps.

1. The employee fills up a leave application, giving his or her employee ID, and start date and end date of leave required.
2. This information then goes to an automated system which validates that the employee is eligible for the requisite number of days of leave. If not, the application is rejected; if the eligibility exists, then the control flow passes on to the next step below.
3. This information goes to the employee's manager who validates that it is okay for the employee to go on leave during that time (for example, there are no critical deadlines coming up during the period of the requested leave).
4. Having satisfied himself/herself with the feasibility of leave, the manager gives the final approval or rejection of the leave application.

The above flow of transactions can again be visualized as a simple state based graph as given in Figure 4.4.

In the above case, each of the states (represented by circles) is an event or a decision point while the arrows or lines between the states represent

Figure 4.4

State graph to
represent workflow.

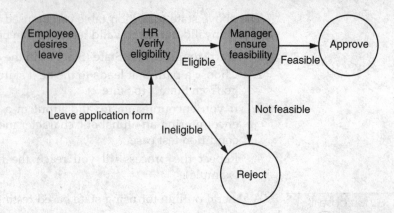

data inputs. Like in the previous example, one can start from the start state
and follow the graph through various state transitions till a "final" state
(represented by a unshaded circle) is reached.

A graph like the one above can also be converted to a state transititon table
using the same notation and method illustrated in the previous example.
Graph based testing such as in this example will be applicable when

1. The application can be characterized by a set of states.
2. The data values (screens, mouse clicks, and so on) that cause the
    transition from one state to another is well understood.
3. The methods of processing within each state to process the input
    received is also well understood.

4.4.7 Compatibility Testing

Testing done to
ensure that the
product features
work consistently with
different infrastructure
components is called
compatibility testing.

In the above sections, we looked at several techniques to test product
features and requirements. It was also mentioned that the test case result are
compared with expected results to conclude whether the test is successful
or not. The test case results not only depend on the product for proper
functioning; they depend equally on the infrastructure for delivering
functionality. When infrastructure parameters are changed, the product
is expected to still behave correctly and produce the desired or expected
results. The infrastructure parameters could be of hardware, software, or
other components. These parameters are different for different customers.
A black box testing, not considering the effects of these parameters on the
test case results, will necessarily be incomplete and ineffective, as it may
not truly reflect the behavior at a customer site. Hence, there is a need for
compatibility testing. This testing ensures the working of the product with
different infrastructure components. The techniques used for compatibility
testing are explained in this section.

The parameters that generally affect the compatibility of the product are

- Processor (CPU) (Pentium III, Pentium IV, Xeon, SPARC, and so on) and the number of processors in the machine
- Architecture and characterstics of the machine (32 bit, 64 bit, and so on)
- Resource availability on the machine (RAM, disk space, network card)
- Equipment that the product is expected to work with (printers, modems, routers, and so on)
- Operating system (Windows, Linux, and so on and their variants) and operating system services (DNS, NIS, FTP, and so on)
- Middle-tier infrastructure components such as web server, application server, network server
- Backend components such database servers (Oracle, Sybase, and so on)
- Services that require special hardware-cum-software solutions (cluster machines, load balancing, RAID array, and so on)
- Any software used to generate product binaries (compiler, linker, and so on and their appropriate versions)
- Various technological components used to generate components (SDK, JDK, and so on and their appropriate different versions)

The above are just a few of the parameters. There are many more parameters that can affect the behavior of the product features. In the above example, we have described ten parameters. If each of the parameters can take four values, then there are forty different values to be tested. But that is not all. Not only can the individual values of the parameters affect the features, but also the permutation and combination of the parameters. Taking these combinations into consideration, the number of times a particular feature to be tested for those combinations may go to thousands or even millions. In the above assumption of ten parameters and each parameter taking on four values, the total number of combinations to be tested is 4^{10}, which is a large number and impossible to test exhaustively.

In order to arrive at practical combinations of the parameters to be tested, a *compatibility matrix* is created. A compatibility matrix has as its columns various parameters the combinations of which have to be tested. Each row represents a unique combination of a specific set of values of the parameters. A sample compatibility matrix for a mail application is given in Table 4.11.

The below table is only an example. It does not cover all parameters and their combinations. Some of the common techniques that are used for performing compatibility testing, using a compatibility table are

1. ***Horizontal combination*** All values of parameters that can coexist with the product for executing the set test cases are grouped together as a row in the compatibility matrix. The values of parameters that can coexist generally belong to different layers/types of infrastructure pieces such as operating system, web server, and so

Table 4.11 Compatibility matrix for a mail application.

Server	Application server	Web server	Client	Browser	MS Office	Mail server
Windows 2000 Advanced Server with SP4 Microsoft SQL Server 2000 with SP3a	Windows 2000 Advanced Server with SP4 and .Net framework 1.1	IIS 5.0	Win2K Professional and Win 2K Terminal Server	IE 6.0 and IE 5.5 SP2	Office 2K and Office XP	Exchange 5.5 and 2K
Windows 2000 Advanced Server with SP4 Microsoft SQL Server 2000 with SP3a	Windows 2000 Advanced Server with SP4 and .Net framework 1.1	IIS 5.0	Win2K Professional and Win 2K Terminal Server	Netscape 7.0,7.1, Safari and Mozilla	Office 2K and Office XP	Exchange 5.5 and 2K
Windows 2003 Enterprise Server Microsoft SQL Server 2000 with SP3a	Windows 2003 Enterprise Server and .Net framework 1.1	IIS 6.0	WinXP Home and Win XP Professional	IE 6.0 and IE 5.5 SP2	Office XP and and Office 2003	Exchange 2K
Windows 2003 Standard Server Microsoft SQL Server 2000 with SP3a	Windows 2003 Standard Server and .Net framework 1.1	IIS 6.0	WinXP Professional and Citrix	IE 6.0,IE 5.5 SP2 and Mozilla	Office XP and Office 2003	Exchange 2003
Windows 2003 Enterprise Server Microsoft SQL Server 2000 with SP3a	Windows 2003 Enterprise Server and .Net framework 1.1	IIS 6.0	Win XP Professional and Win2003 Terminal	IE 6.0,IE 5.5 SP2 and Safari	Office XP and Office 2003	Exchange 2K

on. Machines or environments are set up for each row and the set of product features are tested using each of these environments.

2. *Intelligent sampling* In the horizontal combination method, each feature of the product has to be tested with each row in the compatibility matrix. This involves huge effort and time. To solve this problem, combinations of infrastructure parameters are combined with the set of features intelligently and tested. When there are problems due to any of the combinations then the test cases are executed, exploring the various permutations and combinations. The selection of intelligent samples is based on information collected on the set of dependencies of the product with the parameters. If the product results are less dependent on a set of parameters, then they are removed from the list of intelligent samples. All other parameters are combined and tested. This method significantly reduces the number of permutations and combinations for test cases.

Compatibility testing not only includes parameters that are outside the product, but also includes some parameters that are a part of the product. For example, two versions of a given version of a database may depend on a set of APIs that are part of the same database. These parameters are also an added part of the compatibility matrix and tested. The compatibility testing of a product involving parts of itself can be further classified into two types.

1. *Backward compatibility testing* There are many versions of the same product that are available with the customers. It is important for the customers that the objects, object properties, schema, rules, reports, and so on, that are created with an older version of the product continue to work with the current version of the same product. The testing that ensures the current version of the product continues to work with the older versions of the same product is called backwad compatibility testing. The product parameters required for the backward compatibility testing are added to the compatibility matrix and are tested.

2. *Forward compatibility testing* There are some provisions for the product to work with later versions of the product and other infrastructure components, keeping future requirements in mind. For example, IP network protocol version 6 uses 128 bit addressing scheme (IP version 4, uses only 32 bits). The data structures can now be defined to accommodate 128 bit addresses, and be tested with prototype implementation of Ipv6 protocol stack that is yet to become a completely implemented product. The features that are part of Ipv6 may not be still available to end users but this kind of implementation and testing for the future helps in avoiding drastic changes at a later point of time. Such requirements are tested as part of forward compatibily testing. Testing the product with a beta version of the operating system, early access version of the developers' kit, and so on are examples of forward compatibility. This type of testing ensures that the risk involved in product for future requirements is minimized.

For compatibility testing and to use the techniques mentioned above, an in-depth internal knowledge of the product may not be required. Compatibility testing begins after validating the product in the basic environment. It is a type of testing that involves high degree of effort, as there are a large number of parameter combinations. Following some of the techniques mentioned above may help in performing compatibility testing more effectively.

4.4.8 User Documentation Testing

User documentation covers all the manuals, user guides, installation guides, setup guides, read me file, software release notes, and online help that are provided along with the software to help the end user to understand the software system.

User documentation testing should have two objectives.

1. To check if what is stated in the document is available in the product.

2. To check if what is there in the product is explained correctly in the document.

When a product is upgraded, the corresponding product documentation should also get updated as necessary to reflect any changes that may affect a user. However, this does not necessarily happen all the time. One of the factors contributing to this may be lack of sufficient coordination between the documentation group and the testing/development groups. Over a period of time, product documentation diverges from the actual behavior of the product. User documentation testing focuses on ensuring what is in the document exactly matches the product behavior, by sitting in front of the system and verifying screen by screen, transaction by transaction and report by report. In addition, user documentation testing also checks for the language aspects of the document like spell check and grammar.

> User documentation is done to ensure the documentation matches the product and vice-versa.

Testing these documents attain importance due to the fact that the users will have to refer to these manuals, installation, and setup guides when they start using the software at their locations. Most often the users are not aware of the software and need hand holding until they feel comfortable. Since these documents are the first interactions the users have with the product, they tend to create lasting impressions. A badly written installation document can put off a user and bias him or her against the product, even if the product offers rich functionality.

Some of the benefits that ensue from user documentation testing are:

1. User documentation testing aids in highlighting problems over-looked during reviews.

2. High quality user documentation ensures consistency of documentation and product, thus minimizing possible defects reported by customers. It also reduces the time taken for each support call— sometimes the best way to handle a call is to alert the customer to the relevant section of the manual. Thus the overall support cost is minimized.

3. Results in less difficult support calls. When a customer faithfully follows the instructions given in a document but is unable to achieve the desired (or promised) results, it is frustrating and often this frustration shows up on the support staff. Ensuring that a product is tested to work as per the document and that it works correctly contributes to better customer satisfaction and better morale of support staff.

4. New programmers and testers who join a project group can use the documentation to learn the external functionality of the product.

5. Customers need less training and can proceed more quickly to advanced training and product usage if the documentation is of high quality and is consistent with the product. Thus high-quality

user documentation can result in a reduction of overall training costs for user organizations.

Defects found in user documentation need to be tracked to closure like any regular software defect. In order to enable an author to close a documentation defect information about the defect/comment description, paragraph/page number reference, document version number reference, name of reviewer, name of author, reviewer's contact number, priority, and severity of the comment need to be passed to the author.

Since good user documentation aids in reducing customer support calls, it is a major contibutor to the bottomline of the organization. The effort and money spent on this effort would form a valuable investment in the long run for the organization.

4.4.9   Domain Testing

White box testing required looking at the program code. Black box testing performed testing without looking at the program code but looking at the specifications. Domain testing can be considered as the next level of testing in which we do not look even at the specifications of a software product but are testing the product, purely based on domain knowledge and expertise in the domain of application. This testing approach requires critical understanding of the day-to-day business activities for which the software is written. This type of testing requires business domain knowledge rather than the knowledge of what the software specification contains or how the software is written. Thus domain testing can be considered as an extension of black box testing. As we move from white box testing through black box testing to domain testing (as shown in Figure 4.5) we know less and less about the details of the software product and focus more on its external behavior.

The test engineers performing this type of testing are selected because they have in-depth knowledge of the business domain. Since the depth in business domain is a prerequisite for this type of testing, sometimes it is easier to hire testers from the domain area (such as banking, insurance, and so on) and train them in software, rather than take software professionals and train them in the business domain. This reduces the effort and time required for training the testers in domain testing and also increases the effectivenes of domain testing.

For example, consider banking software. Knowing the account opening process in a bank enables a tester to test that functionality better. In this case, the bank official who deals with account opening knows the attributes of the people opening the account, the common problems faced, and the solutions in practice. To take this example further, the bank official might have encountered cases where the person opening the account might not have come with the required supporting documents or might be unable to fill up the required forms correctly. In such cases, the bank official may

Figure 4.5

Context of white box, black box and domain testing.

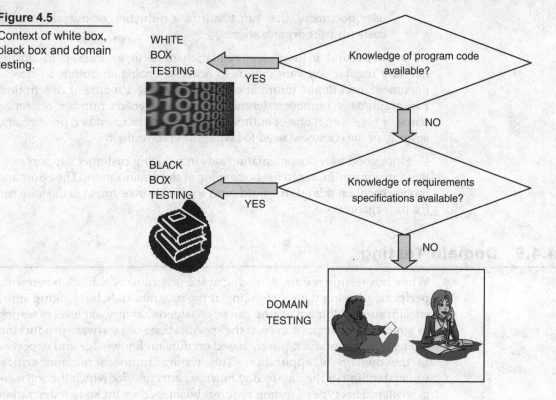

have to engage in a different set of activities to open the account. Though most of these may be stated in the business requirements explicitly, there will be cases that the bank official would have observed while testing the software that are not captured in the requirement specifications explicitly. Hence, when he or she tests the software, the test cases are likely to be more thorough and realistic.

Domain testing is the ability to design and execute test cases that relate to the people who will buy and use the software. It helps in understanding the problems they are trying to solve and the ways in which they are using the software to solve them. It is also characterized by how well an individual test engineer understands the operation of the system and the business processes that system is supposed to support. If a tester does not understand the system or the business processes, it would be very difficult for him or her to use, let alone test, the application without the aid of test scripts and cases.

> Domain testing exploits the tester's domain knowledge to test the suitability of the product to what the users do on a typical day.

Domain testing involves testing the product, not by going through the logic built into the product. The business flow determines the steps, not the software under test. This is also called "business vertical testing." Test cases are written based on what the users of the software do on a typical day.

Let us further understand this testing using an example of cash withdrawal functionality in an ATM, extending the earlier example on banking software. The user performs the following actions.

Step 1: Go to the ATM.

Step 2: Put ATM card inside.

Step 3: Enter correct PIN.

Step 4: Choose cash withdrawal.

Step 5: Enter amount.

Step 6: Take the cash.

Step 7: Exit and retrieve the card.

In the above example, a domain tester is not concerned about testing everything in the design; rather, he or she is interested in testing everything in the business flow. There are several steps in the design logic that are not necessarily tested by the above flow. For example, if you were doing other forms of black box testing, there may be tests for making sure the right denominations of currency are used. A typical black box testing approach for testing the denominations would be to ensure that the required denominations are available and that the requested amount can be dispensed with the existing denominations. However, when you are testing as an end user in domain testing, all you are concerned with is whether you got the right amount or not. (After all, no ATM gives you the flexibility of choosing the denominations.) When the test case is written for domain testing, you would find those intermediate steps missing. Just because those steps are missing does not mean they are not important. These "missing steps"(such as checking the denominations) are expected to be working *before* the start of domain testing.

Black box testing advocates testing those areas which matter more for a particular type or phase of testing. Techniques like equivalence partitioning and decision tables are useful in the earlier phases of black box testing and they catch certain types of defects or test conditions. Generally, domain testing is done after all components are integrated and after the product has been tested using other black box approaches (such as equivalence partitioning and boundary value analysis). Hence the focus of domain testing has to be more on the business domain to ensure that the software is written with the intelligence needed for the domain. To test the software for a particular "domain intelligence," the tester is expected to have the intelligence and knowledge of the practical aspects of business flow. This will reflect in better and more effective test cases which examine realistic business scenarios, thus meeting the objective and purpose of domain testing.

4.5   CONCLUSION

Performing black box testing without applying a methodology is similar to looking at the map without knowing where you are and what your destination is.

In this chapter, we have seen several techniques for performing black box testing. These techniques are not mutually exclusive. In a typical product testing, a combination of these testing techniques will be used to maximize effectiveness. Table 4.12 summarizes the scenarios under which each of these techniques will be useful. By judiciously mixing and matching these different techniques, the overall costs of other tests done downstream, such as integration testing, system testing, and so on, can be reduced.

Table 4.12   Scenarios for black box testing techniques.

When you want to test scenarios that have...	The most effective black box testing technique is likely to be...
Output values dictated by certain conditions depending upon values of input variables	Decision tables
Input values in ranges, with each range exhibiting a particular functionality	Boundary value analysis
Input values divided into classes (like ranges, list of values, and so on), with each class exhibiting a particular functionality	Equivalence partitioning
Checking for expected and unexpected input values	Positive and negative testing
Workflows, process flows, or language processors	Graph based testing
To ensure that requirements are tested and met properly	Requirements based testing
To test the domain expertise rather than product specification	Domain testing
To ensure that the documentation is consistent with the product	Documentation testing

REFERENCES

[MYER-79] and [BEIZ-90] discuss the various types of black box testing with detailed examples. [GOOD-75] is one of the early works on the use of tools like decision tables for the choice of test cases. [PRES-97] provides a comprehensive coverage of all black box testing approaches.

PROBLEMS AND EXERCISES

1. Consider the lock and key example discussed in the text. We had assume that there is only one key for the lock. Assume that the lock requires two keys to be inserted in a particular order. Modify the sample requirements given in Table 4.1 to take care of this condition. Correspondingly, create the Traceability Matrix akin to what is in Table 4.2.

2. In each of the following cases, identify the most appropriate black box testing technique that can be used to test the following requirements:

   a. "The valid values for the gender code are 'M' or 'F'."

   b. "The number of days of leave per year an employee is eligible is 10 for the first three years, 15 for the next two years, and 20 from then on."

   c. "Each purchase order must be initially approved by the manager of the employee and the head of purchasing. Additionally, if it is a capital expense of more than $10,000, it should also be approved by the CFO."

   d. "A file name should start with an alphabetic character, can have upto 30 alphanumeric characters, optionally one period followed by upto 10 other alphanumeric characters."

   e. "A person who comes to bank to open the account may not have his birth certificate in English; in this case, the officer must have the discretion to manually override the requirement of entering the birth certificate number."

3. Consider the example of deleting an element from a linked list that we considered in Problem 4 of the exercises in Chapter 3. What are the boundary value conditions for that example? Identify test data to test at and around boundary values.

4. A web-based application can be deployed on the following environments:

   a. OS (Windows and Linux)

   b. Web server (IIS 5.0 and Apache)

   c. Database (Oracle, SQL Server)

   d. Browser (IE 6.0 and Firefox)

   How many configurations would you have to test if you were to exhaustively test all the combinations? What criteria would you use to prune the above list?

5. A product usually associated with different types of documentation — installation document (for installing the product), administration document, user guide, etc. What would be the skill sets required

to test these different types of documents? Who would be best equipped to do each of these testing?

6. An input value for a product code in an inventory system is expected to be present in a product master table. Identify the set of equivalence classes to test these requirements.

7. In the book, we discussed examples where we partitioned the input space into multiple equivalence classes. Identify situations where the equivalence classes can be obtained by partitioning the output classes.

8. Consider the date validation problem discussed in Chapter 3. Assuming you have no access to the code, derive a set of test cases using any of the techniques discussed in this chapter. Present your results in the form of a table as given below

Test data	Reason for choosing the data	Applicable Black Box Testing Technique	Expected Result

9. A sample rule for creating a table in a SQL database is given below: The statement should start with the syntax

```
CREATE TABLE <table name>
```

This should be followed by an open paranthesis, a comma separated list of column identifiers. Each column identifier should have a mandatory column name, a mandatory column type (which should be one of NUMER, CHAR, and DATE) and an optional column width. In addition, the rules dictate:

a. Each of the key words can be abbreviated to 3 characters or more

b. The column names must be unique within a table

c. The table names should not be repeated.

For the above set of requirements, draw a state graph to derive the initial test cases. Also use other techniques like appropriate to check a–c above

Integration Testing

CHAPTER 5

In this chapter—

- ✓ What is integration testing
- ✓ Integration testing as a type of testing
- ✓ Integration testing as a phase of testing
- ✓ Scenario testing
- ✓ Defect bash
- ✓ Conclusion

5.1   WHAT IS INTEGRATION TESTING?

A system is made up of multiple components or modules that can comprise hardware and software. *Integration* is defined as the set of interactions among components. Testing the *interaction* between the modules and interaction with other systems externally is called integration testing. Integration testing starts when two of the product components are available and ends when all component interfaces have been tested. The final round of integration involving all components is called Final Integration Testing (FIT), or system integration.

Integration testing is both a type of testing and a phase of testing. As integration is defined to be a set of interactions, all defined interactions among the components need to be tested. The architecture and design can give the details of interactions *within* systems; however, testing the interactions *between* one system and another system requires a detailed understanding of how they work *together*. This knowledge of integration (that is, how the system or modules work together) depends on many modules and systems. These diverse modules could have different ways of working when integrated with other systems. This introduces complexity in procedures and in what needs to be done. Recognizing this complexity, a phase in testing is dedicated to test these interactions, resulting in the evolution of a process. This ensuing phase is called the integration testing phase.

Since integration testing is aimed at testing the interactions among the modules, this testing—just like white box, black box, and other types of testing—comes with a set of techniques and methods, which we will see in the following sections. Hence integration testing is also viewed as a type of testing (and thus fits into the canvas of this part of the book).

> Integration is both a phase and a type of testing.

In the next section, we will look at integration as a type of testing and in the section thereafter, we will view integration as a phase of testing.

5.2   INTEGRATION TESTING AS A TYPE OF TESTING

Integration testing means testing of interfaces. When we talk about interfaces, there are two types of interfaces that have to be kept in mind for proper integration testing. They are *internal* interfaces and *exported* or *external* interfaces.

Internal interfaces are those that provide communication across two modules within a project or product, internal to the product, and not exposed to the customer or external developers. Exported interfaces are those that are visible outside the product to third party developers and solution providers.

One of the methods of achieving interfaces is by providing Application Programming Interfaces (APIs). APIs enable one module to call another module. The calling module can be internal or external. For example, JDBC is an example of an API used by a Java program to make certain SQL calls. Even though both the API and interfaces appear to be similar, it is important to realize that integration is the *purpose* to be achieved while API is a *means* of achieving the purpose. API is just one of the means of providing an interface between two modules. One can think of other means of integration among the various modules: Some of these could be simple function calls, public functions, and some could be facets of programming language constructs like global variables and some could be operating system constructs like semaphares and shared memory. In this chapter, we will not discuss the details of the vehicles used for integration (as it is primarily a development issue), but rather look at how we can test the interfaces (which is the focus for testing).

Not all the interfaces may be available at the same time for testing purposes, as different interfaces are usually developed by different development teams, each having their own schedules. In order to test the interfaces, when the full functionality of the component being introduced is not available, *stubs* are provided. A stub simulates the interface by providing the appropriate values in the appropriate format as would be provided by the actual component being integrated.

Integration testing is done with test cases, which goes through the internal and exported interfaces, and tests the functionality of the software. Internal interfaces are for other developers inside an organization and external interfaces are for third party developers or other users outside the group. Testing for internal interfaces requires a complete understanding of architecture and high-level design (HLD) and how they impact the software functionality. In cases where exported interfaces are provided from the software, one needs to understand the purpose of those interfaces, why they are provided, and how they are actually used by developers and solution integrators. Hence a knowledge of design, architecture, and usage is a must for integration testing.

Initially, the exported (or external) interfaces were provided through APIs and *Software Development Kits* (SDKs). The use of SDKs required an understanding of the programming language on which the API/SDK is provided. Later, the interfaces became available through scripting languages, without the need for SDKs. (Some of the popular scripting languages include Perl, Tcl/Tk). These scripting languages eliminated or minimized the effort in learning the languages in which the API was written. This also made it possible for the interfaces to be called from programming language environments different from the one in which the interface was originally written. This significantly simplified the usage of exported interfaces. For testing interfaces, we now have dynamically created scripts, which can be changed at run time, by a few clicks of the mouse.

All these have made the use of interfaces a lot more widespread. The number of purposes for which the interfaces are provided have been on the increase. These interfaces are becoming increasingly generic in nature and

Integration testing type focuses on testing interfaces that are "implicit and explicit" and "internal and external."

not getting tied to a specific application or language. This has resulted in increasing the permutations and combinations of scenarios of usage of the interfaces. Thus, the complexity of integration testing—that is, testing of the various scenarios of usage of interfaces—has also increased significantly.

While discussing about interfaces we need to keep in mind that not all interactions between the modules are known and explained through interfaces. Some of the interfaces are documented and some of them are not. This gives rise to another classification of interfaces, that is, implicit and explicit interfaces. Explicit interfaces are documented interfaces and implicit interfaces are those which are known internally to the software engineers but are not documented. The testing (white box/black box) should look for both implicit and explicit interfaces and test all those interactions.

A question that often arises in the mind of a test engineer is whether integration testing is a black box or a white box testing approach. In most cases, the most appropriate answer is to say integration testing is a black box testing approach. However, in situations where architecture or design documents do not clear by explain all interfaces among components, the approach can include going through the code and generating some additional test cases, and mixing them with other test cases generated using black box testing approaches. This approach could be termed as the "*gray box testing*" approach.

Let us illustrate this with an example. Figure 5.1 shows a set of modules and the interfaces associated with them. The coloured figure is available on page 460. The solid lines represent explicit interfaces and the dotted lines

Figure 5.1

A set of modules and interfaces.

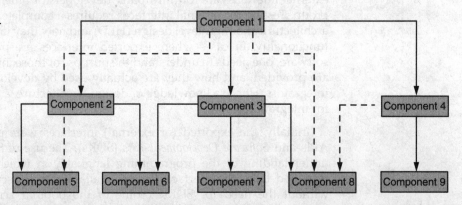

represent implicit interfaces, based on the understanding of architecture, design, or usage.

From Figure 5.1 it is clear that there are at least 12 interfaces between the modules to be tested (9 explicit and 3 implicit). Now a question that comes to the mind is in what order do these interfaces need to be tested. There are several methodologies available, to in decide the *order* for integration testing. These are as follows.

1. Top-down integration
2. Bottom-up integration

3. Bi-directional integration
4. System integration

5.2.1 Top-Down Integration

Integration testing involves testing the topmost component interface with other components in same order as you navigate from top to bottom, till you cover all the components.

To understand this methodology better, let us assume, a new product/software development where components become available one after another in the order of component numbers specified in the Figure 5.2. The coloured figure is available on page 461. The integration starts with testing the interface between Component 1 and Component 2. To complete the integration testing, all interfaces mentioned in Figure 5.2 covering all the arrows, have to be tested together. The order in which the interfaces are to be tested is depicted in Table 5.1. The coloured format of Table 5.1 is available on page 480.

In an incremental product development, where one or two components gets added to the product in each increment, the integration testing

Figure 5.2

Example of top down integrations.

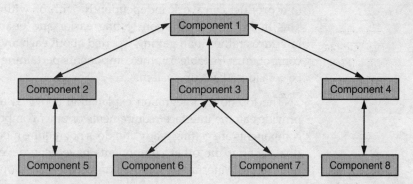

Table 5.1 Order of testing interfaces for the example in Figure 5.2.

Step	Interfaces tested
1	1–2
2	1–3
3	1–4
4	1–2–5
5	1–3–6
6	1–3–6–(3–7)
7	(1–2–5)–(1–3–6–(3–7))
8	1–4–8
9	(1–2–5)–(1–3–6–(3–7))–(1–4–8)

methodology pertains to only to those new interfaces that are added and those related interfaces that are impacted by the changes or increment in the product. Therefore, not all the steps in the above table need to be repeated for integration testing in that case. For example, in Figure 5.2 let us assume one component (component 8), is added for the current release; all other components are tested before for the previous release. If that addition has an impact on the functionality of component 5, then integration testing for the current release needs to include only steps 4, 7, 8, and 9.

To optimize the number of steps in integration testing, steps 6 and 7 can be combined and executed as a single step. Similarly, steps 8 and 9 also can be combined and tested in a single step. Combining steps does not a mean reduction in the number of interfaces tested. It just means an optimization in the elapsed time, as we do not have to wait for steps 6 and 8 to get over to start with testing steps 7 and 9 respectively.

If a set of components and their related interfaces can deliver functionality without expecting the presence of other components or with minimal interface requirement in the software/product, then that set of components and their related interfaces is called as a *"sub-system."* Each sub-system in a product can work independently with or without other sub-systems. This makes the integration testing easier and enables focus on required interfaces rather than getting worried about each and every combination of components. In Table 5.1, the components pertaining to steps 4, 6, and 8 can be considered as sub-systems.

The top-down integration explanation above assumes that component 1 provides all the interface requirements of other components even while other components are getting ready and does not require modification at a later stage (that is, after the other components have been developed). This approach reflects the Waterfall or V model of software development.

If a component at a higher level requires a modification every time a module gets added to the bottom, then for each component addition integration testing needs to be repeated starting from step 1. This may be a requirement for an iterative model of software development. Hence, whatever may be the software development model, top-down integration can be still applied with appropriate repetition in integration testing.

The order in which the interfaces are tested may change a bit in Figure 5.2 if different methods of traversing are used. A *breadth first* approach will get you component order such as 1–2, 1–3, 1–4 and so on and a *depth first* order will get you components such as 1–2–5, 1–3–6, and so on. A breadth first approach was used in Table 5.1 as we have assumed that the components become available in the order of component numbers. But it need not be in the same order for following this integration methodology.

5.2.2 Bottom-up Integration

Bottom-up integration is just the opposite of top-down integration, where the components for a new product development become available in reverse order, starting from the bottom. In Figure 5.3, (coloured figure on page 461) the components are assumed to be available in the order of their number.

Note: *Double arrows in Figure 5.3 denotes both the logical flow of components and integration approach. Logic flow is from top to bottom, and integration path is from bottom to top.*

The navigation in bottom-up integration starts from component 1 in Figure 5.3, covering all sub-systems, till component 8 is reached. The order in which the interfaces have to be tested is depicted in Table 5.2.

The number of steps in the bottom-up approach can be optimized into four steps, by combining steps 2 and 3 and by combining steps 5–8, as shown in Table 5.2 below. The coloured format is available on page 480.

As explained before, in top-down integration, for an incremental product development, only the impacted and added interfaces need to be tested, covering all sub-systems and system components.

Figure 5.3

Example of bottom-up integration. Arrows pointing down depict logic flow; arrows pointing up indicate integration paths.

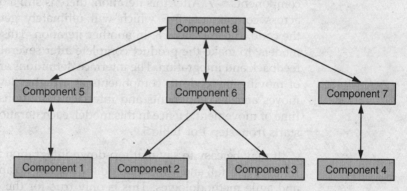

Table 5.2 Order of interfaces tested using bottom up integration for Figure 5.3.

Step	Interfaces tested
1	1–5
2	2–6, 3–6
3	2–6–(3–6)
4	4–7
5	1–5–8
6	2–6–(3–6)–8
7	4–7–8
8	(1–5–8)–(2–6–(3–6)–8)–(4–7–8)

One difference between Figure 5.2 and Figure 5.3 is that in the latter the arrows are two-way arrows. The arrows from top to bottom (that is, downward-pointing arrows) indicate interaction or control flow. The arrows from bottom to top (that is, upward-pointing arrows) indicate integration approach or integration path. What it means is that the logic flow of the product can be different from the integration path. While the logic flow or interaction in this case is going from up to down, the integration path is going from down to up. This approach allows a combination of integration approaches to be followed for the same product.

The iterative and agile model is an example to explain the different paths for logic flow and integration approach. In this model, a product development organization needs to demonstrate the product functionalities at regular intervals to customers for getting their feedback. One way to increase the frequency of delivery is to make each of the components independent. Some portion of the code is duplicated across components to demonstrate each of the components separately to the customer. The code duplication is not only for demonstrating the product but also for independent testing. In the above example, components 5–8 are developed as independent components with duplicated common code. After testing and approval from customer, the common code gets pushed into components at a higher level, say to components 5–7. After this iteration, there is still a duplication of this code across components 5–7 which will ultimately get removed by moving the code to component 8, in another iteration. This is one of the evolving models, to make the product complete after several iterations of customer feedback and integration. The interface definitions are done only at the time of moving the code to components at a higher level. The common code moves across components and interface definitions are made only at the time of movement. Hence in this model, each iteration of integration testing starts from step 1 of Table 5.2.

It may be easy to say that top-down integration approach is best suited for the Waterfall and V models and the bottom-up approach for the iterative and agile methodologies. This is only true for the examples taken above, and from a process perspective. In a practical scenario the approach selected for integration depends more on the design and architecture of a product and on associated priorities. Additionally, the selection of a right integration approach needs to consider several other perspectives such as availability of components, technology used, process, testing skills, and resource availability.

5.2.3 Bi-Directional Integration

Bi-directional integration is a combination of the top-down and bottom-up integration approaches used together to derive integration steps.

Look at Figure 5.4. The coloured figure is available on page 462. In this example, let us assume the software components become available in the order mentioned by the component numbers. The individual components

Figure 5.4
Bi-directional
integration.

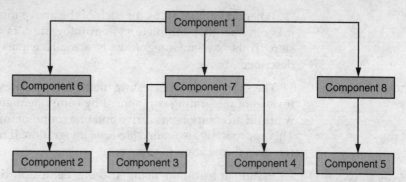

1, 2, 3, 4, and 5 are tested separately and bi-directional integration is performed initially with the use of stubs and drivers. Drivers are used to provide upstream connectivity while stubs provide downstream connectivity. A driver is a function which redirects the requests to some other component and stubs simulate the behavior of a missing component. After the functionality of these integrated components are tested, the drivers and stubs are discarded. Once components 6, 7, and 8 become available, the integration methodology then focuses only on those components, as these are the components which need focus and are new. This approach is also called "*sandwich integration.*"

The steps for integration testing, using this approach is given in Table 5.3. The coloured format is available on page 480.

Table 5.3 Steps for integration using sandwich testing.

Step	Interfaces tested
1	6–2
2	7–3–4
3	8–5
4	(1–6–2)–(1–7–3–4)–(1–8–5)

As you can see from the table, steps 1–3 use a bottom-up integration approach and step 4 uses a top-down integration approach for this example.

An area where this approach comes in handy is when migrating from a two-tier to a three-tier environment. In the product development phase when a transition happens from two-tier architecture to three-tier architecture, the middle tier (components 6–8) gets created as a set of new components from the code taken from bottom-level applications and top-level services.

5.2.4 System Integration

System integration means that all the components of the system are integrated and tested as a single unit. Integration testing, which is testing of interfaces, can be divided into two types:

✠ Components or sub-system integration
✠ Final integration testing or system integration

When looking at steps for each of the above integration methodologies, it is obvious that complete system integration is also covered as the last step. Thus, system integration is actually a part of every methodology described above.

The salient point this testing methodology raises, is that of optimization. Instead of integrating component by component and testing, this approach waits till all components arrive and one round of integration testing is done. This approach is also called *big-bang* integration. It reduces testing effort and removes duplication in testing.

Big bang integration is ideal for a product where the interfaces are stable with less number of defects.

System integration using the big bang approach is well suited in a product development scenario where the majority of components are already available and stable and very few components get added or modified. In this case, instead of testing component interfaces one by one, it makes sense to integrate all the components at one go and test once, saving effort and time for the multi-step component integrations.

While this approach saves time and effort, it is also not without disadvantages. Some of the important disadvantages that can have a bearing on the release dates and quality of a product are as follows.

1. When a failure or defect is encountered during system integration, it is very difficult to locate the problem, to find out in which interface the defect exists. The debug cycle may involve focusing on specific interfaces and testing them again.

2. The ownership for correcting the root cause of the defect may be a difficult issue to pinpoint.

3. When integration testing happens in the end, the pressure from the approaching release date is very high. This pressure on the engineers may cause them to compromise on the quality of the product.

4. A certain component may take an excessive amount of time to be ready. This precludes testing other interfaces and wastes time till the end.

As a result of all these factors, the choice of the method of integration testing becomes extremely crucial. A judicious combination of the above methods would be needed to achieve effectiveness in the time and quality of integration testing.

5.2.5 Choosing Integration Method

Table 5.4 gives some broad level guidelines on selecting the integration method. As mentioned in the above discussions, the integration method depends not only on the process, development model, but also on various other aspects.

Table 5.4 Guidelines on selection of integration method.

S.No.	Factors	Suggested integration method
1	Clear requirements and design	Top-down
2	Dynamically changing requirements, design, architecture	Bottom-up
3	Changing architecture, stable design	Bi-directional
4	Limited changes to existing architecture with less impact	Big bang
5	Combination of above	Select one of the above after careful analysis

5.3   INTEGRATION TESTING AS A PHASE OF TESTING

As we saw in the beginning of this chapter, integration testing as a *phase of testing* starts from the point where two components can be tested together, to the point where all the components work together as a complete system delivering system/product functionality. In the integration testing phase, the focus is not only on whether functionality of the components work well, but also on whether they work *together* and deliver sub-system and system functionality.

The integration testing phase focuses on finding defects which predominantly arise because of *combining* various components for testing, and should not be focused on for component or few components. Integration testing as a type focuses on testing the interfaces. This is a subset of the integration testing phase. When a sub-system or system components are put together (or integrated), the defects not only arise because of interfaces, but also for various other reasons such as usage, incomplete understanding of product domain, user errors, and so on. Hence the integration testing phase needs to focus on interfaces as well as usage flow. It is very important to note this point to avoid confusion between integration testing type and integration testing phase.

> All testing activities that are conducted from the point where two components are integrated to the point where all system components work together, are considered a part of the integration testing phase.

Integration testing as a phase involves different activities and different types of testing have to be done in that phase. This is a testing phase that should ensure completeness and coverage of testing for functionality. To achieve this, the focus should not only be on planned test case execution but also on unplanned testing, which is termed as "ad hoc testing." As we saw in the chapter, Principles of Testing (Chapter 1), there is no end to testing, and quality cannot depend only on pre-written test cases; ad hoc testing becomes important to integration testing phase. There are different terminologies associated with ad hoc testing, such as exploratory testing, monkey testing, out of the box testing, and so on (Chapter 10). All these tests perform the same functions during integration testing phase, that is, uncover or unearth those defects which are not found by planned test case execution. This approach helps in locating some problems which are difficult to find by test teams but also difficult to imagine in the first place. The approach also helps in generating a comfort feeling on the software and getting an overall acceptance of the product from all internal users of the system.

The integration testing phase involves developing and executing test cases that cover multiple components and functionality. When the functionality of different components are combined and tested together for a sequence of related operations, they are called *scenarios*. Scenario testing is a planned activity to explore different usage patterns and combine them into test cases called scenario test cases. We will see scenario testing in more detail in the next section.

5.4 SCENARIO TESTING

Scenario testing is defined as a *"set of realistic user activities that are used for evaluating the product."* It is also defined as the testing involving customer scenarios.

There are two methods to evolve scenarios.

1. System scenarios
2. Use-case scenarios/role based scenarios

5.4.1 System Scenarios

System scenario is a method whereby the set of activities used for scenario testing covers several components in the system. The following approaches can be used to develop system scenarios.

Story line Develop a story line that combines various activities of the product that may be executed by an end user. A user enters his or her office, logs into the system, checks mail, responds to some mails, compiles some programs, performs unit testing and so on. All these typical activities carried out in the course of normal work when coined together become a scenario.

Life cycle/state transition Consider an object, derive the different transitions/modifications that happen to the object, and derive scenarios to cover them. For example, in a savings bank account, you can start with opening an account with a certain amount of money, make a deposit, perform a withdrawal, calculate interest, and so on. All these activities are applied to the "money" object, and the different transformations, applied to the "money" object becomes different scenarios.

Deployment/implementation stories from customer Develop a scenario from a known customer deployment/implementation details and create a set of activities by various users in that implementation.

Business verticals Visualize how a product/software will be applied to different verticals and create a set of activities as scenarios to address specific vertical businesses. For example, take the purchasing function. It may be done differently in different verticals like pharmaceuticals, software houses, and government organizations. Visualizing these different types of tests make the product "multi-purpose."

Battle ground Create some scenarios to justify that "the product works" and some scenarios to "try and break the system" to justify "the product doesn't work." This adds flavor to the scenarios mentioned above.

The set of scenarios developed will be more effective if the majority of the approaches mentioned above are used in combination, not in isolation. Scenario should not be a set of disjointed activities which have no relation to each other. Any activity in a scenario is always a continuation of the previous activity, and depends on or is impacted by the results of previous activities. Effective scenarios will have a combination of current customer implementation, foreseeing future use of product, and developing ad hoc test cases. Considering only one aspect (current customer usage or future customer requirements, for instance) would make scenarios ineffective. If only current customer usage is considered for testing, new features may not get tested adequately. Considering only the future market for scenarios may make the scenarios test only the new features and some of the existing functionality may not get tested. A right mix of scenarios using the various approaches explained above is very critical for the effectiveness of scenario testing.

Coverage is always a big question with respect to functionality in scenario testing. This testing is not meant to cover different permutations and combinations of features and usage in a product. However, by using a simple technique, some comfort feeling can be generated on the coverage of activities by scenario testing. The following activity table (Table 5.5) explains the concept with an example.

Table 5.5 Coverage of activities by scenario testing.

End-user activity	Frequency	Priority	Applicable environments	No. of times covered
1. Login to application	High	High	W2000, W2003, XP	10
2. Create an object	High	Medium	W2000,XP	7
3. Modify parameters	Medium	Medium	W2000,XP	5
4. List object parameters	Low	Medium	W2000,XP, W2003	3
5. Compose email	Medium	Medium	W2000,XP	6
6. Attach files	Low	Low	W2000,XP	2
7. Send composed mail	High	High	W2000,XP	10

From the table, it is clear that important activities have been very well covered by set of scenarios in the system scenario test. This kind of table also helps us to ensure that all activities are covered according to their frequency of usage in customer place and according to the relative priority assigned based on customer usage.

5.4.2   Use Case Scenarios

A use case scenario is a stepwise procedure on how a user intends to use a system, with different user roles and associated parameters. A use case scenario can include stories, pictures, and deployment details. Use cases are useful for explaining customer problems and how the software can solve those problems without any ambiguity.

A use case can involve several roles or class of users who typically perform different activities based on the role. There are some activities that are common across roles and there are some activities that are very specific and can be performed only by the use belonging to a particular role. Use case scenarios term the users with different roles as *actors*. What the product should do for a particular activity is termed as *system behavior*. Users with a specific role to interact between the actors and the system are called *agents*.

To explain the concept of use case scenarios, let us take the example of withdrawing cash from a bank. A customer fills up a check and gives it to an official in the bank. The official verifies the balance in the account from the computer and gives the required cash to the customer. The customer in this example is the actor, the clerk the agent, and the response given by the computer, which gives the balance in the account, is called the system response. This is depicted in Figure 5.5. The coloured figure is available on page 462.

This way of describing different roles in test cases helps in testing the product without getting into the details of the product. In the above example, the actor (who is the customer) need not know what the official is doing and what command he is using to interact with the computer. The

Figure 5.5

Example of a use case scenario in a bank.

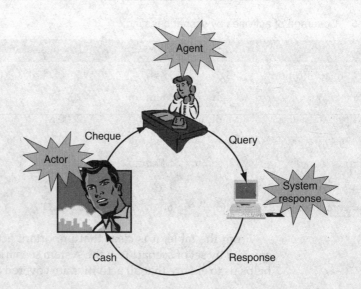

actor is only concerned about getting the cash. The agent (who is the official) is not concerned about the logic of how the computer works. He or she is only interested in knowing from the computer whether he or she can give the cash or not. However, the system behavior (computer logic) needs to be tested before applying the sequence of agent activities and actor activities. In this example, the activities performed by the actor and the agent can be tested by testers who do not have much knowledge of the product. Testers who have in-depth knowledge of the product can perform the system behavior part of testing. They need to know the logic of how the code works and whether or not the system response is accurate.

As mentioned earlier, actor and agent are roles that represent different types (classes) of users. Simulating different types of users again needs a clear understanding of business and the system response for each of the user needs a clear understanding of how the product is implemented. Hence, testers using the use case model, with one person testing the actions and other person testing the system response, complement each other's testing as well as testing the business and the implementation aspect of the product at the same time.

The agent part of the use cases are not needed in all cases. In a completely automated system involving the customer and the system, use cases can be written without considering the agent portion. Let us extend the earlier example of cash withdrawal using an ATM. Table 5.6 illustrates how the actor and system response can be described in the use case.

Table 5.6 Actor and system response in use case for ATM cash withdrawal.

Actor	System response
User likes to withdraw cash and inserts the card in the ATM machine	Request for password or Personal Identification Number (PIN)
User fills in the password or PIN	Validate the password or PIN Give a list containing types of accounts
User selects an account type	Ask the user for amount to withdraw
User fills in the amount of cash required	Check availability of funds Update account balance Prepare receipt Dispense cash
Retrieve cash from ATM	Print receipt

This way of documenting a scenario and testing makes it simple and also makes it realistic for customer usage. Use cases are not used only for testing. In some product implementations, use cases are prepared prior to the design and coding phases, and they are used as a set of requirements for design and coding phases. All development activities are performed based on use case documentation. In extreme programming models these are termed as *user stories* and form the basis for architecture/design and coding phases. Hence, use cases are useful in combining the business perspectives and implementation detail and testing them together.

5.5   DEFECT BASH

Defect bash is an ad hoc testing where people performing different roles in an organization test the product together at the same time. This is very popular among application development companies, where the product can be used by people who perform different roles. The testing by all the participants during defect bash is not based on written test cases. What is to be tested is left to an individual's decision and creativity. They can also try some operations which are beyond the product specifications. Defect bash brings together plenty of good practices that are popular in testing industry. They are as follows.

1. Enabling people *"Cross boundaries and test beyond assigned areas"*
2. Bringing different people performing different roles together in the organization for testing—*"Testing isn't for testers alone"*
3. Letting everyone in the organization use the product before delivery—*"Eat your own dog food"*
4. Bringing fresh pairs of eyes to uncover new defects—*"Fresh eyes have less bias"*
5. Bringing in people who have different levels of product under-standing to test the product together randomly—*"Users of software are not same"*
6. Let testing doesn't wait for lack of/time taken for documentation—*"Does testing wait till all documentation is done?"*
7. Enabling people to say "system works" as well as enabling them to "break the system"—*"Testing isn't to conclude the system works or doesn't work"*

Even though it is said that defect bash is an ad hoc testing, not all activities of defect bash are unplanned. All the activities in the defect bash are planned activities, except for what to be tested. It involves several steps.

Step 1   Choosing the frequency and duration of defect bash

Step 2   Selecting the right product build

Step 3   Communicating the objective of each defect bash to everyone

Step 4   Setting up and monitoring the lab for defect bash

Step 5   Taking actions and fixing issues

Step 6   Optimizing the effort involved in defect bash

5.5.1 Choosing the Frequency and Duration of Defect Bash

Defect bash is an activity involving a large amount of effort (since it involves large a number of people) and an activity involving huge planning (as is evident from the above steps). Frequent defect bashes will incur low return on investment, and too few defect bashes may not meet the objective of finding all defects. Duration is also an important factor. Optimizing the small duration is a big saving as a large number of people are involved. On the other hand if the duration is small, the amount of testing that is done may not meet the objective.

5.5.2 Selecting the Right Product Build

Since the defect bash involves a large number of people, effort and planning, a good quality build is needed for defect bash. A regression tested build (see Chapter 8) would be ideal as all new features and defect fixes would have been already tested in such a build. An intermediate build where the code functionality is evolving or an untested build will make the purpose and outcome of a defect bash ineffective. Where a large number of people are involved, a good quality product build gives confidence on the product and progress. Also, when testers doing a defect bash uncover an excessive number of defects or very severe defects, the confidence of the testers falls and the perception of the product being unstable lingers on for long.

5.5.3 Communicating the Objective of Defect Bash

Even though defect bash is an ad hoc activity, its purpose and objective have to be very clear. Since defect bash involves people performing different roles, the contribution they make has to be focused towards meeting the purpose and objective of defect bash. The objective should be to find a large number of uncovered defects or finding out system requirements (CPU, memory, disk, and so on) or finding the non-reproducible or random defects, which could be difficult to find through other planned tests. Defects that a test engineer would find easily should not be the objective of a defect bash. Once they are told in advance, the members of defect bash team will be in a better position to contribute towards stated objectives.

5.5.4 Setting Up and Monitoring the Lab

Since defect bashes are planned, short term and resource intensive activities, it makes sense to setup and monitor a laboratory for this purpose. Finding out the right configuration, resources (hardware, software, and set of people to perform defect bash) are activities that have to be planned carefully before a bash actually starts. Since the effort involved is more, it is critical to ensure that the right setup is done, so that everyone can perform the desired set of activities on the software. The majority of defect bash fail due to inadequate hardware, wrong software configurations, and perceptions related to performance and scalability of the software. During defect bash, the product parameters and system resources (CPU, RAM, disk, network) need to be monitored for defects and also corrected so that users can continue to use the system for the complete duration of the defect bash.

There are two types of defects that will emerge during a defect bash. The defects that are in the product, as reported by the users, can be classified as *functional defects*. Defects that are unearthed while monitoring the system resources, such as memory leak, long turnaround time, missed requests, high impact and utilization of system resources, and so on are called *non-functional defects*. Defect bash is a unique testing method which can bring out both functional and non-functional defects. However, if the lab is not set up properly or not monitored properly, there is a chance that some of the non-functional defects may not get noticed at all.

5.5.5   Taking Actions and Fixing Issues

The last step, is to take the necessary corrective action after the defect bash. Getting a large number of defects from users is the purpose and also the normal end result from a defect bash. Many defects could be duplicate defects. However, different interpretations of the same defect by different users, and the impact of the same defect showing up differently in different places, make them difficult to be called duplicates. Since there could be a large number of defects, the approach to fix problems from a defect bash should not be at a per defect level. It is difficult to solve all the problems if they are taken one by one and fixed in code. The defects need to be classified into issues at a higher level, so that a similar outcome can be avoided in future defect bashes. There could be one defect associated with an issue and there could be several defects that can be called as an issue. An example of an issue can be "In all components, all inputs for employee number have to be validated before using them in business logic." This enables all defects from different components to be grouped and classified as one issue. All the issues reported from a defect bash need to be taken through a complete code and design inspections, analyzed, and fixed together in places where a defect could evolve from. So the outcome of a defect bash can also be used for preventing defects for future defect bashes.

5.5.6   Optimizing the Effort Involved in Defect Bash

Since a defect bash involves a large number of people, spending much effort is normal for conducting defect bashes. There are several ways to optimize the effort involved in a defect bash if a record of objectives and outcome is kept. Having a tested build, keeping the right setup, sharing the objectives, and so on, to save effort and meet the purpose have been already discussed. Another approach to reduce the defect bash effort is to conduct "micro level" defect bashes before conducting one on a large scale. Some of the more evident defects will emerge at micro level bashes.

Since a defect bash is an integration testing phase activity, it can be experimented by integration test team before they open it up for others. To prevent component level defects emerging during integration testing, a micro level defect bash can also be done to unearth feature level defects, before the product can be taken into integration. Hence, a defect bash can be further classified into

1. Feature/component defect bash
2. Integration defect bash
3. Product defect bash

To explain the effort saved by the defect bash classification, let us take three product defect bashes conducted in two hours with 100 people. The total effort involved is 3*2*100 = 600 person hours. If the feature/component test team and integration test team, that has 10 people each, can participate in doing two rounds of micro level bashes, which can find out one third of defects that are expected, then effort saving is 20% with respect to the following calculation.

> A defect bash is an ad hoc testing, done by people performing different roles in the same time duration during the integration testing phase, to bring out all types of defects that may have been left out by planned testing.

Total effort involved in two rounds of product bashes—400 man hours

Effort involved in two rounds of feature bash (2*2*10)—40

Effort involved in two rounds of integration bash (2*2*10)—40

Effort saved = 600 – (A + B + C) = 600 – 480 = 120 person hours, or 20%

This is only an approximate calculation, as the effort involved in the steps mentioned earlier in this section (Steps 1–6) also need to be included for each defect bash. Those steps have to be repeated for each defect bash, irrespective of whether they are at feature level or integration level or product level.

5.6   CONCLUSION

Integration testing is both a *type of testing* and a *phase of testing*. Integration testing starts after each of the components are tested alone and delivered, using black box testing approaches discussed in Chapter 4. All components tested and working do not mean they will continue to work the same way after they are put together and integrated. This is an important phase/type of testing that is often ignored by many organizations. Owing to project pressure and delay in development schedules, integration testing may get diluted as it is performed in between component and system testing phases. A separate test team focusing on integration testing is an initiative recently taken by several companies to provide to integration testing the focus it has deserved for a long time. Integration testing, if done properly, can reduce the number of defects that will be found in the system testing phase, a phase that is explained in the following chapter.

REFERENCES

[MYER-79] is one of the earliest comparisons of the various integration approaches. [YEWU-2001] also provides a good reference for different approaches to integration testing.

PROBLEMS AND EXERCISES

1. For each of the systems characterized by the descriptions below, decide which type of integration is best suited for testing

    a. A product is evolving in versions and each version introduces new features that are fairly insulated from other features, i.e., the existing features are stable and do not get affected much by the additions

    b. A product is made of components with clearly defined interfaces. Hence, the stubs and drivers are available right from day one.

    c. A product provides standard database query and display facilities. The query facility implements standard JDBC interfaces, while the display facility provides flexibility to interface multiple platforms and display systems (like Windows, Macintosh, etc)

2. Consider a typical university academic information system. Identify the typical agents, actors, and the expected system behavior for the various types of use cases in this system

3. Consider a product which evolves is versions, each version taking approximately six months to release to the market. When would you initiate each type of defect bash for a version? Clearly state the assumptions you made while making that decision.

4. Which of the approaches given in the text would you use to arrive at system scenarios for the following cases:

    a. A customer recounts, "During the last version implementation, I had difficulty in migrating data from the previous version - it failed while backing up data for the customer master and while adding extra columns for the discounts table."

    b. A product is being deployed in the FMCG industry and in the retail sales industry and should be customizable to each.

    c. A test engineer performs unit testing, updates the defect repositories, sends emails to the components owners, chats with them and updates his log.

5. Give examples to show cases where integration testing can be taken as a white box approach (i.e., with access to code) and to show cases where it can be taken as a black box approach (i.e., no access to code).

System and Acceptance Testing

CHAPTER 6

In this chapter—

- ✓ System testing overview
- ✓ Why do system testing
- ✓ Functional versus non-functional testing
- ✓ Functional system testing
- ✓ Non-functional testing
- ✓ Acceptance testing
- ✓ Summary of testing phases

6.1   SYSTEM TESTING OVERVIEW

> The testing conducted on the complete integrated products and solutions to evaluate system compliance with specified requirements on functional and non-functional aspects is called system testing.

System testing is defined as a testing phase conducted on the complete integrated system, to evaluate the system compliance with its specified requirements. It is done after unit, component, and integration testing phases.

A system is a complete set of integrated components that together deliver product functionality and features. A system can also be defined as a set of hardware, software, and other parts that together provide product features and solutions. In order to test the entire system, it is necessary to understand the product's behavior as a whole. System testing helps in uncovering the defects that may not be directly attributable to a module or an interface. System testing brings out issues that are fundamental to design, architecture, and code of the whole product.

System testing is the only phase of testing which tests the both functional and non-functional aspects of the product. On the functional side, system testing focuses on real-life customer usage of the product and solutions. System testing simulates customer deployments. For a general-purpose product, system testing also means testing it for different business verticals and applicable domains such as insurance, banking, asset management, and so on.

On the non-functional side, system brings in different testing types (also called quality factors), some of which are as follows.

1. **Performance/Load testing**   To evaluate the time taken or response time of the system to perform its required functions in comparison with different versions of same product(s) or a different competitive product(s) is called performance testing. This type of testing is explained in the next chapter.

2. **Scalability testing**   A testing that requires enormous amount of resource to find out the maximum capability of the system parameters is called scalability testing. This type of testing is explained in subsequent sections of this chapter.

3. **Reliability testing**   To evaluate the ability of the system or an independent component of the system to perform its required functions repeatedly for a specified period of time is called reliability testing. This is explained in subsequent sections of this chapter.

4. **Stress testing**   Evaluating a system beyond the limits of the specified requirements or system resources (such as disk space, memory, processor utilization) to ensure the system does not break down unexpectedly is called stress testing. This is explained in subsequent sections of this chapter.

5. **Interoperability testing**   This testing is done to ensure that two or more products can exchange information, use the information, and work closely. This is explained in subsequent sections of this chapter.

6. **Localization testing**   Testing conducted to verify that the localized product works in different languages is called localization testing. This is explained in Chapter 9, Internationalization Testing.

The definition of system testing can keep changing, covering wider and more high-level aspects, depending on the context. A solution provided to a customer may be an integration of multiple products. Each product may be a combination of several components. A supplier of a component of a product can assume the independent component as a system in its own right and do system testing of the component. From the perspective of the product organization, integrating those components is referred to as sub-system testing. When all components, delivered by different component developers, are assembled by a product organization, they are tested together as a system. At the next level, there are solution integrators who combine products from multiple sources to provide a complete integrated solution for a client. They put together many products as a system and perform system testing of this integrated solution. Figure 6.1 illustrates the system testing performed by various organizations from their own as well as from a global perspective. The coloured figure is available on page 463.

Figure 6.1

Different perspectives of system testing.

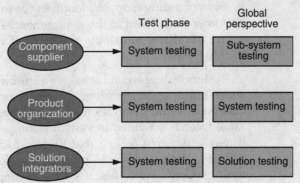

System testing is performed on the basis of written test cases according to information collected from detailed architecture/design documents, module specifications, and system requirements specifications. System test cases are created after looking at component and integration test cases, and are also at the same time designed to include the functionality that tests the system together. System test cases can also be developed based on user stories, customer discussions, and points made by observing typical customer usage.

System testing may not include many negative scenario verification, such as testing for incorrect and negative values. This is because such negative testing would have been already performed by component and integration testing and may not reflect real-life customer usage.

System testing may be started once unit, component, and integration testing are completed. This would ensure that the more basic program logic errors and defects have been corrected. Apart from verifying the business requirements of the product, system testing is done to ensure that the product is ready for moving to the user acceptance test level.

6.2   WHY IS SYSTEM TESTING DONE?

An independent test team normally does system testing. This independent test team is different from the team that does the component and integration testing. The system test team generally reports to a manager other than the project manager to avoid conflict of interest and to provide freedom to individuals doing system testing. Testing the product with an independent perspective and combining that with the perspectives of the customer makes system testing unique, different, and effective. System testing by an independent team removes the bias on the product and inducting a "fresh pair of eyes" through an independent system test team helps in locating problems missed out by component and integration testing.

The behavior of the complete product is verified during system testing. Tests that refer to multiple modules, programs, and functionality are included in system testing. Testing the complete product behavior is critical as it is wrong to believe that individually tested components will work together when they are put together.

System testing helps in identifying as many defects as possible before the customer finds them in the deployment. This is the last chance for the test team to find any remaining product defects before the product is handed over to the customer.

System testing is conducted with an objective to find product level defects and in building the confidence before the product is released to the customer. Component and integration testing phases focus on finding defects. If the same focus is provided in system testing and significant defects are found, it may generate a feeling that the product is unstable (especially because system testing is closer to product release than component or integration testing). Contrary to this, if system testing uncovers few defects, it raises questions on the effectiveness and value of system testing phase. Hence, system testing strives to always achieve a balance between the objective of finding defects and the objective of building confidence in the product prior to release.

Since system testing is the last phase of testing before the release, not all defects can be fixed in code due to time and effort needed in development and testing and due to the potential risk involved in any last-minute changes. Hence, an impact analysis is done for those defects to reduce the risk of releasing a product with defects. If the risk of the customers getting exposed to the defects is high, then the defects are fixed before the release; else, the product is released as such. The analysis of defects and their classification into various categories also gives an idea about the kind of defects that will be found by the customer after release. This information helps in planning some activities such as providing workarounds, documentation on alternative approaches, and so on. Hence, system testing helps in reducing the risk of releasing a product.

System testing is highly complementary to other phases of testing. The component and integration test phases are conducted taking inputs from functional specification and design. The main focus during these testing phases are technology and product implementation. On the other hand, customer scenarios and usage patterns serve as the basis for system testing. Thus system testing phase complements the earlier phases with an explicit focus on customers. The system testing phase helps in switching this focus of the product development team towards customers and their use of the product.

To summarize, system testing is done for the following reasons.

1. Provide independent perspective in testing
2. Bring in customer perspective in testing
3. Provide a "fresh pair of eyes" to discover defects not found earlier by testing
4. Test product behavior in a holistic, complete, and realistic environment
5. Test both functional and non-functional aspects of the product
6. Build confidence in the product
7. Analyze and reduce the risk of releasing the product
8. Ensure all requirements are met and ready the product for acceptance testing.

6.3 FUNCTIONAL VERSUS NON-FUNCTIONAL TESTING

Functional testing involves testing a product's functionality and features. Non-functional testing involves testing the product's quality factors. System testing comprises both functional and non-functional test verification.

Functional testing helps in verifying what the system is supposed to do. It aids in testing the product's features or functionality. It has only two results as far as requirements fulfillment is concerned—met or not met. If requirements are not properly enumerated, functional requirements may be understood in many ways. Hence, functional testing should have very clear expected results documented in terms of the behavior of the product. Functional testing comprises simple methods and steps to execute the test cases. Functional testing results normally depend on the product, not on the environment. It uses a pre-determined set of resources and configuration except for a few types of testing such as compatibility testing where configurations play a role, as explained in Chapter 4. Functional testing requires in-depth customer and product knowledge as well as domain knowledge so as to develop different test cases and find critical defects, as the focus of the testing is to find defects. Failures in functional testing normally result in fixes in the code to arrive at the right behavior. Functional testing is performed in all phases of testing such as unit testing, component testing, integration testing, and system testing. Having said that, the functional testing done in the system testing phase (functional system testing) focuses on product features as against component features and interface features that get focused on in earlier phases of testing.

Non-functional testing is performed to verify the quality factors (such as reliability, scalability etc.). These quality factors are also called non-functional requirements. Non-functional testing requires the expected results to be documented in qualitative and quantifiable terms. Non-functional testing requires large amount of resources and the results are different for different configurations and resources. Non-functional testing is very complex due to the large amount of data that needs to be collected and analyzed. The focus on non-functional testing is to qualify the product and is not meant to be a defect-finding exercise. Test cases for non-functional testing include a clear pass/fail criteria. However, test results are concluded both on pass/fail definitions and on the experiences encountered in running the tests.

Apart from verifying the pass or fail status, non-functional tests results are also determined by the amount of effort involved in executing them and any problems faced during execution. For example, if a performance test met the pass/fail criteria after 10 iterations, then the experience is bad and test result cannot be taken as pass. Either the product or the non-functional testing process needs to be fixed here.

Non-functional testing requires understanding the product behavior, design, and architecture and also knowing what the competition provides. It also requires analytical and statistical skills as the large amount of data generated requires careful analysis. Failures in non-functional testing affect the design and architecture much more than the product code. Since non-functional testing is not repetitive in nature and requires a stable product, it is performed in the system testing phase.

The points discussed in the above paragraphs are summarized in Table 6.1.

Some of the points mentioned in Table 6.1 may be seen as judgmental and subjective. For example, design and architecture knowledge is needed for functional testing also. Hence all the above points have to be taken as guidelines, not dogmatic rules.

Since both functional and non-functional aspects are being tested in the system testing phase, the question that can be asked is "What is the right proportion of test cases/effort for these two types of testing?" Since functional testing is a focus area starting from the unit testing phase while non-functional aspects get tested only in the system testing phase, it is a good idea that a majority of system testing effort be focused on the non-functional aspects. A 70%–30% ratio between non-functional and functional testing can be considered good and 50%–50% ratio is a good starting point. However, this is only a guideline, and the right ratio depends more on the context, type of release, requirements, and products.

Table 6.1 Functional testing versus non-functional testing.

Testing aspects	Functional testing	Non-functional testing
Involves	Product features and functionality	Quality factors
Tests	Product behavior	Behavior and experience
Result conclusion	Simple steps written to check expected results	Huge data collected and analyzed
Results varies due to	Product implementation	Product implementation, resources, and configurations
Testing focus	Defect detection	Qualification of product
Knowledge required	Product and domain	Product, domain, design, architecture, statistical skills
Failures normally due to	Code	Architecture, design, and code
Testing phase	Unit, component, integration, system	System
Test case repeatability	Repeated many times	Repeated only in case of failures and for different configurations
Configuration	One-time setup for a set of test cases	Configuration changes for each test case

6.4 FUNCTIONAL SYSTEM TESTING

As explained earlier, functional testing is performed at different phases and the focus is on product level features. As functional testing is performed at various testing phases, there are two obvious problems. One is *duplication* and other one is *gray area*. Duplication refers to the same tests being performed multiple times and gray area refers to certain tests being missed out in all the phases. A small percentage of duplication across phases is unavoidable as different teams are involved. Performing cross-reviews (involving teams from earlier phases of testing) and looking at the test cases of the previous phase before writing system test cases can help in minimizing the duplication. A small percentage of duplication is advisable, as different people from different teams test the features with different perspectives, yielding new defects.

Gray areas in testing happen due to lack of product knowledge, lack of knowledge of customer usage, and lack of co-ordination across test teams. Such gray areas in testing make defects seep through and impact customer usage. A test team performing a particular phase of testing may assume that a particular test will be performed by the next phase. This is one of the reasons for such gray areas. In such cases, there has to be a clear guideline for team interaction to plan for the tests at the earliest possible phase. A test case moved from a later phase to an earlier phase is a better alternative than delaying a test case from an earlier phase to a later phase, as the purpose of testing is to find defects as early as possible. This has to be done after completing all tests meant for the current phase, without diluting the tests of the current phase.

There are multiple ways system functional testing is performed. There are also many ways product level test cases are derived for functional testing. Some of the common techniques are given below.

1. Design/architecture verification
2. Business vertical testing
3. Deployment testing
4. Beta testing
5. Certification, standards, and testing for compliance.

6.4.1   Design/Architecture Verification

In this method of functional testing, the test cases are developed and checked against the design and architecture to see whether they are actual *product-level test cases*. Comparing this with integration testing, the test cases for integration testing are created by looking at interfaces whereas system level test cases are created first and verified with design and architecture to check whether they are product-level or component-level test cases. The integration test cases focus on interactions between modules or components whereas the functional system test focuses on the behavior of the complete product. A side benefit of this exercise is ensuring completeness of the product implementation. This technique helps in validating the product features that are written based on customer scenarios and verifying them using product implementation. If there is a test case that is a customer scenario but failed validation using this technique, then it is moved appropriately to component or integration testing phases. Since functional testing is performed at various test phases, it is important to reject the test cases and move them to an earlier phase to catch defects early and avoid any major surprise at a later phases. Some of the guidelines used to reject test cases for system functional testing include the following.

1. Is this focusing on code logic, data structures, and unit of the product? (If yes, then it belongs to unit testing.)
2. Is this specified in the functional specification of any component? (If yes, then it belongs to component testing.)
3. Is this specified in design and architecture specification for integration testing? (If yes, then it belongs to integration testing.)
4. Is it focusing on product implementation but not visible to customers? (This is focusing on implementation—to be covered in unit/component/integration testing.)
5. Is it the right mix of customer usage and product implementation? (Customer usage is a prerequisite for system testing.)

6.4.2 Business Vertical Testing

General purpose products like workflow automation systems can be used by different businesses and services. Using and testing the product for different business verticals such as insurance, banking, asset management, and so on, and verifying the business operations and usage, is called "business vertical testing." For this type of testing, the procedure in the product is altered to suit the process in the business. For example, in loan processing, the loan is approved first by the officer and then sent to a clerk. In claim processing, the claim is first worked out by a clerk and then sent to an officer for approval. User objects such as clerk and officer are created by the product and associated with the operations. This is one way of customizing the product to suit the business. There are some operations that can only be done by some user objects; this is called role-based operations. It is important that the product understands the business processes and includes *customization* as a feature so that different business verticals can use the product. With the help of the customization feature, a general workflow of a system is altered to suit specific business verticals.

Another important aspect is called *terminology*. To explain this concept let us take the example of e-mail. An e-mail sent in the insurance context may be called a claim whereas when an e-mail is sent in a loan-processing system, it is called a loan application. The users would be familiar with this terminology rather than the generic terminology of "e-mail." The user interface should reflect these terminologies rather than use generic terminology e-mails, which may dilute the purpose and may not be understood clearly by the users. An e-mail sent to a blood bank service cannot take the same priority as an internal e-mail sent to an employee by another employee. These differentiations need to be made by the product using the profile of the sender and the mail contents. Some e-mails or phone calls need to be tracked by the product to see whether they meet service level agreements (SLAS). For example, an e-mail to a blood bank service needs as prompt a reply as possible. Some of the mails could be even automated mail replies based on rules set in the e-mail management system for meeting the SLAs. Hence the terminology feature of the product should call the e-mail appropriately as a claim or a transaction and also associate the profile and properties in a way a particular business vertical works.

Yet another aspect involved in business vertical testing is *syndication*. Not all the work needed for business verticals are done by product development organizations. Solution integrators, service providers pay a license fee to a product organization and sell the products and solutions using their name and image. In this case the product name, company name, technology names, and copyrights may belong to the latter parties or associations and the former would like to change the names in the product. A product should provide features for those syndications in the product and they are as tested part of business verticals testing.

Business vertical testing can be done in two ways—simulation and replication. In simulation of a vertical test, the customer or the tester assumes requirements and the business flow is tested. In replication, customer data and process is obtained and the product is completely customized, tested, and the customized product as it was tested is released to the customer.

As discussed in the chapter on integration testing, business verticals are tested through scenarios. Scenario testing is only a method to evolve scenarios and ideas, and is not meant to be exhaustive. It's done more from the perspective of interfaces and their interaction. Having some business verticals scenarios created by integration testing ensures quick progress in system testing, which is done with a perspective of end-to-end scenarios. In the system testing phase, the business verticals are completely tested in real-life customer environment using the aspects such as customization, terminology, and syndication described in the above paragraphs.

6.4.3 Deployment Testing

System testing is the final phase before product delivery. By this time the prospective customers and their configuration would be known and in some cases the products would have been committed for sale. Hence, system testing is the right time to test the product for those customers who are waiting for it. The short-term success or failure of a particular product release is mainly assessed on the basis of on how well these customer requirements are met. This type of deployment (simulated) testing that happens in a product development company to ensure that customer deployment requirements are met is called *offsite deployment*.

Deployment testing is also conducted after the release of the product by utilizing the resources and setup available in customers' locations. This is a combined effort by the product development organization and the organization trying to use the product. This is called *onsite deployment*. Even though onsite deployment is not conducted in the system testing phase, it is explained here to set the context. It is normally the system testing team that is involved in completing the onsite deployment test. Onsite deployment testing is considered to be a part of acceptance testing (explained later in this chapter) and is an extension of offsite deployment testing.

Onsite deployment testing is done at two stages. In the first stage (Stage 1), actual data from the live system is taken and similar machines and configurations are mirrored, and the operations from the users are rerun on the mirrored deployment machine. This gives an idea whether the enhanced or similar product can perform the existing functionality without affecting the user. This also reduces the risk of a product not being able to satisfy existing functionality, as deploying the product without adequate testing can cause major business loss to an organization. Some deployments use *intelligent recorders* to record the transactions that happen on a live system and commit these operations on a mirrored system and then compare the results against the live system. The objective of the recorder is to help in keeping the mirrored and live system identical with respect to business transactions. In the second stage (Stage 2), after a successful first stage, the mirrored system is made a live system that runs the new product. Regular backups are taken and alternative methods are used to record the incremental transactions from the time mirrored system became live. The recorder that was used in the first stage can also be used here. However, a different method to record the incremental transaction is advised, for sometimes failures can happen due to recorder also. This stage helps to avoid any major failures since some of the failures can be noticed only after an extended period of time. In this stage, the live system that was used earlier and the recorded transactions from the time mirrored system became live, are preserved to enable going back to the old system if any major failures are observed at this stage. If no failures are observed in this (second) stage of deployment for an extended period (for example, one month), then the onsite deployment is considered successful and the old live system is replaced by the new system. Stages 1 and 2 of deployment testing are represented in Figure 6.2. The coloured figure is available on page 463.

Figure 6.2

Stages of deployment testing.

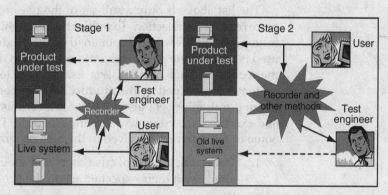

In Stage 1 of Figure 6.2, it can be seen that the recorder intercepts the user and live system to record all transactions. All the recorded transactions from the live system are then played back on the product under test under the supervision of the test engineer (shown by dotted lines). In Stage 2, the test engineer records all transactions using a recorder and other methods and plays back on the old live system (shown again by dotted lines).

6.4.4   Beta Testing

Developing a product involves a significant amount of effort and time. Delays in product releases and the product not meeting the customer requirements are common. A product rejected by the customer after delivery means a huge loss to the organization. There are many reasons for a product not meeting the customer requirements. They are as follows.

1.   There are implicit and explicit requirements for the product. A product not meeting the implicit requirements (for example, ease of use) may mean rejection by the customer.

2. Since product development involves a good amount of time, some of the requirements given at the beginning of the project would have become obsolete or would have changed by the time the product is delivered. Customers' business requirements keep changing constantly and a failure to reflect these changes in the product makes the latter obsolete.

3. The requirements are high-level statements with a high degree of ambiguity. Picking up the ambiguous areas and not resolving them with the customer results in rejection of the product.

4. The understanding of the requirements may be correct but their implementation could be wrong. This may mean reworking the design and coding to suit the implementation aspects the customer wants. If this is not done in time, it may result in rejection of the product.

5. Lack of usability and documentation makes it difficult for the customer to use the product and may also result in rejection.

The list above is only a sub-set of the reasons and there could be many more reasons for rejection. To reduce the risk, which is the objective of system testing, periodic feedback is obtained on the product. One of the mechanisms used is sending the product that is under test to the customers and receiving the feedback. This is called *beta testing*. This testing is performed by the customer and helped by the product development organization. During the entire duration of beta testing, there are various activities that are planned and executed according to a specific schedule. This is called a *beta program*. Some of the activities involved in the beta program are as follows.

1. Collecting the list of customers and their beta testing requirements along with their expectations on the product.

2. Working out a beta program schedule and informing the customers. Not all the customers in the list need to agree to the start date and end date of the beta program. The end date of a beta program should be reasonably before the product release date so that the beta testing defects can be fixed before the release.

3. Sending some documents for reading in advance and training the customer on product usage.

4. Testing the product to ensure it meets "beta testing entry criteria." The customers and the product development/management groups of the vendor together prepare sets of entry/exit criteria for beta testing.

5. Sending the beta product (with known quality) to the customer and enable them to carry out their own testing.

6. Collecting the feedback periodically from the customers and prioritizing the defects for fixing.

7. Responding to customers' feedback with product fixes or documentation changes and closing the communication loop with the customers in a timely fashion.

8. Analyzing and concluding whether the beta program met the exit criteria.

9. Communicate the progress and action items to customers and formally closing the beta program.

10. Incorporating the appropriate changes in the product.

Deciding on the entry criteria of a product for beta testing and deciding the timing of a beta test poses several conflicting choices to be made. Sending the product too early, with inadequate internal testing will make the customers unhappy and may create a bad impression on quality of product. Sending the product too late may mean too little a time for beta defect fixes and this one defeats the purpose of beta testing. Late integration testing phase and early system testing phase is the ideal time for starting a beta program.

It is quite possible that customers discontinue the beta program after starting it or remain passive, without adequately using the product and giving feedback. From the customers' perspective, it is possible that beta testing is normally just one of their activities and it may not be high on their priority list. Constant communication with the customers is necessary to motivate them to use the product and help them whenever they are facing problems with the product. They should also be made to see the benefits of participating in the beta program. The early exposure they get to emerging technologies, the competitive business advantages that can come from these technologies, and the image of the beta customer as a pioneer in the adoption of these technologies should all be impressed upon the customers. Once the customers see the beta program as a win-win program for them as well as for the vendor (rather than be viewed only as a test bed for the product), their motivation to actively participate in the program increases. Defects reported in beta programs are also given the same priority and urgency as that of normal support calls, with the only difference being that the product development/engineering department is likely to have a more direct interaction with the beta customers. Failure in meeting beta testing objectives or in giving timely fixes may mean some customers rejecting the product. Hence, defect fixes are sent to customers as soon as problems are reported and all necessary care has to be taken to ensure the fixes meets the requirements of the customer.

One other challenge in beta programs is the choice of the number of beta customers. If the number chosen are too few, then the product may not get a sufficient diversity of test scenarios and test cases. If too many beta customers are chosen, then the engineering organization may not be able to cope up with fixing the reported defects in time. Thus the number of beta customers should be a delicate balance between providing a diversity of product usage scenarios and the manageability of being able to handle their reported defects effectively.

Finally, the success of a beta program depends heavily on the willingness of the beta customers to exercise the product in various ways, knowing fully well that there may be defects. This is not an easy task. As mentioned earlier, the beta customers must be motivated to see the benefits they can get. Only customers who can be thus motivated and are willing to play the role of trusted partners in the evolution of the product should participate in the beta program.

6.4.5   Certification, Standards and Testing for Compliance

A product needs to be certified with the popular hardware, operating system, database, and other infrastructure pieces. This is called certification testing. A product not working with any of the popular hardware or software or equipment, may be unsuitable for current and future use. The sales of a product depend on whether it was certified with the popular systems or not. The product has to work with the popular systems, as the customer would have already invested heavily on those. Not only should the product co-exist and run with the current versions of these popular systems, but the product organization should also document a commitment (in the form of a roadmap) to continue to work with the future versions of the popular systems. This is one type of testing where there is equal interest from the product development organization, the customer, and certification agencies to certify the product. However, the onus of making sure the certification happens rests with the product development organization. The certification agencies produce automated test suites to help the product development organization. The product development organization runs those certification test suites and corrects the problems in the product to ensure that tests are successful. Once the tests are successfully run, the results are sent to the certification agencies and they give the certification for the product. The test suite may be rerun by the certification agencies to verify the results, in which case the product under test should be sent along with the test results.

There are many standards for each technology area and the product may need to conform to those standards. This is very important as adhering to these standards makes the product interact easily with other products. This also helps the customer not to worry too much about the products future compatibility with other products. As explained, there are many standards for each technology area and the product development companies select the standards to be implemented at the beginning of the product cycle. Following all the standards may not be possible and sometime there may be some non-functional issues (for example, performance impact) because of which certain standards may not get implemented. Standards can be evolving also (for example, Ipv6 in networking and 3G in mobile technology) and finer details are worked out as and when some implementations kick off. Some of the standards are evolved by the open community and published as public domain standards (for example, Open LDAP standard). Tools associated with those open standards can be used free of cost to verify the standard's implementation. Testing the product to ensure that these standards are properly implemented is called *testing for standards*. Once the product is tested for a set of standards, they are published in the release documentation for the information of the customers so that they know what standards, are implemented in the product.

There are many contractual and legal requirements for a product. Failing to meet these may result in business loss and bring legal action against the organization and its senior management. Some of these requirements could be contractual obligations and some statutory requirements. Failing to meet these could severely restrict the market for the product. For example, it may not be possible to bid for US government organizations if usability guidelines (508 Accessibility Guidelines) are not met. Testing the product for contractual, legal, and statutory compliance is one of the critical activities of the system testing team. The following are some examples of compliance testing.

✠ **Compliance to FDA**   This act by the food and drug administration requires that adequate testing be done for products such as cosmetics, drugs, and medical sciences. This also requires that all the test reports along with complete documentation of test cases, execution information for each test cycle along with supervisory approvals be preserved for checking adequacy of tests by the FDA.

✠ **508 accessibility guidelines**   This accessibility set of guidelines requires the product to meet some requirements for its physically challenged users. These guidelines insist that the product should be as accessible to physically challenged people as it is to people without those disabilities.

✠ **SOX (Sarbanes–Oxley's Act)**   This act requires that products and services be audited to prevent financial fraud in the organization. The software is required to go through all transactions and list out the suspected faulty transactions for analysis. The testing for this act helps the top executives by keeping them aware of financial transactions and their validity.

✠ **OFAC and Patriot Act**   This act requires the transactions of the banking applications be audited for misuse of funds for terrorism.

The terms certification, standards and compliance testing are used interchangeably. There is nothing wrong in the usage of terms as long as the objective of the testing is met. For example, a certifying agency helping an organization to meet standards can be called as both certification testing and standards testing (for example, Open LDAP is both a certification and a standard).

6.5   NON-FUNCTIONAL TESTING

In Section 6.3, we have seen how non-functional testing is different from functional testing. The process followed by non-functional testing is similar to that of functional testing but differs from the aspects of complexity, knowledge requirement, effort needed, and number of times the test cases are repeated. Since repeating non-functional test cases involves more time, effort, and resources, the process for non-functional testing has to be more robust stronger than functional testing to minimize the need for repetition. This is achieved by having more stringent entry/exit criteria, better planning, and by setting up the configuration with data population in advance for test execution.

6.5.1   Setting Up the Configuration

The biggest challenge, setting up the configuration, is common to all types of non-functional testing. There are two ways the setup is done—simulated environment and real-life customer environment. Due to varied types of customers, resources availability, time involved in getting the exact setup, and so on, setting up a scenario that is exactly real-life is difficult. Even though using real-life customer environment is a crucial factor for the success of this testing, due to several complexities involved, simulated setup is used for non-functional testing where actual configuration is difficult to get. Setting up a configuration is a challenge for the following reasons.

1.   Given the high diversity of environments and variety of customers, it is very difficult to predict the type of environment that will be used commonly by the customers.

2.   Testing a product with different permutations and combinations of configurations may not prove effective since the same combination of environment may not used by the customer and testing for several combinations involves effort and time. Furthermore, because of the diversity of configurations, there is a combinatorial explosion in the number of configurations to be tested.

3.   The cost involved in setting up such environments is quite high.

4.   Some of the components of the environment could be from competing companies products and it may not be easy to get these.

5.   The people may not have the skills to set up the environment.

6.   It is difficult to predict the exact type and nature of data that the customer may use. Since confidentiality is involved in the data used by the customer, such information is not passed on to the testing team.

In order to create a "near real-life" environment, the details regarding customer's hardware setup, deployment information and test data are collected in advance. Test data is built based on the sample data given. If it is a new product, then information regarding similar or related products is collected. These inputs help in setting up the test environment close to the customer's so that the various quality characteristics of the system can be verified more accurately.

6.5.2 Coming up with Entry/Exit Criteria

Coming up with entry and exit criteria is another critical factor in non-functional testing. Table 6.2 gives some examples of how entry/exit criteria can be developed for a set of parameters and for various types of non-functional tests. Meeting the entry criteria is the responsibility of the previous test phase (that is, integration testing phase) or it could be the objective of dry-run tests performed by the system testing team, before accepting the product for system testing.

6.5.3 Balancing Key Resources

Memory
Network
Disk
CPU
Juggler

This section intends to discuss the concepts of non-functional testing with respect to four key resources—CPU, disk, memory, and network. The four resources are related to each other and we need to completely understand their relationship to implement the strategy for non-functional testing.

These four resources in a computer require equal attention as they need to be judiciously balanced to enhance the quality factors of the product. All these resources are interdependent. For example, if the memory requirements in the system are addressed, the need for CPU may become more intensive. This in turn may result in multiple cycles of upgrade as the requirements of the customers keep increasing. The demand for all these resources tends to grow when a new release of the product is produced as software becomes

Table 6.2 Typical entry/exit criteria for non-functional tests.

Type of test	Parameters	Sample entry criteria	Sample exit criteria
Scalability	Maximum limits	Product should scale up to one million records or 1000 users	Product should scale up to 10 million records or 5000 users
Performance test	• Response time • Throughput • Latency	Query for 1000 records should have a response time less than 3 seconds	Query for 10,000 records should have response time less than 3 seconds
Reliability	• Failures per iteration • Failures per test duration	There should be less than 2% failures when queries are run on 1000 records for 24 hours	There should be less than 0.1% failures when queries are run on 1000 records for 48 hours
Stress	System when stressed beyond the limits	Product should be able to withstand 25 clients login happening simultaneously for 5 hours in a configuration that can take only 20 clients	Product should be able to withstand 100 clients login simultaneously for 5 hours in a configuration that can take only 100 clients

more and more complex. Software is meant not only for computers but also for equipment such as cell phones; hence upgrading the resources is not easy anymore.

Often, customers are perplexed when they are told to increase the number of CPUs, memory, and the network bandwidth for better performance, scalability, and other non-functional aspects. This perception of arbitrariness is created when the rationale and measurable guidelines to specify the level of performance/scalability improvement to be expected when resources are adjusted, is not provided. Hence, when asking customers to upgrade the resources one important aspect return on investment needs to be justified clearly. The question that remains in the customer's mind is, "What will I get when I upgrade?" If the product is well tested, then for every increment of addition to a resource, there will be a corresponding improvement in the product for non-functional aspects, thus justifying to the customer the additional requirement.

It is important to understand and acknowledge customers' views about the resources the product intensively uses and the resources that are critical for product usage. It is easy to tell the customer, "Product A is CPU intensive, product B requires more memory, and product C requires better bandwidth," and so on. However, some of the products that run on a particular server could be from multiple vendors but they may be expected to run together on the same machine. Hence, it is very difficult for the customer to increase all the resources in the server, as all the products are expected to run in the same server, at the same time. Similarly, multiple applications can run on client machines sharing resources.

It is equally important to analyze from the perspective of the product organization that software is becoming more complex as more and more features get added for every release using different and latest technologies. Unless proper resources are assigned for the product, the better aspects of the product can not be seen.

As there are many perspectives of resources, many relationships between resources and varied requirements for non-functional testing, certain basic assumptions about the resources have to be made by the testing team and validated by the development team and by the customers before starting the testing. Without these assumptions being validated, there cannot be any good conclusion that can be made out of non-functional testing. The following are some examples of basic assumptions that can be made about resources and configuration.

1. The CPU can be fully utilized as long as it can be freed when a high priority job comes in.

2. The available memory can be completely used by the product as long as the memory is relinquished when another job requires memory.

3. The cost of adding CPU or memory is not that expensive as it was earlier. Hence resources can be added easily to get better performance as long as we can quantify and justify the benefits for each added resource.

4. The product can generate many network packets as long as the network bandwidth and latency is available and does not cost much. There is a difference in this assumption that most of the packets generated are for LAN and not for WAN. In the case of WAN or routes involving multiple hops, the packets generated by the product need to be reduced.

5. More disk space or the complete I/O bandwidth can be used for the product as long as they are available. While disk costs are getting cheaper, IO bandwidth is not.

6. The customer gets the maximum return on investment (ROI) only if the resources such as CPU, disk, memory, and network are optimally used. So there is intelligence needed in the software to understand the server configuration and its usage.

7. Graceful degradation in non-functional aspects can be expected when resources in the machine are also utilized for different activities in the server.

8. Predictable variations in performance or scalability are acceptable for different configurations of the same product.

9. Variation in performance and scalability is acceptable when some parameters are tuned, as long as we know the impact of adjusting each of those tunable parameters.

10. The product can behave differently for non-functional factors for different configurations such as low-end and high-end servers as long as they support return on investment. This in fact motivates the customers to upgrade their resources.

Once such sample assumptions are validated by the development team and customers, then non-functional testing is conducted.

6.5.4   Scalability Testing

The objective of scalability testing is to find out the maximum capability of the product parameters. As the exercise involves finding the maximum, the resources that are needed for this kind of testing are normally very high. For example, one of the scalability test case could be finding out how many client machines can simultaneously log in to the server to perform some operations. In Internet space, some of the services can get up to a million access to the server. Hence, trying to simulate that kind of real-life scalability parameter is very difficult but at the same time very important.

At the beginning of the scalability exercise, there may not be an obvious clue about the maximum capability of the system. Hence a high-end configuration is selected and the scalability parameter is increased step by step to reach the maximum capability.

The design and architecture give the theoretical values, and requirements from the customers mention the maximum capability that is expected. The scalability exercise first verifies the lower number of these two. When the requirements from the customer are more than what design/architecture can provide, the scalability testing is suspended, the design is reworked, and scalability testing resumed to check the scalability parameters. Hence, the requirements, design, and architecture together provide inputs to the scalability testing on what parameter values are to be tested.

Contrary to other types of testing, scalability testing does not end when the requirements are met. The testing continues till the maximum capability of a scalable parameter is found out for a particular configuration. Having a highly scalable system that considers the future requirements of the customer helps a product to have a long lifetime. Otherwise, each time there are new requirements, a major redesign and overhaul takes place in the product and some stable features may stop working because of those changes, thus creating quality concerns. The cost and effort involved in such product developments are very high.

Failures during scalability test include the system not responding, or the system crashing, and so on. But whether the failure is acceptable or not has to be decided on the basis of business goals and objectives. For example, a product not able to respond to 100 concurrent users while its objective is to serve at least 200 users simultaneously is considered a failure. When a product expected to withstand only 100 users fails when its load is increased to 200, then it is a passed test case and an acceptable situation.

Scalability tests help in identifying the major bottlenecks in a product. When resources are found to be the bottlenecks, they are increased after validating the assumptions mentioned in Section 6.5.3. If the bottlenecks are in the product, they are fixed. However, sometimes the underlying infrastructure such as the operating system or technology can also become bottlenecks. In such cases, the product organization is expected to work with the OS and technology vendors to resolve the issues.

Scalability tests are performed on different configurations to check the product's behavior. For each configuration, data are collected and analyzed. An example of a data collection template is given below.

On completion of the tests, the data collected in the templates are analyzed and appropriate actions are taken. For example, if CPU utilization approaches to 100%, then another server is set up to share the load or another CPU is added to the server. If the results are successful, then the tests are repeated for 200 users and more to find the maximum limit for that configuration.

Some of the data needs analysis on a finer granularity. For example, if the maximum CPU utilization is 100% but only for a short time and if for the rest of the testing it remained at say 40%, then there is no point in adding one more CPU. But, the product still has to be analyzed for the sudden

Given configuration
RAM—512 MB
Cache size—200 MB
Number of users—100 (Scalable parameter)
With/without indexing—With indexing

No. of records	Start time	End time	Average time taken to add a record	Disk used	CPU used	Memory	Records/sec	Server configuraction
0–1 million records								
1–10 million records								

spike in the CPU utilization and it has to be fixed. This exercise requires the utilization data to be collected periodically as in the template given above. By looking at how often the spikes come about, and by analyzing the reasons for these spikes, an idea can be formed of where the bottleneck is and what the corrective action should be. Thus, merely increasing the resources is not an answer to achieving better scalability.

In scalability testing, the demand on resources tends to grow exponentially when the scalability parameter is increased. Resources growth is exponential when the scalability parameter increases. The scalability reaches a saturation point beyond which it cannot be improved (see Figure 6.3). This is called the maximum capability of a scalability parameter. Even though resources may be available, product limitation may not allow scalability. This is called a product bottleneck. Identification of such bottlenecks and removing them in the testing phase as early as possible is a basic requirement for resumption of scalability testing.

Figure 6.3

Variation of resources with the scalability parameter.

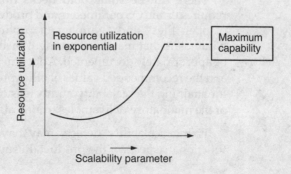

Time (hrs)	CPU utilization	Memory utilization	Network utilization (number of packets sent)
01:00			
01:05			
01:10			
01:15			
01:20			

As explained earlier, scalability testing may also require an upgrading of resources. When there are no product bottlenecks, resources need to be upgraded to complete scalability testing. As explained earlier, when as the resources are upgraded, the return on investment study is carried out to find out if the returns justify the cost of upgrading the resources. The following are a few assumptions that can be kept in mind to carry out such an ROI study. The numbers and percentages used in the assumptions are only guideline values and will have to be modified depending on the product and context.

✠ Scalability should increase 50% when the number of CPUs is doubled from minimum requirement and 40% thereafter, till a given number of CPUs are added. Such a test will be applicable if the product is CPU intensive.

✠ Scalability should increase 40% when memory is doubled from the minimum requirement and 30% thereafter. This will be applicable if the product is memory intensive.

✠ Scalability should increase by at least 30% when the number of NIC cards or network bandwidth are doubled. This aspect has to be tested if the product is network intensive.

✠ Scalability should increase by at least 50% when the I/O bandwidth is doubled. This aspect has to be tested if the product is I/O intensive.

There can be some bottlenecks during scalability testing, which will require certain OS parameters and product parameters to be tuned. "Number of open files" and "Number of product threads" are some examples of parameters that may need tuning. When such tuning is performed, it should be appropriately documented. A document containing such tuning parameters and the recommended values of other product and environmental parameters for attaining the scalability numbers is called a *sizing guide*. This guide is one of the mandatory deliverables from scalability testing.

Fixing scalability defects may have some impact on the other non-functional aspects of the product. In such cases reliability testing (discussed in the next section) should take care of monitoring parameters like response time, throughput, and so on, and taking necessary action. Scalability should not be achieved at the cost of any other quality factor. Hence it is advised that the test engineer discusses the results with people who are performing other functional and non-functional testing and aggregate the findings.

Another important aspect of scalability is the experience associated with doing it. Scalability testing requires significant resources and is expensive. It is ideal that the scalability requirements be met in few iterations of testing and in quick time. If, during scalability testing, plenty of "tweaking" is required to be done to the product, tunable parameters, and resources, it indicate lack of planning and lack of understanding of product behavior. A detailed study of the product and a set of problems anticipated along with probable solutions is a prerequisite to getting a good experience/feel for such testing.

6.5.5   Reliability Testing

As defined earlier, reliability testing is done to evaluate the product's ability to perform its required functions under stated conditions for a specified period of time or for a large number of iterations. Examples of reliability include querying a database continuously for 48 hours and performing login operations 10,000 times.

The *reliability of a product* should not be confused with *reliability testing*. Producing a reliable product requires sound techniques, good discipline, robust processes, and strong management, and involves a whole gamut of activities for every role or function in a product organization. The reliability of a product deals with the different ways a quality product is produced, with very few defects by focusing on all the phases of product development and the processes. Reliability here is an all-encompassing term used to mean all the quality factors and functionality aspects of the product. This perspective is related more to the overall way the product is developed and has less direct relevance to testing. This product reliability is achieved by focusing on the following activities.

1. **Defined engineering processes**   Software reliability can be achieved by following clearly defined processes. The team is mandated to understand requirements for reliability right from the beginning and focuses on creating a reliable design upfront. All the activities (such as design, coding, testing, documentation) are planned, taking into consideration the reliability requirements of the software.

2. **Review of work products at each stage**   At the end of each stage of the product development life cycle, the work products produced are reviewed. This ensures early detection of error and their fixes as soon as they are introduced.

3. **Change management procedures**   Many errors percolate to the product due to improper impact analysis of changes made to the product. Changes received late during the product development

life cycle can prove harmful. There may not be adequate time for regression testing and hence the product is likely to have errors due to changes. Hence, having a clearly defined change management procedure is necessary to deliver reliable software.

4. **Review of testing coverage** Allocating time for the different phases and types of testing can help in catching errors as and when the product is being developed, rather than after the product is developed. All the testing activities are reviewed for adequacy of time allotted, test cases, and effort spent for each type of testing.

5. **Ongoing monitoring of the product** Once the product has been delivered, it is analyzed proactively for any possibly missed errors. In this case the process as well as the product is fixed for missed defects. This prevents the same type of defects from reappearing.

Reliability testing, on the other hand, refers to testing the product for a continuous period of time. Performing good reliability testing does not ensure a reliable product on its own, as there are various other requirements for a product to be reliable, as mentioned in the earlier paragraphs. Reliability testing only delivers a "reliability tested product" but not a reliable product. The main factor that is taken into account for reliability testing is defects. The defects found through testing are closely monitored and they are compared with defects removed in the earlier phases and analyzed for why they were not caught earlier. Defects are tracked in order to guide the product as well as the test process, and also to determine the feasibility of release of the software. At the beginning of the project, a criterion for reliability is set for the maximum number of defects allowed. The actual number of defects found during various durations of running tests are compared to find out how well the product is doing compared with the criterion. This is depicted in Figure 6.4.

In Figure 6.4, it can be seen that the product is very close to meeting the reliability criteria towards the end. Figure 6.4 (a) suggests that the progress towards meeting the criteria is smooth, whereas in Figure 6.4 (b), the transition contains spikes. These spikes indicate that defects in the product for the reliability tests go up and down periodically. This may be a pointer to indicate that the defect fixes are creating new defects in the system. Analyzing the spikes and taking action to avoid the spikes, both from the

Figure 6.4

Reliability criteria showing (a) smooth the progress and (b) spikes.

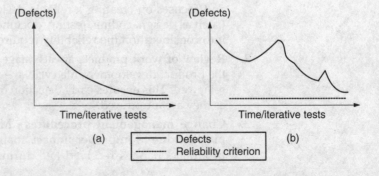

(a)   (b)

process and from the product perspective, will help in meeting reliability criteria in an effective and repeatable way.

Reliability should not be achieved at the cost of some other quality factor. For example, when operations are repeated, they may fail sometimes due to race conditions. They may be resolved by introducing "sleep" between statements. This approach has a definite impact on performance. Hence, collecting and analyzing the data of reliability testing should also include other quality factors so that the impact can be analyzed in a holistic manner. Figure 6.5 gives an example of reliability impact on performance.

Figure 6.5

Reliability impact on performance.

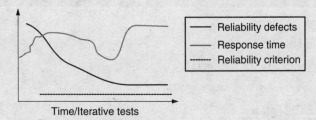

In the above graph, while reliability seems to approach the desired value, response time seems to be erratic. An effective analysis of the system test results should consider not only the (positive) aspect of the convergence of reliability criteria to the desired values but should also analyze why performance is erratic. Reliability testing brings out those errors which arise because of certain operations being repeated. Memory leak is a problem that is normally brought out by reliability testing. At the end of repeated operations sometimes the CPU may not get released or disk and network activity may continue. Hence, it is important to collect data regarding various resources used in the system before, during, and after reliability test execution, and analyze those results. Upon completion of the reliability tests, the resource utilization of the product should drop down to the pre-test level of resource utilization. This verifies whether the resources are relinquished after the use by the product. The following table gives an idea on how reliability data can be collected.

The data for the above table is collected periodically and plotted in charts to analyze the behavior of each parameter. The failure data helps in plotting up the reliability chart explained above and are compared against the criteria. Resource data such as CPU, memory, and network data are collected to analyze the impact of reliability on resources.

Figure 6.6 illustrates resource utilization over a period of time the reliability tests are executed.

Figure 6.6

Resource utilization over a period of execution of reliability tests.

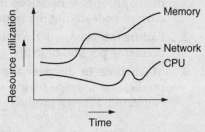

Configuration details
Memory—1 GB
Processors—2,850 MHz
N/W Bandwidth—100 Mbps

Test data	25 clients	60 clients	100 clients
Total iterations:			
Total fail:			
Peak memory utilization (MB):			
Mean memory utilization (MB):			
Peak CPU utilization:			
Mean CPU utilization:			
Packets received at server:			
Packets sent from server:			

The chart in Figure 6.6 indicates that network utilization is constant during reliability testing whereas the memory and CPU utilization are going up. This needs analysis and the causes need to be fixed. The CPU and memory utilization must be consistent through out the test execution. If they keep on increasing, other applications on the machine can get affected; the machine may even run out of memory, hang, or crash, in which case the machine needs to be restarted. Memory buildup problems are common among most server software. These kinds of problems require a lot of time and effort to get resolved.

There are different ways of expressing reliability defects in charts.

1. **Mean time between failures** is the average time elapsed from between successive product failures. Details on the time a product failed have to be maintained to understand its reliability for a specified time frame. For example, if the product fails, say, for every 72 hours, then appropriate decisions may have to be taken on backing out the current code, fixing the issue, and then deploying the same.

2. **Failure rate** is provided as a function that gives the number of failures occurring per unit time (the graphs above depict this measurement).

3. **Mean time to discover the next K faults** is the measure used to predict the average length of time until the next K faults are encountered. When a product is unstable, the time taken to find K faults

will be less and when the product becomes stable, the time taken to find K faults will be more indicating an, increasing trend.

Use of real-life scenario yields more applicable results in reliability. Since reliability is defined as executing operations over a period of time, it should not be taken for granted that all operations need to be repeated. Some operations such as configuration, backup, and restore operations are performed rarely and they should not be selected for reliability. Rather, the operations that are highly and most frequently used and a mix of operations (scenarios) that reflect the daily activities of the customer should be considered for reliability testing. For example, log in-log out operations are important operations that need to be reliability tested. But no real user will keep on doing log in/log out as a sequence. Some operations are normally performed between log in and log out. Typically, a user may check a few mails, sending a few instant messages, and so on. Such a combination of activities represents a typical real-life customer usage. It is this type of combination of activities that must be subjected to reliability testing. When multiple users use the system from different clients, it reflects the scenario on the server side, where some operations are done repeatedly in a loop. Hence, selecting a test for reliability test should consider the scenario closer to real-life usage of the product.

To summarize, a "reliability tested product" will have the following characteristics.

1. No errors or very few errors from repeated transactions.
2. Zero downtime.
3. Optimum utilization of resources.
4. Consistent performance and response time of the product for repeated transactions for a specified time duration.
5. No side-effects after the repeated transactions are executed.

6.5.6 Stress Testing

Stress testing is done to evaluate a system beyond the limits of specified requirements or resources, to ensure that system does not break. Stress testing is done to find out if the product's behavior degrades under extreme conditions and when it is denied the necessary resources. The product is over-loaded deliberately to simulate the resource crunch and to find out its behavior. It is expected to gracefully degrade on increasing the load, but the system is not expected to crash at any point of time during stress testing.

Stress testing helps in understanding how the system can behave under extreme (insufficient memory, inadequate hardware) and realistic situations. System resources upon being exhausted may cause such situations. This helps to know the conditions under which these tests fail so that the maximum limits, in terms of simultaneous users, search criteria, large number of transactions, and so on can be known.

Extreme situations such as a resource not being available can also be simulated. There are tools that can simulate "hogging of memory," generate packets for flooding the network bandwidth, create processes that can take all the CPU cycles, keep reading/writing to disks, and so on. When these tools are run along with the product, the number of machines needed for stress testing can be reduced. However, the use of such tools may not bring out all stress-related problems of the product. Hence, after the simulation exercise (using the tools) is over, it is recommended that the tests should be repeated without the use of such tools.

The process, data collection, and analysis required for stress testing are very similar to those of reliability testing. The difference lies in the way the tests are run. Reliability testing is performed by keeping a constant load condition till the test case is completed; the load is increased only in the next iteration of the test case. In stress testing, the load is generally increased through various means such as increasing the number of clients, users, and transactions till and beyond the resources are completely utilized. When the load keeps on increasing, the product reaches a stress point when some of the transactions start failing due to resources not being available. The failure rate may go up beyond this point. To continue the stress testing, the load is slightly reduced below this stress point to see whether the product recovers and whether the failure rate decreases appropriately. This exercise of increasing/decreasing the load is performed two or three times to check for consistency in behavior and expectations.

Sometimes, the product may not recover immediately when the load is decreased. There are several reasons for this.

1. Some transactions may be in the wait queue, delaying the recovery.
2. Some rejected transactions many need to be purged, delaying the recovery.
3. Due to failures, some clean-up operations may be needed by the product, delaying the recovery.
4. Certain data structures may have got corrupted and may permanently prevent recovery from stress point.

The time required for the product to quickly recover from those failures is represented by *MTTR* (*Mean time to recover*). The recovery time may be different for different operations and they need to be calculated

Figure 6.7

Stress testing with variable load.

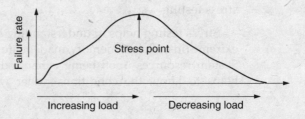

Figure 6.8

MTTR for different
operations.

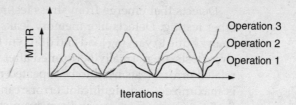

as appropriate. As explained earlier, several iterations of tests/different
operations are conducted around the stress point and MTTR is calculated
from the mean (average) and plotted as in Figure 6.8.

In Figure 6.8, the MTTR peaks and comes down as the load is increased/
decreased around the stress point. It can also be noticed that Operation 1
is consistent with recovery time on all iterations (as it touches zero when
load is reduced and mean time is consistent across iterations), whereas
Operation 2 does not recover fully after first iteration, and recovery time
slightly increases over iterations in Operation 3.

Instead of plotting MTTR for each operation, the average recovery time
of all operations can be taken and the mean plotted.

As indicated earlier, the same tests, data collection sheets, and processes
as used in reliability testing can be used for stress testing as well. One
differentiating factor as explained earlier was variable load. Another factor
that differentiates stress testing from reliability testing is mixed operations/
tests. Different types of tests that utilize the resources are selected and used
in stress testing. Hence, numerous tests of various types run on the system
in stress testing. However, the tests that are run on the system to create stress
point need to be closer to real-life scenario. The following guidelines can be
used to select the tests for stress testing.

1. **Repetitive tests**   Executing repeated tests ensures that at all times
   the code works as expected. There are some operations that are
   repeatedly executed by the customer. A right mix of these operations
   and transactions need to be considered for stress testing.

2. **Concurrency**   Concurrent tests ensure that the code is exercised in
   multiple paths and simultaneously. The operations that are used by
   multiple users are selected and performed concurrently for stress
   testing.

3. **Magnitude**   This refers to the amount of load to be applied to
   the product to stress the system. It can be a single operation being
   executed for a large volume of users or a mix of operations distributed
   over different users. The operations that generate the amount of load
   needed are planned and executed for stress testing.

4. **Random variation**   As explained earlier, stress testing depends
   on increasing/decreasing variable load. Tests that stress the system
   with random inputs (in terms of number of users, size of data),
   at random instances and random magnitude are selected and
   executed as part of stress testing.

Defects that emerge from stress testing are usually not found from any other testing. Defects like memory leaks are easy to detect but difficult to analyze due to varying load and different types/mix of tests executed. Hence, stress tests are normally performed after reliability testing. To detect stress-related errors, tests need to be repeated many times so that resource usage is maximized and significant errors can be noticed. This testing helps in finding out concurrency and synchronization issues like deadlocks, thread leaks, and other synchronization problems.

6.5.7　Interoperability Testing

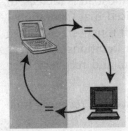

Interoperability testing is done to ensure the two or more products can exchange information, use information, and work properly together.

Systems can be interoperable unidirectional (the exchange of information is one way) or bi-directional (exchange of information in both ways). For example, the text available in a text editor can be exported into a Microsoft Word application using the "Insert->File" option. But a picture available in Microsoft Word cannot be exported into text editor. This represents one-way interoperability. The two-way interoperability is represented by exchange of information between email management (Microsoft Outlook) and Microsoft Word, where information can be cut and pasted on both directions.

The terms "interoperability" and "integration" are used interchangeably but this is incorrect. Integration is a *method* and interoperability is the *end result*. Integration pertains to only one product and defines interfaces for two or more components. Unless two or more products are designed for exchanging information, interoperability cannot be achieved. As explained in the chapter on integration testing, there is only a thin line of difference between various types of testing. It is reproduced in Table 6.4 with more explanations and specific context.

Table 6.4　Where different types of testing belong.

Description of testing	Belongs to
Testing interfaces between product components	Integration testing
Testing information exchange between two or more products	Interoperability testing
Testing the product with different infrastructure pieces such as OS, Database, Network	Compatibility testing
Testing whether the objects/binaries created with old version of the product work with current version	Backward compatibility testing
Testing whether the product interfaces work with future releases of infrastructure pieces	Forward compatibility testing
Testing whether the API interfaces of the product work with custom-developed components	API/integration testing

Interoperability attains more importance in the context of Internet, which is characterized by a seamless co-existence and inter-operation of multiple computers and multiple pieces of software. Hence, it is essential for more and more products to be interoperable so that they can communicate with almost all the operating systems, browsers, development tools, compilers, applications, and so on. Products need to prove that they are interoperable to whatever degree possible so that they can be integrated with other systems.

There are no real standard methodologies developed for interoperability testing. There are different variants of interoperable testing one system with another, one to many, and multi-dimensional interoperability testing. Following technical standards like SOAP (Simple object access protocol), eXtensible Markup Language (XML) and some more from W3C (World Wide Web Consortium) typically aid in the development of products using common standards and methods. But standards conformance is not enough for interoperability testing, as standards alone do not ensure consistent information exchange and work flow. Some popular products may not have implemented all the standards. But the product under test needs to interoperate with those popular products due to pressing business need.

The following are some guidelines that help in improving inter-operability.

1. **Consistency of information flow across systems**   When an input is provided to the product, it should be understood consistently by all systems. This would enable a smooth, correct response to be sent back to the user. For example, when data structures are used to pass information across systems, the structure and interpretation of these data structures should be consistent across the system.

2. **Changes to data representation as per the system requirements** When two different systems are integrated to provide a response to the user, data sent from the first system in a particular format must be modified or adjusted to suit the next system's requirement. This would help the request to be understood by the current system. Only then can an appropriate response be sent to the user.

    For example, when a *little end-ian* machine passes data to a *big end-ian* machine, the byte ordering would have to be changed.

3. **Correlated interchange of messages and receiving appropriate responses**   When one system sends an input in the form of a message, the next system is in the waiting mode or listening mode to receive the input. When multiple machines are involved in information exchange, there could be clashes, wrong response, deadlocks, or delays in communication. These aspects should be considered in architecting/designing the product, rather than leave it to be found as a surprise during the later phases.

4. **Communication and messages**   When a message is passed on from a system A to system B, if any and the message is lost or gets

garbled the product should be tested to check how it responds to such erroneous messages. The product must not crash or hang. It should give useful error messages to the user requesting him to wait for sometime until it recovers the connection. As multiple products are involved, a generic error message such as "Error from remote machine" will be misleading and not value adding. The user need not know where the message is coming from but needs to understand the cause of the message and the necessary corrective action.

5. **Meeting quality factors**   When two or more products are put together, there is an additional requirement of information exchange between them. This requirement should not take away the quality of the products that would have been already met individually by the products. Interoperability testing needs to verify this perspective.

The responsibility for interoperability lies more on the architecture, design, and standards of various products involved in the domain. Hence, testing for interoperability yields better results only if the requirements are met by development activities such as architecture, design, and coding. Interoperability testing should be restricted to qualify the information exchange rather than finding defects and fixing them one after another.

Interoperability among products is a collective responsibility and the effort of many product organizations. All product organizations are expected to work together to meet the purpose of interoperability. There are standards organizations that focus on interoperability standards which help the product organizations to minimize the effort involved in collaborations. They also assist in defining, implementing, and certifying the standards implementation for interoperability.

6.6   ACCEPTANCE TESTING

Acceptance testing is a phase after system testing that is normally done by the customers or representatives of the customer. The customer defines a set of test cases that will be executed to qualify and accept the product. These test cases are executed by the customers themselves to quickly judge the quality of the product before deciding to buy the product. Acceptance test cases are normally small in number and are not written with the intention of finding defects. More detailed testing (which is intended to uncover defects) is expected to have been completed in the component, integration, and system testing phases, prior to product delivery to the customer. Sometimes, acceptance test cases are developed jointly by the customers and product organization. In this case, the product organization will have complete understanding of what will be tested by the customer for acceptance testing. In such cases, the product organization tests those test cases in advance as part of the system test cycle itself to avoid any later surprises when those test cases are executed by the customer.

In cases where the acceptance tests are performed by the product organization alone, acceptance tests are executed to verify if the product meets the acceptance criteria defined during the requirements definition phase of the project. Acceptance test cases are black box type of test cases. They are directed at verifying one or more acceptance criteria.

Acceptance tests are written to execute near real-life scenarios. Apart from verifying the functional requirements, acceptance tests are run to verify the non-functional aspects of the system also.

Acceptance test cases failing in a customer site may cause the product to be rejected and may mean financial loss or may mean rework of product involving effort and time.

6.6.1 Acceptance Criteria

6.6.1.1 Acceptance criteria—Product acceptance During the requirements phase, each requirement is associated with acceptance criteria. It is possible that one or more requirements may be mapped to form acceptance criteria (for example, all high priority requirements should pass 100%). Whenever there are changes to requirements, the acceptance criteria are accordingly modified and maintained.

Acceptance testing is not meant for executing test cases that have not been executed before. Hence, the existing test cases are looked at and certain categories of test cases can be grouped to form acceptance criteria (for example, all performance test cases should pass meeting the response time requirements).

Testing for adherence to any specific legal or contractual terms is included in the acceptance criteria. Testing for compliance to specific laws like Sarbanes–Oxley can be part of the acceptance criteria.

6.6.1.2 Acceptance criteria—Procedure acceptance Acceptance criteria can be defined based on the procedures followed for delivery. An example of procedure acceptance could be documentation and release media. Some examples of acceptance criteria of this nature are as follows.

1. User, administration and troubleshooting documentation should be part of the release.

2. Along with binary code, the source code of the product with build scripts to be delivered in a CD.

3. A minimum of 20 employees are trained on the product usage prior to deployment.

These procedural acceptance criteria are verified/tested as part of acceptance testing.

6.6.1.3 Acceptance criteria–Service level agreements Service level agreements (SLA) can become part of acceptance criteria. Service level agreements are generally part of a contract signed by the customer and product organization. The important contract items are taken and verified as part of acceptance testing. For example, time limits to resolve those defects can be mentioned part of SLA such as

- ✠ All major defects that come up during first three months of deployment need to be fixed free of cost;
- ✠ Downtime of the implemented system should be less than 0.1%;
- ✠ All major defects are to be fixed within 48 hours of reporting.

With some criteria as above (except for downtime), it may look as though there is nothing to be tested or verified. But the idea of acceptance testing here is to ensure that the resources are available for meeting those SLAs.

6.6.2　Selecting Test Cases for Acceptance Testing

As mentioned earlier, the test cases for acceptance testing are selected from the existing set of test cases from different phases of testing. This section gives some guideline on what test cases can be included for acceptance testing.

1. **End-to-end functionality verification**　Test cases that include the end-to-end functionality of the product are taken up for acceptance testing. This ensures that all the business transactions are tested as a whole and those transactions are completed successfully. Real-life test scenarios are tested when the product is tested end-to-end.

2. **Domain tests**　Since acceptance tests focus on business scenarios, the product domain tests are included. Test cases that reflect business domain knowledge are included.

3. **User scenario tests**　Acceptance tests reflect the real-life user scenario verification. As a result, test cases that portray them are included.

4. **Basic sanity tests**　Tests that verify the basic existing behavior of the product are included. These tests ensure that the system performs the basic operations that it was intended to do. Such tests may gain more attention when a product undergoes changes or modifications. It is necessary to verify that the existing behavior is retained without any breaks.

5. **New functionality**　When the product undergoes modifications or changes, the acceptance test cases focus on verifying the new features.

6. **A few non-functional tests**　Some non-functional tests are included and executed as part of acceptance testing to double-check that the non-functional aspects of the product meet the expectations.

7. **Tests pertaining to legal obligations and service level agreements** Tests that are written to check if the product complies with certain legal obligations and SLAs are included in the acceptance test criteria.

8. **Acceptance test data** Test cases that make use of customer real-life data are included for acceptance testing.

6.6.3 Executing Acceptance Tests

> Acceptance testing is done by the customer or by the representative of the customer to check whether the product is ready for use in the real-life environment.

As explained before, sometimes the customers themselves do the acceptance tests. In such cases, the job of the product organization is to assist the customers in acceptance testing and resolve the issues that come out of it. If the acceptance testing is done by the product organization, forming the acceptance test team becomes an important activity.

An acceptance test team usually comprises members who are involved in the day-to-day activities of the product usage or are familiar with such scenarios. The product management, support, and consulting team, who have good knowledge of the customers, contribute to the acceptance testing definition and execution. They may not be familiar with the testing process or the technical aspect of the software. But they know whether the product does what it is intended to do. An acceptance test team may be formed with 90% of them possessing the required business process knowledge of the product and 10% being representatives of the technical testing team. The number of test team members needed to perform acceptance testing is very less, as the scope and effort involved in acceptance testing is not much when compared to other phases of testing.

As mentioned earlier, acceptance test team members may or may not be aware of testing or the process. Hence, before acceptance testing, appropriate training on the product and the process needs to be provided to the team. This training can be given to customers and other support functions irrespective of who does the acceptance tests, as the effort involved is the same. The acceptance test team may get the help of team members who developed/tested the software to obtain the required product knowledge. There could also be in-house training material that could serve the purpose.

The role of the testing team members during and prior to acceptance test is crucial since they may constantly interact with the acceptance team members. Test team members help the acceptance members to get the required test data, select and identify test cases, and analyze the acceptance test results. During test execution, the acceptance test team reports its progress regularly. The defect reports are generated on a periodic basis.

Defects reported during acceptance tests could be of different priorities. Test teams help acceptance test team report defects. Showstopper and high-priority defects are necessarily fixed before software is released. In case major defects are identified during acceptance testing, then there is a risk of missing the release date. When the defect fixes point to scope or requirement changes, then it may either result in the extension of the release date to include the feature in the current release or get postponed to subsequent releases. All resolution of those defects (and unresolved defects) are discussed with the acceptance test team and their approval is obtained for concluding the completion of acceptance testing.

6.7   SUMMARY OF TESTING PHASES

The purpose of this section is to summarize all the phases of testing and testing types we have seen so far in different chapters.

6.7.1   Multiphase Testing Model

Various phases of testing have been discussed in this chapter and previous chapters. When these phases of testing are performed by different test teams, the effectiveness of the model increases. However the big question in front of this model is in knowing when to start and finish each of the testing phases. This section addresses some guidelines that can be used to start/complete each of the testing phases. The transition to each of the testing phase is determined by a set of entry and exit criteria. The objective of the entry and exit criteria is to allow parallelism in testing and, at the same time, give importance to the quality of the product to decide the transitions. Having very mild entry criteria or very strict entry criteria have their own disadvantages. When the criteria are too mild, all the testing phases start at the same time representing one extreme where the same problem is reported by multiple teams, increasing the duplication of defects and making multiple teams wait for bug fixes. This results in releasing a bad quality product and lack of ownership on issues. It also creates a repetition of test cases at various phases when a new build arrives. It may prove counter-productive to the next phase of testing in case the quality requirements of that phase are not met. Having too strict entry criteria solves this problem but a lack of parallelism in this case creates a delay in the release of the product. These two extreme situations are depicted in the Figure 6.9. The coloured figure is available on page 464.

The right approach is to allow product quality to decide when to start a phase and entry criteria should facilitate both the quality requirements for a particular phase and utilize the earliest opportunity for starting a particular phase. The team performing the earlier phase has the ownership to meet the entry criteria of the following phase. This is depicted in Figure 6.10. The coloured figure is available on page 464.

Some sample entry and exit criteria are given in tables 6.5, 6.6, and 6.7. Please note that there are no entry and exit criteria for unit testing as it starts soon after the code is ready to compile and the entry criteria for component testing can serve as exit criteria for unit testing. However, unit test regression continues till the product is released. The criteria given below enables the product quality to decide on starting/completing test phases at the same time and creates many avenues for allowing parallelism among test phases.

Figure 6.9

Relationship of entry
criteria to time lines.

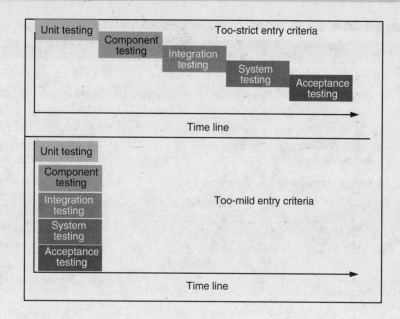

Figure 6.10

Entry criteria to balance
parallelism with quality.

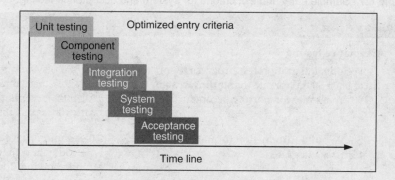

Table 6.5 Sample entry and exit criteria for component testing.

Entry criteria	Exit criteria
Component testing	
Periodic unit test progress report showing 70% completion rate	No extreme and critical outstanding defects in features
Stable build (installable) with basic features working	All 100% component test cases executed with at least 98% pass ratio
Component test cases ready for execution	Component test progress report (periodic) and defect trend sorted based on features and analyzed.
	Component level performance and load testing report and analysis of the same.

Table 6.6 Sample entry and exit criteria for integration testing.

Entry criteria	Exit criteria
Integration testing	
Periodic component test progress report (with at least 50% completion ratio) with at least 70% pass rate	No extreme and critical defects outstanding to be fixed
Stable build (installable/upgradeable) with all features integrated	All 100% integration test cases executed with at least 98% pass ratio
Defect arrival showing downward trend	Integration test progress report showing good progress and defects showing consistent downward trend
	Performance, load test report for all critical features within acceptable range
	Product in release format (including documents, media, and so on)

Table 6.7 Sample entry and exit criteria for system and acceptance testing.

Entry criteria	Exit criteria
Acceptance testing	
Periodic integration test progress report with at least 50% pass rate for starting system testing, 90% pass rate for starting acceptance testing	All 100% system test cases executed with at least 98% pass ratio All 100% acceptance test cases executed with 100% pass rate
Stable build (production format) with all features integrated	Test summary report all phases consolidated (periodic) and they are analyzed and defect trend showing downward trend for last four weeks
Defect arrival trend showing downward movement	Metrics (quality and progress metrics) showing product readiness for release
No extreme and critical defects outstanding	Performance, load test report for all critical features, system

6.7.2 Working Across Multiple Releases

As explained earlier, separate test teams for each phase of testing increases effectiveness. It also creates an opportunity for a test team to work on multiple releases at the same time. This way the test teams can be utilized completely. For example, when exit criteria is met for component test team, they can get on to next release of component testing while the integration and system test teams are focusing the on current release. This allows

Figure 6.11

Exploiting parallelism across test phases to work on multiple releases simultaneously.

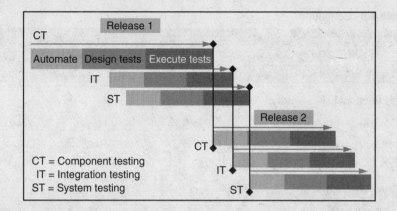

a part of the test team to work on the next release while the testing for current release is in progress. This is one way to reduce the overall elapsed time for releases, exploiting the overlap and parallelism among the test phases. Figure 6.11 depicts this concept. This figure takes into account only a few major activities of a testing team such as automation, test case creation, and test execution to explain the concept. The coloured figure is available on page 465.

6.7.3 Who Does What and When

Table 6.8 gives an overview of when what tests are executed.

Table 6.8 The when and what of tests.

Type of testing	Unit testing	Component testing	Integration testing	System and acceptance testing
Static analysis/memory leak/code complexity	☑	✓		
Internationalization	☑	✓		
Compatibility (Forward/backward)		☑		
Localization testing				☑
Interoperability			✓	☑
API/interface testing			☑	
Performance testing				☑
Load testing				☑
Reliability				☑

Table 6.8 Continued.

Type of testing	Unit testing	Component testing	Integration testing	System and acceptance testing
Functionality/usability	✓	☑	✓	✓
White box testing	☑	✓		
Black box testing	✓	☑	✓	✓
Daily build and smoke testing	☑			
Buddy testing	☑			
Defect bash			☑	
Scenario testing			☑	✓
Acceptance testing				☑
Regression testing		☑		☑
Exploratory testing	☑	☑		☑
Pair testing	☑	☑		
Ad hoc testing	☑	☑	☑	☑
Scalability testing				☑

☑ – Full

✓ – Partial

REFERENCES

There are several terminologies and definitions that associated with system and acceptance testing. The glossary of terms found in [IEEE-1994] is a step closer to what is being discussed as a topic and definition in this chapter. This chapter tries to take a practical approach with several types of testing. The methodology for reliability testing in [UMES-2002] is used in this chapter with more examples and details.

PROBLEMS AND EXERCISES

1. Which category of system testing applies to each of the following cases:

   a. A customer has given his transaction load and throughput requirements. You are to recommend an appropriate hardware and software configuration for the customer.

b. Your product is a web-based product with a highly seasonal usage. You want to understand the product behavior and performance even at loads much more than the maximum expected usage so as to prepare for future expansion.

c. Your product is expected to run continuously and never stop functioning.

d. You have bought a special reporting software that runs on top of an Oracle database. Recently Oracle came up with a new version and the reporting software should be tested to work with this new version.

e. ou are to measure and publish performance characteristics of your product:

2. Classify the following as functional and non-functional testing:

a. Testing of documentation of the product to match the product behavior

b. Verification that a payroll system satisfies local tax laws

c. Testing of the screens for user friendliness

d. Performance qualification of a product

e. Ensuring a certain percentage of code coverage for a product

3. Which of the following are "product level tests cases" as explained in the text? If not, identify which level it belongs

a. This test is to ensure that the customizations made on top of an ERP package which in turn runs on a particular version of a database are working correctly.

b. In a payroll system, tests are done only for the tax calculation module.

c. In a database package, there are options to specify different sort algorithms. The correct behavior of each of these algorithms has to be verified.

4. Consider a revolutionary, path-breaking product that comes about which opens up completely new methods of usage that the users are not used to. How would you characterize "acceptance testing" in such a case? What are some of the challenges do you foresee in such acceptance testing? How would you overcome such challenges?

5. You are advising a customer, "based on the tests conducted, the memory should be doubled and the network bandwidth has to be quadrupled." What kind of objective data would you give to substantiate your recommendation? If the customer asks you to justify your answer in a tabular or graphical form, stating all your assumptions, how would you go about?

6. Your initial tests indicated that a product went through a spike in CPU usage, but in general otherwise, the CPU usage was below

average. What tests would you do to further narrow down and identify the cause for the spike?

7. Which of the following test scenarios would you subject to stress tests:

   a. Users making ad hoc queries to a database

   b. Students logging on to find results of examinations on the net on the result day

   c. Users in a customer service center taking orders for various customers, entering credit notes, handling complaints, etc.

8. In the Internet space, we talk of "e services," wherein, there are different "services" registered on the net (like travel service, hotel booking services, etc.). Consider the testing challenges of putting together a "bigger" service composed of these atomic services. For example, consider putting together a comprehensive travel booking that uses airline booking from (the existing) travel service, and from the (existing) hotel booking service. What kind of testing challenges should you expect when you put together and use such composite services? Consider all phases/types of testing, given that a user who buys your comprehensive service may hold you responsible for the end-to-end functionality.

9. Consider a piece of embedded software that is part of a consumer gadget like a TV. Which of the types of system testing discussed in this chapter would you perform and at what times? What extra challenges would you foresee vis à vis say testing a conventional financial application or a system software product like a database or operating system?

Performance Testing

C H A P T E R 7

In this chapter—

7.1   INTRODUCTION

In this Internet era, when more and more of business is transacted online, there is a big and understandable expectation that all applications run as fast as possible. When applications run fast, a system can fulfill the business requirements quickly and put it in a position to expand its business and handle future needs as well. A system or a product that is not able to service business transactions due to its slow performance is a big loss for the product organization, its customers, and its customers' customers. For example, it is estimated that 40% of online marketing/ shopping for consumer goods in the USA happens over a period of November—December. Slowness or lack of response during this period may result in losses to the tune of several million dollars to organizations. In yet another example, when examination results are published on the Internet, several hundreds of thousands of people access the educational websites within a very short period. If a given website takes a long time to complete the request or takes more time to display the pages, it may mean a lost business opportunity, as the people may go to other websites to find the results. Hence, performance is a basic requirement for any product and is fast becoming a subject of great interest in the testing community.

7.2   FACTORS GOVERNING PERFORMANCE TESTING

There are many factors that govern performance testing. It is critical to understand the definition and purpose of these factors prior to under-standing the methodology for performance testing and for analyzing the results.

As explained in the previous section, a product is expected, to handle multiple transactions in a given period. The capability of the system or the product in handling multiple transactions is determined by a factor called *throughput*. Throughput represents the number of requests/business transactions processed by the product in a specified time duration. It is important to understand that the throughput (that is, the number of transactions serviced by the product per unit time) varies according to the load the product is subjected to. Figure 7.1 is an example of the throughput of a system at various load conditions. The load to the product can be increased by increasing the number of users or by increasing the number of concurrent operations of the product.

In the above example, it can be noticed that initially the throughput keeps increasing as the user load increases. This is the ideal situation for any product and indicates that the product is capable of delivering more when there are more users trying to use the product. In the second part of the graph, beyond certain user load conditions (after the bend), it can be noticed that the throughput comes down. This is the period when the users of the

Figure 7.1

Throughput of a system at various load conditions.

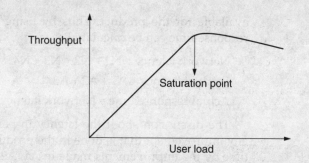

Figure 7.2

Example of latencies at various levels—network and applications.

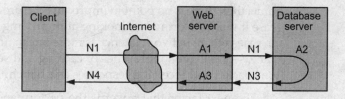

system notice a lack of satisfactory response and the system starts taking more time to complete business transactions. The "optimum throughput" is represented by the saturation point and is the one that represents the maximum throughput for the product.

Throughput represents how many business transactions can be serviced in a given duration for a given load. It is equally important to find out how much time each of the transactions took to complete. As was explained in the first section, customers might go to a different website or application if a particular request takes more time on this website or application. Hence measuring "response time" becomes an important activity of performance testing. *Response time* can be defined as the delay between the point of request and the first response from the product. In a typical client-server environment, throughput represents the number of transactions that can be handled by the server and response time represents the delay between the request and response.

In reality, not all the delay that happens between the request and the response is caused by the product. In the networking scenario, the network or other products which are sharing the network resources, can cause the delays. Hence, it is important to know what delay the product causes and what delay the environment causes. This brings up yet another factor for performance—*latency*. Latency is a delay caused by the application, operating system, and by the environment that are calculated separately. To explain latency, let us take an example of a web application providing a service by talking to a web server and a database server connected in the network. See Figure 7.2.

In the above example, latency can be calculated for the product that is running on the client and for the network that represents the infrastructure available for the product. Thus by using the above picture, latency and response time can be calculated as

Network latency = N1 + N2 + N3 + N4

Product latency = A1 + A2 + A3

Actual response time = Network latency + Product latency

The discussion about the latency in performance is very important, as any improvement that is done in the product can only reduce the response time by the improvements made in A1, A2, and A3. If the network latency is more relative to the product latency and if that is affecting the response time, then there is no point in improving the product performance. In such a case it will be worthwhile looking at improving the network infrastructure. In cases where network latency is more or can not be improved, the product can use intelligent approaches of caching and sending multiple requests in one packet and receiving responses as a bunch.

The next factor that governs the performance testing is *tuning*. Tuning is a procedure by which the product performance is enhanced by setting different values to the parameters (variables) of the product, operating system, and other components. Tuning improves the product performance without having to touch the source code of the product. Each product may have certain parameters or variables that can be set a run time to gain optimum performance. The default values that are assumed by such product parameters may not always give optimum performance for a particular deployment. This necessitates the need for changing the values of parameters or variables to suit the deployment or for a particular configuration. Doing performance testing, tuning of parameters is an important activity that needs to be done before collecting actual numbers.

Yet another factor that needs to be considered for performance testing is performance of competitive products. A very well-improved performance of a product makes no business sense if that performance does not match up to the competitive products. Hence it is very important to compare the throughput and response time of the product with those of the competitive products. This type of performance testing wherein competitive products are compared is called *benchmarking*. No two products are the same in features, cost, and functionality. Hence, it is not easy to decide which parameters must be compared across two products. A careful analysis is needed to chalk out the list of transactions to be compared across products, so that an apples-to-apples comparison becomes possible. This produces meaningful analysis to improve the performance of the product with respect to competition.

One of the most important factors that affect performance testing is the availability of resources. A right kind of configuration (both hardware and software) is needed to derive the best results from performance testing and for deployments. The exercise to find out what resources and configurations are needed is called *capacity planning*. The purpose of a capacity planning exercise is to help customers plan for the set of hardware and software resources prior to installation or upgrade of the product. This exercise also sets the expectations on what performance the customer will get with the available hardware and software resources.

> The testing performed to evaluate the response time, throughput, and utilization of the system, to execute its required functions in comparison with different versions of the same product(s) or a different competitive product(s) is called performance testing.

To summarize, performance testing is done to ensure that a product

✠ processes the required number of transactions in any given interval (throughput);

✠ is available and running under different load conditions (availability);

✠ responds fast enough for different load conditions (response time);

✠ delivers worthwhile return on investment for the resources—hardware and software—and deciding what kind of resources are needed for the product for different load conditions (capacity planning); and

✠ is comparable to and better than that of the competitors for different parameters (competitive analysis and benchmarking).

7.3 METHODOLOGY FOR PERFORMANCE TESTING

Performance testing is complex and expensive due to large resource requirements and the time it takes. Hence, it requires careful planning and a robust methodology. Performance testing is ambiguous because of the different people who are performing the various roles having different expectations. Additionally, a good number of defects that get uncovered during performance testing may require design and architecture change. Finally, a fix for a performance defect may even cause some functionality to stop working, thereby requiring more effort during regression. For these reasons, this section focuses on various steps and guidelines for doing a performance testing in a methodical way. A methodology for performance testing involves the following steps.

1. Collecting requirements
2. Writing test cases
3. Automating performance test cases
4. Executing performance test cases
5. Analyzing performance test results
6. Performance tuning
7. Performance benchmarking
8. Recommending right configuration for the customers (Capacity Planning)

7.3.1   Collecting Requirements

Collecting requirements is the first step in planning the performance testing. Typically, functionality testing has a definite set of inputs and outputs, with a clear definition of expected results. In contrast, performance testing generally needs elaborate documentation and environment setup and the expected results may not well known in advance. As a result of these differences, collecting requirements for performance testing presents some unique challenges.

Firstly, a performance testing requirement should be testable—not all features/functionality can be performance tested. For example, a feature involving a manual intervention cannot be performance tested as the results depend on how fast a user responds with inputs to the product. A performance test can only be carried out for a completely automated product.

Secondly, a performance-testing requirement needs to clearly state what factors needs to be measured and improved. As discussed in the previous section, performance has several factors such as response time, latency, throughput, resource utilization, and others. Hence, a requirement needs to associate the factors or combination of factors that have to be measured and improved as part of performance testing.

Lastly, performance testing requirement needs to be associated with the actual number or percentage of improvement that is desired. For example, if a business transaction, say ATM money withdrawal, should be completed within two minutes, the requirement needs to document the actual response time expected. Only then can the pass/fail status of a performance testing be concluded. Not having the expected numbers for the appropriate parameter (response time, throughput, and so on) renders performance testing completely futile, as there is no quantitative measure of success and nothing can be concluded or improved in the end.

Given the above challenges, a key question is how requirements for performance testing can be derived. There are several sources for deriving performance requirements. Some of them are as follows.

1. **Performance compared to the previous release of the same product** A performance requirement can be something like "an ATM withdrawal transaction will be faster than the previous release by 10%."

2. **Performance compared to the competitive product(s)** A performance requirement can be documented as "ATM withdrawal will be as fast as or faster than competitive product XYZ."

3. **Performance compared to absolute numbers derived from actual need** A requirement can be documented such as "ATM machine should be capable of handling 1000 transactions per day with each transaction not taking more than a minute."

4. **Performance numbers derived from architecture and design**
The architect or a designer of a product would normally be in a much better position than anyone else to say what is the performance expected out of the product. The architecture and design goals are based on the performance expected for a particular load. Hence, there is an expectation that the source code is written in such a way that those numbers are met.

There are two types of requirements performance testing focuses on— *generic requirements* and *specific requirements*. Generic requirements are those that are common across all products in the product domain area. All products in that area are expected to meet those performance expectations. For some of the products they are mandated by SLAs (Service Level Agreements) and standards. The time taken to load a page, initial response when a mouse is clicked, and time taken to navigate between screens are some examples of generic requirements. Specific requirements are those that depend on implementation for a particular product and differ from one product to another in a given domain. An example of specific performance requirement is the time taken to withdraw cash in an ATM. During performance testing both generic and specific requirements need to be tested.

As discussed earlier, the requirements for performance testing also include the load pattern and resource availability and what is expected from the product under different load conditions. Hence, while documenting the expected response time, throughput, or any other performance factor, it is equally important to map different load conditions as illustrated in the example in Table 7.1.

Beyond a particular load, any product shows some degradation in performance. While it is easy to understand this phenomenon, it will be very difficult to do a performance test without knowing the degree of degradation with respect to load conditions. Massive degradation in performance beyond a degree is not acceptable by users. For example, ATM cash withdrawal taking one hour to complete a transaction (regardless of reason or load) is not acceptable. In such a case, the customer who requested the transaction would have waited and left the ATM and the money may

Table 7.1 Example of performance test requirements.

Transaction	Expected response time	Loading pattern/throughput	Machine configuration
ATM cash withdrawal	2 sec	Upto 10,000 simultaneous access by users	Pentium IV/512MB RAM/broadband network
ATM cash withdrawal	40 sec	Upto 10,000 simultaneous access by users	Pentium IV/512 MB RAM/dial-up network
ATM cash withdrawal	4 sec	More than 10,000 but below 20,000 simultaneous access by users	Pentium IV/512MB RAM/broadband network

get disbursed to the person who reaches the ATM next! The performance values that are in acceptable limits when the load increases are denoted by a term called *"graceful performance degradation."* A performance test conducted for a product needs to validate this graceful degradation also as one of the requirement.

7.3.2 Writing Test Cases

The next step involved in performance testing is writing test cases. As was briefly discussed earlier, a test case for performance testing should have the following details defined.

1. List of operations or business transactions to be tested
2. Steps for executing those operations/transactions
3. List of product, OS parameters that impact the performance testing, and their values
4. Loading pattern
5. Resource and their configuration (network, hardware, software configurations)
6. The expected results (that is, expected response time, throughput, latency)
7. The product versions/competitive products to be compared with and related information such as their corresponding fields (steps 2–6 in the above list)

Performance test cases are repetitive in nature. These test cases are normally executed repeatedly for different values of parameters, different load conditions, different configurations, and so on. Hence, the details of what tests are to be repeated for what values should be part of the test case documentation.

While testing the product for different load patterns, it is important to increase the load or scalability gradually to avoid any unnecessary effort in case of failures. For example, if an ATM withdrawal fails for ten concurrent operations, there is no point in trying it for 10,000 operations. The effort involved in testing for 10 concurrent operations may be several times lesser than that of testing for 10,000 operations. Hence, a methodical approach is to gradually improve the concurrent operations by say 10, 100, 1000, 10,000, and so on rather than trying to attempt 10,000 concurrent operations in the first iteration itself. The test case documentation should clearly reflect this approach.

Performance testing is a laborious process involving time and effort. Not all operations/business transactions can be included in performance testing. Hence, all test cases that are part of performance testing have to be assigned different priorities so that high priority test cases can be completed before others. The priority can be absolute as indicated by the customers or relative within the test cases considered for performance testing. Absolute priority is indicated by the requirements and the test team normally assigns relative priority. While executing the test cases, the absolute and relative priorities are looked at and the test cases are sequenced accordingly.

7.3.3 Automating Performance Test Cases

Automation is an important step in the methodology for performance testing. Performance testing naturally lends itself to automation due to the following characteristics.

1. Performance testing is repetitive.

2. Performance test cases cannot be effective without automation and in most cases it is, in fact, almost impossible to do performance testing without automation.

3. The results of performance testing need to be accurate, and manually calculating the response time, throughput, and so on can introduce inaccuracy.

4. Performance testing takes into account several factors. There are far too many permutations and combination of those factors and it will be difficult to remember all these and use them if the tests are done manually.

5. The analysis of performance results and failures needs to take into account related information such as resource utilization, log files, trace files, and so on that are collected at regular intervals. It is impossible to do this testing and perform the book-keeping of all related information and analysis manually.

As we will see in the chapter on test automation (Chapter 16), there should not be any hard coded data in automated scripts for performance testing. Such hard coding may impact the repeatability nature of test cases and may require change in automation script, taking more time and effort.

End-to-end automation is required for performance testing. Not only the steps of the test cases, but also the setup required for the test cases, setting different values to parameters, creating different load conditions, setting up and executing the steps for operations/transactions of competitive product, and so on have to be included as part of the automation script. While automating performance test cases, it is important to use standard tools and practices. Since some of the performance test cases involve comparison with the competitive product, the results need to be consistent, repeatable, and accurate due to the high degree of sensitivity involved.

7.3.4 Executing Performance Test Cases

Performance testing generally involves less effort for execution but more effort for planning, data collection, and analysis. As discussed earlier, 100% end-to-end automation is desirable for performance testing and if that is achieved, executing a performance test case may just mean invoking certain automated scripts. However, the most effort-consuming aspect in execution is usually data collection. Data corresponding to the following points needs to be collected while executing performance tests.

1. Start and end time of test case execution
2. Log and trace/audit files of the product and operating system (for future debugging and repeatability purposes)
3. Utilization of resources (CPU, memory, disk, network utilization, and so on) on a periodic basis
4. Configuration of all environmental factors (hardware, software, and other components)
5. The response time, throughput, latency, and so on as specified in the test case documentation at regular intervals

Another aspect involved in performance test execution is *scenario testing*. A set of transactions/operations that are usually performed by the user forms the scenario for performance testing. This particular testing is done to ensure whether the mix of operations/transactions concurrently by different users/machines meets the performance criteria. In real life, not all users perform the same operation all the time and hence these tests are performed. For example, not all users withdraw cash from an ATM; some of them query for account balance; some make deposits, and so on. In this case this scenario (with different users executing different transactions) is executed with the existing automation that is available and related data is collected using the existing tools.

What performance a product delivers for different configurations of hardware and network setup, is another aspect that needs to be included during execution. This requirement mandates the need for repeating the tests for different configurations. This is referred to as *configuration performance tests*. This test ensures that the performance of the product is compatible with different hardware, utilizing the special nature of those configurations and yielding the best performance possible. For a given configuration, the product has to give the best possible performance, and if the configuration is better, it has to get even better. Table 7.2 illustrates an example of this type

Table 7.2 Sample configuration performance test.

Transaction	Number of users	Test environment
Querying ATM account balance	20	RAM 512 MB, P4 Dual Processor; Operating system—Windows NT Server
ATM cash withdrawal	20	RAM 128 MB, P4 Single Processor Operating system—Windows 98
ATM user profile query	40	RAM 256 MB, P3 Quad Processor Operating system—Windows 2000

Figure 7.3

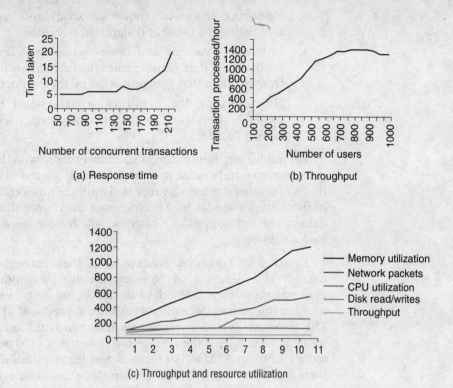

(a) Response time

(b) Throughput

(c) Throughput and resource utilization

of test. The performance test case is repeated for each row in the following table and factors such as response time and throughput are recorded and analyzed.

Once performance tests are executed and various data points are collected, the next step is to plot them. As explained earlier, performance test cases are repeated for different configurations and different values of parameters. Hence, it makes sense to group them and plot them in the form of graphs and charts. Plotting the data helps in making a quick analysis which would otherwise be difficult to do with only the raw data. Figure 7.3 above illustrates how performance data can be plotted. The coloured figure is available on page 465.

7.3.5   Analyzing the Performance Test Results

Analyzing the performance test results require multi-dimensional thinking. This is the most complex part of performance testing where product knowledge, analytical thinking, and statistical background are all absolutely essential.

Before analyzing the data, some calculations of data and organization of the data are required. The following come under this category.

1.   Calculating the mean of the performance test result data
2.   Calculating the standard deviation

3. Removing the noise (noise removal) and re-plotting and re-calculating the mean and standard deviation

4. In terms of caching and other technologies implemented in the product, the data coming from the cache need to be differentiated from the data that gets processed by the product, and presented

5. Differentiating the performance data when the resources are available completely as against when some background activities were going on.

For publishing the performance numbers, there is one basic expectation—performance numbers are to be reproducible for the customers. To ensure this, all performance tests are repeated multiple times and the average/mean of those values are taken. This increases the chance that the performance data can be reproduced at a customer site for the same configuration and load condition.

Repeatability not only depends on taking the average/mean of performance data. It also depends on how consistently the product delivers those performance numbers. Standard deviation can help here. It may indicate whether the performance numbers can be reproduced at the customer site. The standard deviation represents how much the data varies from the mean. For example, if the average response time of 100 people withdrawing money from an ATM is 100 seconds and the standard deviation is 2, then there is greater chance that this performance data is repeatable than in a case where the standard deviation is 30. Standard deviation close to zero means the product performance is highly repeatable and performance values are consistent. Higher the standard deviation, more is the variability of the product performance.

When there are a set of performance numbers that came from multiple runs of the same test, there could be situations where in a few of the iterations, some errors were committed by the scripts, software, or a human. Taking such erroneous executions into account may not be appropriate and such values need to be ignored. Moreover, when a set of values is plotted on a chart, one or two values that are out of range may cause the graph to be cluttered and prevent meaningful analysis. Such values can be ignored to produce a smooth curve/graph. The process of removing some unwanted values in a set is called *noise removal*. When some values are removed from the set, the mean and standard deviation needs to be re-calculated.

The majority of the server-client, Internet, and database applications store the data in a local high-speed buffer when a query is made. This enables them to present the data quickly when the same request is made again. This is called *caching*. The performance data need to be differentiated according to where the result is coming from—the server or the cache. The data points can be kept as two different data sets—one for cache and one coming from server. Keeping them as two different data sets enables the performance data to be extrapolated in future, based on the hit ratio expected in deployments.

For example, assume that data in a cache can produce a response time of 1000 microseconds and a server access takes 1 microsecond and 90% of the time a request is satisfied by the cache. Then the average response time is $(0.9) \times 1000 + 0.1 \times 1 = 900.1$ µs. The mean response time is thus calculated as a weighted average rather than a simple mean.

Some "time initiated activities" of the product or background activities of the operating system and network may have an effect on the performance data. An example of one such activity is garbage collection/defragmentation in memory management of the operating system or a compiler. When such activities are initiated in the background, degradation in the performance may be observed. Finding out such background events and separating those data points and making an analysis would help in presenting the right performance data.

Once the data sets are organized (after appropriate noise removal and after appropriate refinement as mentioned above), the analysis of performance data is carried out to conclude the following.

1. Whether performance of the product is consistent when tests are executed multiple times

2. What performance can be expected for what type of configuration (both hardware and software), resources

3. What parameters impact performance and how they can be used to derive better performance (Please refer to the section on performance tuning)

4. What is the effect of scenarios involving several mix of operations for the performance factors

5. What is the effect of product technologies such as caching on performance improvements (Please refer to the section on performance tuning)

6. Up to what load are the performance numbers acceptable and whether the performance of the product meets the criteria of "graceful degradation"

7. What is the optimum throughput/response time of the product for a set of factors such as load, resources, and parameters

8. What performance requirements are met and how the performance looks when compared to the previous version or the expectations set earlier or the competition

9. Sometime high-end configuration may not be available for performance testing. In that case, using the current set of performance data and the charts that are available through performance testing, the performance numbers that are to be expected from a high-end configuration should be extrapolated or predicted.

7.3.6   Performance Tuning

Analyzing performance data helps in narrowing down the list of parameters that really impact the performance results and improving product performance. Once the parameters are narrowed down to a few, the performance test cases are repeated for different values of those parameters to further analyze their effect in getting better performance. This performance-tuning exercise needs a high degree of skill in identifying the list of parameters and their contribution to performance. Understanding each parameter and its impact on the product is not sufficient for performance tuning. The combination of parameters too cause changes in performance. The relationship among various parameters and their impact too becomes very important to performance tuning.

There are two steps involved in getting the optimum mileage from performance tuning. They are

1.   Tuning the product parameters and
2.   Tuning the operating system and parameters

There are a set of parameters associated with the product where the administrators or users of the product can set different values to obtain optimum performance. Some of the common practices are providing a number of forked processes for performing parallel transactions, caching and memory size, creating background activities, deferring routine checks to a later point of time, providing better priority to a highly used operation/transaction, disabling low-priority operations, changing the sequence or clubbing a set of operations to suit the resource availability, and so on. Setting different values to these parameters enhances the product performance. The product parameters in isolation as well as in combination have an impact on product performance. Hence it is important to

1.   Repeat the performance tests for different values of each parameter that impact performance (when changing one parameter you may want to keep the values of other parameters unchanged).
2.   Sometimes when a particular parameter value is changed, it needs changes in other parameters (as some parameters may be related to each other). Repeat the performance tests for a group of parameters and their different values.
3.   Repeat the performance tests for default values of all parameters (called *factory settings* tests).
4.   Repeat the performance tests for low and high values of each parameter and combinations.

There is one important point that needs to be noted while tuning the product parameters. Performance tuning provides better results only for a particular configuration and for certain transactions. It would have achieved the performance goals, but it may have a side-effect on functionality or on some non-functional aspects. Therefore, tuning may be counter-productive to other situations or scenarios. This side-effect of tuning product parameters needs to be analyzed and such side-effects also should be included as part of the analysis of this performance-tuning exercise.

Tuning the OS parameters is another step towards getting better performance. There are various sets of parameters provided by the operating system under different categories. Those values can be changed using the appropriate tools that come along with the operating system (for example, the Registry in MS-Windows can be edited using `regedit.exe`). These parameters in the operating system are grouped under different categories to explain their impact, as given below.

1. File system related parameters (for example, number of open files permitted)

2. Disk management parameters (for example, simultaneous disk reads/writes)

3. Memory management parameters (for example, virtual memory page size and number of pages)

4. Processor management parameters (for example, enabling/disabling processors in multiprocessor environment)

5. Network parameters (for example, setting TCP/IP time out)

As explained earlier, not only each of the in parameters but also their combinations, have different effects on product performance. As before, the performance tests have to be repeated for different values of each and for a combination of OS parameters. While repeating the tests, the OS parameters need to be tuned before application/product tuning is done.

There is one important point that needs to be remembered when tuning the OS parameters for improving product performance. The machine on which the parameter is tuned, may have multiple products and applications that are running. Hence, tuning an OS parameter may give better results for the product under test, but may heavily impact the other products that are running on the same machine. Hence, OS parameters need to be tuned only when the complete impact is known to all applications running in the machine or they need to be tuned only when it is absolutely necessary, giving big performance advantages. Tuning OS parameters for small gains in performance is not the right thing to do.

The products are normally supported on more than one platform. Hence, the performance tuning procedure should consider the OS parameters and their effect on all supported platforms for the product.

The charts in Figure 7.4 are examples of what can be achieved by the performance-tuning exercise. In the charts the expected results (performance requirements), performance results without tuning (represented as normal), and tuned results (represented as high) are plotted together. These charts help in analyzing the effect of tuning with varying resource availability such as CPU and memory. These tests can also be repeated for different load conditions and plotted as yet another set of performance data points.

Figure 7.4

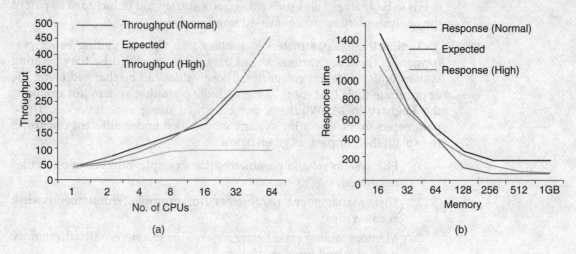

(a)

(b)

From the throughput chart, Figure 7.4 (a), you can see that the expectations on performance was met after tuning up to 32 CPU configurations and the product has issue with 64 CPU configuration. In the response time graph, Figure 7.4 (b), the expectations of before tuning and after tuning are met in both the cases, as long as the memory is 128 MB or more. Where the expectations are not met, the problems should be analyzed and resolved. The coloured figure is available on page 466.

The results of performance tuning are normally published in the form of a guide called the "*performance tuning guide*" for customers so that they can benefit from this exercise. The guide explains in detail the effect of each product and OS parameter on performance. It also gives a set of guideline values for the combination of parameters and what parameter must be tuned in which situation along with associated warnings of any wrong tuning exercise.

7.3.7 Performance Benchmarking

Performance benchmarking is about comparing the performance of product transactions with that of the competitors. No two products can have the same architecture, design, functionality, and code. The customers and types of deployments can also be different. Hence, it will be very difficult to compare two products on those aspects. End-user transactions/scenarios could be one approach for comparison. In general, an independent test team or an independent organization not related to the organizations of the products being compared does performance benchmarking. This does away with any bias in the test. The person doing the performance benchmarking needs to have the expertise in all the products being compared for the tests to be executed successfully. The steps involved in performance benchmarking are the following:

1. Identifying the transactions/scenarios and the test configuration
2. Comparing the performance of different products
3. Tuning the parameters of the products being compared fairly to deliver the best performance
4. Publishing the results of performance benchmarking

As mentioned earlier, as the first step, comparable (apples-to-apples) transactions/scenarios are selected for performance benchmarking. Normally, the configuration details are determined well in advance and hence test cases are not repeated for different configurations. Generally, the test cases for all the products being compared are executed in the same test bed. However, two to three configurations are considered for performance benchmarking just to ensure that the testing provides the breadth required to cover realistic scenarios.

Once the tests are executed, the next step is to compare the results. This is where the understanding of the products being compared becomes essential. Equal expertise level in all the products is desirable for the person doing the tests. The tunable parameters for the various products may be completely different and understanding those parameters and their impact on performance is very important in doing a fair comparison of results. This is one place where bias can come in. A well tuned product, A, may be compared with a product B with no parameter tuning, to prove that the product A performs better than B. It is important that in performance benchmarking all products should be tuned to the same degree.

From the point of view of a specific product there could be three outcomes from performance benchmarking. The first outcome can be positive, where it can be found that a set of transactions/scenarios outperform with respect to competition. The second outcome can be neutral, where a set of transactions are comparable with that of the competition. The third outcome can be negative, where a set of transaction under-perform compared to that of the competition. The last outcome may be detrimental for the success of the product, hence, the performance tuning exercise described in the previous section needs to be performed for this set of transactions using the same configuration internally by the product organization. If tuning helps in this case, it at least helps in bringing down the criticality of the failure; else it requires the performance defects to be fixed and a subset of test cases for performance benchmarking to be repeated again. Even though it was said that tuning as an exercise needs to be repeated for the third outcome, it need not be limited only to that situation. Tuning can be repeated for all situations of positive, neutral, and negative results to derive the best performance results. Repeating the performance tuning may not be always possible. If neutral agencies (as benchmarks are done) are involved, then they may just bring out the apples-to-apples comparison and may not do tuning. In such cases, the test teams will take care of repeating the tests.

The results of performance benchmarking are published. There are two types of publications that are involved. One is an internal, confidential publication to product teams, containing all the three outcomes described above and the recommended set of actions. The positive outcomes of performance benchmarking are normally published as marketing collateral, which helps as a sales tool for the product. Also benchmarks conducted by independent organizations are published as audited benchmarks.

7.3.8   Capacity Planning

If performance tests are conducted for several configurations, the huge volume of data and analysis that is available can be used to predict the configurations needed for a particular set of transactions and load pattern. This reverse process is the objective of capacity planning. Performance configuration tests are conducted for different configurations and performance data are obtained. In capacity planning, the performance requirements and performance results are taken as input requirements and the configuration needed to satisfy that set of requirements are derived.

Capacity planning necessitates a clear understanding of the resource requirements for transactions/scenarios. Some transactions of the product associated with certain load conditions could be disk intensive, some could be CPU intensive, some of them could be network intensive, and some of them could be memory intensive. Some transactions may require a combination of these resources for performing better. This understanding of what resources are needed for each transaction is a prerequisite for capacity planning.

If capacity planning has to identify the right configuration for the transactions and particular load patterns, then the next question that arises is how to decide the load pattern. The load can be the actual requirement of the customer for immediate need (short term) or the requirements for the next few months (medium term) or for the next few years (long term). Since the load pattern changes according to future requirements, it is critical to consider those requirements during capacity planning. Capacity planning corresponding to short-, medium-, and long-term requirements are called

1.   Minimum required configuration;
2.   Typical configuration; and
3.   Special configuration.

A *minimum required* configuration denotes that with anything less than this configuration, the product may not even work. Thus, configurations below the minimum required configuration are usually not supported. A *typical* configuration denotes that under that configuration the product will work fine for meeting the performance requirements of the required load pattern and can also handle a slight increase in the load pattern. A *special* configuration denotes that capacity planning was done considering all future requirements.

There are two techniques that play a major role in capacity planning. They are *load balancing* and *high availability*. Load balancing ensures that the multiple machines available are used equally to service the transactions. This ensures that by adding more machines, more load can be handled by the product. Machine clusters are used to ensure availability. In a cluster there are multiple machines with shared data so that in case one machine goes down, the transactions can be handled by another machine in the cluster. When doing capacity planning, both load balancing and availability factors are included to prescribe the desired configuration.

The majority of capacity planning exercises are only interpretations of data and extrapolation of the available information. A minor mistake in the analysis of performance results or in extrapolation may cause a deviation in expectations when the product is used in deployments. Moreover, capacity planning is based on performance test data generated in the test lab, which is only a simulated environment. In real-life deployment, there could be several other parameters that may impact product performance. As a result of these unforeseen reasons, apart from the skills mentioned earlier, experience is needed to know real-world data and usage patterns for the capacity planning exercise.

7.4 TOOLS FOR PERFORMANCE TESTING

There are two types of tools that can be used for performance testing—functional performance tools and load tools.

Functional performance tools help in recording and playing back the transactions and obtaining performance numbers. This test generally involves very few machines.

Load testing tools simulate the load condition for performance testing without having to keep that many users or machines. The load testing tools simplify the complexities involved in creating the load and without such load tools it may be impossible to perform these kinds of tests. As was mentioned earlier, this is only a simulated load and real-life experience may vary from the simulation.

We list below some popular performance tools:

✠ Functional performance tools

- WinRunner from Mercury
- QA Partner from Compuware
- Silktest from Segue

✠ Load testing tools

- Load Runner from Mercury
- QA Load from Compuware
- Silk Performer from Segue

There are many vendors who sell these performance tools. The references at the end of the book point to some of the popular tools.

Performance and load tools can only help in getting performance numbers. The utilization of resources is another important parameter that needs to be collected. "Windows Task Manager" and "top" in Linux are examples of tools that help in collecting resource utilization. Network performance monitoring tools are available with almost all operating systems today to collect network data.

7.5   PROCESS FOR PERFORMANCE TESTING

Performance testing follows the same process as any other testing type. The only difference is in getting more details and analysis. As mentioned earlier, the effort involved in performance testing is more and tests are generally repeated several times. The increased effort reflects in increased costs, as the resources needed for performance testing is quite high. A major challenge involved in performance testing is getting the right process so that the effort can be minimized. A simple process for performance testing tries to address these aspects in Figure 7.5.

Ever-changing requirements for performance is a serious threat to the product as performance can only be improved marginally by fixing it in the code. As mentioned earlier, a majority of the performance issues require rework or changes in architecture and design. Hence, it is important to collect the requirements for performance earlier in the life cycle and address them, because changes to architecture and design late in the cycle are very expensive. While collecting requirements for performance testing, it is important to decide whether they are testable, that is, to ensure that the performance requirements are quantified and validated in an objective way. If so, the quantified expectation of performance is documented. Making the requirements testable and measurable is the first activity needed for the success of performance testing.

Figure 7.5

Process for performance testing.

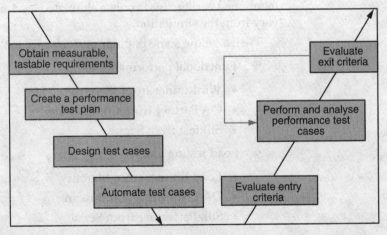

The next step in the performance testing process is to create a performance test plan. This test plan needs to have the following details.

1. **Resource requirements** All additional resources that are specifically needed for performance testing need to be planned and obtained. Normally these resources are obtained, used for performance test, and released after performance testing is over. Hence, the resources need to be included as part of the planning and tracked.

2. **Test bed (simulated and real life), test-lab setup** The test lab, with all required equipment and software configuration, has to be set up prior to execution. Performance testing requires a large number of resources and requires special configurations. Hence, setting up both the simulated and real-life environment is time consuming and any mistake in the test-bed setup may mean that the complete performance tests have be repeated. Hence, it has to be a part of the planning exercise and tracked.

3. **Responsibilities** Performance defects, as explained earlier, may cause changes to architecture, design, and code. Additionally, the teams facing the customers normally communicate requirements for performance. Multiple teams are involved in the successful execution of performance tests and all the teams and people performing different roles need to work together if the objectives of performance have to be met. Hence, a matrix containing responsibilities must be worked out as part of the performance test plan and communicated across all teams.

4. **Setting up product traces, audits, and traces (external and internal)** Performance test results need to be associated with traces and audit trails to analyze the results and defects. What traces and audit trials have to be collected is planned in advance and is an associated part of the test plan. This is to be planned in advance, because enabling too many traces and audit traces may start impacting the performance results.

5. **Entry and exit criteria** Performance tests require a stable product due to its complexity and the accuracy that is needed. Changes to the product affect performance numbers and may mean that the tests have to be repeated. It will be counter-productive to execute performance test cases before the product is stable or when changes are being made. Hence, the performance test execution normally starts after the product meets a set of criteria. The set of criteria to be met are defined well in advance and documented as part of the performance test plan. Similarly, a set of exit criteria is defined to conclude the results of performance tests.

Designing and automating the test cases form the next step in the performance test process. Automation deserves a special mention as this step because it is almost impossible to perform performance testing without automation.

Entry and exit criteria play a major role in the process of performance test execution. At regular intervals during product development, the entry criteria are evaluated and the test is started if those criteria are met. There can be a separate set of criteria for each of the performance test cases. The entry criteria need to be evaluated at regular intervals since starting the tests early is counter-productive and starting late may mean that the performance objective is not met on time before the release. At the end of performance test execution, the product is evaluated to see whether it met all the exit criteria. If some of the criteria are not met, improvements are made to the product and the test cases corresponding to the exit criteria are re-executed with an objective to fill the gap. This process is repeated till all the exit criteria are met.

Each of the process steps for the performance tests described above are critical because of the factors involved (that is, cost, effort, time, and effectiveness). Hence, keeping a strong process for performance testing provides a high return on investment.

7.6 CHALLENGES

Performance testing is not a very well understood topic in the testing community. There are several interpretations of performance testing. Some organizations separate performance testing and load testing and conduct them at different phases of testing. While it may be successful in some situations, sometimes separating these two causes complications. When there is a need to compare these functional performance numbers with load testing numbers, it becomes difficult as the build used is different and the timeline (when the timeline is different, the quality of product may also be different) is also different as they were performed at two different phases. In this case, an apples-to-apples comparison is not possible.

The availability of skills is a major problem facing performance testing. As discussed at several places of this chapter, product knowledge, knowledge of competition, tools usage, automation, process, knowledge on statistics, and analytical skills are needed to do performance testing. This is one of the longest lists of skills that are required for any type of testing discussed till now. Training the engineers on these skills and making them available for a long duration for doing performance testing will help in meeting these skills.

Performance testing requires a large number and amount of resources such as hardware, software, effort, time, tools, and people. Even large organizations find these resources that are needed to meet the objectives of performance testing scarce. Even if they are available, it is so only for a short duration. This is yet another challenge in performance testing. Looking at the resources available and trying to meet as many objectives as possible is what is expected from the teams executing performance tests.

Performance test results need to reflect real-life environment and expectations. But due to the nature of tools which only simulate the environment, the test lab that works in a controlled environment, and data sets which may not have all fields populated the same way as the customer has, repeating the performance test results in the real-life customer deployments is a big challenge. Adequate care to create a test bed as close to a customer deployment is another expectation for performance tests.

Selecting the right tool for the performance testing is another challenge. There are many tools available for performance testing but not all of them meet all the requirements. Moreover, performance test tools are expensive and require additional resources to install and use. Performance tools also expect the test engineers to learn additional meta-languages and scripts. This throws up another challenge for performance testing.

Interfacing with different teams that include a set of customers is yet another challenge in performance testing. Not only the customers but also the technologists give performance test requirements and development teams. Performance testing is conducted to meet the expectations of customers, architects, and development team. As a business case, the performance of the product need to match up with the competition. As expectations keep growing from all directions, it will be difficult to meet all of them at one go. Sustained effort is needed if the majority of performance expectations have to be met.

Lack of seriousness on performance tests by the management and development team is another challenge. Once all functionalities are working fine in a product, it is assumed that the product is ready to ship. Due to various reasons specified, performance tests are conducted after the features are stable, and the defects that come out of these tests need to be looked into very seriously by the management. Since it may be too late to fix some defects or due to release pressures or due to fixes needed in design and architecture that may need a big effort in regression or various other reasons, generally some of the defects from these tests are postponed to the next release. It defeats the purpose of performance tests. A high degree of management commitment and directive to fix performance defects before product release are needed for successful execution of performance tests.

 REFERENCES

Performance testing is a type of testing that is easy to understand but difficult to perform due to amount of information and effort needed. There are several materials available on the web, explaining the cause and method for performance testing. This chapter tries to be unique among those, by covering the process and methodology from practical perspective. More details on the tools and associated information can be obtained from the web sites pointed to in the Bibliography and References at the end of the book.

PROBLEMS AND EXERCISES

1. In each of the following cases, which performance factor is likely to be most important?

    a. All the transactions in a bank should be processed by end of each day and by that evening the end of day cash reconciliation should be done.

    b. The users coming in to a bank should have their transactions completed in under 5 minutes.

    c. Users are accessing a remote file system from a client that has no processing power and are typing a file name. Since the processing is done at the remote file server, every character typed in is sent to the server and returned back.

2. Each product has different tuning parameters. For each of the following cases, identify the important tuning parameters; Which documents/sources would you go through to find out these parameters?

    a. Operating system (e.g., Windows XP)

    b. Database (e.g., Oracle)

    c. A network card (e.g., a Wireless LAN card)

3. How are collecting requirements for performance testing different from say collecting requirements for functional testing like black box testing? Distinguish by the sources used, methods used, tools used and the skill sets required

4. Most product types in software like databases, networks, etc. have standard performance benchmarks. For example, TPCB benchmarks characterize the transaction rates. Look up the Internet and prepare a consolidated report on the industry standard benchmarks for the various types of database transactions, compilers and other types of software that is of interest to you.

5. There are a number of performance test automation tools available in the market. For your organization, prepare a checklist of what you would expect from a performance test automation tool. Using this checklist, make a comparison of the various possible automation tools.

6. "Staffing people for performance testing is arguably the most difficult" – Justify this statement based on the skill sets, attitude, and other parameters.

Regression Testing

CHAPTER 8

In this chapter—

- ✓ What is regression testing
- ✓ Types of regression testing
- ✓ When to do regression testing
- ✓ How to do regression testing
- ✓ Best practices in regression testing

8.1 WHAT IS REGRESSION TESTING?

Doctor: Congratulations! The stomach ulcer that was bothering you and preventing digestion is now completely cured!

Patient: That is fine, doctor, but I have got such a bad mouth ulcer that I can't eat anything. So there is nothing to digest!

Software undergoes constant changes. Such changes are necessitated because of defects to be fixed, enhancements to be made to existing functionality, or new functionality to be added. Anytime such changes are made, it is important to ensure that

1. The changes or additions work as designed; and
2. The changes or additions do not break something that is already working and should continue to work.

Regression testing is designed to address the above two purposes. Let us illustrate this with a simple example.

> Regression testing is done to ensure that enhancements or defect fixes made to the software works properly and does not affect the existing functionality.

Assume that in a given release of a product, there were three defects—D1, D2, and D3. When these defects are reported, presumably the development team will fix these defects and the testing team will perform tests to ensure that these defects are indeed fixed. When the customers start using the product (modified to fix defects D1, D2, and D3), they may encounter new defects—D4 and D5. Again, the development and testing teams will fix and test these new defect fixes. But, in the process of fixing D4 and D5, as an unintended side-effect, D1 may resurface. Thus, the testing team should not only ensure that the fixes take care of the defects they are supposed to fix, but also that they do not break anything else that was already working.

Regression testing enables the test team to meet this objective. Regression testing is important in today's context since software is being released very often to keep up with the competition and increasing customer awareness. It is essential to make quick and frequent releases and also deliver stable software. Regression testing enables that any new feature introduced to the existing product does not adversely affect the current functionality.

Regression testing follows *selective re-testing* technique. Whenever the defect fixes are done, a set of test cases that need to be run to verify the defect fixes are selected by the test team. An impact analysis is done to find out what areas may get impacted due to those defect fixes. Based on the impact analysis, some more test cases are selected to take care of the impacted areas. Since this testing technique focuses on reuse of existing test cases that have already been executed, the technique is called selective re-testing. There may be situations where new test cases need to be developed to take care of some impacted areas. However, by and large, regression testing reuses the test cases that are available, as it focuses on testing the features that are already available and tested at least once already.

8.2   TYPES OF REGRESSION TESTING

Before going into the types of regression testing, let us understand what a "build" means. When internal or external test teams or customers begin using a product, they report defects. These defects are analyzed by each developer who make individual *defect fixes*. The developers then do appropriate unit testing and check the defect fixes into a Configuration Management (CM) System. The source code for the complete product is then compiled and these defect fixes along with the existing features get consolidated into the build. *A build thus becomes an aggregation of all the defect fixes and features that are present in the product.*

There are two types of regression testing in practice.

1. Regular regression testing
2. Final regression testing

A *regular regression testing* is done between test cycles to ensure that the defect fixes that are done and the functionality that were working with the earlier test cycles continue to work. A regular regression testing can use more than one product build for the test cases to be executed.

A "final regression testing" is done to validate the final build before release. The CM engineer delivers the final build with the media and other contents exactly as it would go to the customer. The final regression test cycle is conducted for a specific period of duration, which is mutually agreed upon between the development and testing teams. This is called the *"cook time"* for regression testing. Cook time is necessary to keep testing the product for a certain duration, since some of the defects (for example, Memory leaks) can be unearthed only after the product has been used for a certain time duration. The product is continuously exercised for the complete duration of the cook time to ensure that such time-bound defects are identified. Some of the test cases are repeated to find out whether there are failures in the final product that will reach the customer. All the defect fixes for the release should have been completed for the build used for the final regression test cycle. The final regression test cycle is more critical than any other type or phase of testing, as this is the only testing that ensures *the same build of the product that was tested reaches the customer*.

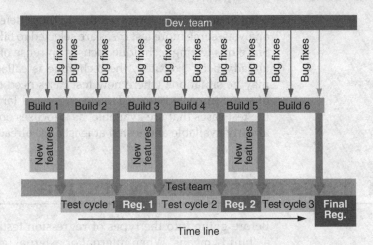

Figure 8.1

Regression testing—
types.

The regression testing types discussed above are represented in Figure 8.1. The coloured figure is available on page 466. *Reg. 1* and *Reg. 2* are regular regression test cycles and final regression is shown as *Final Reg.* in the figure.

8.3   WHEN TO DO REGRESSION TESTING?

Whenever changes happen to software, regression testing is done to ensure that these do not adversely affect adversely the existing functionality. A regular regression testing can use multiple builds for the test cases to be executed. However, an unchanged build is highly recommended for final regression testing. The test cases that failed due to the defects should be included for future regression testing.

Regression testing is done between test cycles to find out if the software delivered is as good or better than the builds received in the past. As testing involves large amount of resources (hardware, software, and people), a quick testing is needed to assess the quality of build and changes to software. Initially a few test engineers with very few machines do regression testing. This prevents a huge loss of effort in situations where the defect fixes or build process affects the existing/working functionality, taking the quality or progress in a negative direction. These kind of side-effects need to be fixed immediately before a large number of people get involved in testing. Regression testing is done whenever such a requirement arises.

It is necessary to perform regression testing when

1.   A reasonable amount of initial testing is already carried out.

2.   A good number of defects have been fixed.

3.   Defect fixes that can produce side-effects are taken care of.

Regression testing may also be performed periodically, as a pro-active measure.

Figure 8.2

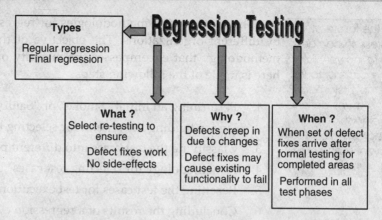

As we will see in Chapter 15, a defect tracking system is used to communicate the status of defect fixes amongst the various stake holders. When a developer fixes a defect, the defect is sent back to the test engineer for verification using the defect tracking system. The test engineer needs to take the appropriate action of closing the defect if it is fixed or reopening it if it has not been fixed properly. In this process what may get missed out are the side-effects, where a fix would have fixed the particular defect but some functionality which was working before has stopped working now. Regression testing needs to be done when a set of defect fixes are provided. To ensure that there are no side-effects, some more test cases have to be selected and defect fixes verified in the regression test cycle. Thus, before a tester can close the defect as fixed, it is important to ensure that appropriate regression tests are run and the fix produces no side-effects. It is always a good practice to initiate regression testing and verify the defect fixes. Else, when there is a side-effect or loss of functionality observed at a later point of time through testing, it will become very difficult to identify which defect fix has caused it.

> Regression testing can be performed irrespective of which test phase the product is in.

From the above discussion it is clear that regression testing is both a planned test activity and a need-based activity and it is done between builds and test cycles. Hence, regression test is applicable to all phases in a software development life cycle (SDLC) and also to component, integration, system, and acceptance test phases.

Figure 8.2 summarizes the contents of the above-mentioned sections.

8.4 HOW TO DO REGRESSION TESTING?

A well-defined methodology for regression testing is very important as this among is the final type of testing that is normally performed just before release. If regression testing is not done right, it will enable the defects to seep through and may result in customers facing some serious issues not found by test teams.

> The failure of regression can only be found very late in the cycle or found by the customers. Having a well-defined methodology for regression can prevent such costly misses.

There are several methodologies for regression testing that are used by different organizations. The objective of this section is to explain a methodology that encompasses the majority of them. The methodology here is made of the following steps.

1. Performing an initial "Smoke" or "Sanity" test
2. Understanding the criteria for selecting the test cases
3. Classifying the test cases into different priorities
4. A methodology for selecting test cases
5. Resetting the test cases for test execution
6. Concluding the results of a regression cycle

8.4.1   Performing an Initial "Smoke" or "Sanity" Test

Whenever changes are made to a product, it should first be made sure that nothing basic breaks. For example, if you are building a database, then any build of the database should be able to start it up; perform basic operations such as queries, data definition, data manipulation; and shutdown the database. In addition, you may want to ensure that the key interfaces to other products also work properly. This has to be done *before* performing any of the other more detailed tests on the product. If, for example, a given build fails to bring up a database, then it is of no use at all. The code has to be corrected to solve this (and any other such basic) problem first, before one can even consider testing other functionality.

Smoke testing consists of

1. Identifying the basic functionality that a product must satisfy;
2. Designing test cases to ensure that these basic functionality work and packaging them into a smoke test suite;
3. Ensuring that every time a product is built, this suite is run successfully before anything else is run; and
4. If this suite fails, escalating to the developers to identify the changes and perhaps change or roll back the changes to a state where the smoke test suite succeeds.

To make sure that problems in smoke testing are detected upfront, some organizations mandate that anytime a developer makes a change, he or she should run the smoke test suite successfully on that build before checking the code into the Configuration Management repository.

Defects in the product can get introduced not only by the code, but also by the build scripts that are used for compiling and linking the programs. Smoke testing enables the uncovering of such errors introduced by (also) the build procedures. This is important, as a research conducted in the past

Figure 8.3

CM defects.

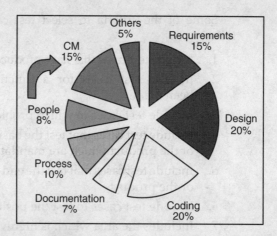

revealed that 15% of defects are introduced by Configuration Management or build-related procedures. This is shown in Figure 8.3. The coloured figure is available on page 467.

8.4.2 Understanding the Criteria for Selecting the Test Cases

Having performed a smoke test, the product can be assumed worthy of being subjected to further detailed tests. The question now is what tests should be run to achieve the dual objective of ensuring that the fixes work and that they do not cause unintended side-effects.

There are two approaches to selecting the test cases for a regression run. First, an organization can choose to have a constant set of regression tests that are run for every build or change. In such a case, deciding what tests to run is simple. But this approach is likely to be sub-optimal because

1. In order to cover all fixes, the constant set of tests will encompass all features and tests which are not required may be run every time; and

2. A given set of defect fixes or changes may introduce problems for which there may not be ready-made test cases in the constant set. Hence, even after running all the regression test cases, introduced defects will continue to exist.

A second approach is to select the test cases dynamically for each build by making judicious choices of the test cases. The selection of test cases for regression testing requires knowledge of

1. The defect fixes and changes made in the current build;

2. The ways to test the current changes;

3. The impact that the current changes may have on other parts of the system; and

4. The ways of testing the other impacted parts.

Some of the criteria to select test cases for regression testing are as follows.

1. Include test cases that have produced the maximum defects in the past
2. Include test cases for a functionality in which a change has been made
3. Include test cases in which problems are reported
4. Include test cases that test the basic functionality or the core features of the product which are mandatory requirements of the customer
5. Include test cases that test the end-to-end behavior of the application or the product
6. Include test cases to test the positive test conditions
7. Includes the area which is highly visible to the users

When selecting test cases, do not select more test cases which are bound to fail and have little or less relevance to the defect fixes. Select more positive test cases than negative test cases for the final regression test cycle. Selecting negative test cases—that is, test cases introduced afresh with the intent of breaking the system—may create some confusion with respect to pinpointing the cause of the failure. It is also recommended that the regular test cycles before regression testing should have the right mix of both positive and negative test cases.

> Regression testing should focus more on the impact of defect fixes than on the criticality of the defect itself.

The selection of test cases for regression testing depends more on the *impact of defect fixes* than the *criticality of the defect* itself. A minor defect can result in a major side-effect and a defect fix for a critical defect can have little or minor side-effect. Hence the test engineer needs to balance these aspects while selecting test cases for regression testing.

Selecting regression test cases is a continuous process. Each time a set of regression tests (also called regression test bed) is to be executed, the test cases need to be evaluated for their suitability, based on the above conditions.

8.4.3 Classifying Test Cases

> It is important to know the relative priority of test cases for a successful test execution.

When the test cases have to be selected dynamically for each regression run, it would be worthwhile to plan for regression testing from the beginning of project, even before the test cycles start. To enable choosing the right tests for a regression run, the test cases can be classified into various *priorities* based on importance and customer usage. As an example, we can classify the test cases into three categories. See Figure 8.4. The coloured figure is available on page 467.

✠   **Priority-0**   These test cases can be called sanity test cases which check basic functionality and are run for accepting the build for further testing. They are also run when a product goes through a major change. These test cases deliver a very high project value to both to product development teams and to the customers.

Figure 8.4

Classification of test
cases—an example.

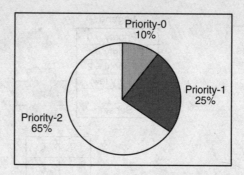

Priority-0
10%

Priority-1
25%

Priority-2
65%

✠ **Priority-1**   Uses the basic and normal setup and these test cases deliver high project value to both development team and to customers.

✠ **Priority-2**   These test cases deliver moderate project value. They are executed as part of the testing cycle and selected for regression testing on a need basis.

8.4.4 Methodology for Selecting Test Cases

Once the test cases are classified into different priorities, the test cases can be selected. There could be several right approaches to regression testing which need to be decided on "case to case" basis. There are several methodologies available in the industry for selecting regression test cases. The methodology discussed in this section takes into account the criticality and impact of defect fixes after test cases are classified into several priorities as explained in the previous section.

Case 1   If the criticality and impact of the defect fixes are low, then it is enough that a test engineer selects a *few* test cases from *test case database* (TCDB), (a repository that stores all the test cases that can be used for testing a product. More information about TCDB in Chapter 15 of this book) and executes them. These test cases can fall under any priority (0, 1, or 2).

Case 2   If the criticality and the impact of the defect fixes are medium, then we need to execute *all Priority-0* and *Priority-1* test cases. If defect fixes need additional test cases (*few*) from Priority-2, then those test cases can also be selected and used for regression testing. Selecting Priority-2 test cases in this case is desirable but not necessary.

Case 3   If the criticality and impact of the defect fixes are high, then we need to execute *all Priority-0, Priority-1* and a *carefully selected subset of Priority-2* test cases.

The cases discussed above are illustrated in Figure 8.5. The coloured figure is available on page 468.

The above methodology requires that the impact of defect fixes be analyzed for all defects. This can be a time-consuming procedure. If, for some reason, there is not enough time and the risk of not doing an impact analysis is low, then the alternative methodologies given below can be considered.

Figure 8.5

Methodology for the selection of test cases.

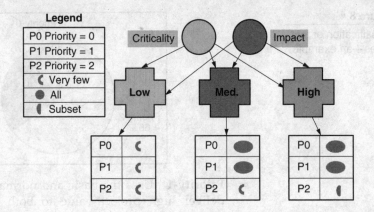

* **Regress all**   For regression testing, all priority 0, 1, and 2 test cases are rerun. This means *all* the test cases in the regression test bed/suite are executed.

* **Priority based regression**   For regression testing based on this priority, all priority 0, 1, and 2 test cases are run in order, based on the availability of time. Deciding when to stop the regression testing is based on the availability of time.

* **Regress changes**   For regression testing using this methodology code changes are compared to the last cycle of testing and test cases are selected based on their impact on the code (gray box testing)

* **Random regression**   Random test cases are selected and executed for this regression methodology.

* **Context based dynamic regression**   A few Priority-0 test cases are selected, and based on the context created by the analysis of those test cases after the execution (for example, find new defects, boundary value) and outcome, additional related cases are selected for continuing the regression testing.

An effective regression strategy is usually a combination of all of the above and not necessarily any of these in isolation.

8.4.5   Resetting the Test Cases for Regression Testing

After selecting the test cases using the above methodology, the next step is to prepare the test cases for execution. For proceeding with this step, a "test case result history" is needed.

In a large product release involving several rounds of testing, it is very important to record what test cases were executed in which cycle, their results, and related information. This is called *test case result history*. This is part of the test case database discussed in Chapter 15.

In many organizations, not all the types of testing nor all the test cases are repeated for each cycle. As mentioned, test case result history provides a wealth of information on what test cases were executed and when. A method or procedure that uses test case result history to indicate some of the test cases be selected for regression testing is called a *reset* procedure. Resetting a test case is nothing but setting a flag called *not run* or *execute again* in test case database (TCDB). The reset procedure also hides the test case results of previous builds for the test cases, so that the test engineer executing the test cases may not be biased by the result history.

Resetting test cases reduces the risk involved in testing defect fixes by making the testers go through all the test cases and selecting appropriate test cases based on the impact of those defect fixes. If there are defect fixes that are done just before the release, the risk is more; hence, more test cases have to be selected.

Resetting of test cases, is not expected to be done often, and it needs to be done with the following considerations in mind.

1. When there is a major change in the product.

2. When there is a change in the build procedure which affects the product.

3. Large release cycle where some test cases were not executed for a long time.

4. When the prodcut is in the final regression test cycle with a few selected test cases.

5. Where there is a situation, that the expected results of the test cases could be quite different from the previous cycles.

6. The test cases relating to defect fixes and production problems need to be evaluated release after release.In case they are found to be working fine, they can be reset.

7. Whenever existing application functionality is removed, the related test cases can be reset.

8. Test cases that consistently produce a positive result can be removed.

9. Test cases relating to a few negative test conditions (not producing any defects) can be removed.

When the above guidelines are not met, we may want to *rerun* the test cases rather than reset the results of the test cases. There are only a few differences between the rerun and reset states in test cases. In both instances, the test cases are executed but in the case of "reset" we can expect a different result from what was obtained in the earlier cycles. In the case of rerun, the test cases are expected to give the same test result as in the past; hence, the management need not be unduly worried because those test cases are executed as a formality and are not expected to reveal any major problem.

Test cases belonging to the "rerun" state help to gain confidence in the product by testing for more time. Such test cases are not expected to fail or affect the release. Test cases belonging to the "reset" state say that the test results can be different from the past, and only after these test cases are executed can we know the result of regression and the release status.

For example, if there is a change in the installation of a product, which does not affect product functionality, then the change can be tested independently by rerunning some test cases and the test cases do not have to be "reset." Similarly, if there is a functionality that underwent a major change (design or architecture or code revamp), then all the related test cases for that functionality need to be "reset," and these test cases have to be executed again. By resetting test cases, the test engineer has no way of knowing their past results. This removes bias and forces the test engineer to pick up those test cases and execute them.

A rerun state in a test case indicates low risk and reset status represents medium to high risk for a release. Hence, close to the product release, it is a good practice to execute the "reset" test cases first before executing the "rerun" test cases.

Reset is also decided on the basis of the stability of the functionalities. If you are in Priority-1 and have reached a stage of comfort level in Priority-0 (say, for example, more than 95% pass rate), then you do not reset Priority-0 test cases unless there is a major change. This is true with Priority-1 test cases when you are in the Priority-2 test phase.

We will now see illustrate the use of the "reset" flag for regression testing in the various phases.

8.4.5.1 Component test cycle phase Regression testing between component test cycles uses only Priority-0 test cases. For each build that enters the test, the build number is selected and all test cases in Priority-0 are reset. The test cycle starts only if all Priority-0 test cases pass.

8.4.5.2 Integration testing phase After component testing is over, if regression is performed between integration test cycles Priority-0 and Priority-1 test cases are executed. Priority-1 testing can use multiple builds. In this phase, the test cases are "reset" only if the criticality and impact of the defect fixes and feature additions are high. A "reset" procedure during this phase may affect all Priority-0 and Priority-1 test cases.

8.4.5.3 System test phase Priority-2 testing starts after all test cases in Priority-1 are executed with an acceptable pass percentage as defined in the test plan. In this phase, the test cases are "reset" only if the criticality and impact of the defect fixes and feature additions are very high. A "reset" procedure during this phase may affect Priority-0, Priority-1, and Priority-2 test cases.

8.4.5.4 Why reset test cases
Regression testing uses a good number of test cases which have already been executed and are associated with some results and assumptions on the result. A "reset" procedure gives a clear picture of how much of testing still remains, and reflects the status of regression testing.

If test cases are not "reset," then the test engineers tend to report a completion rate and other results based on previous builds. This is because of the basic assumption that multiple builds are used in each phase of the testing and a gut feeling that if something passed in the past builds, it will pass in future builds also. Regression testing does not go with an assumption that "Future is an extension of the past." Resetting as a procedure removes any bias towards test cases because resetting test case results prevents the history of test cases being viewed by testers.

8.4.6   Concluding the Results of Regression Testing

> Everyone monitors regression test results as this testing not only indicates about defects and but also their fixes.

Apart from test teams, regression test results are monitored by many people in an organization as it is done after test cycles and sometimes very close to the release date. Developers also monitor the results from regression as they would like to know how well their defect fixes work in the product. Hence, there is a need to understand a method for concluding the results of regression.

Since regression uses test cases that have already executed more than once, it is expected that 100% of those test cases pass using the same build, if defect fixes are done right. In situations where the pass percentage is not 100, the test manager can compare with the previous results of the test case to conclude whether regression was successful or not.

✵ If the result of a particular test case was a pass using the previous builds and a fail in the current build, then regression has failed. A new build is required and the testing must start from scratch after resetting the test cases.

✵ If the result of a particular test case was a fail using the previous builds and a pass in the current build, then it is safe to assume the defect fixes worked.

✵ If the result of a particular test case was a fail using the previous builds and a fail in the current build and if there are no defect fixes for this particular test case, it may mean that the result of this test case should not be considered for the pass percentage. This may also mean that such test cases should not be selected for regression.

✵ If the result of a particular test case is a fail using the previous builds but works with a documented workaround and if you are satisfied with the workaround, then it should considered as a pass for both the system test cycle and regression test cycle.

✠   If you are not satisfied with the workaround, then it should be considered as a fail for a system test cycle but may be considered as a pass for regression test cycle.

This is illustrated in Table 8.1.

Table 8.1   Conclude the results of a regression test cycle.

Current result from regression	Previous result(s)	Conclusion	Remarks
FAIL	PASS	FAIL	Need to improve the regression process and code reviews
PASS	FAIL	PASS	This is the expected result of a good regression to say defect fixes work properly
FAIL	FAIL	FAIL.	Need to analyze why defect fixes are not working. "Is it a wrong fix?" Also should analyze why this test is rerun for regression
PASS (with a work-around)	FAIL	Analyze the workaround and if satisfied mark result as PASS	Workarounds also need a good review as they can also create side-effects
PASS	PASS	PASS	This pattern of results gives a comfort feeling that there are no side-effects due to defect fixes

8.5   BEST PRACTICES IN REGRESSION TESTING

Practice 1:Regression can be used for all types of releases.

Regression methodology can be applied when

1.   We need to assess the quality of product between test cycles (both planned and need based);

2.   We are doing a major release of a product, have executed all test cycles, and are planning a regression test cycle for defect fixes; and

3.   We are doing a minor release of a product (support packs, patches, and so on) having only defect fixes, and we can plan for regression test cycles to take care of those defect fixes.

There can be multiple cycles of regression testing that can be planned for every release. This applies if defect fixes come in phases or to take care of some defect fixes not working with a specific build.

Practice 2: Mapping defect identifiers with test cases improves regression Quality.

When assigning a fail result to a test case during test execution, it is a good practice to enter the defect identifier(s) (from the defect tracking system) along so that you will know what test cases to be executed when a defect fix arrives. Please note that there can be multiple defects that can come out of a particular test case and a particular defect can affect more than one test case.

Even though ideally one would like to have a mapping between test cases and defects, the choice of test cases that are to be executed for taking care of side-effects of defect fixes may still remain largely a manual process as this requires knowledge of the interdependences amongst the various defect fixes.

As the time passes by and with each release of the product, the size of the regression test cases to be executed grows. It has been found that some of the defects reported by customers in the past were due to last-minute defect fixes creating side-effects. Hence, selecting the test case for regression testing is really an art and not that easy. To add to this complexity, most people want maximum returns with minimum investment on regression testing.

Practice 3: Create and execute regression test bed daily.

To solve this problem, as and when there are changes made to a product, regression test cases are added or removed from an existing suite of test cases. This suite of test cases, called regression suite or regression test bed, is run when a new change is introduced to an application or a product. The automated test cases in the regression test bed can be executed along with nightly builds to ensure that the quality of the product is maintained during product development phases.

Practice 4: Ask your best test engineer to select the test cases.

It was mentioned earlier that the knowledge of defects, products, their interdependences and a well-structured methodology are all very important to select test cases. These points stress the need for selecting the right person for the right job. The most experienced person in the team or the most talented person in the team may do a much better job of selecting the right test cases for regression than someone with less experience. Experience and talent can bring in knowledge of fragile areas in the product and impact the analysis of defects.

Please look at the pictures below. In the first picture, the tiger has been put in a cage to prevent harm to human kind. In the second picture, some members of a family are lie inside the mosquito net as prevention against from mosquitoes.

The same strategy has to be adopted for regression. Like the tiger in the cage, all defects in the product have to be identified and fixed. This is what *"detecting defects in your product"* means. All the testing types discussed in the earlier chapters and regression testing adopt this technique to find each defect and fix it.

The photograph of the family under the mosquito net signifies *"protecting your product from defects."* The strategy followed here is of defect prevention. There are many verification and quality assurance activities such as reviews and inspections (discussed in Chapter 3), that try to do this.

Practice 5:Detect defects, and protect your product from defects and defect fixes.

Another aspect related to regression testing is *"protecting your product from defect fixes."* As discussed earlier, a defect that is classified as a minor defect may create a major impact on the product when it gets fixed into the code. It is similar to what a mosquito can do to humans (impact), even though its size is small. Hence, it is a good practice to analyze the impact of defect fixes, irrespective of size and criticality, before they are incorporated into the code. The analysis of an impact due to defect fixes is difficult due to lack of time and the complex nature of the products. Hence, it is a good practice to limit the amount of changes in the product when close to the release date. This will prevent the product from defects that may seep in through the defect fixes route, just as mosquitoes can get into the mosquito net through a small hole there. If you make a hole for a mosquito to get out of the net, it also opens the doors for new mosquitoes to come into the net. Fixing a problem without analyzing the impact can introduce a large number of defects in the product. Hence, it is important to insulate the product from defects as well as defect fixes.

If defects are detected and the product is protected from defects and defect fixes, then regression testing becomes effective and efficient.

REFERENCES

This chapter is written based on one of earlier paper published as in [SRINI-2003]. Some of the definitions used in this chapter are closer to [IEEE-1994] and may be a good place to look for templates and guidelines for performing regression testing.

PROBLEMS AND EXERCISES

1. A product for automating payroll is slated to be released in March. The following are some of the features. For these, identify which of them would you put through smoke tests in the three months

leading up to the product release in March, assuming that there will be one more maintenance release in September.

    a. Screens for entering employee information

    b. Statutory year-end reports

    c. Calculating the pay slip details for a month

    d. Screens for maintaining address of the employee

2. A product has some test cases that are rarely run, ostensibly "because of lack of time." Discuss the pros and cons of running such dormant tests as a part of regression.

3. Which of the test cases given below for inclusion in a given regression cycle?

    a. Version 7 of the product is being released and there are tests cases for new features to be introduced in this version.

    b. Version 6 had a number of defects in the buffer management module and Version 7 builds on top of this module.

    c. Version 6 had a fairly stable (i.e., very few defects) in the user interface module and there have been very little changes in this module in Version 7.

    d. Version 7 went through a Beta test cycle and during Beta tests, some important customer usage scenarios were found to uncover defects in the product.

    e. The product is a database software and has features like database startup, basic SQL query and multi-site query.

4. We discussed ways of prioritizing test cases. Using the suggestions given in the text, prioritize the test cases as P0/P1/P2.

    a. A test cases for a network product that tests basic flow control and error control.

    b. A test case for a database software that tests all the options of a join query.

    c. A test case for a file system that checks allocation of space that is not contiguous.

    d. A test case that tests the startup of OS with normal parameters

    d. A test case that tests the startup of an application in a "safe mode," something that is not done very often.

    f. A test case corresponding to a feature that has undergone significant change in the current version.

    g. A test case corresponding to a stable feature that has not uncovered any major defects.

5. If during regression run, you are hard pressed for time, discuss the pros and cons of the various methodologies of regress (regress all, regress changes, etc) discussed in the text.

6. A regression test engineer presented the following results. Discuss the efficacy of the choice of regression tests and of the development process:

    a. The tests for print facility produced no defects in the previous version and has not produced any defects in this version.

    b. The defects in tests for multi-currency continue in the current version.

    c. The feature expedited delivery had new defects in the current version.

7. Discuss the difference in regression testing for a major release versus minor release of a product.

8. We have discussed in this chapter as well as in Chapter 15, details of Test Case Data Base and Configuration Management Repository and a Defect Repository. Discuss how you can establish a link between these three repositories to automatically choose the most optimal regression tests for a given release.

Internationalization (I₁₈n) Testing

CHAPTER 9

In this chapter—

9.1   INTRODUCTION

The market for software is becoming truly global. The advent of Internet has removed some of the technology barriers on widespread usage of software products and has simplified the distribution of software products across the globe. However, the ability of a software product to be available and usable in the local languages of different countries will significantly influence its rate of adoption. Thus, there is a paradoxical yet reasonable requirement for a software to support different languages (such as Chinese, Japanese, Spanish) and follow their conventions. This chapter deals with what needs to be done, both from development and testing perspectives in order to make a software product usable in different languages and countries. Building software for the international market, supporting multiple languages, in a cost-effective and timely manner is a matter of using internationalization standards throughout the software development life cycle—from requirements capture through design, development, testing, and maintenance. The guidelines given in this chapter help in reducing the time and effort required to make a software product support multiple languages, by building it right the first time with sufficient flexibility to support multiple languages.

If some of the guidelines are not followed in the software life cycle for internationalization, the effort and additional costs to support every new language will increase significantly over time. Testing for internationalization is done to ensure that the software does not assume any specific language or conventions associated with a specific language. Testing for internationalization has to be done in various phases of the software life cycle. We will go into the details of these in Section 9.3. We will first provide a basic primer on the terminology used in internationalization.

9.2   PRIMER ON INTERNATIONALIZATION

9.2.1   Definition of Language

To explain the terms that are used for internationalization, we need to understand what a *language* is. A language is a tool used for communication Internationalization—and this chapter—focuses mostly on human languages (such as Japanese, English, and so on) and not on computer languages (such as Java, C, and so on), which has a set of characters (alphabet), a set of (valid) words formed from these characters, and grammar (rules on how to coin words and sentences). In addition, a language also has semantics or the meaning associated with the sentences. For the same language, the spoken usage, word usage, and grammar could vary from one country to another. However, the characters/alphabet may remain the same in most cases. Words can have a different set of characters to mean the same thing for different countries that speak the same language. For example, "color" is spelt thus in US English while it is spelt as "colour" in UK English.

9.2.2   Character Set

This section outlines some of the standards that are used to represent characters of different languages in the computer. The purpose of this section is to introduce the idea of different character representations. A detailed understanding of how exactly each character is represented and a knowledge of internals are not required for understanding this chapter.

ASCII   ASCII stands for American Standard Code for Information Interchange. It is a byte representation (8 bits) for characters that is used in computers. ASCII used seven bits to represent all characters that were used by the computer. Using this method, 128 ($2^7 = 128$) characters were represented in binary. ASCII was one of the earliest binary character representation for computers. Later ASCII was extended to include the unused eighth bit, that enabled 256 ($2^8 = 256$) characters to be represented in the binary. This representation included more punctuation symbols, European characters and special characters. Extended ASCII also helped *accented characters* (for example, ñáéíóú) to be represented. Accented characters are those English-like ASCII characters which have special meaning in European and western languages.

Double-Byte Character Set (DBCS)   English characters were represented using a single byte in ASCII. Some languages such as Chinese and Japanese have many different characters that cannot be represented in a byte. They use two bytes to represent each character; hence the name DBCS. In a single-byte notation, only 256 different characters can be represented (in binary), whereas in the DBCS scheme, 65,536 (2^{16}) different characters can be represented.

Unicode   ASCII or DBCS may be sufficient to encode all the characters of a single language. But they are certainly not sufficient to represent all the characters of *all* the languages in the world. The characters for all the languages need to be stored, interpreted, and transmitted in a standard way. Unicode fills this need effectively. *Unicode provides a unique number to every character no matter what platform, program or language.* Unicode uses fixed-width, 16-bit worldwide character encoding that was developed, maintained, and promoted by the Unicode Consortium. This allows unique encoding for each language by representing the characters, thereby allowing it to be handled the same way—sorted, searched, and manipulated. *Unicode Transformation Format (UTF)* specifies the algorithmic mapping for the language characters of different languages to be converted into Unicode. The Unicode Consortium recognizes many of the languages and locales (discussed in the next sub-section) existing in the world. Each character of every language is assigned a unique number. Such a provision aids

Table 9.1 Move towards unicode for Windows operating system.

Microsoft operating system	Path to internationalization
Windows 3.1	ANSI
Windows 95	ANSI and limited Unicode
Windows NT 3.1	First OS based on Unicode
Windows NT 4.0	Display of Unicode characters
Windows NT 5.0	Display and input of Unicode characters

greatly in internationalizing software. All software applications and platforms are moving towards Unicode. As an example, the information in Table 9.1 explains the path taken by various versions of Microsoft Windows to Unicode.

9.2.3 Locale

Commercial software not only needs to remember the language but also the country in which it is spoken. There are conventions associated with the language which need to be taken care of in the software. There could be two countries speaking the same language with identical grammar, words, and character set. However, there could still be variations, such as currency and date formats. A *locale* is a term used to differentiate these parameters and conventions. A locale can be considered as a subset of a language that defines its behavior in different countries or regions. For example, English is a language spoken in USA and India. However, the currency symbol used in the two countries are different ($ and Rs respectively). The punctuation symbols used in numbers are also different. For example, 1,000,000 is represented in USA as 1,000,000 and as 10,00,000 in India.

Software needs to remember the locale, apart from language, for it to function properly. There could also be several currencies used in a country speaking the same language (for example, Euro and Franc are two currencies used in France, where the language is French). There could be several date formats also. A locale is a term which means all of these and more that may be important. For these reasons, a language can have multiple locales.

9.2.4 Terms Used in This Chapter

Internationalization ($I_{18}n$) is predominantly used as an umbrella term to mean all activities that are required to make the software available for international market. This includes both development and testing activities. In the short form $I_{18}n$, the subscript 18 is used to mean that there are 18 characters between "I" and the last "n" in the word "internationalization." The testing that is done in various phases to ensure that all those activities are done right is called internationalization testing or $I_{18}n$ testing.

Globalization = Internation-alization + Localization

Localization ($L_{10}n$) is a term used to mean the translation work of all software resources such as messages to the target language and conventions. In the short form $L_{10}n$, the subscript 10 is used to indicate that there are 10 characters between "L" and "n" in the word "localization." This translation of messages and documentation is done by a set of language experts who understand English (by default, all messages of the software are in English) and the target language into which the software is translated. In cases where an accurate translation is needed, the messages along with the context of usage is given to the $L_{10}n$ team.

Globalization ($G_{11}n$) is a term that is not very popular but used to mean internationalization and localization. This term is used by a set of organizations, which would like to separate the internationalization from the localization set of activities. This separation may be needed because the localization activities are handled by a totally different set of language experts (per language), and these activities are generally outsourced. Some companies use the term I18n, to mean only the coding and testing activities, not the translation.

9.3   TEST PHASES FOR INTERNATIONALIZATION TESTING

Testing for internationalization requires a clear understanding of all activities involved and their sequence. Since the job of testing is to ensure the correctness of activities done earlier by other teams, this section also elaborates on activities that are done outside the testing teams. Figure 9.1 depicts the various major activities involved in internationalization testing, using different colored boxes. The coloured figure is available on page 468. The boxes in yellow are the testing activities done by test engineers, the activity in the blue box is done by developers; and the activities in the pink boxes are done by a team called the localization team (which we will revisit later in this chapter). We will now go into details of each of these activities.

Figure 9.1

Major activities in internationalization testing.

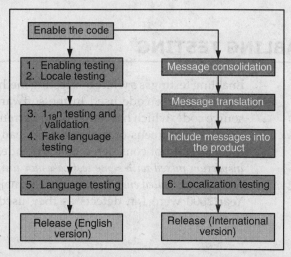

Figure 9.2

Phases of SDLC
V model related to
internationalization
activities.

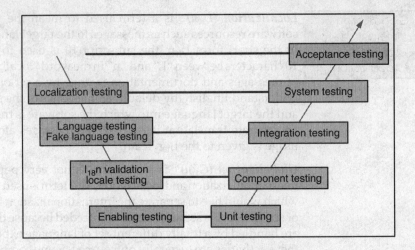

The testing for internationalization is done in multiple phases in the project life cycle. Figure 9.2 further elaborates the SDLC V model described in Chapter 2, and how the different phases of this model are related to various $I_{18}n$ testing activities. The coloured figure is available on page 469. Please note that the enabling testing is done by the developer as part of the unit testing phase.

Some important aspects of internationalization testing are

1. Testing the code for how it handles input, strings, and sorting items;

2. Display of messages for various languages; and

3. Processing of messages for various languages and conventions.

These aspects are the main points of discussion in the following sections.

9.4 ENABLING TESTING

Enabling testing is a white box testing methodology, which is done to ensure that the source code used in the software allows internationalization. A source code, which has hard-coded currency format and date format, fixed length GUI screens or dialog boxes, read-and-print messages directly on the media is not considered enabled code. A*n activity of code review or code inspection mixed with some test cases for unit testing, with an objective to catch $I_{18}n$ defects is called enabling testing.* The majority of the defects found during Year 2000 were $I_{18}n$ defects as they used hard-coded formats. Enabling testing uses a checklist. Some items to be kept in the review checklist for enabling testing are as follows.

✠ Check the code for APIs/function calls that are not part of the $I_{18}n$ API set. For example, printf () and scanf () are functions in C which are not $I_{18}n$ enabled calls. NLSAPI, Unicode and GNU gettxt define some set of calls which are to be used. (Some companies use prewritten parser/scripts to catch those obvious problems of non-internationalized functions used.)

✠ Check the code for hard-coded date, currency formats, ASCII code, or character constants.

✠ Check the code to see that there are no computations (addition, subtraction) done on date variables or a different format forced to the date in the code.

✠ Check the dialog boxes and screens to see whether they leave at least 0.5 times more space for expansion (as the translated text can take more space).

✠ Ensure region-cultural-based messages and slang are not in the code (region-based messages are hard to translate into other languages).

✠ Ensure that no string operations are performed in the code (sub-string searches, concatenation, and so on) and that only system-provided internationalization APIs used for this purpose.

✠ Verify that the code does not assume any predefined path, file names. or directory names in a particular language for it to function.

✠ Check that the code does not assume that the language characters can be represented in 8 bits, 16 bits, or 32 bits (some programs use bit shift operations of C language to read the next character, which are not allowed).

✠ Ensure that adequate size is provided for buffers and variables to contain translated messages.

✠ Check that bitmaps and diagrams do not have embedded translatable text (that needs to be translated).

✠ Ensure that all the messages are documented along with usage context, for the use of translators.

✠ Ensure that all the resources (such as bitmaps, icons, screens, dialog boxes) are separated from the code and stored in resource files.

✠ Check that no message contains technical jargon and that all messages are understood even by the least experienced user of the product. This also helps in translating messages properly.

✠ If the code uses scrolling of text, then the screen and dialog boxes must allow adequate provisions for direction change in scrolling such as top to bottom, right to left, left to right, bottom to top, and so on as conventions are different in different languages. For example, Arabic uses "right to left" direction for reading and "left to right" for

Figure 9.3

Reading and scrolling
direction.

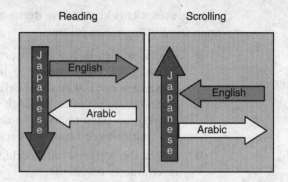

scrolling. [Please note that scrolling direction is generally opposite to reading direction as indicated in Figure 9.3. The coloured figure is available on page 469.]

Of all the phases in internationalization testing, the enabling testing phase generally finds the largest number of $I_{18}n$ defects, if done right. At the time of design and initial coding itself, adequate care has to be taken to ensure that all items in the checklist and other requirements for $I_{18}n$ are met. Code enabling for $I_{18}n$ should not be postponed beyond the coding phase. If the product development team follows the approach of first developing (coding) the product and then incorporating $I_{18}n$ requirements as a separate phase, it would prove counter-productive and inefficient. This is so because in such cases the code would have to be modified to a large extent for $I_{18}n$ (after the basic functionality is incorporated). Hence, all the testing phases, starting from unit testing to final acceptance testing, need to be repeated as the changes would impact the basic functionality of the software.

> The objective of enabling testing is to verify the code for $I_{18}n$ standards during unit testing.

9.5 LOCALE TESTING

Once the code has been verified for $I_{18}n$ and the enabling test is completed, the next step is to validate the effects of locale change in the product. A locale change affects date, currency format, and the display of items on screen, in dialog boxes and text. *Changing the different locales using the system settings or environment variables, and testing the software functionality, number, date, time, and currency format is called locale testing.* As explained earlier, each language can have multiple locales, and all such combinations need to be taken into account for locale testing. The locale settings in the machine need to be changed every time for each combination to test functionality and display.

Whenever a locale is changed, the tester needs to understand the changes to software functionality. It requires knowledge of code enabling. If the code is not enabled correctly, each and every feature of the product with each locale has to be tested. However, in a practical scenario, every functionality is assigned a priority (high, medium, and low) and the tests are executed based on the priority of the functionality. The priority is assigned keeping in mind the importance of the functionality to international customers and the impact. Since locale testing is performed as part of the component testing phase in the SDLC V model (see Figure 9.2 above), relative priority can be assigned to each component for I$_{18}$n testing. This allows more focus for locale testing of those functionality which are important to customers and to the components that are not enabled right. Some of the items to be checked in locale testing are as follows.

1. All features that are applicable to I$_{18}$n are tested with different locales of the software for which they are intended. Some activities that need *not* be considered for I$_{18}$n testing are auditing, debug code, log of activities, and such features which are used only by English administrators and programmers.

2. Hot keys, function keys, and help screens are tested with different applicable locales. (This is to check whether a locale change would affect the keyboard settings.)

3. Date and time format are in line with the defined locale of the language. For example, if US English locale is selected, the software should show mm/dd/yyyy date format.

4. Currency is in line with the selected locale and language. For example, currency should be AUS$ if the language is AUS English.

5. Number format is in line with selected locale and language. For example, the correct decimal punctuations are used and the punctuation is put at the right places.

6. Time zone information and daylight saving time calculations (if used by the software) are consistent and correct.

> Locale testing focuses on testing the conventions for number, punctuations, date and time, and currency formats.

Locale testing is not as elaborate procedure as enabling testing or other phases of testing which are discussed in this chapter. The focus of locale testing is limited to changing the locales and testing the date, currency formats, and the keyboard hot keys for the functionality that are important. Note that one can change the locale of the server or client by using the setup of the operating system. For example, in Microsoft Windows 2000, the locale can be changed by clicking "Start->Settings->Control Panel->Regional options."

9.6   INTERNATIONALIZATION VALIDATION

I$_{18}$n validation is different from I$_{18}$n testing. I$_{18}$n testing is the superset of all types of testing that are discussed in this chapter. I$_{18}$n validation is performed with the following objectives.

1. The software is tested for functionality with ASCII, DBCS, and European characters.

2. The software handles string operations, sorting, sequencing operations as per the language and characters selected.

3. The software display is consistent with characters which are non-ASCII in GUI and menus.

4. The software messages are handled properly.

Here the real challenge of testing is with the non-ASCII characters and how they impact the software. For this purpose, language-specific keyboards and tools that can generate non-ASCII characters are used. IME (Input Method Editor) is a software tool available on Microsoft platforms. This tool can be used for entering non-English characters into a software. It helps in generating non-English ASCII characters. On Unix/Linux platforms, there are plenty of such tools available for free downloads. Many of the tools come with a "soft keyboard," which enables the users to type the characters in the target language. Figure 9.4 below, shows an IME soft keyboard layout for entering Japanese (Katakana) characters. The coloured figure is available on page 470.

Figure 9.4

IME soft keyboard for Japanese.

A checklist for the $I_{18}n$ validation includes the following.

✠ The functionality in all languages and locales are the same.

✠ Sorting and sequencing the items to be as per the conventions of language and locale.

✠ The input to the software can be in non-ASCII or special characters using tools such as IME and can be entered and functionality must be consistent.

✠ The display of the non-ASCII characters in the name are displayed as they were entered.

✠ The cut or copy-and-paste of non-ASCII characters retain their style after pasting, and the software functions as expected.

✠ The software functions correctly with different languages words/ names generated with IME and other tools. For example, log in should work with English user name and German user name with some accented characters.

7. The documentation contains consistent documentation style, punctuations, and all language/locale conventions are followed for every target audience.

8. All the runtime messages in the software are as per the language, country terminology and usage along with proper punctuations; for example, the punctuations for numbers are different for different countries The currency amount 123456789.00 should get formatted as 123,456,789.00 in USA and as 12,34,56,789.00 in India).

> I$_{18}$n validation focuses on component functionality for input/output of non-English messages.

The internationalization validation phase is introduced to take care of all interface-related issues on messages and functionality in all the components as the next phase involves integration of all components. It is important that the above testing is performed on all the components prior to proceeding to the next level of testing which is fake language testing.

9.7 FAKE LANGUAGE TESTING

Fake language testing uses software translators to catch the translation and localization issues early. This also ensures that switching between languages works properly and correct messages are picked up from proper directories that have the translated messages. Fake language testing helps in identifying the issues proactively before the product is localized. For this purpose, all messages are consolidated from the software, and fake language conversions are done by tools and tested. The fake language translators use English-like target languages, which are easy to understand and test. This type of testing helps English testers to find the defects that may otherwise be found only by language experts during localization testing. Figure 9.5 illustrates fake language testing. The coloured figure is available on page 470.

Figure 9.5
Fake language testing.

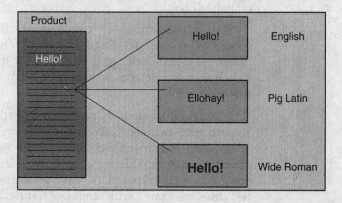

In the figure, there are two English-like fake languages used (Pig Latin and Wide Roman). A message in the program, "Hello," is displayed as "Ellohay" in Pig Latin and "Hello" in Wide Roman. This helps in identifying whether the proper target language has been picked up by the software when language is changed dynamically using system settings.

The following items in the checklist can be used for fake language testing.

1. Ensure software functionality is tested for at least one of the European single-byte fake language (Pig Latin).
2. Ensure software functionality is tested for at least one double-byte language (Wide Roman).
3. Ensure all strings are displayed properly on the screen.
4. Ensure that screen width, size of pop-ups, and dialog boxes are adequate for string display with the fake languages.

> Fake language testing helps in simulating the functionality of the localized product for a different language, using software translators.

9.8   LANGUAGE TESTING

> Language testing focuses on testing the English product with a global environment of products and services functioning in non-English.

Language testing is the short form of "language compatibility testing." This ensures that software created in English can work with platforms and environments that are English and non-English. For example, if a software application was developed for Microsoft Windows, then the software is tested with different available language settings of Microsoft Windows. Since the software is not localized at this stage, it still continues to print and interact using English messages. This testing is done to ensure that the functionality of the software is not broken on other language settings and it is still compatible.

Figure 9.6 illustrates the language testing and various combinations of locales that have to be tested in a client-server architecture. As shown in the figure, for language testing, one of the European languages is selected to represent accented character, one language for double-byte representation, and one default language which is English. The coloured figure is available on page 471.

Testing majority of the combinations illustrated in the figure ensures compatibility for the English software to work in different language platforms. While testing, it is important to look for locale-related issues, as some of the defects that escaped from locale testing may show up in this testing.

It is also important to understand that there are many code page, bit stream, and message conversions taking place for internationalization when data is transmitted between machines or between software and operating system. This may cause some issues in functionality. Since data conversions are taking place, it is a good practice to have some performance test cases associated with language testing. The software is expected to give

Figure 9.6

Language testing and locale combinations that have to be tested in a client server architecture.

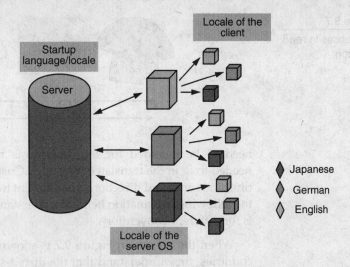

similar performance, irrespective of the language used for the software, operating system, or their combinations. This needs to be verified during language testing.

Language testing should at least have the following checklist

1. Check the functionality on English, one non-English, and one double-byte language platform combination.

2. Check the performance of key functionality on different language platforms and across different machines connected in the network.

9.9 LOCALIZATION TESTING

When the software is approaching the release date, messages are consolidated into a separate file and sent to multilingual experts for translation. A set of *build tools* consolidates all the messages and other resources (such as GUI screens, pictures) automatically, and puts them in separate files. In Microsoft terminology these are called resource files, on some other platforms these are called as message database. As discussed before, the messages for translation need to be sent along with the context in which they are used, so that they can get translated better. The multilingual experts may not be aware of the software or their target customers; it is, therefore, better that the messages do not contain any technology jargons.

Localization is a very expensive and labor-intensive process. Not all messages that belong to the software need to be translated. Some of the messages could be for administrators and developers and may not be for the target user. Such messages need not be translated and should be excluded from the file used for translation. While translating, not only the messages but also resources such as GUI screens, dialog boxes, icons, and bitmaps

Figure 9.7

Differences in read direction.

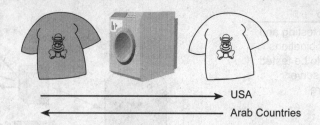

USA

Arab Countries

need to be included for localization, as resizing and customization are needed to fit in the translated messages. Customization is important as scroll directions and read directions are different in some languages. Figure 9.7 and the following explanation helps to understand how important customization is for different conventions.

When the picture in Figure 9.7 is shown to people in English-speaking countries, they understand that the dirty t-shirt on the left-hand side when put inside the washing machine becomes a clean t-shirt as shown on the right-hand side. This is so because conventionally these countries read from left to right. If the same picture is shown to people in Arab countries, they may understand that a clean t-shirt when put inside the washing machine becomes dirty, as their reading direction from is right to left! The coloured figure is available on page 471.

> After L$_{10}$n, the product becomes truly global, functioning in different languages and works with other global products.

Hence customization of resources is very critical for localizing the software. Not only the software but also the documentation needs to be localized for the target language and conventions.

The next step after localization is to conduct localization testing. As explained earlier, after translating the messages, documents, and customizing the resources, a cycle of testing is conducted to check whether the software functions as expected in the localized environment. This is called *localization testing*. This testing requires language experts who can understand English, the target language, and have knowledge of the software and how it functions. The following checklist may help in doing localization testing.

- ✠ All the messages, documents, pictures, screens are localized to reflect the native users and the conventions of the country, locale, and language.
- ✠ Sorting and case conversions are right as per language convention. For example, sort order in English is A, B, C, D, E, whereas in Spanish the sort order is A, B, C, CH, D, E. See Figure 9.8. The coloured figure is available on page 471.
- ✠ Font sizes and hot keys are working correctly in the translated messages, documents, and screens.
- ✠ Filtering and searching capabilities of the software work as per the language and locale conventions.
- ✠ Addresses, phone numbers, numbers, and postal codes in the localized software are as per the conventions of the target user.

Figure 9.8

Sort order in English and Spanish.

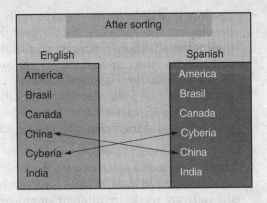

9.10 TOOLS USED FOR INTERNATIONALIZATION

There are several tools available for internationalization. These largely depend on the technology and platform used. For example, the tools used for client-server technology is different from those for web services technology using Java. Table 9.2 gives some sample free tools available. The requirements for $I_{18}n$ testing can vary with product and platform. Therefore, an organization should conduct a detailed study of the available tools before choosing an appropriate one.

Table 9.2 Sample tools for internatinalization.

S.No.	Sample list of tools for Microsoft OS	Name of tool for Linux OS	Purpose
1	MS localization Studio	GNU gettxt ()	Enabling and enabling testing
2	http://BabelFish.Altavista.com	http://BabelFish.Altavista.com	Fake language testing
3	MS regional settings	LANG and set of environment variables	Locale testing
4	IME	Unicode IME (several variants exist, coming from different companies)	$I_{18}n$ validation
5	http://www.snowcrest.net/donnelly/piglatin.html	http://www.snowcrest.net/donnelly/piglatin.html	Fake language testing (e.g. Pig Latin)

9.11 CHALLENGES AND ISSUES

There are many challenges and issues attached to the activities listed in this chapter. The first issue is regarding ownership. A number of software engineering professionals think that $I_{18}n$ and $L_{10}n$ are the issues of the translation team. This is not true. The ownership of making the product available in the market with or without $I_{18}n$ is with everyone developing the software. As we saw through this chapter, the effort for internationalization is spread all through the software development life cycle. Hence, the responsibility is not confined to a single translation team. Many organizations assume that they can afford to have a separate effort planned to make the necessary modification for $I_{18}n$ once developed in English. Again, as we have seen in this chapter, this will prove counter-productive and inefficient in the long run.

$I_{18}n$ believes in *"Doing it right the first time."* Doing it later or releasing a support pack or a patch or a fix at a later point of time cannot be considered as the same software, release, or even feasible. The $I_{18}n$ effort of ensuring the software works in different languages cannot be carried over to the next release. Similarly, localization testing is the only testing phase which can be postponed to the next release, if the English version of the product has been released.

There are several interpretations of the terminology, activities, and phases. The variations are fine, as long as the objectives of the discussions in the chapter are met. There is only a thin line of difference among the several testing activities described in this chapter. Test engineers can merge two or three types of $I_{18}n$ testing and do them together. For example, locale testing, internationalization validation, and fake language testing can be merged to mean "$I_{18}n$ testing."

$I_{18}n$ testing is not a subject which is as well understood as are other types of testing. Lack of standard tools and clarity for $I_{18}n$ testing further complicates the subject. The development community has similar challenges as there are many variations. This gives rise to a challenge as well as an opportunity to research and develop models and methodologies which will resolve these issues. This chapter is only the proverbial tip of the iceberg in this area.

REFERENCES

Internationalization ($I_{18}n$) is still not a term which is well understood by students and practitioners. This chapter takes additional care to introduce those terminologies and explains various activities involved in detail. To understand $I_{18}n$, [uni-2005] is a good site. This site has useful information for reading and understanding the concepts and procedures involved in $I_{18}n$ testing.

PROBLEMS AND EXERCISES

1. Identify at least one language each where the text scrolling is from bottom to top, left to right and right to left.

2. Why Internationalization and localization are denoted as $I_{18}n$ and $L_{10}n$?

3. What is the specific role of configuration management in internationalization?

4. List two of the fake languages and the corresponding tools that can be used for them?

5. What is the primary skill that is needed for doing localization testing?

6. Why is the role of Unicode very unique in internationalization?

7. List the activities of Internationalization in unit, component, integration and system test phases.

Ad hoc Testing

CHAPTER 10

In this chapter—

- ✓ Overview of ad hoc testing
- ✓ Buddy testing
- ✓ Pair testing
- ✓ Exploratory testing
- ✓ Iterative testing
- ✓ Agile and extreme testing
- ✓ Defect seeding
- ✓ Conclusion

10.1 OVERVIEW OF AD HOC TESTING

We have seen in previous chapters that there are many techniques and types of tests that aid in unearthing a large number of defects, thereby improving the quality of the product and minimizing the risk of releasing a product. All the types of testing explained in the previous chapters are part of planned testing and are carried out using certain specific techniques (for example, boundary value analysis). In this chapter, we will look into a family of test types which are carried out in an unplanned manner (hence the name ad hoc testing). We will discuss the characteristics of ad hoc testing and their relative positioning vis-à-vis planned testing activities in the later part of this section. We will then cover other related types of ad hoc testing—buddy testing, exploratory testing, pair testing, iterative testing, agile and extreme testing, and defect seeding—in the subsequent sections. We conclude the chapter with a comparison of all these methods and the scenarios wherein each of these methods may (and may not) add value.

Planned testing, such as the ones we have discussed in the previous chapters, are driven by test engineers and their understanding of the product at a particular time frame. The product under test is assumed to be working in a particular pattern, as specified by the requirements document and other specifications. The validity of this assumption can be checked when the product is implemented and ready to test. The more the test engineers work with the product, the better their understanding becomes. By the time the implemented system is completely understood, it may be too late and there may not be adequate time for a detailed test documentation. Hence, there is a need for testing not only based on planned test cases but also based on better understanding gained with the product.

Some of the issues faced by planned testing are as follows.

1. Lack of clarity in requirements and other specifications
2. Lack of skills for doing the testing
3. Lack of time for test design

Firstly, after some of the planned test cases are executed, the clarity on the requirements improves. However, the test cases written earlier may not reflect the better clarity gained in this process. Secondly, after going through a round of planned test execution, the skills of the test engineers become better but the test cases may not have been updated to reflect the improvement in skills. Lastly, the lack of time for test design affects the quality of testing, as there could be missing perspectives.

Planned testing enables catching certain types of defects. Though planned tests help in boosting the tester's confidence, it is the tester's "intuition" that often finds critical defects. This is because none of the specifications can be considered complete to provide all the perspectives that are needed for testing. As we saw in domain testing in Chapter 4, sometimes testing without the specifications and making a domain expert test the product can bring in new perspectives and help unearth new types of defects. These perspectives evolve dynamically when testers think "out of the box." It is possible that some of the most critical perspectives may be missed in planned testing, which get identified by testers later. Hence, a tester's intuition plays a significant role. Furthermore, as mentioned earlier, the intuition and extra skills that a tester acquires as he or she gets better clarity of the product, is not reflected in the test cases that have already been designed.

Ad hoc testing attempts to bridge the above gaps. It is done to explore the undiscovered areas in the product by using intuition, previous experience in working with the product, expert knowledge of the platform or technology, and experience of testing a similar product. It is generally done to uncover defects that are not covered by planned testing.

Ad hoc testing does not make use of any of the test case design techniques like equivalence partitioning, boundary value analysis, and so on.

As we have seen in Chapter 1, the "pesticide paradox" explains the situation where the surviving pests in a farm create resistance to a particular pesticide. The situation required the farmer to use a different type of pesticide every time for the next crop cycle. Similarly, product defects get tuned to planned test cases and those test cases may not uncover defects in the next test cycle unless new perspectives are added. Therefore, planned test cases requires constant update, sometimes even on a daily basis, incorporating the new learnings. However, updating test cases very frequently may become (or be perceived as) a time consuming and tedious job. In such a situation ad hoc testing comes handy—to test those perspectives without requiring to formally and immediately update the test cases.

Figure 10.1 shows the various steps of ad hoc testing and illustrates the basic differences between ad hoc testing and planned testing. The coloured figure is available on page 472. One of the most fundamental differences between planned testing and ad hoc testing is that test execution and test report generation takes place *before* test case design in ad hoc testing. This testing gets its name by virtue of the fact that execution precedes design.

Figure 10.1

Ad hoc testing versus planned testing.

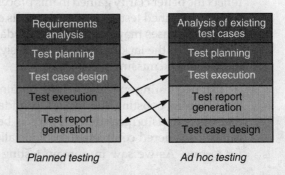

Requirements analysis		Analysis of existing test cases
Test planning	⟷	Test planning
Test case design		Test execution
Test execution		Test report generation
Test report generation		Test case design
Planned testing		*Ad hoc testing*

Since ad hoc testing brings in new perspectives, it is necessary to know what is already covered in the existing planned testing activities and also what changes in the product can cause changes in the testing functions.

Constant interaction with developers and other project team members may lead to a better understanding of the product from various perspectives. Since ad hoc tests require better understanding of the product, it is important to stay "connected." Project review meetings can be another place for picking up information on the product.

Many times, due to lack of communication, changes in requirements may not be informed to the test team. When the test engineer does not know the requirements changes, it is possible to miss a few tests. This may result in a few undetected defects. It is possible to unintentionally miss some perspectives due to the changed requirements. By the time the changed requirements are noticed, it may be too late to include them in the planned test cases.

Interaction with developers and other team members may help in getting only a set of perspectives. Sometimes such an interaction may bias the people in the testing team. They may get carried away by what developers and other team members say. Hence, it is important to constantly question the test cases and also interact with people outside the organization (for example, customers), to find different ways of using the product and use them in ad hoc testing.

We have been referring to the earlier testing activities as "planned testing." This does not mean ad hoc testing is an unplanned activity. Ad hoc testing is a planned activity; only the test cases are not documented to start with. Ad hoc testing can be performed on a product at any time, but the returns from ad hoc testing are more if they are run after running planned test cases. Ad hoc testing can be planned in one of two ways.

1. After a certain number of planned test cases are executed. In this case, the product is likely to be in a better shape and thus newer perspectives and defects can be uncovered. Since ad hoc testing does not require all the test cases to be documented immediately, this provides an opportunity to catch multiple missing perspectives with minimal time delay.

2. Prior to planned testing. This will enable gaining better clarity on requirements and assessing the quality of the product upfront.

The objective in either case should be to plan in such a way that ad hoc testing supplements and complements the other testing activities to uncover new perspectives with minimal time delay.

It has been mentioned that ad hoc testing does not require the test cases to be documented. This is applicable only for the test execution phase. After test execution, ad hoc testing requires all the perspectives that were tested to be documented as a set of test cases. These test cases will become part of the planned test execution for the next cycle. Following this method ensures two things: First, the perspectives gained in one round of ad hoc testing are formally captured and not lost. Second, the subsequent rounds of ad hoc testing bring in new perspectives, without repeating the same things. This ensures that ad hoc testing is intuitive every time. Obviously, if the same perspectives are covered again and again, then it is not ad hoc testing at all.

Ad hoc testing can be used to switch the context of software usage frequently to cover more functionality in less time. For example, instead of testing a given functionality end-to-end, ad hoc testing may cause a tester to jump across different functionalities and different screens. This is what is called "random sampling test." This testing involves using the features of the software randomly in different components, without worrying about what features are to be tested and their coverage in each component. Since this technique simulates the behavior of monkeys jumping from one tree to another in search of (hopefully!) a better fruit, assuming that all the fruit on a given tree are similar, this is also called *"monkey testing."*

While it has been mentioned above that ad hoc testing is normally performed in conjunction with planned testing, it raises the question of what is the appropriate effort distribution between planned and ad hoc test efforts. Relying entirely on regular test cases or relying entirely on ad hoc testing is not a good idea. A judicious combination of the two (say, 95% effort in regular testing and 5% on ad hoc testing, if requirements are fairly stable and clear) usually proves more effective than relying exclusively on one or the other. In situations where the requirements are not clear and missing, the ad hoc testing effort increases correspondingly.

> Testing done without using any formal testing technique is called ad hoc testing.

Ad hoc testing is done as a confidence measure just before the release, to ensure there are no areas that got missed out in testing. Ad hoc testing can involve looking at areas that were tested by regular testing and focus on areas that were missed in a planned way. It is still called ad hoc testing as the test cases are not documented.

Although there are many advantages in ad hoc testing, there are also a few drawbacks. Some of these disadvantages and their resolution are discussed in Table 10.1.

Ad hoc testing is applicable for all testing phases. It is performed during unit testing to improve requirements clarity, identify missing code and to detect defects early. It is performed during component and integration test phases to uncover defects not caught earlier by planned test cases. During the system and acceptance test phases, ad hoc testing is performed to gain confidence in the product and to catch costly defects that may have been missed.

Table 10.1 Drawbacks of ad hoc testing and their resolution.

Drawback	Possible resolution
Difficult to ensure that the learnings gleaned in ad hoc testing are used in future	• Document ad hoc tests after test completion
Large number of defects found in ad hoc testing	• Schedule a meeting to discuss defect impacts • Improve the test cases for planned testing
Lack of comfort on coverage of ad hoc testing	• When producing test reports combine planned test and ad hoc test • Plan for additional planned test and ad hoc test cycles
Difficult to track the exact steps	• Write detailed defect reports in a step-by-step manner • Document ad hoc tests after test execution
Lack of data for metrics analysis	• Plan the metrics collection for both planned tests and ad hoc tests

There are different variants and types of testing under ad hoc testing. They are described in the following sections.

10.2 BUDDY TESTING

This type of testing uses the "buddy system" practice wherein two team members are identified as *buddies*. The buddies mutually help each other, with a common goal of identifying defects early and correcting them.

A developer and a tester usually become buddies. It may be advantageous to team up people with good working relationship as buddies to overcome any apprehensions. On the other hand, if this is mapped to a complete agreement of views and approaches between the buddies, the diversity required between the two may not be achieved. This may make buddy testing less effective. Buddying people with good working relationships yet having diverse backgrounds is a kind of a safety measure that improves the chances of detecting errors in the program very early.

Buddies should not feel mutually threatened or get a feeling of insecurity during buddy testing. They are trained (if required) on the philosophy and objective of buddy training (that is, to find and correct defects in the product early). They also should be made to appreciate that they have a responsibility to one another. They also have to agree on the modalities and the terms of working before actually starting the testing work. They stay close together to be able to follow the agreed plan.

The code is unit tested to ensure what it is supposed to do before buddy testing starts. After the code is successfully tested through unit testing the developer approaches the testing buddy. Starting buddy testing before completing unit testing may result in a lengthy review session for the buddy on a code that may not meet specified requirements. This in turn may erode the confidence of the buddy and cause unnecessary rework.

The buddy can check for compliance to coding standards, appropriate variable definitions, missing code, sufficient inline code documentation, error checking, and so on. Buddy testing uses both white box and black box testing approaches. The buddy, after testing, generates specific review comments and points out specific defects. These are passed on to the developer. The more specific the feedback, the easier it is for the developer to fix the defects. The buddy may also suggest ideas to fix the code when pointing out an error in the work product.

The developer reviews the comments and, if the buddies agree, the appropriate changes are implemented. Or else both of them discuss the comments and come to a conclusion. While arriving at the conclusions and action items, it is necessary not to take an egoistic or personal view of the defects and review comments. That is why a good personal chemistry between the buddies is essential for the success of buddy testing.

A buddy test may help avoid errors of omission, misunderstanding, and miscommunication by providing varied perspectives or interactive exchanges between the buddies. Buddy testing not only helps in finding errors in the code but also helps the tester to understand how the code is written and provides clarity on specifications. It helps the tester, who worked as a buddy, to come out with a better testing strategy for a subsequent planned testing.

> A developer and tester working as buddies to help each other on testing and in understanding the specifications is called buddy testing.

Buddy testing is normally done at the unit test phase, where there are both coding and testing activities. It is done for new or critical modules in the product where the specification is not clear to buddies who perform different roles as developer and tester.

10.3   PAIR TESTING

For this type of testing, two testers pair up to test a product's feature on the same machine. The objective of this exercise is to maximize the exchange of ideas between the two testers. When one person is executing the tests, the other person takes notes. The other person suggests an idea or helps in providing additional perspectives.

It may not be mandatory for one person to stick one role continuously for an entire session. They can swap roles of "tester" and "scribe" during a session. They can mutually decide on the modus operandi. One person can pair with multiple persons during a day at various points of time for testing. Pair testing is usually a focused session for about an hour or two. During this session, the pair is given a specific area to focus and test. It is up to the pair to decide on the different ways of testing this functionality.

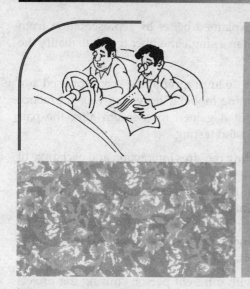

Let us take an example of two people traveling in a car in a new area to find a place, with one person driving the car and another person navigating with the help of a map.

In the above example, finding the new place (like finding defects in the unexplored area of the product) becomes easier as there are two people putting their heads together with specific roles such as navagation and driving assigned between them.

> Pair testing is testing done by two testers working simultaneously on the same machine to find defects in the product.

Pair testing takes advantage of the concept as explained in the above example. The presence of one senior member can also help in pairing. This can cut down on the time spent on the learning curve of the product. Also, it enables better training to be given to the team member. The impact of the requirements can be fully understood and explained to the less experienced individual. As can be inferred from the above discussion, the objective of pair testing is to identify defects by exchange of ideas. It may prove effective when two members work very well together and share a good understanding.

Pair testing can be done during any phase of testing. It encourages idea generation right from the requirements analysis phase, taking it forward to the design, coding, and testing phases. Testers can pair together during the coding phase to generate various ideas to test the code and various components. After completion of component testing, during integration, testers can be paired to test the interfaces together. Pair testing during system testing ensures that product level defects are found and addressed. Defect reproduction becomes easy in pair testing as both testers can discuss and produce the steps for reproduction.

When the product is in a new domain and not many people have the desired domain knowledge, pair testing is useful. Pair testing helps in getting feedback on their abilities from each other. This testing can be used to coach the inexperienced members in the team by pairing them with experienced testers. It may be difficult to provide training to all the members when the project schedules are very tight. Pair testing can resolve this issue by providing constant, continuous guidance to new members from the more experienced one.

Whenever planned testing does not uncover critical defects, the product is tested further to explore latent defects. Pair testing can track those elusive defects that are not caught by a single person testing. A defect found during such pair testing may be explained better by representation from two members. This may be better than a single member trying to justify the defect and its context.

Pair testing is an extension of the "pair programming" concept used as a technique in the extreme programming model. Pair testing was in practice much before pair programming but it gained momentum after the pair concept was proven for both coding and testing.

As we have seen earlier, pair testing requires interaction and exchange of ideas between two individuals. True to the dictum that two heads are better than one, there is a higher chance of significant defects getting reported early on. This enables fixing of such critical defects early in the project. Most often the pair finds a defect together. During such situations, an understanding of the requirements or product's functionality between the two helps in not reporting defects that are not important.

Since the team members pair with different persons during the project life cycle, the entire project team can have a good understanding of each other. In addition to making the knowledge of the different components more widespread across the team, this also fosters better teamwork. Project status meetings and team meetings may now have a new meaning since everyone is focused on the entire product delivery (as against attitudes such as "this is *my* module, *my* program, *my* test case/test plan").

10.3.1　Situations When Pair Testing Becomes Ineffective

Having discussed the advantages, there are a few situations when it may not be advisable to do pair testing.

During pairing, teaming up individual high performers may lead to problems. It may be possible that during the course of the session, one person takes the lead and other has a laidback attitude. This may not produce the desired results. In case the pair of individuals in the team are ones who do not try to understand and respect each other, pair testing may lead to frustration and domination.

When one member is working on the computer and the other is playing the role of a scribe, if their speed of understanding and execution does not match, it may result in loss of attention. It may become difficult to catch up at a later stage. Pair testing may result in delays (if not properly planned) due to the time spent on interactions with the testers.

Sometimes pairing up juniors with experienced members may result in the former doing tasks that the senior may not want to do. At the end of the session, there is no accountability on who is responsible for steering the work, providing directions, and delivering of results.

10.4   EXPLORATORY TESTING

Another technique to find defects in ad hoc testing is to keep exploring the product, covering more depth and breadth. Exploratory testing tries to do that with specific objectives, tasks, and plans. Exploratory testing can be done during any phase of testing.

Exploratory testers may execute their tests based on their past experiences in testing a similar product, or a product of similar domain, or a product in a technology area. They also leverage their past experience of finding defects in the previous product release and check if the same problems persist in the current version.

A developer's knowledge of a similar technology can help in the unit testing phase to explore the limitations or the constraints imposed by that technology. Exploratory testing can be used to test software that is untested, unknown, or unstable. It is used when it is not obvious what the next test should be and/or when we want to go beyond the obvious tests. Exploring can happen not only for functionality but also for different environments, configuration parameters, test data, and so on.

Since there is large creative element to exploratory testing, similar test cases may result in different kinds of defects when done by two different individuals.

10.4.1   Exploratory Testing Techniques

There are many ways of doing exploratory testing. Often, some common techniques are used without realizing that such a technique is being used.

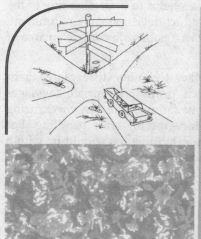

Let us take an example of someone driving a car to a place in a new area without a map. The person driving the car will use various common techniques to reach the place, such as

❋   Getting a map of the area

❋   Traveling in some random direction to figure out the place

❋   Calling up and asking a friend for the route

❋   Asking for directions by going to a nearby gas station

The same analogy can be extended to exploratory testing. As shown in the Figure 10.2, there are several ways to perform exploratory testing.

Figure 10.2

Exploratory test
techniques.

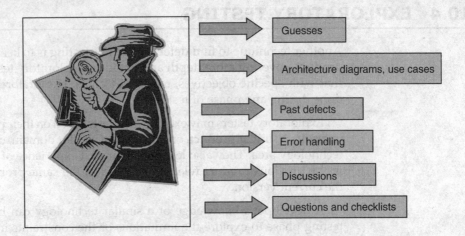

Guesses

Architecture diagrams, use cases

Past defects

Error handling

Discussions

Questions and checklists

Guesses are used to find the part of the program that is likely to have
more errors. Previous experience on working with a similar product or
software or technology helps in guessing. This is because the tester would
have already faced situations to test a similar product or software. Those
tests from guesses are used on the product to check for similar defects.

A second technique for exploration is the usage of *architecture diagrams*
and *use cases*. Architecture diagrams depict the interactions and relationships
between different components and modules. Use cases give an insight of the
product's usage from the end user's perspective. A use case explains a set of
business events, the input required, people involved in those events and the
expected output. Exploration technique may use these diagrams and use
cases to test the product.

A third technique for exploring is based on the *study of past defects*. Studying
the defects reported in the previous releases helps in understanding of the
error prone functionality/modules in a product development environment.
Defect reports of the previous releases act as a pointer to explore an area of
the product further.

Error handling in the product is another technique to explore. Error
handling is a portion of the code which prints appropriate messages
or provides appropriate actions in case of failures. We can check using
exploratory tests for various scenarios for graceful error handling. For
example, in the case of a catastrophic error, termination should be with a
meaningful error message. In case of an action by the user that is invalid or
unexpected, the system may misbehave. Error handling provides a message
or corrective action in such situations. Tests can be performed to simulate
such situations to ensure that the product's code takes care of this aspect.

A fifth exploratory test technique is based on the understanding of
the product from *discussions*. Exploration may be planned based on the
understanding of the system during project discussions or meetings.
Plenty of information can be picked up during these meetings regarding

implementation of different requirements for the product. They can be noted and used while testing. Information can also be noted from various presentations of the product implementation such as architecture and design presentations, or even presentations made to customers.

The last technique uses *questionnaires and checklists* to perform the exploration. Questions like "what, when, how, who and why" can provide leads to explore areas in the product. To understand the implementation of functionality in a product, open-ended questions like "what does this module do," "when is it being called or used," "how is the input processed," "who are the users of this module," and so on can be asked. Such questions will provide insights to what more can be tested.

For exploratory testing, a detailed plan can be created specifying the areas to be tested, objectives, and time and effort to be spent. Focus could also be put on the test environment and system configuration parameters.

During test execution, areas are identified where there may be more problems and they are probed further. The exploration technique can consider various combinations of inputs, environments, or system configuration parameters.

Inviting subject matter experts for exploratory testing may yield good results. A group of project team members (developers, test engineers, business representatives, technical writers) may be teamed up to test a particular module or functionality. With their varied backgrounds, exploration may find more defects. Whenever there are non-documented behavior or unanswered questions regarding the functionality of the product, exploring as a team will be more effective.

10.5 ITERATIVE TESTING

As we have seen in Chapter 2, the iterative (or spiral) model is where the requirements keep coming and the product is developed iteratively for each requirement. The testing associated for this process is called iterative testing.

One of the biggest challenges in testing for this model is in ensuring that all the requirements that are tested continue to work when a new requirement is given. Hence, iterative testing requires repetitive testing. When a new requirement or a defect fix is done, it may have an impact on other requirements that have already been tested. As the new requirements may involve a large number of changes at the product level, the majority of these tests are executed manually because automation in this case is very difficult. Iterative testing aims at testing the product for all requirements, irrespective of the phase they belong to in the spiral model.

Unlike the waterfall model, schedules, efforts involved are dependent on the features introduced in that iteration. Customers have a usable product at the end of every iteration. It is possible to stop the product development at any particular iteration and market the product as an independent entity. Since a product undergoes all the phases of the life cycle each time, errors due to omission or misunderstanding can also be corrected at regular intervals.

Customers and the management can notice the impact of defects and the product functionality at the end of each iteration. They can take a call to proceed to the next level or not, based on the observations made in the last iteration.

A test plan is created at the beginning of the first iteration and updated for every subsequent iteration. This can broadly define the type and scope of testing to be done for each of the iterations. This is because the product goes through a series of iterations and the testing time for the later iterations increases substantially. Also, some type of tests that are performed in later iterations may not be possible to perform during earlier iterations. For example, performance or load testing may come under the scope of testing only during the last few iterations when the product becomes complete. Hence test plan preparation becomes an important activity during the beginning phase. It may help to get concurrence from the different groups on the test plan prepared so that everyone is in sync. This document gets updated after each iteration since the scope of testing, type of testing, and the effort involved vary (more details on test planning in Chapter 15 of the book).

Developers create unit test cases to ensure that the program developed goes through complete testing. Unit test cases are also generated from black box perspective to more completely test the product. After each iteration, unit test cases are added, edited, or deleted to keep up with the revised requirement for the current phase.

Regression tests may be repeated at least every alternate iteration (if not every iteration) so that the current functionality is preserved. Since iterative testing involves repetitive test execution of tests that were run for the previous iterations, it becomes a tiresome exercise for the testers. In order

Let us take an example of a person driving without a route map, trying to count the number of restaurants in an area. When he reaches the multiway junction, he may take one road at a time and search for restaurants on that road. Then he can go back to the multiway junction and try a new road. He can continue doing this till all the roads have been explored for counting the restaurants.

to avoid the monotony and to increase test efficiency, tests that need to be carried forward to all the iterations may be automated, wherever possible.

The iterative model thus focuses on delivering the product in small increments in short, regular intervals. One issue that may crop up for the team is the co-ordination of defect fixes. A defect found in one iteration may be fixed in the same build or carried forward, based on the priority decided by the customer. Assume that a defect was found in the second iteration and was not fixed until the fifth. There is a possibility that the defect may no longer be valid or could have become void due to revised requirements during the third, fourth, and fifth iterations. Another possibility is that a functionality that worked during the third iteration may fail during the fifth iteration. Hence, testing efforts increase as the iterations increase.

In the above example, counting the number of restaurants starts from the first road visited. The results of the search can be published at the end of each iteration and released.

This is the same concept that is used in iterative testing to develop the product for each incoming requirement and delivering in small increments. Agile and extreme testing, the next section, makes use of some concepts of the iterative model. The overlap in the content between this model and agile is intentional.

10.6 AGILE AND EXTREME TESTING

Call attendant: Our process requires the person for whom the certificate is issued to come and sign the form.

Caller: I understand your process, but I am asking you for a death certificate of my grandfather.

Agile and extreme (XP) models take the processes to the extreme to ensure that customer requirements are met in a timely manner. In this model, customers partner with the project teams to go step by step in bringing the project to completion in a phased manner. The customer becomes part of the project team so as to clarify any doubts/questions.

Agile and XP methodology emphasizes the involvement of the entire team, and their interactions with each other, to produce a workable software that can satisfy a given set of features. As a result of such interactions, all ideas are exchanged. Software is delivered as small releases, with features being introduced in increments. As the changes are introduced incrementally, responding to the changes becomes very easy.

Agile testing has a rather radical change in the testing arena where the team no longer works as a "group of testers." Test engineers no longer need to send test documents and defect reports and wait for inputs from the other members in the project. When testers pair with developers, they may concentrate on the program's functionality from a technology perspective. While when they pair with customers, they act like a subject matter expert on the product. Testers form a bridge between the customers (who know the business) and the developers (who know the technology) to explain their different perspectives. Testers thus become the essential glue that brings together the customer perspectives of product requirements and developer perspectives of technology and implementation.

A typical XP project day starts with a meeting called the *stand up meeting*. At the start of each day, the team meets to decide on the plan of action for the day. During this meeting, the team brings up any clarifications or concerns. These are discussed and resolved. The entire team gets a consistent view of what each team member is working on. Testers present to the project team the progress of the project based on the test results. Other points of discussion could be missing requirements or overshooting of estimates due to an issue or time spent on various activities the previous day. The stand up meetings being daily meetings enable quick reactions to changes.

Even though the roles of testers and developers are presented as though they are different, in the XP model there is no hard boundary between their roles. People cross boundaries and perform different roles in XP model. The high degree of communication and teamwork makes this transition possible.

10.6.1   XP Work Flow

There are different steps involved in following the XP methodology. This section presents the process flow for a XP product release. The different activities involved in XP work flow are as follows.

1. Develop user stories
2. Prepare acceptance test cases
3. Code
4. Test
5. Refactor
6. Delivery

The XP work flow is depicted in Figure 10.3.

Figure 10.3

XP work flow.

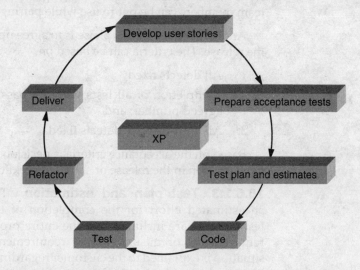

10.6.1.1 Develop and understand user story

Customer requirements in XP projects are given as *story lines*. These story lines are short sentences that describe a feature or a functionality to be developed. They are put up on small cards called as "index cards."

During story line discussion, test engineers prepare a list of questions on the stories to make it complete and understood by all present. Notes are taken on the answers provided, they may be used while preparing acceptance test cases.

Whenever there are requests for performance or load testing, a separate story line might help in providing details of the requirements for those tests.

10.6.1.2 Prepare acceptance tests

The next step is to prepare *acceptance tests*, based on the user stories understood. Test engineers sit with customers and develop acceptance test cases. In some situations, customers can themselves prepare acceptance test cases. Test data for acceptance tests can be given by customers to match production data. Acceptance tests can include test scenarios to cover the system end-to-end. Test engineers may present their analysis of the requirements to the customer. They get added to the acceptance test cases. Testers can team up with customers to develop cases with negative scenarios also.

Developers can review these test cases so that their perspective on the implementation of these stories is known. Customers review and give their consent to the acceptance test cases. Based on their feedback, acceptance tests are fine-tuned. Once these cases are baselined, they act as a reference point for everyone regarding requirements for that release. These test cases are shared with everyone in the team.

During this exchange-of-ideas session, testers pick up a lot of information from the customers. The knowledge gained from interaction with various team members can be put to use while pairing with developers.

Another activity of this phase is to agree upon the acceptance criteria for the release. The criteria can be based on

1. All defects fixed;
2. Completion of all tests with x% pass rate, where x is a mutually agreed number; and
3. All high-priority defects fixed.

Based on the acceptance criteria, a decision is taken whether to go for the next iteration in the release or stop the workflow.

10.6.1.3 Test plan and estimation The next step is to prepare an estimated effort for the completion of this exercise. Efforts for the testing tasks are included into the entire project effort. In case of missed requirements or misunderstood requirements after the estimation, the situation is explained to the customer regarding additional efforts involved. The customer may decide either to pass on the missed requirements to the next iteration or release. Alternatively, he or she may approve including these requirements into the current iteration, while approving additional effort for the current release.

10.6.1.4 Code The third step in this process is to start the *coding*. But before the start of coding, test engineers work with the developers to prepare unit test cases. Test plan and test cases are developed based on discussions and interactions with the different groups. Unit test cases are revisited after the completion of an iteration due to revised requirements. The code is written, based on unit test cases and not based on specifications alone.

10.6.1.5 Test Once developers complete the coding, test cases are executed. Test results are documented and defects found in the iteration are tracked. Whenever defects are being fixed, testers pair up with developers to work on the defect fixes. Test status is discussed in the stand up meeting, where detailed findings on defect metrics are presented. Defect metrics are more oriented towards the functionality that works and the functionality that needs to be focused on rather than on the number of defects.

Test cases are updated based on the revised requirements after each iteration. They may be deleted, edited, or newly included. Test engineers can work on testing the performance, stress, installation, and load testing when required. Regression tests can be run to verify that the functionality of the previous iterations works in this iteration.

10.6.1.6 Refactor During the different iterations within a small release, requirements and changing priorities are revised. In order to meet such changes, *refactoring* is required. Refactor is a method of correcting whatever work product exists to reflect the current changes. During this phase, test cases may need to be added, modified, or deleted. It may be helpful to involve the customer while refactoring test cases.

10.6.1.7 Automate While the developers are working on code fixes for the changed requirements, or defects fixes, testers can focus on the tests that can be automated so that they can be run in the next iteration. This would reduce the test execution effort significantly. An appropriate automation strategy that works for the user story given for that release may need to be identified.

10.6.1.8 Accepted and delivered The customer runs acceptance tests (with or without a tester) and notes down the results. Based on the test results, it may be decided to develop new stories for the next iteration or release.

As mentioned above, acceptance is decided on the basis of the acceptance criteria agreed upon at the beginning of the project. Defects that remain and if they are non-critical may get into the next iteration. There may be a few unresolved non-critical defects that can go to next iteration, based on the effort involved in fixing them. The customer approves all unresolved defects from the current iteration.

10.6.2 Summary with an Example

Let us take an example of automobile manufacturing. Traditionally, an automobile has four wheels, a steering wheel, brake, a pedal to accelerate the car, and a transmission system. These are the basic features of any automobile. Over the years, several new features have been introduced in an incremental way, but the basic features and purpose of those features do not change much. However, every manufacturer releases new models many times in a year with new features.

These frequent releases make the customers happy and they keep upgrading their cars. Thus the automobile industry is always growing and improving.

Technically, it may be easier to drive the car by using a joystick, but customers are used to driving the car using the steering wheel. Importance is given only to those requirements that the customers ask for.

The incremental requirements for the car are always obtained from the customers, using feedback mechanisms. Customers test them and they are involved in the development of new features.

Extreme programming and testing uses the concept from the above example to make releases frequently and in a controlled way by involving customers. Small adjustments are made in the requirements and in the software to reduce cost, time, and effort. The policies/concepts that are followed in extreme programming and testing are as follows.

1. Cross boundaries—developers and testers cross boundaries to perform various roles.
2. Make incremental changes—both product and process evolves in an incremental way.
3. Travel light—least overhead possible for development and testing.
4. Communicate—more focus on communication.
5. Write tests before code—unit tests and acceptance tests are written before the coding and testing activities respectively. All unit tests should run 100% all the time. Write code from test cases.
6. Make frequent small releases.
7. Involve customers all the time.

10.7   DEFECT SEEDING

Error seeding is also known as *bebugging*. It acts as a reliability measure for the release of the product.

Usually one group of members in the project injects the defects while an other group tests to remove them. The purpose of this exercise is while finding the known seeded defects, the unseeded/unearthed defects may also be uncovered. Defects that are seeded are similar to real defects. Therefore, they are not very obvious and easy to detect.

Defects that can be seeded may vary from severe or critical defects to cosmetic errors. This is because this (defect seeding) may be used as a predictor of the percentage of defect types and to make it difficult for the inspecting team to distinguish seeded defects from the actual ones.

> Defect seeding is a method of intentionally introducing defects into a product to check the rate of its detection and residual defects.

Defect seeding may act as a guide to check the efficiency of the inspection or testing process. It serves as a confidence measure to know the percentage of defect removal rates. It acts as a measure to estimate the number of defects yet to be discovered in the system.

For example, assume that 20 defects that range from critical to cosmetic errors are seeded on a product. Suppose when the test team completes testing, it has found 12 seeded defects and 25 original defects. The total number of defects that may be latent with the product is calculated as follows.

$$\text{Total latent defects} = (\text{Defects seeded} / \text{Defects seeded found}) * \text{Original defects found}$$

So, the number of estimated defects, based on the above example = $(20/12)*25 = 41.67$

Based on the above calculations, the number of estimated defects yet to be found is 42.

When a group knows that there are seeded defects in the system, it acts as a challenge for them to find as many of them as possible. It adds new energy into their testing. In case of manual testing, defects are seeded before the start of the testing process. When the tests are automated, defects can be seeded any time.

It may be useful to look at the following issues on defect seeding as well.

1. Care should be taken during the defect seeding process to ensure that all the seeded defects are removed before the release of the product.

2. The code should be written in such a way that the errors introduced can be identified easily. Minimum number of lines should be added to seed defects so that the effort involved in removal becomes reduced.

3. It is necessary to estimate the efforts required to clean up the seeded defects along with the effort for identification. Effort may also be needed to fix the real defects found due to the injection of some defects.

It may be worthwhile to note injecting defects based on an existing defect may not yield the desired results. That is, the developers would have taken care of such defects and fixed them in earlier releases.

It may not be possible to inject requirements defects (such as incomplete or missing requirements). Whereas, we observe that many a times, requirements defects form a major category of defects. This defect seeding may not be effective for this type of defect.

10.8 CONCLUSION

In this chapter, we have seen different methods of ad hoc testing. Table 10.2 summarizes the scenarios under which each of these techniques will be useful.

Table 10.2 Methods and effectiveness of ad hoc testing techniques.

When you want to ...	The most effective ad hoc testing technique to follow
Randomly test the product after all planned test cases are done	Monkey testing
Capture the programmatic errors early by developers and testers working together	Buddy testing
Test the new product/domain/technology	Exploratory testing
Leverage on the experience of senior testers and to exploit the ideas of newcomers	Pair testing
Deal with changing requirements	Iterative testing
Make frequent releases with customer involvement in product development	Agile/extreme testing
Get an approximate idea of the effectiveness of the testing process	Defect seeding

REFERENCES

Ad hoc testing is widely performed but has only very less documentation available. Iterative programming model and agile methodologies follow good number of ad hoc testing approaches. [MARI-2001] is a good place to start with pair testing and [BACH-2003] explains the exploratory testing in detail.

PROBLEMS AND EXERCISES

1. How do ad hoc test cases move into planned test cases over time?
2. Can the ad hoc test cases be white box tests? If so, identify the conditions under which this will be useful
3. At which phase of testing is buddy testing likely to capture most defects? Why?
4. What skills are required to perform monkey testing?

5. We described buddy testing and pair testing as two types of ad hoc tests. Describe how you could combine the two for even more effectiveness.

6. In each of the following cases, which of the ad hoc testing methods discussed in the book will be most appropriate?

   a. A small organization where testers and developers work closely together

   b. Where you want to develop awareness of testing of given modules amongst multiple testers

   c. A product evolving in multiple releases, features being iteratively added from one release to another

   d. A new breakthrough product is being developed and tested

Part **THREE**

Select Topics in Specialized Testing

This part of the book discusses two specialized aspects of testing. Chapter 11 discusses testing of object oriented systems. We discuss here how the types of tests discussed in the previous parts have to be adapted to fit into the needs of object oriented systems. The other chapter in this part, Chapter 12, discusses usability and accessibility testing. This is becoming increasingly important to meet the nebulous user interface expectations of users and also because legal frameworks are demanding that products be fit for use by people with physical challenges.

Testing of Object-Oriented Systems

CHAPTER 11

In this chapter—

- ✓ Introduction
- ✓ Primer on object-oriented software
- ✓ Differences in OO testing

11.1   INTRODUCTION

In the previous chapters, we have considered the various phases and types of testing. The tools, techniques, and processes discussed encompass most types of software. In this chapter, we will address the adaptations of these to a specific type of software systems—Object-Oriented (OO) systems. We provide an introduction to the terminology and concepts of OO in Section 11.2. This section is not intended to be an exhaustive coverage of OO concepts, rather just set the context quickly. This can be skipped by readers already familiar with OO terminology. Section 11.3 takes each of the basic OO concepts and addresses what needs to be done differently from the testing perspective.

11.2   PRIMER ON OBJECT-ORIENTED SOFTWARE

In this section, we will look at some of the basic concepts of OO systems that are relevant for testing. It is not the aim of this section to provide an exhaustive coverage of all OO concepts. Rather, the goal is to highlight the major concepts that cause some modifications and additions to the approach of testing that we have seen so far.

Earlier languages such as C—called procedure-oriented languages—are best characterized by the title of a book [WIRT-70] that came in the 1970s called *Algorithms + Data Structures = Programs*.

These programming languages were *algorithm-centric* in that they viewed the program as being driven by an algorithm that traced its execution from start to finish, as shown in Figure 11.1. *Data was an external entity* that was operated upon by the algorithm. Fundamentally, this class of programming languages was characterized by

1.   Data being considered as separate from the operations or program and
2.   Algorithm being the driver, with data being subsidiary to the algorithm.

Figure 11.1

Conventional algorithm centric programming languages.

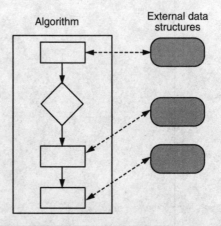

Algorithm   External data structures

From a testing perspective, testing a conventional procedure-oriented system therefore entailed testing the algorithm, treating data as secondary to testing the algorithm flow.

As against this, there are two fundamental paradigm shifts in OO languages and programming: First, the language is data- or *object-centric*. Second, as shown in Figure 11.2, there is no separation between data and the methods that operate on the data. *The data and the methods that operate on the data go together as one indivisible unit.*

Classes form the fundamental building blocks for OO systems. A class is a representation of a real-life object. Each class (or the real-life object it represents) is made up of *attributes* or *variables* and *methods* that operate on the variables. For example, a real-life object called a rectangle is characterized by two attributes, length and breadth. Area and perimeter are two of the operations or methods that can be performed on the rectangle object. The variables and the methods together define a `rectangle` class.

For the moment, let us not focus too much on the syntax and semantics of the code segment given below. A class definition like the below just provides a *template* that indicates the attributes and functions of an object. These attributes and methods (that is, the template) apply to all the *objects* of that class. A specific instance of the object is created by a new *instantiation*. Objects are the dynamic instantiation of a class. Multiple objects are instantiated using a given (static) class definition. Such specific instantiations are done using a *constructor* function. Most classes have a method (for example, called `new`) that is supposed to create a new instantiation of the class. After a new instantiation is created, the various methods of the class are invoked by

Figure 11.2

Object centric language—algorithm and data tightly coupled.

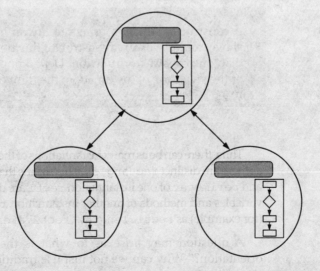

Example 11.1: Simple class definition

```
Class rectangle
  {
    private int length, breadth;
    public:
    new(float length, float breadth)
    {
        this->length = length;
        this->breadth = breadth;
    }
    float area()
    {
        return (length*breadth);
    }
    float perimeter()
    {
        return (2*(length+breadth));
    }
};
```

passing *messages* to the instantiated objects using the appropriate parameters, for example,

rect1.area() or rect2.new(l1,b1). In the case of the first example, the method called area does not require any parameters whereas in the second example, creating a new rectangle requires specification of its length and breadth.

Example 11.2: Constructor function

A constructor function brings to life an instance of the class. In the above example, **new** is a constructor function. Each class can have more than one constructor function. Depending on the parameters passed or the *signature* of the function, the right constructor is called.

Thus, there can be as many instantiations of the rectangle class in a program as there are distinct rectangles. This means that the length, breadth, area, and perimeter of one instantiation rect1 are different from the corresponding variables and methods of another instantiation rect2. Thus they are referred to (for example) as rect1.length, rect2.area, and so on.

A question may arise as to what is the big deal about this "object orientation?" Why can we not just use traditional programming languages and have two functions (or subroutines) called `area` and `perimeter` and call these from anywhere else in the code? The basic difference is that in an object-oriented language, the functions `area` and `perimeter` (and the variables `length` and `breadth`) do not have a life of existence without a specific instantiation `rect1` of the class `Rectangle`. In the case of a conventional programming language representing `Area` and `Perimeter` as two functions (and the variables `length` and `breadth` as parts of some global data structure) gives them existence independent of an instantiation of the object `Rectangle`. This may cause unpredictable results. For example, the variables `length` and `breadth` can be manipulated in unexpected (and incorrect) ways. Or, the functions `Perimeter` and `Area` may be called for inappropriate objects. In contrast, in an object-oriented language, since the variables and methods are specific to a particular instantiation of the object, it achieves better protection for the variables and methods.

Not all the data and not all the methods become publicly visible outside of the class. Some of the data and some of the methods are *encapsulated* within the class. This makes sure that the data and methods that are private to the implementation of the method is not accessible to the outside world. This increases the predictability of what transformations can happen to a data item. Also, the public methods provide the only operations that can be applied on the contents of the objects. This further minimizes the chances of any accidental or malicious changes to the contents of objects.

The methods are glued onto the object and do not stand out independently. Thus, the methods provide the *only* operations that can be done on the object. In other words, a user of the classes knows only the external interface of the calculation of area or perimeter, but has no details about the implementation of the methods. That is, the implementation of the methods is hidden from the user. This enables the person writing the methods to optimize the implementation without changing the external behavior. This is called *encapsulation*.

Both the methods and the variables (or data structures) that make up an object can be encapsulated. When variables are encapsulated, the only way to access the encapsulated variables are from within the object. Such *private* variables are not visible outside the object. This provides further protection against accidental modification of variables.

Different objects in real life have different traits that characterize each object. For example, while a rectangle requires two parameters (length and breadth) to characterize it, a square is characterized by just one value—its side. Similarly, a circle is also characterized by one value—its radius. But all these objects, despite their differences, also have some common characteristics—all these are plane figures and all these have two characteristics called perimeter (which measures the sum of the lengths of the object's boundaries) and area (which measures the plane area occupied by the figure). The specific ways in which area or perimeter is calculated varies from shape to shape. Thus, a general object (class) called

Example 11.3: Encapsulation

Encapsulation provides the right level of abstraction about the variables and methods to the outside world. In the example given below, the length and breadth (surrounded by ovals) are private variables, which means that they cannot be directly accessed from a calling program. The methods new, area, and perimeter (shown in rectangles) are public methods, in that they can be called from outside the class.

```
Class rectangle
    {
        private int length, breadth;

        public:

        new(float length, float breadth)

        {
            this->length = length;
            this->breadth = breadth;
        }
        float area()

        {
            return (length*breadth);
        }
        float perimeter()

        {
            return (2*(length+breadth));
        }
    };
```

plane objects has two attributes called perimeter and area that apply to all plane objects, even if the method of calculating the area and perimeter are different for different plane objects. A specific type of plane figure (for example, Rectangle) *inherits* these functions from the parent object (plane objects) and modifies them as needed to suit its specific needs. Similarly, another plane figure, circle, inherits the two functions and redefines them to suit its need (for example, perimeter = $2*\pi*r$ and area = $\pi*r^2$).

A major strength of OO systems lies in its ability to define new classes from existing classes, with some of the properties of the new class being

Example 11.4: Example to show inheritance

Inheritance enables the derivation of one class from another without losing sight of the common features. Rather than view `rectangle`, `circle`, and so on as unrelated shapes, the example below looks at these as derived from a class called **plane objects**. Regardless of the object, they all have attributes called area and `perimeter`.

```
Class plane_objects
{
   public float area();
   public float perimeter();
   Class rectangle
      {
         private float length, breadth;
         public:
            new(float length, float breadth)
            {
               this->length = length;
               this->breadth = breadth;
            }
            float area()
            {
               return (length*breadth);
            }
            float perimeter()
            {
               return (2*(length+breadth));
            }
      };
   Class circle
      {
         private float radius;
         public:
            new(float radius)
            {
               this->radius = radius;
            }
            float area()
            {
               return (22/7*radius*radius);
            }
            float perimeter()
            {
               return (2*22/7*radius);
            }
      };
}
```

similar to the existing class and some of the properties being different. This ability is called *inheritance*. The original class is called the parent class (or super-class) and the new class is called a child class (or derived class, or sub-class).

Inheritance allows objects (or at least parts of the object) to be reused. A derived class inherits the properties of the parent class—in fact, of all the parent classes, as there can be a hierarchy of classes. Thus, for those properties of the parent class that are inherited and used as is, the development and testing costs can be saved.

In the above example of an object `rectangle` being inherited from a general class called `plane figure`, we saw that the two derived classes (`rectangle` and `circle`) both have methods named `area` and `perimeter`. The specific inputs and logic of course is different for the methods in the `circle` class vis-à-vis those in the `rectangle` class, even though the names of the methods are the same. This means that even though the method names are the same for circle and rectangle, their actual meaning is dependent on the context of the class from which they are called. This property of two methods—in different classes—having the same name but performing different functions is called *polymorphism*.

As can be inferred from the above discussion, a method is to be associated with an object. One way to specify the object associated with the method is to specify it directly. For example, `rect1.area()`. In this case, it is easy to see which specific method is being called on what class. A more subtle variation is the case of *dynamic binding*.

Assume there is a variable called `ptr` and it is assigned the address of an object at run time. In this case, we will not be able to ascertain which method is being called by just looking at the code. The value of `ptr` is known only at run-time and hence defies any static analysis of the code for testing. We will revisit the challenges posed by polymorphism and dynamic binding for testing in the next section.

As mentioned earlier, procedure-oriented programming are algorithm-centric. Control flows from top to bottom of a "main" program, operating on data structures as they proceed. However, an object-oriented program integrates data and methods. Control flow takes place by passing *messages* across the different objects. A message is nothing but an invocation of a method of an instantiation of a class (i.e. an object) by passing appropriate parameters.

The paradigm shift from algorithm-centric, control-based approach of procedure-oriented programming to object-centric, message-based approach of object-oriented programming changes the way the programs are to be written or tested.

A second difference that the message-based approach brings in is that these messages can be passed to the instantiations only after the instantiation is created. Messages passed to objects that are not instantiated can result in run-time errors. Such errors are difficult to catch by the static testing methods we have discussed so far.

Yet another difference in control flow and testing of OO systems arises from exceptions. Each class may have a set of exceptions that are raised as error conditions, in response to erroneous messages and conditions. For example, when a parameter passed to an object is invalid, the object may raise an exception. Such transfer of control to the exception code may cause a break in the sequence of program flow, which needs to be tested. When a class is nested into other classes, there may be a nested exceptions. It is important for an object to follow the code corresponding to the right exception by going up the nesting hierarchy. When a programmer is not aware of the interaction between the multiple levels of nesting, these exceptions can produce undesirable results. It is important to test the various nesting of exceptions.

11.3   DIFFERENCES IN OO TESTING

We looked at various salient aspects of object-oriented programming in the previous section. We will now go into the details of how these aspects affect testing.

From a testing perspective, the implication is that testing an OO system should tightly integrate data and algorithms. The dichotomy between data and algorithm that drove the types of testing in procedure-oriented languages has to be broken.

Testing OO systems broadly covers the following topics.

1.   Unit testing a class
2.   Putting classes to work together (integration testing of classes)
3.   System testing
4.   Regression testing
5.   Tools for testing OO systems

11.3.1   Unit Testing a Set of Classes

As a class is built before it is "published" for use by others, it has to be tested to see if it is ready for use. Classes are the building blocks for an entire OO system. Just as the building blocks of a procedure-oriented system have to be unit tested individually before being put together, so also the classes have to be unit tested. In this section, we will see the special reasons why these building blocks should be unit tested even more thoroughly for OO and then look at the conventional methods that apply to OO systems and proceed to techniques and methods that are unique to OO systems.

11.3.1.1 Why classes have to be tested individually first   In the case of OO systems, it is even more important (than in the case of procedure-oriented systems) to unit test the building blocks (classes) thoroughly for the following reasons.

1. A class is intended for heavy reuse. A residual defect in a class can, therefore, potentially affect every instance of reuse.

2. Many defects get introduced at the time a class (that is, its attributes and methods) gets defined. A delay in catching these defects makes them go into the clients of these classes. Thus, the fix for the defect would have to be reflected in multiple places, giving rise to inconsistencies.

3. A class may have different features; different clients of the class may pick up different pieces of the class. No one single client may use all the pieces of the class. Thus, unless the class is tested as a unit first, there may be pieces of a class that may never get tested.

4. A class is a combination of data and methods. If the data and methods do not work in sync at a unit test level, it may cause defects that are potentially very difficult to narrow down later on.

5. Unlike procedural language building blocks, an OO system has special features like inheritance, which puts more "context" into the building blocks. Thus, unless the building blocks are thoroughly tested stand-alone, defects arising out of these contexts may surface, magnified many times, later in the cycle. We will see details of these later in the chapter.

11.3.1.2 Conventional methods that apply to testing classes   Some of the methods for unit testing that we have discussed earlier apply directly to testing classes. For example:

1. Every class has certain variables. The techniques of boundary value analysis and equivalence partitioning discussed in black box testing can be applied to make sure the most effective test data is used to find as many defects as possible.

2. As mentioned earlier, not all methods are exercised by all the clients, The methods of function coverage that were discussed in white box testing can be used to ensure that every method (function) is exercised.

3. Every class will have methods that have procedural logic. The techniques of condition coverage, branch coverage, code complexity, and so on that we discussed in white box testing can be used to make sure as many branches and conditions are covered as possible and to increase the maintainability of the code.

4. Since a class is meant to be instantiated multiple times by different clients, the various techniques of stress testing discussed in Chapter 6, System and Acceptance Testing, can be performed for early detection of stress-related problems such as memory leaks.

We had discussed state based testing in Chapter 4, Black Box Testing. This is especially useful for testing classes. Since a class is a combination of data and methods that operate on the data, in some cases, it can be visualized as an object going through different states. The messages that are passed to the class act as inputs to trigger the state transition. It is useful to capture this view of a class during the design phase so that testing can be more natural. Some of the criteria that can be used for testing are:

✠ Is every state reached at least once?

✠ Is every message (that is, input that causes a state transition) generated and tested?

✠ Is every state transition achieved at least once?

✠ Are illegal state transitions tested?

11.3.1.3 Special considerations for testing classes The above methods were the common ones applicable from procedure-oriented systems. Given the nature of objects that are instantiated by classes (that these objects have to be tested via message passing), how do we test these instantiations at the unit level?

In order to test an instantiated object, messages have to be passed to various methods. In what sequence does one pass the messages to the objects? One of the methods that is effective for this purpose is the *Alpha–Omega* method. This method works on the following principles.

1. Test the object through its life cycle from "birth to death" (that is, from instantiation to destruction). An instance gets instantiated by a constructor method; then the variables get set to their values. During the course of execution, the values may get modified and various methods executed. Finally, the instantiation is destroyed by a destructor method.

2. Test the simple methods first and then the more complex methods. Since the philosophy of building OO systems is to have a number of reusable objects, it is likely that the more complex methods will build upon the simpler methods. Thus, it makes sense to test the simpler methods first, before testing the more complex methods.

3. Test the methods from private through public methods. Private methods are methods that are not visible outside the object/class. Thus, these are the implementation-oriented methods, which deal with the logic of the method and are the building blocks of the entire system. Also, private methods are insulated from the callers (or clients). This reduces the dependencies in testing and gets the building blocks in a more robust state before they are used by clients.

4. Send a message to every method at least once. This ensures that every method is tested at least once.

The Alpha–Omega method achieves the above objective by the following steps.

1. Test the constructor methods first. Each class may get constructed by multiple constructor messages, based on its signatures. These are different ways of creating instances of the object. When there are multiple constructors, all the constructor methods should be tested individually.

2. Test the **get** methods or **accessor** methods. Accessor methods are those that retrieve the values of variables in an object for use by the calling programs. This ensures that the variables in the class definition are accessible by the appropriate methods.

3. Test the methods that modify the object variables. There are methods that test the contents of variables, methods that set/update the contents of variables, and methods that loop through the various variables. As can be inferred, these methods are increasingly complex, keeping in mind the principles laid down earlier.

4. Finally, the object has to be destroyed and when the object is destroyed, no further accidental access should be possible. Also, all the resources used by the object instantiation should be released. These tests conclude the lifetime of an instantiated object.

There are also other special challenges that are unique to testing classes that do not arise for unit testing procedure-oriented systems. We will discuss these now.

As discussed earlier, encapsulation is meant to hide the details of a class from the clients of the class. While this is good from an implementation and usage perspective, it makes things difficult from a testing perspective, because the inside behavior of the encapsulated part is less visible to the tester. In the case of a procedure-oriented language, one can "get under the hood" of the implementation and get more visibility into the program behavior. Deprived of this flexibility, white box testing of classes with encapsulation becomes difficult.

As mentioned earlier, a class can actually be a part of a class hierarchy. A class can

1. Inherit certain variables and methods from its parent class;

2. Redefine certain variables and methods from its parent class; and

3. Define new variables and methods that are specific to it and not applicable to the parent.

Since a class is made up of all three of the above categories of variables and methods, strictly speaking, every new class will have to be tested for *all* the variables and methods. However, in reality, a more incremental method may be more effective and sufficient. When a class is introduced for the first time, all the variables and methods have to be tested fully, using the conventional unit testing means discussed. From then on, whenever a class is derived from a parent class, the following will have to be tested because they are appearing for the first time.

1. The changes made to the base class variables methods and attributes have to be tested again, as these have changed.

2. New variables and methods that have been introduced in an inherited class have to be tested afresh.

For the first case, that is, modified attributes, the existing test cases for the parent may or may not be reusable. In the plane figures examples discussed earlier, even when the area and perimeter of a circle are tested, it does not tell anything about the same methods for a rectangle, even though both are derived from the same parent class.

While it is obvious that any changes or additions to class attributes in a child class have to be independently tested, the question that is arises, what do we do about testing the attributes that are inherited from a parent and *not* changed by a child class? Strictly speaking, it should not be necessary to test these again, because in theory, these have not changed. However, given that these unchanged variables and methods could have undesirable side-effects when mixed with the changes, some selective re-testing of the (unmodified) parent class elements will also have to be done with a derived class. How does one decide which of the unchanged elements should be re-tested? Some possible choices are as follows.

1. Whenever an unmodified variable is referenced in a new or modified method, test cases for the unmodified variable can become a possible candidate for re-testing. This helps to find out any unintended use of the unmodified variable.

2. Whenever an unmodified method is called in a new or modified method, this unmodified method is a candidate for re-test. If the new or modified method does not yield the correct results, it may indicate that the unmodified method probably has to be redefined in the child class containing the new method. Alternatively, the original method may have to be generalized to be able to accommodate the requirements of the new child class.

The above method of testing all the changes or new additions thoroughly at the point of creation and selective re-testing of other unchanged attributes is called *incremental class testing*. Such an approach strives to balance the need for exhaustive testing with the risks associated with not testing something that has (apparently) not changed.

While inheritance is supposed to make it easier to define new objects in terms of existing ones, it also introduces a potential source of defect. Consider a class with several levels of nesting. The innermost class may have very little code but might inherit a lot of variables and methods from the classes higher up in the hierarchy. This means that there is a lot of context that makes up the child class and this context cannot be ascertained by looking at the class in question in isolation. This is similar to the case of using global variables in a procedure-oriented languages. Since a nested class may freely access its parent's methods and variables, tests for nested classes should necessarily have access to information about the parent classes.

There are two other forms of classes and inheritance that pose special challenges for testing—multiple inheritance and abstract classes.

The examples discussed so far have assumed that a child class can be derived from only one immediate parent class. Certain languages support what is called *multiple inheritance*—where a child class is derived from two parent classes, much as a human child derives its nature from the genes of both the parents. This property of multiple inheritance presents some interesting testing issues. For example, consider a child class A that is derived from its two parent classes P1 and P2. It is quite possible that both P1 and P2 will have variables and methods of the same name but performing different functions. Assume there is a method with name X in both P1 and P2 (performing different functions). When a child class is inherited from these two parent classes, the child class may

1. Use X from either P1 or P2, or
2. Modify X by itself, thus making the modified X as the default meaning for X, overriding in X from both P1 and P2.

The second case is similar to changed classes in single inheritance and therefore definitely needs to be tested. For the first case, X has not changed, but it may be considered as a candidate for re-testing. Given that the possibility of side-effects has doubled because of the multiple inheritance, there is a greater scope for defects in this case. Thus, from a testing perspective, multiple inheritance requires more thorough testing.

There are cases where a particular method with a published interface must exist for any redefinition of a class, but the specific implementation of the method is completely left to the implementer. For example, consider a method that sorts a given array of integers and returns the sorted list in another array. The interfaces to the sort routine are clearly defined—an input array of integers and an output array of integers. Such a method is called *virtual method*. A class that has a virtual method is called an *abstract class*. A virtual method has to be implemented afresh for every new child class inherited from the parent class.

What implications do abstract class and virtual functions pose for testing? An abstract class cannot be instantiated directly because it is not complete and only has placeholders for the virtual functions. A *concrete class* with no abstract functions has to be redefined from the abstract class and it is those instances of concrete classes that have to be tested. Since the same virtual function may be implemented differently for different concrete classes, test cases for the different implementations of an abstract class cannot, in general, be reused. However, the advantage that virtual functions and abstract classes bring to testing is that they provide definitions of the interfaces that the function should satisfy. This interface should be unchanged for different implementations. Thus, this interface provides a good starting point for testing the concrete classes.

11.3.2   Putting Classes to Work Together—Integration Testing

In all of the above discussion, we have taken testing at a class level. An OO system is not a collection of discrete objects or classes but these objects or classes should coexist, integrate, and communicate with another. Since OO systems are designed to be made up of a number of smaller components or classes that are meant to be reused (with necessary redefinitions), testing that classes work *together* becomes the next step, once the basic classes themselves are found to be tested thoroughly. More often than not, it is not an individual class that is tested individually as a unit, but a collection of related classes that always go together. This is not very different from procedure-oriented languages, where it may not always be a single source file, but a collection of related files performing related functions that is tested as a unit. In the case of OO systems, because of the emphasis on reuse and classes, testing this integration unit becomes crucial.

In the case of a procedure-oriented system, testing is done by giving different data to exercise the control flow path. The control flow path is determined by the functions called by the program, from start to finish. As has been discussed before, in an OO system, the way in which the various classes communicate with each other is through messages. A message of the format

```
<instance name>.<method name>.<variables>
```

calls the method of the specified name, in the named instance, or object (of the appropriate class) with the appropriate variables. Thus, it is not possible to describe the flow of testing by merely listing out the function names through which execution proceeds. In fact, the name of the method does not uniquely identify the control flow while testing an OO system. Methods with the same name perform different functions. As we saw earlier, this property by which the meaning of a function or an operator varies with context and the same operation behaves differently in different circumstances is called polymorphism. From a testing perspective, polymorphism is especially challenging because it defies the conventional definition of code coverage and static inspection of code. For example, if there are two classes called square and circle, both may have a method called area. Even though the function is called area in both cases, and even though both the functions accept only one parameter, the meaning of the parameter is different depending on the context of the method called (radius for a circle and side for a square). The behavior of the method is also entirely different for the two cases. Thus, if we have tested the method **area** for a square, it has no implication on the behavior of area of a circle. They have to be independently tested.

A variant of polymorphism called *dynamic binding* creates special challenges for testing. If, in the program code, we were to explicitly refer to `square.area` and `circle.area`, then it will be obvious to the tester that these are two different functions and hence have to be tested according to the context where each is being used. In dynamic binding, the specific class for which a message is intended is specified at run time. This is especially challenging to test in languages that allow the use of pointers (for example, C++). Assuming that the pointer to a specific object is stored in a pointer variable called `ptr`, then `ptr->area(i)` will resolve at run time to the method `area` of the appropriate object type pointed to by `ptr`. If `ptr` were to point to a `square` object, then the method invoked will be `square.area(i)` (and `i` is considered as the side of the square). If `ptr` points to a `circle` object, the methods invoked will be `circle.area(i)` (and `i` is considered as the radius of the circle). What this means is that typical white box testing strategies like code coverage will not be of much use in this case. In the above example, one can achieve code coverage of the line

`ptr->area(i)` with `ptr` pointing to a `square` object. But if `ptr` is not tested pointing to a `circle` object, it leaves that part of the code which calculates the area of a circle completely untested, even though the lines of code in the calling program have already been covered by tests.

In addition to addressing encapsulation and polymorphism, another question that arises is in what order do we put the classes together for testing? This question is similar to what was encountered in integration testing of procedure-oriented systems. The various methods of integration like top-down, bottom-up, big bang, and so on can all be applicable here. The extra points to be noted about integration testing OO systems are that

1. OO systems are inherently meant to be built out of small, reusable components. Hence integration testing will be even more critical for OO systems.

2. There is typically more parallelism in the development of the underlying components of OO systems; thus the need for frequent integration is higher.

3. Given the parallelism in development, the sequence of availability of the classes will have to be taken into consideration while performing integration testing. This would also require the design of stubs and harnesses to simulate the function of yet-unavailable classes.

11.3.3   System Testing and Interoperability of OO Systems

Object oriented systems are by design meant to be built using smaller reusable components (i.e. the classes). This heavy emphasis on reuse of existing building blocks makes system testing even more important for OO systems than for traditional systems. Some of the reasons for this added importance are:

1. A class may have different parts, not all of which are used at the same time. When different clients start using a class, they may be

using different parts of a class and this may introduce defects at a later (system testing) phase

2. Different classes may be combined together by a client and this combination may lead to new defects that are hitherto uncovered.

3. An instantiated object may not free all its allocated resource, thus causing memory leaks and such related problems, which will show up only in the system testing phase.

The different types of integration that we saw in Chapter 5 also apply to OO systems. It is important to ensure that the classes and objects interoperate and work together as a system. Since the complexity of interactions among the classes can be substantial, it is important to ensure that proper unit and component testing is done before attempting system testing. Thus, proper entry and exit criteria should be set for the various test phases before system testing so as to maximize the effectiveness of system testing.

11.3.4   Regression Testing of OO Systems

Taking the discussion of integration testing further, regression testing becomes very crucial for OO systems. As a result of the heavy reliance of OO systems on reusable components, changes to any one component could have potentially unintended side-effects on the clients that use the component. Hence, frequent integration and regression runs become very essential for testing OO systems. Also, because of the cascaded effects of changes resulting from properties like inheritance, it makes sense to catch the defects as early as possible.

11.3.5   Tools for Testing of OO Systems

There are several tools that aid in testing OO systems. Some of these are

1. Use cases
2. Class diagrams
3. Sequence diagrams
4. State charts

We will now look into the details of each of these.

11.3.5.1   Use cases   We have covered use cases in Chapter 4, on Black Box Testing. To recap, use cases represent the various tasks that a user will perform when interacting with the system. Use cases go into the details of the specific steps that the user will go through in accomplishing each task and the system responses for each steps. This fits in place for the object oriented paradigm, as the tasks and responses are akin to messages passed to the various objects.

11.3.5.2 Class diagrams Class diagrams represent the different entities and the relationship that exists among the entities. Since a class is a basic building block for an OO system, a class diagram builds upon the classes of a system. There are a number of parts in a class diagram. We list a few here that are important from the testing perspective.

A class diagram has the following elements.

Boxes Each rectangular box represents a class. The various elements that make up a class are shown in the compartments within the class rectangle.

Association It represents a relationship between two classes by a line. A relationship may be something like "every employee works in one and only department" or "an employee may participate in zero or more projects." Thus, an association can be 1–1, 1–many, many–1, and so on. The multiplicity factor for either side is shown on either side of the association line.

Generalization It represents child classes that are derived from parent classes, as discussed in inheritance earlier in the chapter.

A class diagram is useful for testing in several ways.

1. It identifies the elements of a class and hence enables the identification of the boundary value analysis, equivalence partitioning, and such tests.

2. The associations help in identifying tests for referential integrity constraints across classes.

3. Generalizations help in identifying class hierarchies and thus help in planning incremental class testing as and when new variables and methods are introduced in child classes.

11.3.5.3 Sequence diagrams We saw earlier that an OO system works by communicating messages across the various objects. A sequence diagram represents a sequence of messages passed among objects to accomplish a given application scenario or use case.

The objects that participate in a task or use case are listed horizontally. The lifetime of an object is represented by a vertical line from top to bottom. A dashed line on top represents object construction/activation, while an X in the end indicates destruction of the object.

The messages are represented by horizontal lines between two objects. There are different types of messages. They can be blocking or non-blocking. Some messages are passed conditionally. Like an IF statement in a programming language, a conditional message gets passed to different objects, based on certain Boolean conditions.

Time progresses as we go down from top to bottom in a sequence diagram.

A sequence diagram helps in testing by

1. Identifying temporal end-to-end messages.
2. Tracing the intermediate points in an end-to-end transaction, thereby enabling easier narrowing down of problems.
3. Providing for several typical message-calling sequences like blocking call, non-blocking call, and so on.

Sequence diagrams also have their limitations for testing—complex interactions become messy, if not impossible, to represent; dynamic binding cannot be represented easily.

11.3.5.4 Activity diagram While a sequence diagram looks at the sequence of messages, an activity diagram depicts the sequence of activities that take place. It is used for modeling a typical work flow in an application and brings out the elements of interaction between manual and automated processes. Since an activity diagram represents a sequence of activities, it is very similar to a flow chart and has parallels to most of the elements of a conventional flow chart.

The entire work flow is visualized as a set of action states, each action state representing an intermediate state of result that makes sense for the application. This is akin to a standard flow chart element of a sequence of steps with no conditional branching in between. Just as in conventional flow charts, decision boxes are diamond-shaped boxes, with each box having two exit paths (one when the Boolean condition in the decision is TRUE and the other when it is FALSE), only one of which will be chosen at run time. Since objects are the target for messages and cause for action, objects are also represented in an activity diagram. The activities are related to each other by control flows, with control flowing from the previous activity to the next, or a message flow, with a message being sent from one action state to an object. Since a decision or multiple control flows potentially cause multiple branches, they are synchronized later.

Given that an activity diagram represents control flow, its relevance for testing comes from

1. The ability to derive various paths through execution. Similar to the flow graph discussed in white box testing, an activity diagram can be used to arrive at the code complexity and independent paths through a program code.
2. Ability to identify the possible message flows between an activity and an object, thereby making the message-based testing discussed earlier more robust and effective.

11.3.5.5 State diagrams We already saw the usefulness of state transition diagrams earlier in this chapter. When an object can be modeled as a state machine, then the techniques of state-based testing, discussed in black box testing and earlier in this chapter, can be directly applied.

11.3.6 Summary

We have discussed in this chapter the concepts of OO systems as they pertain to testing. We have seen how the general techniques of testing discussed in earlier chapters can be adapted for OO testing. Table 11.1 below summarizes these discussions.

Table 11.1 Testing methods and tools for key OO concepts.

Key OO concept	Testing methods and tools
Object orientation	• Tests need to integrate data and methods more tightly
Unit testing of classes	• BVA, equivalence partitioning, and so on for testing variables • Code coverage methods for methods • Alpha–Omega method of exercising methods • Activity diagram for testing methods • State diagram for testing the states of a class • Stress testing to detect memory leaks and similar defects when a class is instantiated and destroyed multiple times
Encapsulation and inheritance	• Requires unit testing at class level and incremental class testing when encapsulating • Inheritance introduces extra context; each combination of different contexts has to be tested • Desk checking and static review is tougher because of the extra context
Abstract classes	• Requires re-testing for every new implementation of the abstract class
Polymorphism	• Each of the different methods of the same name should be tested separately • Maintainability of code may suffer
Dynamic binding	• Conventional code coverage has to modified to be applicable for dynamic binding • Possibility of unanticipated run time defects higher
Inter-object communication via messages	• Message sequencing • Sequence diagrams
Object reuse and parallel development of objects	• Needs more frequent integration tests and regression tests • Integration testing and unit testing are not as clearly separated as in the case of a procedure-oriented language • Errors in interfaces between objects likely to be more common in OO systems and hence needs through interface testing

REFERENCES

[BOOC-94] provides the required foundations to object orientation concepts. [BOOC-99] covers the various diagrams like collaboration diagram and also integrates these use cases, UML, and other key concepts into a unified process. [GRAH-94] is one of the sources for the methods for testing classes like Alpha–Omega method. [BIND-2000] provides a very comprehensive and detailed coverage of all the issues pertaining to testing object oriented systems.

PROBLEMS AND EXERCISES

1. The idea of not decoupling data and algorithms was given as a key differentiator between algorithm centric systems and object centric systems. What special challenges does this approach present from a testing perspective?

2. What role would test data generators play in testing object oriented systems?

3. In the example of plane figures given in the text, there was no redefinition of a method. Consider a case when a child class redefines a method of a parent class. What considerations would this introduce for testing?

4. "OO languages that do not support the use of pointers make testing easier"—comment on this statement

5. Consider a class that is nested five levels deep and the each level just redefines one method. What kind of problems do you anticipate in testing such classes and the instantiated objects?

6. Why do integration and system testing assume special importance for an object oriented system?

7. What are some of the differences in the approaches to regression testing that one can expect for object oriented systems vis-à-vis traditional/procedure-oriented systems?

Usability and Accessibility Testing

CHAPTER 12

In this chapter—

12.1 WHAT IS USABILITY TESTING?

Hit any key to continue!

Hit any key to abort!

Hit any key to retry!

Usability testing attempts to characterize the "look and feel" and usage aspects of a product, from the point of view of users. Most types of testing we have discussed are objective in nature. There is a debate whether usability testing really belongs to the realm of testing at all. Some of the factors that fuel this debate are as follows.

1. Usability and look-and-feel aspects are subjective in nature and cannot always be objectively measured

2. Perceptions of "good usability" varies from user to user. For example, while a system administrator or a developer would consider use of command line flags as good user interface, an end-user will want everything in terms of GUI elements such as menus, dialog boxes, and so on.

3. User interface can be construed as a design time activity. If a particular user interface does not meet the users' needs, it is really a problem with not gathering the right requirements or not translating the requirements into the right design.

For all the above reasons, there is a view that usability can only be validated and cannot be tested. Regardless of the semantics of whether usability is a testing activity or a validation activity, some of the characteristics of "usability testing" or "usability validation" are as follows.

1. Usability testing tests the product from the users' point of view. It encompasses a range of techniques for identifying how users actually interact with and use the product.

2. Usability testing is for checking the product to see if it is easy to use for the various categories of users.

3. Usability testing is a process to identify discrepancies between the user interface of the product and the human user requirements, in terms of the pleasantness and aesthetics aspects.

> The testing that validates the ease of use, speed, and aesthetics of the product from the user's point of view is called usability testing

If we combine all the above characterizations of the various factors that determine usability testing, then the common threads are

1. Ease of use
2. Speed
3. Pleasantness and aesthetics

Usability testing addresses these three aspects from the point of view of a user. Combining these characterizations, usability testing can be formally defined.

From the above definition it is easy to conclude that

1. Something that is easy for one user may not be easy for another user due to different types of users a product can have.
2. Something what is considered fast (interms of say, response time) by one user may be slow for another user as the machines used by them and the expectations of speed can be different.
3. Something that is considered beautiful by someone may look ugly to another.
4. A view expressed by one user of the product may not be the view of another.

For these reasons, usability remains subjective, as mentioned earlier. However, if a product can incorporate the different views and requirements of the entire user base, it can become a successful product. Throughout the industry, usability testing is gaining momentum as sensitivity towards usability in products is increasing and it is very difficult to sell a product that does not meet the usability requirements of the users. There are several standards (for example, accessibility guidelines), organizations, tools (for example, Microsoft Magnifier), and processes that try to remove the subjectivity and improve the objectivity of usability testing.

12.2 APPROACH TO USABILITY

When doing usability testing, certain human factors can be represented in a quantifiable way and can be tested objectively. The number of mouse clicks, number of sub-menus to navigate, number of keystrokes, number of commands to perform a task can all be measured and checked as a part of usability testing. Obviously, if there are too many mouse clicks or too many commands to execute a user task, then the product would not be considered easy to use.

Usability improvements sometimes can be very marginal but can give huge benefits, with the number of users for the product increasing. For example, when a Philips (or a star) screwdriver was invented, it saved only few milliseconds per operation to adjust the screwdriver to the angle of

Figure 12.1

Flat versus Philips
screwdriver.

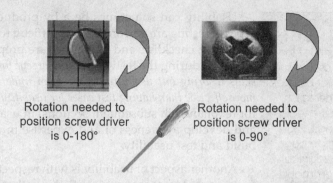

Rotation needed to
position screw driver
is 0-180°

Rotation needed to
position screw driver
is 0-90°

the screw compared to a "flat" screwdriver. See Figure 12.1. However, its repeated use by multiple users saved several person years of effort. That's why marginal usability improvements should not be ignored. Something marginal to the product organization may mean big usability advantage to users. Let us extend this example to a software product that enables data entry operators to take customer orders. If one can reduce the number of mouse clicks by, say, three for each order, when a few hundred thousand orders are entered, the savings in the overall time taken can be substantial.

Usability testing is not only for product binaries or executables. It also applies to documentation and other deliverables that are shipped along with a product. The release media should also be verified for usability. Let us take an example of a typical AUTORUN script that automatically brings up product setup when the release media is inserted in the machine. Sometimes this script is written for a particular operating system version and may not get auto executed on a different OS version. Even though the user can bring up the setup by clicking on the setup executable manually, this extra click (and the fact that the product is not automatically installed) may be considered as an irritant by the person performing the installation.

Generally, the people best suited to perform usability testing are

1. Typical representatives of the actual user segments who would be using the product, so that the typical user patterns can be captured, and

2. People who are new to the product, so that they can start without any bias and be able to identify usability problems. A person who has used the product several times may not be able to see the usability problems in the product as he or she would have "got used" to the product's (potentially inappropriate) usability.

Hence, a part of the team performing usability testing is selected from representatives outside the testing team. Inviting customer-facing teams (for example, customer support, product marketing) who know what the customers want and their expectations, will increase the effectiveness of usability testing.

> A right approach for usability is to test every artifact that impacts users—such as product binaries, documentation, messages, media—covering usage patterns through both graphical and command user interfaces, as applicable.

Usability can sometimes be a by-product and get noticed when other types of testing are performed. It is difficult to develop test cases for usability. Generally, checklists and guidelines are prepared for usability and they are observed during the testing. *Having an eye for detail, intuition and the building skills to bring out usability defects from underneath will make usability testing more effective than having test cases for usability*. There are many things to look for (explained in subsequent sections) in usability and it is essential to train and develop awareness of and expertise in usability in the organization to build and test usability.

Another aspect of usability is with respect to *messages* that a system gives to its users. Messages are classified into three types—*informational, warning, and error*. Usability depends on the type of error message. When there is an informational message, the message is verified to find out whether an end-user can understand that message and associate it with the operation done and the context. When there is a warning, such a message is checked for why it happened and what to do to avoid the warning. Whenever there is an error message, three things are looked for—what is the error, why that error happened, and what to do to avoid or work around that error.

Usability is not only for correct usage. It is not right to say that a product will be usable/or behave correctly only when the user has not made a mistake and that the product can behave wrongly (or in a user-unfriendly manner) when a user makes a mistake. A system should intelligently detect and avoid wrong usage and if a wrong usage cannot be avoided, it should provide appropriate and meaningful messages to steer the user to the right path. Hence, usability should go through both positive and negative testing—that is, both correct and incorrect usage of the product.

Usability should not be confused with graphical user interface (GUI). Usability is also applicable to non-GUI interface such as command line interfaces (CLI). A large number of Unix/Linux users find CLIs more usable than GUIS. SQL command is another example of a CLI, and is found more usable by database users. Hence, usability should also consider CLI and other interfaces that are used by the users.

12.3   WHEN TO DO USABILITY TESTING?

The most appropriate way of ensuring usability is by performing the usability testing in two phases. First is design validation and the second is usability testing done as a part of component and integration testing phases of a test cycle.

When planning for testing, the usability requirements should be planned in parallel, upfront in the development cycle, similar to any other type of testing. Generally, however, usability is an ignored subject (or at least given less priority) and is not planned and executed from the beginning

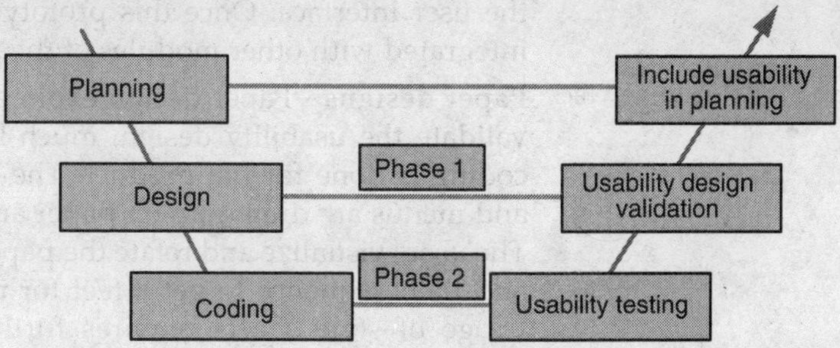

Figure 12.2
Phases and activities of usability testing.

of the project. When there are two defects—one on functionality and other on usability—the functionality defect is usually given precedence. This approach is not correct as usability defects may demotivate users from using the software (even if it performs the desired function) and it may mean a huge financial loss to the product organization if users reject the product. Also, postponing usability testing in a testing cycle can prove to be very expensive as a large number of usability defects may end up as needing changes in design and needing fixes in more than one screen, affecting different code paths. All these situations can be avoided if usability testing is planned upfront. The phases and activities of usability testing are given in Figure 12.2.

A product has to be designed for usability. A product designed only for functionality may not get user acceptance. A product designed for functionality may also involve a high degree of training, which can be minimized if it is designed for both functionality and usability. In the first phase of usability testing, this aspect of usability design is validated.

Usability design is verified through several means. Some of them are as follows.

- **Style sheets** Style sheets are grouping of user interface design elements. Use of style sheets ensures consistency of design elements across several screens and testing the style sheet ensures that the basic usability design is tested. Style sheets also include frames, where each frames is considered as a separate screen by the user. Style sheets are reviewed to check whether they force font size, color scheme, and so on, which may affect usability.
- **Screen prototypes** Screen prototype is another way to test usability design. The screens are designed as they will be shipped to the customers, but are not integrated with other modules of the product. Therefore, this user interface is tested independently without integrating with the functionality modules. This prototype will have other user interface functions simulated such as screen navigation, message display, and so on. The prototype gives an idea of how exactly the screens will look and function when the product is released. The test team and some real-life users test this prototype and their ideas for improvements are incorporated in

the user interface. Once this prototype is completely tested, it is integrated with other modules of the product.

✠ **Paper designs**   Paper design explores the earliest opportunity to validate the usability design, much before the actual design and coding is done for the product. The design of the screen, layout, and menus are drawn up on paper and sent to users for feedback. The users visualize and relate the paper design with the operations and their sequence to get a feel for usage and provide feedback. Usage of style sheets requires further coding, prototypes need binaries and resources to verify, but paper designs do not require any other resources. Paper designs can be sent through email or as a printout and feedback can be collected.

✠ **Layout design**   Style sheets ensure that a set of user interface elements are grouped and used repeatedly together. Layout helps in arranging different elements on the screen dynamically. It ensures arrangement of elements, spacing, size of fonts, pictures, justification, and so on, on the screen. This is another aspect that needs to be tested as part of usability design.

If an existing product is redesigned or enhanced, usability issues can be avoided by using the existing layout, as the user who is already familiar with the product will find it more usable. Making major usability changes to an existing product (for example, reordering the sequence of buttons on a screen) can end up confusing users and lead to user errors.

In the second phase, tests are run to test the product for usability. Prior to performing the tests, some of the actual users are selected (who are new to the product and features) and they are asked to use the product. Feedback is obtained from them and the issues are resolved. Sometimes it could be difficult to get the real users of the product for usability testing. In such a case, the representatives of users can be selected from teams outside the product development and testing teams—for instance, from support, marketing, and sales teams.

When to do usability also depends on the type of the product that is being developed. For example, client applications (Windows client32) designed for LAN environments are generally very rich in features and every screen tries to accomplish various tasks and they provide a lot of information. Web services go the other way and the amount of information and the list of tasks in each screen is limited to enable fast loading of the web pages. The usability activities are performed at different stages for these types of applications. Table 12.1 lists the differences in the way client and web services are developed and tested in general.

As indicated in Table 12.1, web application interfaces are designed before designing functionality. That gives adequate time for doing two phases of usability testing (phase 1 and phase 2). In the case of client application, the user interface becomes available only after functionality is available. As

Table 12.1 Development and testing of client applications and web application.

Client application	Web application
Step 1: Design for functionality	**Step 1:** Design for user interface
Step 2: Perform coding for functionality	**Step 2:** Perform coding for user interface (prototype)
Step 3: Design for user interface	**Step 3:** Test user interface (Phase 1)
Step 4: Perform coding for user interface	**Step 4:** Design for functionality
Step 5: Integrate user interface with functionality	**Step 5:** Perform coding for functionality
Step 6: Test the user interface along with functionality (Phase 1 and 2)	**Step 6:** Integrate user interface with functionality
	Step 7: Test user interface along with functionality (Phase 2)

user interface coding is the last-leg activity, not much of design validation can be done in a separate phase. Therefore, phase 1 and 2 are merged and done together. At the same time, there is no hard and fast rule that client application cannot have a user interface design prior to functionality. This is only a common practice that can be changed as more and more focus is put on usability.

Testing alone cannot make the product completely usable. The product has to be designed, coded, tested for usability; furthermore, the usability aspects should be reviewed by real users for getting maximum benefits.

There are several phases of testing that were explained in earlier chapters. The responsibility for usability testing is spread across all the testing phases and all the testing teams. Usability cannot be "added on" to a product—it should be planned upfront and must be tested throughout. Hence, usability as a requirement can be indirectly tested (while direct testing is performed by a test team) starting from day one of product development and can continue till the product is released. Everyone performing various roles in product development needs to contribute to the various perspectives and requirements of usability.

> A "usable product" is always the result of mutual collaboration from all the stakeholders, for the entire duration of the project.

12.4 HOW TO ACHIEVE USABILITY?

If anybody expects the users to explicitly report usability problems, it is not likely to happen. Users who are frustrated by the user interface may evolve some clever workarounds (or even stop using part of the product!). However, involving the users proactively on user interface design can yield good results. User interface requirements cannot be expressed in terms of words. One has to use the product to get a feel of its usability. That is why involving the customers to give feedback on all the user interface requirements upfront or during the design (or even requirements gathering) phase is essential. Of course, this is not always possible because

1.   The users may not have the time or bandwidth to participate in this exercise.

2.   There may be a number of users who may give conflicting requirements and it would not be possible to satisfy everyone.

3.   In the case of breakthrough products, the users may not even be able to visualize the usage of the product. Hence, the feedback may not be directly relevant.

There can be different categories of users. Some users can be experts, some can be beginners, and some novices. Expert users usually do not report usability problems. Instead they invent workarounds and adapt themselves to the product though they hope for a better product. Beginners generally get impacted because of lack of usability but still they do not report usability problems as they are eager to learn more about the product. They are generally in two minds whether the problems are due to usability or due to their being new to the product. Within each category of users the expectations could be still different. Novice users report plenty of usability issues but some of them may get ignored because they do not have adequate skills to use the product. Irrespective of the category of users, the product is expected to be usable by all.

There is also an additional dimension to the categories of users. In addition to all of the above, the product is expected to be usable to another category of challenged users such as those who are hearing impaired, vision impaired, and mobility impaired. The type of usability that deals with overall-, visual-, and motion-challenged users is called *accessibility testing*. It is explained in Section 12.7.

In order to create to a product that is usable for all categories of the users, at least one user from each category must be involved in usability testing. As explained earlier, it is not always possible to get each type of user for usability testing. For that reason, part of the team for usability testing is picked up from different teams, to replicate and test different categories of real end-users.

It was explained earlier that many categories of users and customers do not report usability defects. It is not just whether the product has a usability defect or not, but also how the user reacts as he or she goes through the product usage. Sometimes these user reactions (for example, an irritated user banging on the keyboard indicates a system that is not responding fast enough) can be even more informative than the actual defect they report. When the users are using the product during usability testing, their activities are closely monitored and all observations are recorded and defects are raised by the test team rather than expecting, every problem to be reported. Recording the operating sequence, screens, and user reactions and making observations needs some equipment to be set up for a *usability lab*. This is explained in Section 12.9. When making observations certain guidelines/

Usability is a habit and a behavior. Just like humans, the products are expected to behave differently and correctly with different users and to their expectations.

checklists are created and verified during usability testing. Some of the items in the checklist are as follows.

1. Do users complete the assigned tasks/operations successfully?
2. If so, how much time do they take to complete the tasks/operations?
3. Is the response from the product fast enough to satisfy them?
4. Where did the users get struck? What problems do they have?
5. Where do they get confused? Were they able to continue on their own? What helped them to continue?

Apart from checklists, the product is also verified for various other usability components such as comprehensibility, consistency, responsiveness, and aesthetics. They are explained in Sections 12.5 and 12.6.

12.5 QUALITY FACTORS FOR USABILITY

In the earlier sections, usability testing, and the approach and methodology for performing usability testing were explained. Some quality factors are very important when performing usability testing. As was explained earlier, usability is subjective and not all requirements for usability can be documented clearly. However focusing on some of the quality factors given below help in improving objectivity in usability testing are as follows.

1. **Comprehensibility**   The product should have simple and logical structure of features and documentation. They should be grouped on the basis of user scenarios and usage. The most frequent operations that are performed early in a scenario should be presented first, using the user interfaces. When features and components are grouped in a product, they should be based on user terminologies, not technology or implementation.

2. **Consistency**   A product needs to be consistent with any applicable standards, platform look-and-feel, base infrastructure, and earlier versions of the same product. Also, if there are multiple products from the same company, it would be worthwhile to have some consistency in the look-and-feel of these multiple products. User interfaces that are different in different operating systems underlying, services irritates the users since they need to become comfortable with different templates and procedures for using each of them. For example, if an operating system uses a template for error message with a set of icons, error number, error message and link to the related documentation, following the same format will make users more comfortable with a product on that operating system. Unless there is a major problem with the user interface of a product, the current interface and usage should be consistent with the earlier versions of the same product. Following some standards for usability helps in meeting the consistency aspect of the usability.

3. **Navigation**   This helps in determining how easy it is to select the different operations of the product. An option that is buried very deep requires the user to travel to multiple screens or menu options to perform the operation. The number of mouse clicks, or menu navigations that is required to perform an operation should be minimized to improve usability. When users get stuck or get lost, there should be an easy option to abort or go back to the previous screen or to the main menu so that the user can try a different route.

4. **Responsiveness**   How fast the product responds to the user request is another important aspect of usability. This should not be confused with performance testing. Screen navigations and visual displays should be almost immediate after the user selects an option or else it could give an impression to the user that there is no progress and cause him or her to keep trying the operation again. Whenever the product is processing some information, the visual display should indicate the progress and also the amount of time left so that the users can wait patiently till the operation is completed. Adequate dialogs and popups to guide the users also improve usability. Responsiveness should not be mistaken for too many popups and dialog boxes. Too many notifications within a short interval works only to reduce usability and may, in fact, slow down responsiveness.

Including some of the quality factors as discussed above in the usability checklist and ensuring that they are designed and tested, will help in achieving a good, usable product.

12.6   AESTHETICS TESTING

Another important aspect in usability is making the product "beautiful." Performing aesthetics testing helps in improving usability further. This testing is important as many of the aesthetics related problems in the product from many organizations are ignored on the ground that they are not functional defects. All the aesthetic problems in the product are generally mapped to a defect classification called "Cosmetic," which is of low priority. Having a separate cycle of testing focusing on aesthetics helps in setting up expectations and also in focusing on improving the look and feel of the user interfaces.

"Beautiful" or not can be a subjective matter (Remember the old adage "Beauty is in the eye of the beholder!"). Something that is acceptable to one person may appear ugly to another person. Adequate care, for the aesthetics aspect of the product can ensure that product is beautiful, at least a product must not end up being termed ugly. Beauty sets the first impression for any product and the perception that beauty is not important for the product may impact product acceptance by users.

However, in many product companies, aesthetics takes a back seat. Aesthetics is not in the external look alone. It is in all the aspects such as messages, screens, colors, and images. A pleasant look for menus, pleasing colors, nice icons, and so on can improve aesthetics. It is generally considered as gold plating, which is not right. Gold plating is normally done after the ornament is ready; aesthetics testing should not be taken as the last leg of testing activity. Some of the aesthetics aspects must be done during the design phase and should not be taken as the last and a low-priority activity before the release.

> It's not possible for all products to measure up with the Taj Mahal for its beauty. Testing for aesthetics can at least ensure the product is pleasing to the eye.

Aesthetics testing can be performed by anyone who appreciates beauty — that means everyone. Involving beauticians, artists, and architects who have regular roles of making different aspects of life beautiful (not just products), serve as experts here in aesthetics testing. Involving them during design and testing phases and incorporating their inputs may improve the aesthetics of the product. For example, the icons used in the product may look more appealing if they are designed by an artist, as they are not meant only for conveying messages but also help in making the product beautiful.

12.7 ACCESSIBILITY TESTING

> Verifying the product usability for physically challenged users is called accessibility testing.

There are a large number of people who are challenged with vision, hearing, and mobility related problems—partial or complete. Product usability that does not look into their requirements would result in lack of acceptance. For such users, alternative methods of using the product have to be provided. There are several tools that are available to help them with alternatives. These tools are generally referred as *accessibility tools* or *assistive technologies*. Accessibility testing involves testing these alternative methods of using the product and testing the product along with accessibility tools. Accessibility is a subset of usability and should be included as part of usability test planning.

Accessibility to the product can be provided by two means.

1. Making use of accessibility features provided by the underlying infrastructure (for example, operating system), called *basic accessibility*, and
2. Providing accessibility in the product through standards and guidelines, called *product accessibility*.

12.7.1 Basic Accessibility

Basic accessibility is provided by the hardware and operating system. All the input and output devices of the computer and their accessibility options are categorized under basic accessibility.

12.7.1.1 Keyboard accessibility A keyboard is the most complex device for vision- and mobility-impaired users. Hence, it received plenty of attention for accessibility. Some of the accessibility improvements were done on hardware and some in the operating system. An example of hardware accessibility improvement is the little protrusion one can find in any keyboard on top of the **F** and **J** keys. This little projection helps vision-impaired users to get a feel and align their fingers for typing. Keyboard keys with different sizes, and providing shortcut function keys are other examples of improving accessibility, provided at the hardware level.

Similarly, the operating system vendors came up with some more improvements in the keyboard. Some of those improvements are usage of *sticky keys, toggle keys* and *arrow keys* for mouse.

Sticky keys To explain the sticky keys concept, let us take an example of <CTRL> <ALT> <DEL>. One of the most complex sequences for vision-impaired and mobility-impaired users is <CTRL> <ALT> <DEL>. This keyboard sequence is used for various purposes such as log in, log out, locking and unlocking machines, shutdown, and bringing up task manager. Sometimes the keyboard sequence is complex for users without disabilities too as it requires holding down two of the keys when pressing the third. This particular sequence requires three fingers to be coordinated from both hands. The sticky keys setting in the operating system removes the requirement for holding the keys. When sticky keys feature is enabled, <CTRL> and <ALT> keys are pressed once and released by the user before pressing the <DEL> key. This allows a single finger operation to complete the sequence.

Filter keys When keys are pressed for more than a particular duration, they are assumed to be repeated. Sometimes this troubles physically challenged users. Some of them may not be as fast as a normal user in pressing and releasing the keys. Filter keys help in either stopping the repetition completely or slowing down the repetition.

Toggle key sound When toggle keys are enabled, the information typed may be different from what the user desires. For example, in a typical Word Processing package, the <INS> key is a toggle; if its normal setting is that characters are inserted, when the key is pressed once and released, it goes into a REPLACE mode, wherein the typed characters overwrite what is already there. Vision-impaired users find it difficult to know the status of these toggle keys. To solve this problem sound is enabled, and the different tones are played when enabling and disabling toggle keys.

Sound keys To help vision-impaired users, there is one more mechanism that pronounces each character as and when they are hit on the keyboard. In some operating systems, this feature is available as part of a *Narrator* utility (discussed below); however, many accessibility tools have this feature.

Arrow keys to control mouse Mobility-impaired users have problems moving the mouse. By enabling this feature, such users will be able to use the keyboard arrow keys for mouse movements. The two buttons of the mouse and their operations too can be directed from the keyboard.

Narrator   Narrator is a utility which provides auditory feedback. For example, it may pronounce the events when they are executed by the users, read out the characters typed, notify the system events by distinguishing sounds, and so on. Since this provides the sound equivalent for keyboard and system events, this feature is considered as one of the significant utilities used for accessibility and increases the accessibility of the product.

12.7.1.2   Screen accessibility

Many of the keyboard accessibility features assist the vision-impaired and mobility-impaired users. These features may not help the hearing-impaired users who require extra visual feedback on the screen. Some accessibility features that enhance usability using the screen are as follows.

Visual sound   Visual sound is the "wave form" or "graph form" of the sound. These visual effects inform the user of the events that happen on the system using the screen.

Enabling captions for multimedia   All multimedia speech and sound can be enabled with text equivalents, and they are displayed on the screen when speech and sound are played.

Soft keyboard   Some of the mobility-impaired and vision-impaired users find it easier to use pointing devices instead of the keyboard. A soft keyboard helps such users by displaying the keyboard on the screen. Characters can be typed by clicking on the keyboard layout on the screen using pointing devices such as the mouse.

Easy reading with high contrast   Vision-impaired users have problems in recognizing some colors and size of font in menu items. A toggle option is provided generally by the operating system to switch to a high contrast mode. This mode uses pleasing colors and font sizes for all the menus on the screen.

12.7.1.3   Other accessibility features

There are many other accessibility features provided at the operating system level. A vision- or mobility-impaired user can find both keyboard and mouse devices difficult to use. In such cases, the option to use any other device should be provided. For example, a joystick device can be used as an alternative to a pointing device and such a pointing device can be used in combination with a soft keyboard to accomplish the things a user desires.

Some of the features explained above try to address users with multiple disabilities. For example, sticky keys remove the need to hold the keys as well as display the status of all sticky keys on the screen on the toolbar portion of the computer.

12.7.2   Product Accessibility

> Sample requirement #1: Text equivalents have to be provided for audio, video, and picture images.

A good understanding of the basic accessibility features is needed while providing accessibility to the product. A product should do everything possible to ensure that the basic accessibility features are utilized by it. For example, providing detailed text equivalent for multimedia files ensures the captions feature is utilized by the product.

A good understanding of basic accessibility features and the requirements of different types users with special needs helps in creating certain guidelines on how the product's user interface has to be designed. These different requirements of different categories of users, their abilities and challenges need to be kept in mind throughout while providing accessibility of the product.

There is much information on various websites on accessibility standards and requirements that can be used to collect the requirements for accessibility. Accessibility standards such as **508** and **W3C** can be referred to for a complete set of requirements. This section takes a few requirements to set the context and to explain the concepts.

This requirement explains the importance of providing text equivalents for picture images and providing captions for audio portions. When an audio file is played, providing captions for the audio improves accessibility for the hearing-impaired. Providing audio clippings improves accessibility impaired users who cannot understand the video streams and pictures. While trying to meet this requirement, the knowledge of accessibility tools comes in handy. For example, people who do not have knowledge of accessibility tools may perceive that there is no visible advantage of providing a text equivalent for a picture because vision-impaired users cannot see either. But when users use tools like the narrator, the associated text is read and produced in audio form whereby the vision-impaired are benefited. A sample picture from the website along with the associated text equivalent is given in Figure 12.3.

Figure 12.3

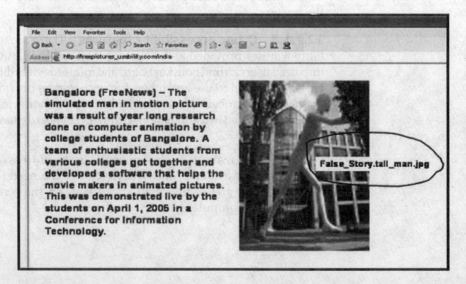

In the above example, even if an impaired user cannot see the picture, the associated tag of the image and text on the left-hand side help the person when tools like narrator are used.

Hence text equivalents for audio (captions), audio descriptions for pictures and visuals become an important requirement for accessibility.

People with low vision would like to see the pages in extra-large fonts for them to use the product comfortably. Hence, a product expecting a particular resolution and font size to display all fields on the screen may face usability issues. There should be adequate spacing between the fields and text so that the messages that appear on the screen do not look cluttered when font size is increased.

Sample requirement #2: Documents and fields should be organized so that they can be read without requiring a particular resolution of the screen, and templates (known as style sheets).

Normally, information on web page is displayed on the screen using templates called style sheets. There are two types of style sheets: internal and external. Internal style sheets are those hard coded sheets that dictate the fields, size, and their positions on the screen. This creates problems for users when they want to adjust the windows and size of fonts. The safest method is to use external style sheets, and programs written for the product should not tamper with user-defined external style sheets.

Sample requirement #3: User interfaces should be designed so that all information conveyed with color is also available without color.

Not only users with low vision but those with good vision too may have problems in identifying the numerous colors and their combinations that are available. This is termed as color blindness. Hence, products using color text, color pictures, and color screens should not use color as the sole method of identification of user interface elements. For example, in the picture in Figure 12.4, the colors (green and red) are used as methods to identify the buttons for different operations. However, color blind users may not be able to select the right button for operations. The right approach would be

Figure 12.4

Color as a method of identification.

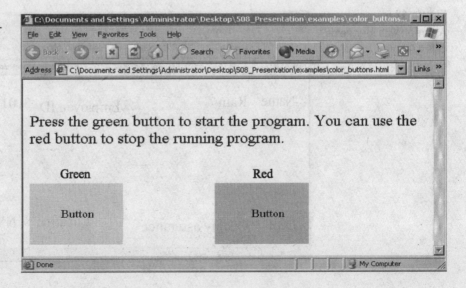

to retain the colors and name the buttons appropriately. In the following example, naming the green button as "Continue" and red button as "Stop" will improve accessibility.

Sample requirement #4: Reduce flicker rate, speed of moving text; avoid flashes and blinking text.

Different people read at different speeds. People with below-average speed in reading may find it irritating to see text that is blinking and flashing as it further impacts reading speed. Even people with good vision find the flashes and flickers beyond a particular frequency uncomfortable. The flickers should be between the frequencies of 2 Hz and 55 Hz, as defined by some of the usability standards.

Some mobility-impaired users and those with nerve-related problems cannot move their eyeballs as fast as others. There may also be other health problems that prevent them from reading as fast as others. In case of rolling and moving text, the speed at which the text rolls or moves should be compatible with the reading capability of the slowest product user or the product should have a feature to alter the speed of moving text.

Sample requirement #5: Reduce physical movement requirements for the users when designing the interface and allow adequate time for user responses.

When designing the user interfaces, adequate care has to be taken to ensure that the physical movement required to use the product is minimized to assist mobility-impaired users. Spreading user interface elements to the corner of the screens should be avoided, as this requires the users to move the pointing devices to the corners, involving effort. Figure 12.5 is an example where four fields are kept in the corners of the screen. The same user interface can be better designed to have the fields one below the other, given that there is adequate space on the screen.

Not only individual screens, but the entire set of screens in totality have to be designed keeping minimum movement requirements in mind. When multiple screens are used in performing a set of operations (say, validating

Figure 12.5

A screen with four fields in the corners.

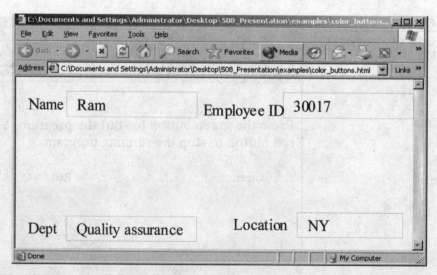

multiple screens of user information), the corresponding sequence of positive responses such as CONTINUE , ACCEPT BACK, EXIT buttons are aligned across screens so that the pointing devices need not be realigned when the screen changes.

As much as possible, user interfaces should expect users to use fewer devices for regular operations. For example, in Figure 12.5, using the keyboard is essential as it expects information to be typed but using a pointing device may be avoided if the <TAB> key can be used to navigate among the fields. Mixing the use of several devices such as keyboard and mouse increases the complexity of user interface.

When a timed response is required, the user should be alerted and given sufficient time to indicate that more time is required. Some users require more time to think and act, as they may be challenged in some fashion. Giving messages in user interface such as "Click on OK button within 5 seconds if information is correct" puts pressure on the users and should be avoided.

The sample requirements given above are some examples to improve accessibility. There are many more requirements like these and they are normally classified on the basis of the technology used for providing the user interface (for example, web-based interface, client-based interface, and so on) in the popular standards (such as **508** guidelines) defined for accessibility. Selecting the right standard for the technology used in the interface will go a long way in improving accessibility.

12.8   TOOLS FOR USABILITY

There are not many tools that help in usability because of the high degree of subjectivity involved in evaluating this aspect. However, there are adequate tools available for accessibility testing. A sample list of usability and accessibility tools is given in Table 12.2. Some of those tools have been explained in the previous sections.

Testing with a black-and-white monitor instead of a color monitor ensures the right combination of colors used and also ensures that the information available with color is also available without color. Some color monitors have a feature to display information in gray scale. Some operating systems have a display setting for black and white. Using this display setting and testing it ensures that information available with color, can be made without color.

Inviting physically challenged users for review of the product also serves as a method and tool to validate product accessibility.

Table 12.2 Sample list of usability and accessibility tools.

Name of the tool	Purpose
JAWS	For testing accessibility of the product with some assistive technologies.
HTML validator	To validate the HTML source file for usability and accessibility standards.
Style sheet validator	To validate the style sheets (templates) for usability standards set by W3C.
Magnifier	Accessibility tool for vision challenged (to enable them to enlarge the items displayed on screen)
Narrator	Narrator is a tool that reads the information displayed on the screen and creates audio descriptions for vision-challenged users.
Soft keyboard	Soft keyboard enables the use of pointing devices to use the keyboard by displaying the keyboard template on the screen.

12.9 USABILITY LAB SETUP

As mentioned earlier, expecting users to give inputs on usability is unlikely to happen. Product developers often ignore usability defects. Users too ignore some of them as they may have faced similar defects and got used to those defects. Hence, expecting the users to give inputs alone will not make a product usable. Observing the "body language" of the users may point to some usability defects, or which may never get reported oterwise.

Not only the body language, the context that is, the screen on which the user got stuck and what event confused the user, and so on, also needs to be associated with the feedback received from the user for those defects to be rectified.

The above points become a compelling reason to set up a usability lab so that all associated information for usability is recorded, observed, and the defects resolved. Figure 12.6 gives some of the key elements of the usability lab.

As illustrated in the figure, a usability lab has two sections—"Recording section" and "Observation section." A user is requested to come to the lab with a prefixed set of operations that are to be performed with the product in the recording section of the lab. The user is explained the product usage and given the documentation in advance. The user comes prepared to perform the tasks. While the whole sequence is recorded, a set of usability experts observe the whole process.

In the observation section, some usability experts sit and observe the user for body language and associate the defects with the screens and events

Figure 12.6

Key elements of a
usability lab.

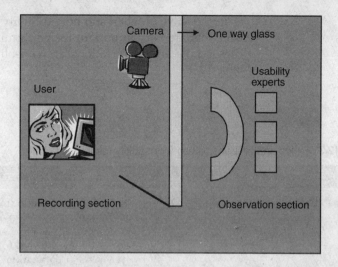

that caused it. The observation is made through a "one-way glass"—the experts can see the user but the user cannot see the experts. This helps avoid any disturbance to the user from the expert's body movements and allows them to be natural. The camera additionally helps in capturing live images of the user and the computer monitor from different angles. After watching the different users use the product, the usability experts suggest usability improvements in the product.

The recorded version of usability testing is used to make further observations after the event, and also to get more information (if needed) for fixing the usability defects.

Therefore, keeping a separate lab for usability serves as a tool for locating more usability defects and in resolving them.

12.10   TEST ROLES FOR USABILITY

Usability testing is not as formal as other types of testing in several companies and is not performed with a pre-written set of test cases/checklists. Various methods adopted by companies for usability testing are as follows.

1. Performing usability testing as a separate cycle of testing.
2. Hiring external consultants (who understand ergonomics and special accessibility needs) to do usability validation.
3. Setting up a separate group for usability to institutionalize the practices across various product development teams and to set up organization-wide standards for usability.

Irrespective of when and how usability testing is done, there are certain skills that are very important for performing full-fledged usability testing. These skills and expectations are consolidated for the different roles in Table 12.3.

Table 12.3 Roles and responsibilities for usability testing.

Role	Responsibility
Usability architect/consultant	• Institutionalizing and improving usability across the organization • Educating, advocating, and obtaining management commitment required for usability, as an initiative area in the organization • Helping in resolving conflicts that arise during the implementation of usability testing across the organization • Creating a communication channel between customers and the organization for getting feedback on usability problems
Usability expert	• Providing the technology guidance needed for performing usability testing • Owning the usability strategy for testing products for usability • Giving technical directions to all people performing usability testing • Establishing usability standards and certifications for product teams
Human factors specialist	• Reviewing the screens and other artifacts for usability • Ensuring consistency across multiple products • Suggesting improvements to enhance user experience • Covering the angle of consistency, effort, and productivity
Graphic designer	• Creating icons, graphic images, and so on needed for user interfaces • Cross-checking the icons and graphic messages on the contexts they are used and verifying whether those images communicate the right meaning
Usability manager/lead	• Estimating, scheduling, and tracking all usability testing activities • Working closely with usability experts to get usability strategy and implement them for projects • Working with customers to obtain feedback on the current version of the product prior to release
Usability test engineer	• Executing usability test based on scripts, scenarios, and test cases • Providing feedback to usability tests from execution perspective as well as user perspective, if possible

12.11 SUMMARY

There is an increasing awareness of usability testing in the industry. Soon, usability testing will become an engineering discipline, a life cycle activity, and a profession or career.

However, usability testing is not without challenges. Often usability testing engineers and consultants are brought in just before an usability test release to complete the formalities and may not improve usability. Even if usability test is done, it is done by engineers who are not adequately skilled/trained on usability. Usability is an evolving area and training is important to keep people up to date with technology.

Several companies plan for usability testing in the beginning of the product life cycle and track them to completion. However, adequate investments interms of training the engineers on standards, tools, lab setup, and so on are ignored. Effectiveness in usability increases only if there is adequate focus on these aspects and if investments are done in training the people on usability aspect and inform such aspects in the product.

Usability is not achieved only by testing. Usability is more in the design and in the minds of the people who contribute to the product. Usability is all about user experiences. Thinking from the perspective of the user all the time during the project will go a long way in ensuring usability.

 ## REFERENCES

Accessibility tools and related documentation available with Microsoft Windows is a good reference material for understanding accessibility. [508] provides 508 guidelines set by the American government. [W3C] explain how the usability standards (with a special focus on web based application) can be built and tested. [Yog-2002] is an article which stresses the importance of Aesthetics testing and the guidelines associated in performing this testing.

 ## PROBLEMS AND EXERCISES

1. What are the different methods by which usability design can be validated?

2. Classify different impaired users and give a summary of how accessibility testing and tools can help them to use the product.

3. What is aesthetics testing and why it is important to include it in usability checklists?

4. Explain the different tools that are available for usability and accessibility. What is the role played by these tools in testing usability?

5. What are the key objectives of setting up usability test lab? In what way it is different from using other traditional labs for testing?

6. Explain different roles that can be played by test professionals in usability testing?

7. Explain the V model and explain how different activities of usability testing can be mapped to the V model?

People and Organizational Issues in Testing

This part of the book discusses two of the oft-ignored aspects of testing that turn out to be the biggest challenges in running testing projects. First, in Chapter 13, we address common people issues faced in testing teams. We discuss candidly some of the "heard in the street" perceptions on testing and see how they are not well founded. We address the question of career paths for people in testing profession and see what needs to be done by the rest of the eco-system to achieve these aspirations. This chapter is followed by Chapter 14, *Organizational Structures for Testing Teams*. Here, we see how to organize testing teams and distribute work among them to provide better accountability and effectiveness. In particular, we discuss the impact of globalization on team structures and work allocation.

Common People Issues

CHAPTER 13

In this chapter—

✓ Perceptions and misconceptions about testing
✓ Comparison between testing and development functions
✓ Providing career paths for testing professionals
✓ The role of the ecosystem and a call for action

13.1　PERCEPTIONS AND MISCONCEPTIONS ABOUT TESTING

In this section, we will look at some of the common "heard in the street" statements about the testing profession. These statements are sometimes made by testing professionals, by the management team, and by academicians. We will look at where these statements come from, the fallacy in the statements, and what can be given as arguments to counter these perceptions. It is important that these misconceptions and perceptions are cleared upfront to build a successful and motivated testing team.

13.1.1　"Testing is not Technically Challenging"

If you are conducting interviews to hire people for performing testing functions, you will generally observe a very bipolar behavior among the candidates. There will be the first set of people—usually a minority—who will approach testing with tremendous pride, commitment, and enjoyment. The second set—unfortunately, a majority—will be those who get into testing, "because they have no choice." They often believe testing is not technically challenging. There are several contributors to this perception. One of the argument given is, "If I look at development functions, I can acquire proficiency in a given programming language and that is considered valuable. On the other hand, testing is simply a routine and repetitive job that does not require any special skills."

This argument may have been true about twenty years ago when most of the testing was manual and the products were somewhat simplistic. In the scenario that prevails today, the testing stream bears a remarkable parallel to the development job functions, as summarized in Table 13.1 and discussed in detail below. (In the next section, we will look at the differences between testing and development functions that contribute to the perceptions and misconceptions discussed here.)

Requires a holistic understanding of the entire product rather than just a single module　Typically, development engineers tend to focus on specific modules. It is possible for them to be somewhat oblivious about the functionality from other modules. Test engineers, in contrast, generally require a more holistic understanding of the product rather than be constrained to a single module or component. This gives an edge to test engineers at becoming domain specialists.

Requires thorough understanding of multiple domains　As the products become more complex and more open and seamlessly integrated with one another, testing requires a deep appreciation of the domains of multiple products. Just like developing a product, an in-depth understanding of the nuances of the domain of application is required for testing as well. In fact, extending the argument presented in the previous paragraph, while most development happens in a compartmentalized manner, testing

Table 13.1 Similarities in the testing and development functions.

Functions in development projects	Corresponding functions in testing projects	Similarities
Requirements specification	Test specification	Both require a thorough understanding of the domain; sometimes testing functions require an even more holistic understanding of the entire system from the users' perspective.
Design	Test design	Test design carries with it all the attributes of product design in terms of architecting the test system, considering reuse, formulating standards, and so on.
Development/coding	Test script development	Involves using the test development and test automation tools.
Testing	Making the tests operational	This would involve well-knit teamwork between the development and testing teams to ensure that the correct results are captured.
Maintenance	Test maintenance	Keeping the tests (regression tests, functional test, and so on) current with changes from maintenance.

may even require a much deeper understanding of the interactions and inter-dependencies amongst multiple domains to be able to simulate real-life scenarios. Thus, testing seems to be even more suited to and challenging for someone who has expertise in product domains.

Specialization in languages Most developers stake their claim at expertise by gaining proficiency in some specific programming language(s) or platform(s). In the early 1990s, most people sought to be experts in C, which moved to C++ and then to Java. Similarly, in terms of platforms, the preferred platforms shifted from mainframes to client-server computing to network-centric computing. Until about ten years ago, people in the testing functions found very little parallel to these kinds of "resume enriching" language skills. Most testing was either manual or used some home-grown tools. The advent of specialized testing languages and tools over the past few years has narrowed this gap about language expertise in testing. Today, the argument that "in testing we don't have any programming" holds no water. In fact, the use of most testing tools requires programming in languages remarkably similar to those that developers use.

Use of tools People in other activities of a software life cycle had access to a wide variety of tools like CASE tools, debuggers, IDEs, and so on. Tools added more "glamor" to their jobs and were "cool" to use. Testing functions offered very little opportunity for using tools. Again, things have changed significantly on this front over the last few years. The standard testing tools available in the market not only support languages that are akin to programming languages, but also provide opportunities for better design and integration with the program code of the product being tested. Given the complexity of tools, sometimes, automating the tests can prove to be more challenging than even developing the code for the product!

Opportunities for conceptualization and out-of-the-box thinking Since testing is viewed as a "destructive" job, there is a perception that there are more opportunities for conceptualization in development functions than in testing functions. As we saw earlier, the process of testing bears a strong parallel with the process of development. Even though testing is considered destructive (in the sense of finding defects in a product), these similarities are enough proof that there are ample opportunities for conceptualization and out-of-the-box thinking. Unfortunately, these similarities most often get completely overlooked by people in seeking a career in testing.

> There is testing in all development and development in all testing.

Significant investments are made in testing today—sometimes a lot more than in development For instance, testing tools are very expensive and obviously, an organization would have to ensure that there is sufficient return on investments on these expensive tools. Hence, it is eminently possible that some of the best talent gets channeled to testing functions.

An internal test tool today could very well be one of those expensive test automation tools of tomorrow! In many organizations, what starts off as an internal tool within a small group expands to be a sizable product, with ramifications and applicability across multiple groups and from there to even becoming a revenue-earning test automation product. This possibility increases the need for a still wider view of the testing functions, from a technical challenge perspective.

In view of all of the above, testing offers sufficient technical challenges for an interested professional to continuously learn, enrich his or her knowledge, and achieve greater heights of personal satisfaction as well as product quality and fulfillment.

We would like to summarize our discussions on the development—testing dichotomy by saying, "there is testing in all development and development in all testing".

13.1.2 "Testing Does Not Provide Me a Career Path or Growth"

A number of organizations have career paths defined for people in the development and other software engineering functions but when it comes to testing functions, the career paths are not clearly laid out. In fact, even the job titles are given as "Development Engineer," "Senior Development Engineer," and so on! From a project life cycle point of view, developers seem to have a natural progression into being a designer, a business analyst, and a domain expert. There is also scope for being a respected "architect." Testing organizations do not always present such obvious opportunities for career growth. This does not mean that there are no career paths for testing professionals. Since we strongly believe that there is an equally lucrative career path for testing professionals, we will revisit this statement and devote the entire next section fully to address the career path choices for testing professionals.

> Testing is not a devil and development is not an angel; opportu-nities abound equally in testing and development.

13.1.3 "I Am Put in Testing—What is Wrong With Me?!"

> If a person is not suitable for development, for the same or similar reason, he or she may not be suitable for testing either.

Since testing is an activity that is closest to releasing the product to customers, it stands to reason that some of the best talent in an organization be deployed to the testing functions and that these functions should be treated on par with other functions. But the (false) "gleam" associated with other job functions sometimes cause not-so-obvious slips in the message conveyed to the team. People are sometimes made to feel that they are in testing because they could not fit in anywhere else! Consider some of the causes and effects of such messages

1. Filling up positions for testing should not be treated as a second string function. If the hiring and allocation policy is such that all the "toppers" in a class (or the candidates from top schools) are allocated to development functions and testing functions get the "leftovers," then obviously the management is sending the wrong signals and reinforcing the wrong message.

2. A person should be assigned to testing only when he or she has the right aptitude and attitude for testing. They should see a career path in testing, as much as developers look for a career path in development.

3. The compensation schemes should not discriminate against any specific function, notably the testing function. When the compensation and reward mechanisms favor the development functions, employees are bound to view the testing function as a means to "graduate to development" rather than look for careers in testing itself.

4. Appropriate recognition should be given to the engineers who participate in activities such as testing, maintenance, and documentation. Recognition is not just in terms of monetary awards or compensation but in the form of visibility. For example, when a product is launched and is successful, how often do we see a "test architect" steal the center stage vis-à-vis the development manager? These invisible job functions sometimes get viewed as "thankless jobs" and hence people want to move out of these functions.

The fact of the matter is that the common sense that is so obvious in all the above arguments is so often missed out because of the baggage of perceptions associated with the nature of testing functions. This erodes team work within the organization and eventually tells on the quality of the product.

13.1.4   "These Folks Are My Adversaries"

> Testing and Development teams should reinforce each other and not be at loggerheads.

Since the main function of testing is to find defects in the products, it is easy for an adversary attitude to develop between the testing team and the development team. The development team start viewing the testing team as people who nitpick their work, while testing teams begin viewing the development teams as giving them products that are not ready for prime time.

13.1.5   "Testing is What I Can Do in the End if I Get Time"

> Testing is not what happens in the end of a project—it happens throughout and continues even beyond a release!

Even though there are different phases of testing that are interspersed throughout the project, testing is still construed as an "end of life cycle" activity. When deadlines are considered sacrosanct, and when it is considered "natural" for developers to take "slightly longer" than what was planned to get the product ready from development, it is the testing team that often takes the brunt of the deadline pressure. The time allocated to testing gets cut and testers often have to put in long hours spanning weekends to meet the deadlines, while ensuring that the product is tested "adequately." After all, when customers report problems, the first question asked is "Why wasn't this defect caught in testing?!"

This double whammy of having to squeeze in a lot of work in high pressure mode (almost incessantly, given the shrinking lifetimes of products) and facing the brunt of attack for product defects has a significantly negative impact on the morale and perceptions of people aspiring to perform testing functions. Some ways of overcoming this problem are

1. Stipulating completion/acceptance criteria for a testing team to accept a product from the development team. For example, an organization may specify some minimum conditions for a product to be considered ready for testing.

2. Giving the testing team the freedom to mandate a minimum quality in the product before it can be released. For example, an organization can have norms which specify the limits on the number and severity of open problems before the product can be released.

13.1.6 "There is No Sense of Ownership in Testing"

> Testing has deliverables just as development has and hence testers should have the same sense of ownership.

When we talk of team structures for product development, we often see roles like "module leader." These are often people who have ownership of the module that is being developed. Even in the maintenance phase, there is ownership at module level or component level. This ownership creates a pride that drives individuals to ensure better quality.

This ownership is sometimes not created for testing functions. A possible contributor to this feeling of lack of ownership is the apparent lack of "deliverables" for testing functions. Development functions produce code and the developers feel that this "touchy feely" code is their creation. This creates a sense of ownership. On the other hand, testers may feel that they only make the code better—or worse! They do not associate themselves with any concrete deliverables. No doubt the testing professional owns the test scripts, test design, and so on but the lack of direct customer exposure of these artifacts does put a damper on the mindset of the testing professionals.

One way to minimize the impact of this problem is to vest the testing team with the authority to decide the state of readiness of the product and make them the final arbiters of quality. Secondly, some of the tests can end up as user acceptance tests or installation verification programs to be shipped with the product and hence the testers get to have some more deliverables in the product. Finally, today's products are pretty complex and require not just the binaries and executables to be shipped but also sample programs and applications. In fact, most product vendors have websites that have sample programs or applications that demonstrate the use of the various features of the product. A test engineer, with a holistic view of product usage, is best suited to write these sample applications. The introduction of these samples in a product release or a website increases the sense of seeing a visible deliverable for the testing process and hence increases ownership in the testing process.

13.1.7 "Testing is Only Destructive"

> Testing is destructive as much it is constructive, like the two sides of a coin.

There is a perception is that test engineers are only working towards "breaking the software" or testing to prove "the product doesn't work." This is not entirely true. This "pessimism" in testing (that is, wanting to find defects) is just one part of the testing job. The pessimism attached to testing should be viewed as professional pessimism or constructive pessimism. Such constructive pessimism together with balanced curiosity is required for constructive product development. The test engineers not only say "something doesn't work," they also point out "what works" in the product. The job of testing is a combination of pointing out what works in the product, "breaking the software" and analyzing the risk of releasing the software with the defects, and providing a mitigation plan by striking a perfect balance across all these perspectives. The balance among these perspectives brings a positive mindset to the test engineer.

Just because the test engineer brings the "bad news" on the product (of things not working), it does not mean the profession is bad or testing is destructive. The very same test engineer can provide the workaround to get over the defect, when the same or similar defects get reported by the customer, saving the company money and image. Knowing a problem is half solving the problem. By reporting a problem in a positive way with adequate data, the test engineers provide a method to solve the problem, without which the problems are difficult to solve on several occasions.

Thus, the job of test engineers is not only to find defects but also prevent defects by proactively reviewing the specifications, design, architecture, and code from the testing angle. Defects can be prevented by providing the test cases in advance to developers so that the code can incorporate all test conditions. This makes testing proactive, constructive, and saves effort in finding and fixing problems. The seemingly destructive nature of testing assumes a constructive dimension by virtue of this contribution towards proactive problem resolution.

13.2 COMPARISON BETWEEN TESTING AND DEVELOPMENT FUNCTIONS

The perceptions and misconceptions discussed above arise because of some significant differences between testing and development functions. Let us look at some of these differences now.

Testing is often a crunch time function Even though there are different phases of testing and different types of testing that get distributed throughout software life cycle, the major thrust on testing usually comes close to product release time. This concentration of testing functions close to product release time throws in some unique planning and management challenges.

Generally more "elasticity" is allowed in projects in earlier phases It is considered almost normal to expect that the development functions will take longer than planned! However, since the final deadline for a product release is seldom compromised, the same amount of elasticity and flexibility that is given for development activities are not usually given for testing activities. Thus, planning testing projects usually affords less flexibility than development projects.

Testing functions are arguably the most difficult ones to staff For all the reasons we are discussing in this chapter, there is a much smaller number of people who take to testing as a career compared to other functions. This makes it difficult to attract and retain top talent for testing functions. However, since testing functions usually take place under time pressure, the uncertainty on the people dimension calls for more exhaustive contingency planning.

Testing functions usually carry more external dependencies than development functions There are two factors that contribute to this. The first factor is that testing comes at the end of a project life cycle. Secondly, testing activities usually have a number of "show stopper" situations wherein the testing activities would come to a standstill until certain defects in the product get fixed. Once the product is retested after the defects are fixed, it may uncover more serious defects, thus increasing the external dependencies even further.

13.3 PROVIDING CAREER PATHS FOR TESTING PROFESSIONALS

We briefly discussed the myth that people believe about the lack of career opportunities in testing. As we saw earlier, there is a pronounced feeling of uncertainty about career paths in the minds of aspiring testing professionals. The objective of this section is to share some of our thoughts on what testing professionals can expect as a career and to re-emphasize that a career in testing could be as rewarding and satisfying as any other career for motivated and competent people. In this section, we present the career progressions that a testing professional may look forward to and the competencies he or she needs to acquire as he or she makes this progression.

When people look for a career path in testing (or for that matter in any chosen profession), some of the areas of progression they look for are

1. Technical challenge;
2. Learning opportunities;
3. Increasing responsibility and authority;
4. Increasing independence;
5. Ability to have a significant influence on an organization's success; and
6. Rewards and recognition.

To go higher up the value chain in each of the above dimensions, we have identified a framework comprising three stages through which an individual goes through.

The first stage is the *follow* stage. At the beginning of this stage, the trust and confidence level between the individual and the organization just starts to evolve. Most professionals, when they start their career with an organization (especially fresh from school), are simply given instructions to be followed. At this stage of their career, they have fairly detailed instructions on what tasks they have to do and how they should go about carrying out the defined tasks. This is required as both the individual and the organization try to get a feel of each other's strengths and evolve a method of working together. Thus at this stage, the work

1. Is fairly task oriented;
2. Comes with detailed instructions; and
3. Leaves little requirement for decision making.

A demonstration of capability in the assigned tasks at the follow stage leads to the individual getting recognized as trustworthy as well as enables the individual to learn the ropes of the tasks that he or she is executing. The individual is ready to move from just executing tasks by following instructions to *formulating* tasks, for himself or herself as well as for others. At this stage of the career, there is an increased focus on

1. Independent decision making;
2. Clarity in communication to assign work for others; and
3. Interacting with other groups.

When an individual reaches the formulating stage, he or she has demonstrated an ability to plan ahead as well as to delegate and monitor work. At this stage, the individual has created a competent next level to take on some of the functions he or she has been performing. This takes him or her to the next stage of playing an *influencing* role to mentor and nurture other individuals. At this influencing stage, the individual becomes a role model. Others in the organization feel comfortable approaching these role models for advice and guidance for the chosen tasks. At this stage, these role models are ready to assume additional responsibilities in other dimensions. When they assume these additional responsibilities, they may begin in the *following* stage for the new areas they are starting off, presumably under the tutelage of an existing role model in the new area.

Let us illustrate this progression for a typical test engineer from a functional point of view. A typical test engineer's career may begin by executing certain manual or automated tests. The job calls for diligently following the given instructions and completing the feedback loop as per the specified process. After some point of time, the test engineer may grow from executing tests to writing the tests scripts using an automated tool. This increases the technical challenge for the test engineer. He or she then moves to test design, which will involve better understanding of the product and the domain. This can in turn lead to formulating standards for designing and coding of tests, thus having a wider impact on testing. Finally, the engineer can reach the influencing stage, where he or she can take part in activities like evaluating test automation tools, interfacing with external product groups, and participating in upstream activities such as design to enhance the effectiveness of testing.

We have presented in Figure 13.1 one possible career progression for testing professionals that takes into account the three stages of growth. An individual starts his or her testing career as a test engineer. During this time,

Figure 13.1

Career progression for testing professionals.

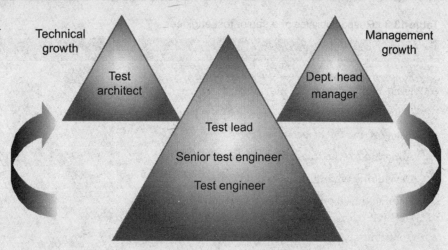

Table 13.2   Responsibilities of a test engineer.

Task	Follow	Formulate	Influence
Following the test processes for executing tests, maintaining tests, and so on	✓		
Filing high-quality defects, usable by developers	✓		
Categorizing defects		✓	
Adhering to schedules specified	✓		
Developing high-quality documentation	✓		

most of the role he or she plays is in the follow stage. In areas like categorizing defects, the test engineer is expected to get involved in formulation, being closest to reality. Table 13.2 above presents the various responsibilities that a test engineer would face.

A test engineer, upon gaining the necessary expertise and demonstrating ability and competence, moves to the role of a senior test engineer. At this level, the individual carries out the activities of a test engineer but with more independence and less supervision. Thus there is a progression to the formulate stage in a number of activities. In addition, there are a few new tasks added, wherein the individual begins to gain familiarity (by being in the follow stage).

The next stage of progression is a test lead, who essentially has module level responsibility for testing a module of a product. The test lead and the module development lead work hand in hand to make sure that the module meets the functions it is supposed to accomplish. A test lead's role involves

Table 13.3   Responsibilities of a senior test engineer.

Task	Follow	Formulate	Influence
Following the test processes for executing tests, maintaining tests, and so on	✓	✓	
Filing high-quality defects, usable by developers	✓	✓	
Categorizing the defects		✓	
Adhering to schedules specified	✓	✓	
Developing high-quality documentation	✓	✓	
Helping development staff in debugging and problem isolation	✓		
Contribution to enhancing processes for testing	✓		
Generation of metrics related to testing	✓		

Table 13.4   Responsibilities of a test lead.

Task	Follow	Formulate	Influence
Review of test cases, test design, and so on at the module level		✓	✓
Planning a test strategy and test plan for the module		✓	
Allocating tasks to individuals		✓	
Monitoring tasks given to individuals	✓	✓	
Making technology and tool choices for module testing		✓	✓
Mentoring team members and assisting them in technical matters			✓
Interaction with development teams for debugging and problem reproduction			✓
Interaction with product documentation teams for debugging and problem reproduction			
Generation and analysis of metrics related to testing at a module level		✓	✓
Overall responsibility for test quality at a module level		✓	✓

a significant amount of influencing and getting the job done by other test engineers and senior test engineers. This role also entails an increase in communication requirements, both within the group as well as with other groups. The test lead becomes the anchor point for people performing downstream testing such as integration testing and system testing.

Table 13.5 Responsibilities of a test manager/department head.

Task	Follow	Formulate	Influence
Planning the test strategy at a product or organizational level		✓	✓
Driving quality at the product or organizational level		✓	✓
Allocation of resources across the board		✓	✓
Making technology and tool choices		✓	✓
Risk management		✓	✓
Inter-group co-ordination		✓	✓
Hiring and retaining top talent into the organization		✓	✓
Helping team members with career planning		✓	✓
Implementing organizational policies	✓	✓	✓
Instilling organizational values in the team		✓	✓
Effective management of meetings		✓	✓
Keeping everyone in sync by effective communication		✓	✓

The test lead position presents a decision point for an individual. He or she has to choose between climbing the technical ladder or the management ladder. On the management ladder, the individual can don the role of a test manager or a department head. In this role, the responsibilities get focused on people issues and higher level strategy issues. Most of the functions are at the influencing and formulating levels. If an individual does not want to climb the management ladder but chooses to rise on the technical front, he or she can take up the option of being a test architect. This role essentially does not contain direct people management responsibilities but focuses more on aspects like providing overall technology direction, being a torchbearer of organizational values, helping in hiring and mentoring top talent in the organization, and playing an active role in the choice of tools for test automation.

These different roles have been found to be quite effective in fulfilling the aspirations of test engineers for a successful career. In order to carry out the required functions at various levels, a good combination of knowledge, skills, and attitude are required. *Knowledge* refers to knowing *what to do* in different situations. *Skill* refers to understanding *how to do* the required things. *Attitude* pertains to being motivated and *wanting* to do the right things. The ability to provide a career path for employees depends crucially on identifying the right combination of knowledge, skills and attitude. Table 13.6 summarizes the various attributes required at each of the job levels.

Table 13.6 Attribute requirements for test professionals at various job levels.

Attribute	Test engineer	Senior test engineer	Test lead	Test manager	Test architect
Knowledge					
Product knowledge	Low	Medium	High	Very high	Very high
Interface knowledge	Medium	High	Very high	Very high	Very high
Competitive information	Low	Low	Not essential but useful	Very high	Very high
Knowledge of test process	High	High	High	High	High
Test tool usage knowledge	High	Very high	High	Medium	High
Industry best practices for testing	Low	Medium	High	Very high	Very high
Test design review	Low	Medium	Medium	High	Very high
Test case review	Low	Medium	High	High	Very high
Process improvements	Low	Medium	Very high	High	Very high
Risk management	Low	Medium	Very high	Very high	Medium
Test automation	High	Very high	Very high	High	Medium
Review of feature requirements and testability	Low	Low	High	Very high	Very high
Generation of test metrics	Low	Low	Very high	Very high	Low
Analysis of metrics	Low	Low	High	Very high	Very high
Evaluation of tools	Low	Low	Medium	High	Very high
Test automation	High	Very high	Very high	High	Medium
Overall release quality	Low	Low	High	Very high	Medium
Skills					
Ability to share knowledge	Medium	Medium	High	High	Very high
Internal communication skills	Medium	Medium	High	Very high	Very high
Cross-group communication skills	Low	Medium	Very high	Very high	Very high
Ability to seek and use feedback	Very high	Very high	High	High	Very high
Keeping immediate manager informed of changes	Very high	Very high	Very high	High	Medium
Ability to prioritize	Low	Low	High	High	High
Ability to raise issues proactively	Very high	Very high	Very high	High	High
Customer focus	Medium	Medium	High	Very high	Very high
Goal setting	Low	Medium	Very high	Very high	High
Ability to work without follow up	Low	Medium	High	Very high	Very high
Effective status reporting	Very high	Very high	Very high	Very high	Very high
Ability to negotiate and influence others	Low	Low	High	Very high	Very high
Awareness of status in interfacing teams	Low	Medium	High	Very high	Very high

Table 13.6 Continued.

Attribute	Test engineer	Senior test engineer	Test lead	Test manager	Test architect
Attitude					
Instilling pride in work	Medium	Medium	High	Very high	Very high
Motivating people by being role models	Low	Medium	High	Very high	Very high
Promoting team work	Low	Low	Medium	Very high	Very high
Setting and tracking challenging goals for self and team	Low	Low	Medium	Very high	High
Providing technical guidance to team	Low	High	Very high	High	Very high
Evolving strategy for testing a feature or module	Low	Low	High	Very high	Very high
Allocating people for tasks	Low	Low	High	Very high	Low

In addition to all the above, every team member, regardless of his or her level in the organization, should have some common traits. These traits include

1. Being a team player and understanding the importance of the success of the team as a whole rather than focusing only on individual interests. As discussed earlier, the success of the testing team depends on uncovering defects before the product is shipped out. This should not be viewed as a function inimical to development. The focus of the entire organization should be to release high-quality products in a timely manner and the testing team members should also keep this overarching goal in mind.

2. Taking initiative. As in most other professions, successful people are those who take initiative, volunteer, experiment, and share their learning with others. Testing profession is no exception to this.

3. Being a continuous learner. With the technology landscape changing rapidly, it is essential that an individual be able to quickly adapt to new technologies, processes, and tools.

4. Being able to react quickly to changes without giving up on proactive planning. Testing will require a lot of flexibility on the part of the team members, especially because it is a downstream activity. They have to be able to respond quickly to changing priorities, delayed handover from development, and flux of employees. At the same time, they should anticipate such contingencies as early as possible, so that they are better prepared to meet the changes.

From the above discussion, it is obvious that fears about the non-viability of testing careers are completely misplaced. There is enough challenge, enough rewards, and enough career opportunities for an aspiring and competent professional to scale great heights in testing.

13.4   THE ROLE OF THE ECOSYSTEM AND A CALL FOR ACTION

The perceptions, misconceptions, and issues discussed so far cannot all be corrected by each and every organization individually. There are collective and much higher-level actions that need to be done. These actions pertain to the entire ecosystem covering the education system, senior management, and the community as a whole. We will look at some of these issues in this section and present a call for action that is required from each of these constituents.

13.4.1   Role of Education System

> The right values can only be more effectively *caught* by the students than be *taught* by the teachers!

The education system does not place sufficient emphasis on testing. Consider some of these facts about what prevails in most universities.

✳ There are formal core courses on programming but only a few universities offer core courses on software testing; most do not have a formal full course on testing and even if they do, it is at best a sparsely populated elective course.

✳ There are "lab courses" for various development tools but none or very few for common testing tools.

✳ Even during courses like Operating Systems and Databases, the emphasis on exercises and practical work is only on the programming aspects, not on appropriately testing the built product. As a result, students end up with a lopsided view that the work of producing an operating system or database ends when coding is completed!

✳ Most "projects" done as a part of the curriculum (for one full semester) never ask for test plans nor look at testing effectiveness. Almost the complete weightage is on coding. Since students work towards where the rewards are, there is almost complete neglect of testing functions. This sets in as a habit that has to be "unlearned" when they start their careers.

✳ Most courses and projects reward individual performance and present very little opportunity for team work, which is so essential for the success of development and test engineers. More importantly, communication and soft skills, which are absolute table stakes for a test engineer, are neither emphasized nor formally taught.

✳ Real-life scenarios like constant churn of changes and the impact of such changes on the quality of the product and the demands placed on testing and quality assurance methods are seldom emphasized. This reduces the student's ability to react quickly to changes.

Some of the things that need to be done to improve the awareness of importance of testing and to inculcate the right knowledge, skills, and attitude towards testing with a sense of urgency are

✠ Making a course on software testing mandatory for all students of computer science, software engineering, and information technology;

✠ Giving extra attention to communication and soft skills during degree programs;

✠ Requiring every practical assignment in every course to focus not just on the programming aspects but also on testing the developed product in a systematic manner; and

✠ Setting aside a certain percentage of marks for project work for developing test plans and presenting appropriate metrics for testing.

Overall, the academic community has to instill the right value systems to appreciate the importance and value of the testing functions. This calls for some attitudinal changes in the academia as well as leading by example by changing the evaluation criteria appropriately.

13.4.2 Role of Senior Management

Fairness to and recognition of testing professionals should not only be **done** but should be **seen to** be done.

The senior management of organizations plays a vital role in the development of test professionals. It is simply not enough to use words like "quality is our top concern" or "people are our top priority." This commitment has to be translated into *visible action*. Some of the concrete steps they can take to achieve this are as follows.

1. Ensuring a fair distribution of appropriately talented people in the testing arena. For example, by allocating some of the best hires from the "Ivy League" schools for testing functions, the senior management sends a strong signal about its commitment to quality and recognition of the importance of testing functions.

2. Not allowing development engineers to look down upon test engineers. They are—and should be treated—as peers, equal stakeholders, and contributors in the success of a product.

3. Encouraging and consciously ensuring that there is active job rotation among development, testing, and support functions. Such job rotation will increase the cohesion in the organization and minimize the chances of testers being "looked down upon."

4. Demonstrating equity in recognition and reward schemes to the top performers in all the functions, including testing.

5. Nurturing talent in test professionals by providing them opportunities to further their knowledge and skills. This can be accomplished by encouraging participation in community activities

> ## How to spot a good tester?
>
> Look for the pride in testing ... if that gleam is not seen in the eye, the fire is not likely to be in the belly.
>
> Look for a clean typo-free resume ... if the candidate does not test his or her own resume well, it is unlikely he or she will test a product well!
>
> Provide a teaser with an option between development and testing ... the die-hard tester will not take the bait!
>
> Examine his or her holistic understanding of the domain of product ... a good tester can understand the big picture better and demonstrate that understanding visibly.

such as conferences and by rewarding people who go in for the various certification programs. This should result in the creation of role models for testing, who are highly visible in the organization and thus motivate more people to take testing as a career.

We will summarize the role of the senior management in fostering testing professionals by adapting a quote from Agatha Christie's *Witness for Prosecution* given in the shaded box at the beginning of the section.

13.4.3 Role of the Community

> As members of test community, do you have pride and sense of equality? Remember, authority is taken, not given!

Regardless of whatever the senior management or academia do, the success of the testing community starts from within. There are a few things that the members of the testing community—the testing professionals—should do in order to showcase and promote the testing profession.

Testers should start with a sense of pride in their job and the realization of their role in a more holistic way, in the bigger picture of the entire product. It is often this lack of internal pride that acts as the biggest bottleneck. This creates an apparent sense of lack of parity with developers and develops into a self-fulfilling prophecy.

The pride in work is best illustrated by an oft-told story given in an inset on the next page.

Testers should themselves see a career in testing rather than view testing as a stopgap arrangement or a means to get into development functions. Hopefully, the career paths outlined in the previous section will motivate people to take up testing as a career.

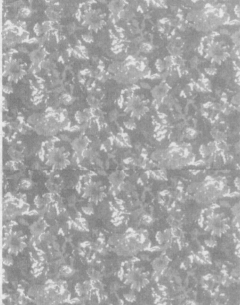

There were three workers working at a construction site.

A passer-by asked the first worker, "What are you doing?"

"Phew, I am just slogging along, as it is my fate," replied the worker.

The passer-by posed the same question to the second worker. "I am breaking stones," the second worker replied.

Then the passer by asked the third worker the same question.

The third worker replied enthusiastically, "I am helping build a cathedral that will soon come up at this site!"

The first worker is like a tester looking at testing as a stopgap arrangement, blaming his fate for not getting into a development job. The second worker is like a person who does testing but does not see its relevance.

The final worker is the one who sees the value in his work and understands the big picture.

Test engineers need not be just followers of technology—they can take an active part in shaping and using new technology. There is a misconception that new technology is difficult to understand for test engineers, and that only "developers" are better equipped to understand it. Sometimes, test engineers are under pressure to learn the technology and test the product at the same time. Learning the product and testing it at the same time may lead to ineffective testing. This scenario must change. A positive scenario would be one in which test engineers understand new technology areas proactively before they are implemented in a product. This can be achieved by being part of the product development team and contributing to ensure that the technology is correctly adopted in the product so as to benefit the customers. Proactive involvement of test engineers in understanding new technology can bring in better user perspective that can enhance the market potential of a product.

One of the reasons why there is a strong fraternity of professionals in development and other software engineering arenas is the existence of communities and forums for sharing experiences and furthering knowledge. There are a number of conferences and symposia that cater to various aspects of development. In contrast, the number of forums devoted purely to testing is very limited. The good news is that this has been changing rapidly over the past few years. It is important to keep up the momentum to create sustained forums for the testing profession. Some of the activities that could be taken up include

✠ Creation of industry-academia collaboration in recognizing champions and spreading the message of the importance of testing;

✠ Institution of awards for stellar contributions to the testing profession; and

✠ Organizing events focused on testing.

A synergy amongst the various stakeholders of the ecosystem described above enhances the chances of spotting aspiring test professionals early, furthering their knowledge, skills, and attitude so that they fit better into the industry. They can then continue to grow in the testing profession and understand the business value of the testing profession and appreciate where they fit in the overall scheme of things.

REFERENCES

The topic of people issues are not discussed at great length in the literature. When it comes to issues facing geographically distributed teams, the material available is even lesser. One of the popular books that focuses on people issues across the board in software engineering is [DEMA-87]. [SRINI-2003] provides insights into the issues involved in building effective test organizations. [RAME-2002] covers the important aspects of managing global software projects and the various organization structures possible for testing as well as other types of projects. [IEEE-2001] was a special issue on global product development. Although the issue does not have any article directly related to testing, the issues pertaining to teams that are geographically distributed discussed here are widely applicable to testing as well. [BURN-2004] discusses the issues of building a test organization on various dimensions of skill development, providing a career path, etc.

PROBLEMS AND EXERCISES

1. What arguments would you give to a person who says that the testing job is not challenging?

2. Through the text, we have been talking of only two job functions and have labeled them—"development" and "testing." Consider the other job functions like support and maintenance.

   a. Compare the career paths and progressions in testing to those in these job functions.

   b. Compare the nature of these new job functions with testing and identify similarities and differences.

3. Discuss how a job rotation among all the job functions—development, maintenance, testing, and support can be rewarding for the employees and worthwhile for the organization.

4. Which of the following statements by senior management would you agree with? Justify your answer

   a. "I will give you a Java development job if you do the testing function for six months."

   b. "Our hiring policy will be to hire under graduate students (freshers) for testing functions; Freshers are not allowed for development functions."

   c. "Every developer will have to rotate to testing and support functions for three months."

   d. "The bonus allocation percentage should be the same for top performers in all the job functions."

5. How will you respond to the following statements by test engineers?

   a. "Both he and I are from the same college and I have got higher grades than him—why is it that he has been given development function whereas I have been put in testing?"

   b. "My performance in the testing role is poor because I told you I am not interested in testing . . . put me in development and see the change in my performance."

   c. "I enjoy testing, show me what new things I can learn in testing."

   d. "I have taken up testing—shouldn't I get a higher compensation?"

6. You are having a set of test engineers from whom you have identified a few who can advance to the level of senior test engineers. List the kind of training programs you will put them to.

7. When a person wants to move laterally from the position of a test architect to that of a test manager,

   a. What challenges should he or she expect?

   b. What training programs will he/she have to undergo?

   c. What changes would the person have to make internally to be successful in the new role?

8. One of the tasks in the management ladder was "driving quality at the product or organizational level." Elaborate on this and break this down into more detailed activities.

Organization Structures for Testing Teams

CHAPTER 14

In this chapter—

- ✓ Dimensions of organization structures
- ✓ Structures in single-product companies
- ✓ Structures for multi-product companies
- ✓ Effect of globalization and geographically distributed teams on product testing
- ✓ Testing services organizations
- ✓ Success factors for testing organizations

14.1 DIMENSIONS OF ORGANIZATION STRUCTURES

In this chapter, we will look at the various organization structures in typical testing organizations. (We discuss only the organization structures directly pertaining to development and testing. Other parts of an organization such as finance, administration, and so on have not been covered.)

Organization structures directly relate to some of the people issues discussed in the previous chapter. In addition, the study of organization structures is important from the point of view of effectiveness because an appropriately designed organization structure can provide accountability to results. This accountability can promote better teamwork among the different constituents and create in better focus in the work. In addition, organization structures provide a road map for the team members to envision their career paths.

We have discussed organization structures based on two dimensions. The first dimension is organization type and the second dimension is on geographic distribution.

We have broadly classified types of organizations into two categories—*product* organizations and *services* organizations. Product organizations produce software products and have a "womb to tomb" (or conception through design, development, testing and maintenance to product obsolescence) responsibility for the entire product. Testing happens to be one of the phases or groups that are within the organization. The product organizations that we will discuss in this chapter are multi-product organizations. Service organizations do not have complete product responsibility. In the testing context, they are external organizations that provide testing services to other organizations that require them. In essence, testing services are outsourced to such organizations. Such testing services organizations provide specialized and committed personnel for testing. They also undertake specialized and niche areas of examining performance testing, internationalization testing, and so on.

A second factor that plays a significant role in deciding organization structures is the geographic distribution of teams. Product or service organizations that are involved in testing can be either single-site or multi-site. In a single-site team, all members are located at one place while in a multi-site team, the team is scattered across multiple locations. Multi-site teams introduce cultural and other factors that influence organization structures.

14.2 STRUCTURES IN SINGLE-PRODUCT COMPANIES

Product companies in general have a high-level organization structure similar to the one shown in Figure 14.1.

Figure 14.1

Organization structure of a multi-product company.

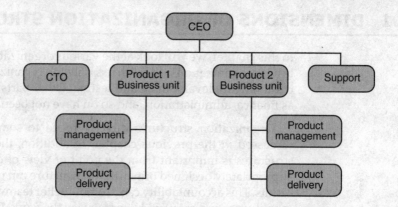

Note: *We have only indicated groups that are directly related to our discussion. We have consciously left out groups such as sales, finance and administration, hardware infrastructure group, and so on.*

The CTO's office sets the high-level technology directions for the company. A business unit is in charge of each product that the company produces. (Sometimes the business unit may also handle related *products* to form a *product line*.) A product business unit is organized into a *product management* group and a *product delivery group*. The product management group has the responsibility of merging the CTO's directions with specific market needs to come out with a product road map. The product delivery group is responsible for delivering the product and handles both the development and testing functions. We use the term "project manager" to denote this head. Sometimes the term "development manager" or "delivery manager" is also used.

Figure 14.1 shows a typical multi-product organization. The internal organization of the delivery teams varies with different scenarios for single- and multi-product companies, as we will discuss below.

14.2.1 Testing Team Structures for Single-Product Companies

Most product companies start with a single product. During the initial stages of evolution, the organization does not work with many formalized processes. The product delivery team members distribute their time among multiple tasks and often wear multiple hats. All the engineers report into the project manager who is in charge of the entire project, with very little distinction between testing function and development functions. Thus, there is only a very thin line separating the "development team and "testing team."

The model in Figure 14.2 is applicable in situations where the product is in the early stages of evolution. We have indicated in Figure 14.2 that a "project manager" handles part or all of a product. We have consciously avoided showing multiple layers of management for the development and

Figure 14.2

Typical organization
structures in early
stages of a product.

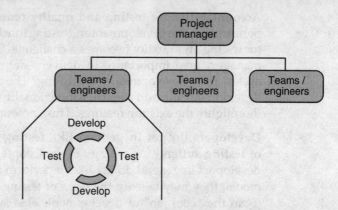

testing functions. This is because, in a small organization in the early stages of development, there is very little management hierarchy and people playing the roles of "managers," "leads" and so on actually are also "engineers" who are expected to act as individual contributors as well.

This model offers some advantages that are well suited to small organizations.

Exploits the rear-loading nature of testing activities Even though testing activities are distributed throughout the project life cycle, the major concentration and pressure points for testing arise during the later part of the project life cycle. Thus, this organization structure provides an automatic load-balancing scheme wherein during the early part of the project, everyone chips in for development and during the later part, they wear a different hat and switch over to testing.

Enables engineers to gain experience in all aspects of life cycle Since an engineer divides his or her time between development and testing, he or she can get to know what is involved in all the life cycle activities. This also makes them appreciate the importance of and difficulties in all the activities and prepares them for a better teamwork when the functions are broken down among different groups.

Is amenable to the fact that the organization mostly only has informal processes An organization in its early days usually has only informal processes and there may not be well-defined entry and exit criteria for products to satisfy to move from one phase to another, say from development to testing. Thus, multiplexing the same resource between development and testing is in line with this informal nature of the organization.

Some defects may be detected early Since the developers perform the testing functions, there is a possibility that they may catch the defects closer to the point of injection (much like what white box testing can do).

This model, however, has some serious disadvantages that cause an organization to move away quickly from it. These disadvantages are as follows.

Accountability for testing and quality reduces Since the same persons perform both the development and testing functions, providing accountability for testing and quality becomes a challenge. Should a developer (or project manager) give importance to delivery dates or should he or she "steal cycles" from development to do testing? The temptation is to spend time on development and add some new functionality, even at the expense of testing thoroughly the existing features. Thus, accountability for testing suffers.

Developers do not in general like testing and hence the effectiveness of testing suffers As we saw in the Chapter 13, People Issues in Testing, developers in general do not like to perform testing activities. Thus, in this model, they may take up the tasks of testing as a "price" they have to pay to do the "cool job" of development. This lack of intrinsic motivation for performing the testing function can have a telling effect on the effectiveness of testing.

Schedule pressures generally compromise testing When push comes to shove, deadlines rule the roost! There are always lots of deadlines to meet and there may not be sufficient time for testing. This, coupled with a typical engineer's preference for development tasks than testing tasks, compromises the quality of testing.

Developers may not be able carry out the different types of tests As we have seen in the earlier chapters there are a number of different types of tests. A developer may not be equipped to carry out all the tests, because such testing may require specialized infrastructure or skills. For example, performance testing may not be an area where a general product developer can perform effectively because he or she would have to be well versed in ascertaining typical workloads, using special tools, and so on. Thus, it would become necessary to separate at least these specialized testing functions into a different group.

As the product matures and the processes evolve, a homogeneous single-product organization doing both development and testing, splits into two distinct groups, one for development and one for testing. These two teams are considered as peer teams and both report to the project manager in charge of the entire product. In this model, some of the disadvantages of the previous model are done away with.

Figure 14.3

Separate groups for testing and development.

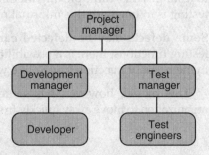

1. There is clear accountability for testing and development. The results and the expectations from the two teams can be more clearly set and demarcated.

2. Testing provides an external perspective. Since the testing and development teams are logically separated, there is not likely to be as much bias as in the previous case for the testers to prove that the product works. This external perspective can lead to uncovering more defects in the product.

3. Takes into account the different skill sets required for testing. As we have seen in the earlier chapters, the skill sets required for testing functions are quite different from that required for development functions. This model recognizes the difference in skill sets and proactively address the same.

There are certain precautions that must be taken to make this model effective. First, the project manager should not buckle under pressure and ignore the findings and recommendations of the testing team by releasing a product that fails the test criteria. Second, the project manager must ensure that the development and testing teams do not view each other as adversaries. This will erode the teamwork between the teams and ultimately affect the timeliness and quality of the product. Third, the testing team must participate in the project decision making and scheduling right from the start so that they do not come in at the "crunch time" of the project and face unrealistic schedules or expectations.

14.2.2   Component-Wise Testing Teams

Even if a company produces only one product, the product is made up of a number of components that fit together as a whole. In order to provide better accountability, each component may be developed and tested by separate teams and all the components integrated by a single integration test team reporting to the project manager. The structure of each of the component teams can be either a coalesced development-testing team (as in the first model above) or a team with distinct responsibilities for testing and development. This is because not all components are of the same complexity, not all components are at the same level of maturity. Hence, an informal mix-and-match of the different organization structures for the different components, with a central authority to ensure overall quality will be more effective. Figure 14.4 depicts this model.

14.3   STRUCTURES FOR MULTI-PRODUCT COMPANIES

When a company becomes successful as a single-product company, it may decide to diversify into other products. In such a case, each of the products is considered as a separate business unit, responsible for all activities of a product. In addition, as before, there will be common roles like the CTO.

Figure 14.4

Component-wise organization.

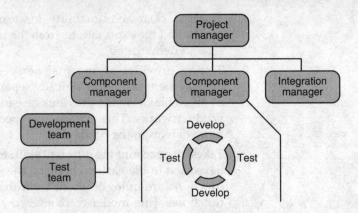

The organization of test teams in multi-product companies is dictated largely by the following factors.

How tightly coupled the products are in terms of technology   If different products exploit similar technology, perhaps there may also be a synergy of testing of these similar products. For example, if an organization is making compilers for different languages, it may be possible to spread the testing resources across the multiple compilers. However, if an organization has a wide coverage of product types—ranging from system software products like operating systems or database to application software products like a payroll system—then it is unlikely that the testing resources can be shared across the products as the skill sets required for the two functions are different.

Dependence among various products   If the dependence among the products is high, then testing of the products would also be necessarily tightly coupled. A change in one product may have a significant impact on the functioning of another product. Thus, it may be necessary to have some overlap among the testing teams of the various products. At least, there may be a need for an organization-wide testing team that performs integration testing of the various dependent products.

How synchronous are the release cycles of products   If the release cycles of the various products are synchronous, it may mean two things. One, there is likely to be some dependency amongst the products. Two, the resources for testing are likely to be demanded at the same time. These appear like two conflicting demands—on the one hand, there needs to be commonality in the testing team because of dependencies (as discussed in the previous paragraph); on the other hand, because the resources are needed for different products at the same time, the resources may have be part of distinct teams with different reporting structures.

Customer base for each product and similarity among customer bases for various products   Since the type of testing and skill sets required for testing depend largely on the nature of the product which in turn is dictated by the customer base, the nature of the latter may have an influence on whether the teams for the different products should be same or different.

Based on the above factors, there are several options available for organizing testing teams for a multi-product company.

1. A central "test think-tank/brain trust" team, which formulates the test strategy for the organization
2. One test team for all the products
3. Different test teams for each product (or related products)
4. Different test teams for different types of tests
5. A hybrid of all the above models

14.3.1 Testing Teams as Part of "CTO's Office"

In a number of situations, the participation of the testing teams comes later in the product life cycle while the design and development teams get to participate early. However, testability of a product is as important (if not more important) as its development. Hence, it makes sense to assign the same level of importance to testing as to development. One way to accomplish this is to have a testing team report directly to the CTO as a peer to the design and development teams. The advantages that this model brings to the table are as follows.

1. Developing a product architecture that is testable or suitable for testing. For example, the non-functional test requirements are better addressed during architecture and design; by associating the testing team with the CTO, there is a better chance that the product design will keep the testing requirements in mind.
2. Testing team will have better product and technology skills. These skills can be built upfront during the product life cycle. In fact, the testing team can even make valuable contributions to product and technology choices.
3. The testing team can get a clear understating of what design and architecture are built for and plan their tests accordingly
4. The technical road map for product development and test suite development will be in better sync.
5. In the case of a multi-product company, the CTO's team can leverage and optimize the experiences of testing across the various product organizations/business units in the company.
6. The CTO's team can evolve a consistent, cost-effective strategy for test automation.
7. As the architecture and testing responsibilities are with the same person, that is the CTO, the end-to-end objectives of architecture such as performance, load conditions, availability requirements, and so on can be met without any ambiguity and planned upfront.

In this model, the CTO handles only the architecture and test teams. The actual development team working on the product code can report to a different person, who has operational responsibilities for the code. This ensures independence to the testing team.

This group reporting to the CTO addresses issues that have organization-wide ramifications and need proactive planning. A reason for making them report to the CTO is that this team is likely to be cross-divisional, and cross-functional. This reporting structure increases the credibility and authority of the team. Thus, their decisions are likely to be accepted with fewer questions by rest the of the organization, without much of a "this decision does not apply to my product as it was decided by someone else" kind of objections.

This structure also addresses career path issues of some of the top test engineers. Oftentimes, people perceive a plateau in the testing profession and harbor a misconception that in order to move ahead in their career, they have to go into development. This model, wherein a testing role reports to the CTO and has high visibility, will motivate them to have a good target to aim for.

In order that such a team reporting to the CTO be effective,

1.   It should be small in number;
2.   It should be a team of equals or at most very few hierarchies;
3.   It should have organization-wide representation;
4.   It should have decision-making and enforcing authority and not just be a recommending committee; and
5.   It should be involved in periodic reviews to ensure that the operations are in line with the strategy.

14.3.2   Single Test Team for All Products

It may be possible to carry out the single-testing-team company model of a single-product company into a multi-product company. Earlier in this section, we discussed some criteria of how to organize testing teams. Based on those criteria, a single testing team for all the products would be possible when the line between the products is somewhat thin.

This model is similar to the case of a single-product team divided into multiple components and each of the components being developed by an independent team. The one major difference between the two is that in the earlier model, the project manager to whom the testing teams reports has direct delivery responsibilities whereas in the case of a multi-product company, since different groups/individuals have delivery responsibilities for different products, the single testing team must necessarily report to a different level. There are two possibilities.

1. The single testing team can form a "testing business unit" and report into this unit. This is similar to the "testing services" model to be discussed in the next section.
2. The testing team can be made to report to the "CTO think-tank" discussed earlier. This may make the implementation of standards and procedures somewhat easier but may dilute the function of the CTO think-tank to be less strategic and more operational.

14.3.3 Testing Teams Organized by Product

In a multi-product company, when the products are fairly independent of one another, having a single testing team may not be very natural. Accountability, decision making, and scheduling may all become issues with the single testing team. The most natural and effective way to organize the teams is to assign complete responsibility of all aspects of a product to the corresponding business unit and let the business unit head figure out how to organize the testing and development teams. This is very similar to the multi-component testing teams model.

Depending on the level of integration required among the products, there may be need for a central integration testing team. This team handles all the issues pertaining to the integration of the multiple products. Such an integration team should be cross-product and hence ideally report into the CTO think-tank.

14.3.4 Separate Testing Teams for Different Phases of Testing

So far, we have viewed "testing" as a single, homogeneous activity. In reality, however, it is not so.

- We have seen that there are different *types* of testing that need to be done—such as black box testing, system testing, performance testing, integration testing, internationalization testing, and so on.
- We have also seen that the skill sets required for performing each of these different test types are quite different from each other. For example, for white box testing, an intimate knowledge of the program code and programming language are needed. For black box testing, knowledge of external functionality is needed.
- Each of these different types of tests may be carried out at different points in time. For example, within internationalization testing, certain activities (such as enabling testing) are carried out early in the cycle and fake language testing is done before the product is localized.

As a result of these factors, it is common to split the testing function into different types and phases of testing. Since the nature of the different types of tests are different and because the people who can ascertain or be directly concerned with the specific types of tests are different, the people

Table 14.1 Organizing people to perform different types of testing.

Type of test	Reports into	Rationale
White box testing	Development team	White box testing is inherently close to code, the developers develop and (should) run the tests themselves.
Black box testing	Testing team	This is the first level of "external testing" that a product gets and hence ideally fits in the scope of the testing team, as described above.
Integration testing	Organization-wide testing team	Integration testing involves putting together multiple components or multiple products. Thus, this should ideally belong to an organization-wide testing team.
System testing	Product management or Product marketing	System testing involves testing in real-life scenarios and hence—like acceptance testing —can be part of the product management or product marketing.
Performance testing	A central benchmarking group	Performance testing (as discussed in Chapter 7) is very specialized. This may also be related to benchmarking and industry standards thereof. In case of a multi-product company, there may also be inter-product dependencies that affect performance.
Acceptance testing	Product management or Product marketing	Acceptance testing is actually a proxy for customer acceptance and hence is rightly carried out by product management or product marketing.
Internationalization testing	Internationalization team and some local teams	Internationalization involves testing at various levels. Some of the levels (as discussed in Chapter 9) involve even knowledge of local languages and conventions. Thus the responsibility of this may be distributed.
Regression testing	All test teams	Some of the regression tests are also run as a part of the smoke tests—these parts may continue to report into the product testing teams and the organization must establish processes to transfer these learnings across the groups.

performing the different types of tests may end up reporting into different groups. A possible way of organizing the people performing the different types of testing is shown in Table 14.1.

Such an organization based on the testing types presents several advantages.

1. People with appropriate skill sets are used to perform a given type of test.

2. Defects can get detected better and closer to the point of injection.

3. This organization is in line with the V model and hence can lead to effective distribution of test resources.

The challenge to watch out for is that the test responsibilities are now distributed and hence it may seem that there is no single point of accountability for testing. The key to address this challenge is to define objectively the metrics for each of the phases or groups and track them to completion.

14.3.5 Hybrid Models

The above models are not mutually exclusive or disjoint models. In practice, a combination of all these models are used and the models chosen change from time to time, depending on the needs of the project. For example, during the crunch time of a project, when a product is near delivery, a multi-component team may act like a single-component team. During debugging situations, when a problem to do with the integration of multiple products comes up, the different product teams may work as a single team and report to the CTO/CEO for the duration of that debugging situation. We would like to view the various organization structures presented above as simply building blocks that can be put together in various permutations and combinations, depending on the need of the situation. The main aim of such hybrid organization structures should be effectiveness without losing sight of accountability.

14.4 EFFECTS OF GLOBALIZATION AND GEOGRAPHICALLY DISTRIBUTED TEAMS ON PRODUCT TESTING

14.4.1 Business Impact of Globalization

Globalization has revolutionized the way we produce and maintain software products. As we discussed earlier in the book.

1. Markets for software products are becoming global. Hence, a global distribution of production of software becomes necessary to exploit the knowledge of the local conditions.

2. Since the markets are global, the needs that a product must satisfy are increasing exponentially. Hence, it is impossible to meet all the demands from resources from just one location.

3. Several countries around the globe have a rich supply of talented people and this needs to be utilized effectively.

4. Some countries offer not only a rich supply of talent pool but also offer cost advantages that makes them a compelling business proposition.

It is increasingly common to find software product teams distributed in multiple countries, working together, developing testing and delivering a single product. Testing in particular tends to be a major beneficiary of globalization and helps maximize the potential of globalization. Several factors contribute to this.

1. In mature organizations, testing is fairly well defined as a process and hence can be handed over to a team anywhere provided they are well trained on the process and are equipped with the necessary technology infrastructure.

2. When test automation is not involved, testing is a manual process and hence it may not be possible to find people in all countries who can or will do the job.

3. When test automation is involved, automation development is usually an activity that has to go on in parallel with testing of the products to be released. This offers a scope for parallelism, which in turn enables use of resources in multiple locations.

4. Testing of older releases of a product is an activity that is perceived as low risk but essential for ensuring the sustenance of existing customers. This makes it possible to choose a low-cost location to perform such activities.

There are essentially two organization structures for distributing testing teams across multiple locations—*Round the Clock Development/Testing Teams Model* and *Testing Competency Center Model*.

14.4.2   Round the Clock Development/Testing Model

The basic premises that drive this model are as follows.

1. Development and testing happen alternately and iteratively, that is a piece of code is developed, tested, and defects removed. This cycle continues until the testing is deemed complete. Since development and testing alternate, they can be viewed as two separate work units.

2. Since development and testing alternate, it may be possible to perform development during one part of the day and testing during the other part.

3. The geographic time difference between two different locations can be exploited to "stretch" the day so that effectively work can be carried on during the night of one location, which is actually day for another location.

Consider an example of a product team split across California and India. Because of the time difference between India and California, effectively, when it is day time in California, it is night time in India and vice versa. If, say, we distribute the work between the two teams with development being done in California and testing being done in India, we will find that we are

Figure 14.5

Work flow between development team in California and testing team in India.

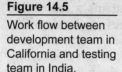
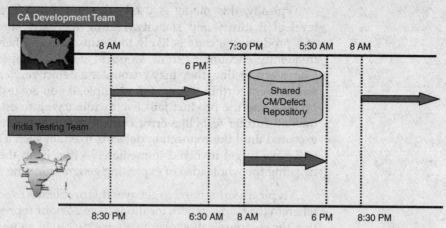

able to get a 24-hour coverage of work across the two teams, without either of the teams having to work continuously for 24-hours at a stretch. In this situation, a typical work flow could be as shown in Figure 14.5.

1. The developers in California work from 8 am to 6 pm their time. The corresponding times in India are 8:30 pm to 6:30 am (next day).

2. Before they sign off for the day, the development team in California check in the latest build into a configuration management repository.

3. The testers in India come to work at 8 am (which is 7:30 pm the previous day in California). They pick up the latest build from the configuration management repository, run whatever tests are required to be run (and possible to run), report the problems encountered into a defect repository. When the testers in India sign off for the day at 6 pm, it is 5:30 am in California. The developers are now ready for their days work to continue to fix the reported defects in the next build and go to the next cycle for the next day.

In the above model, we have actually stretched the day to be almost completely utilized—we have a gap of about three hours in a 24-hour window where no activity is taking place. This model can be extended to have multiple testing teams in multiple locations to utilize these hours also. However, one has to be careful that the communication overheads do not overwhelm the utilization of time.

This model is very natural and effective when

1. Testing as a process is well established and there is no need for developer intervention to make a test run successfully.

2. There is a communication channel available between the two teams during any part of the day or night. This is required so that when one team needs to get clarifications from the other team, they do not end up playing mail tags, wasting time.

Typically, this model is used when the product attains a reasonable level of maturity and stability. During the early stages of development of a product, the code is likely to be unstable and hence testing will very frequently encounter "show stopper" defects. That is, when the testing team starts testing, they may encounter a defect very early in the cycle that will prevent further testing. For example, if you are testing a network layer product and the product fails even while trying to establish a connection, then all further tests like error control, flow control, and so on cannot be executed until the connection defect is fixed. In such a case, the developers will have to get involved immediately—that is, in their night time—thus negating the whole idea of exploiting geographic time difference.

A typical workaround to get over this problem is to adopt a "shift" system wherein the teams in both locations have 24-hour representation. Even with this, the communication overheads arising out of an unstable product make this model unviable early in the product cycle.

14.4.3   Testing Competency Center Model

In this model, a logical organization called the Testing Competency Center is created. This organization could potentially span multiple locations to effectively exploit time difference and/or available skill sets. This Center is highly specialized in testing. It has the final say in the quality of the product and release readiness. The Testing Competency Center model has two variants.

In the first variant, the Center is a shared (and often scarce) resource that is shared across multiple product development groups. As mentioned before, this center has testing competency that is not available elsewhere. Hence, there is a demand for the services of this group. Product development groups "book" the time of this group in advance. With the high skill level of the group and the highly matured processes that this group has, the recommendations of this group are highly regarded by the management. This group could be internal to an organization or can be an external organization of high standing in the testing arena. One can regard this group or Center as a "certifying authority" whose "blessing" is needed before a product can be released. In other words, certification by this Center adds credibility to the product. This model is not to gain cost savings. In fact, it may even be expensive because of the specialized nature of the group. This model is not to exploit the time zone advantages. The placement of the group in any location or locations is determined purely by the availability of talent pool. This model can apply to product as well as service companies.

Another variant of the Testing Competency Center is to have a set of dedicated testing resources that gets involved in the full cycle of testing activities, right from the early stages of the project. This typically follows the process and structure given below.

1. The members of this Center get involved in planning for testing activities right from the early stages of product conception. Any activity that involves testing of a product always entails participation from members of this Center. Note that the physical location of the Center itself is immaterial in this variant.

2. When product functionality and release are being planned, the product team and the testing team from this Center identify and prioritize the product features to be tested and the location where each feature would be tested. This process ensures that the most important features get a higher priority for testing and that the right resources at the right location get involved in testing the right features at the right time.

3. Some of the factors for selecting features to be tested and allocating them to the various locations of the Center are

    (i)   Past experience in using similar features;

    (ii) Skill sets for performing the functions, including using the required test automation tools; and

    (iii) Availability of hardware and software resources (including local availability of support for these resources).

4. The testing team members from the Center spend time with the development team (and, if necessary, the product management team), early in the cycle, understanding the details of the product features allocated for testing. During this time, they get trained on the external and where necessary, internal aspects of the product. This forms the basis for the test planning and test case design.

5. The test case design thus generated gets translated to test cases by a larger team at the Center location(s). They also execute the tests to verify that the tests are tested (true to the dictum we saw in Chapter 1 to "test the tests first"). This creates the first baseline for the test cases.

6. If the product is fairly stable, then the test teams at the Center location(s) can also undertake the repeated testing of the code, as it evolves. If not, there may be a small team co-located with development team that will do the repeated execution in the early stages.

7. The Center in parallel undertakes the automation of the test cases and, over time, the running of the automated tests is done as a part of the build. Since this is automated, the exact location of the server is immaterial.

This second variant is most applicable when a product is undergoing version changes, which are usually upgrades with new features added/ enhanced. In this variant, since the center is focused on developing testing as a competency, it is somewhat similar to "testing as a service" model, discussed later in this chapter.

14.4.4   Challenges in Global Teams

Cultural challenges   Whenever a global team works together, culture and language pose major barriers for communication. Without effective communication, the divide between development and testing will only widen. When a testing team is set up in a new location, it is important for the teams on both the locations to get a mutual appreciation of the culture, language accents, and so on. Some of the ways to achieve this are given below.

1. Planning periodic travel by the members from one location to another: Testing offers natural means to plan such travels—such as acceptance testing, integration testing of modules developed in multiple locations, training on new products to be tested. From a long-term team building perspective, it is important to plan such travel into the project and ensure that before and when an individual travels, he or she gets exposed to the cultural and language aspects of the other location.

2. Periodic video and audio conference calls.

Work allocation challenges   When teams are distributed, it is important to have clear work allocation policies that are articulated upfront and understood consistently by all the teams. There should not be a perception that all the "cool work" goes to one location while all the "not-so-cool work" goes to another location. The entire team must take pride in what they do. Only then can they perform effectively and develop themselves and make the product successful.

Parity across teams   When teams across different geographies work on similar tasks, they expect parity in the way they are treated and in their compensation and reward systems. "Parity" can be a debatable term. Firstly, the teams in different locations would like to have parity in job content. Next, the teams would like parity in ownership, authority and delegation, freedom, and so on. Last, they would also expect reasonable parity in terms of compensation and reward systems. A person working in USA may get a salary in terms of dollars whereas a person working in India may be getting a salary in Indian Rupees, which would not be the same in absolute value as what his or her US counterpart gets. Given the difference in purchasing levels and the economies of the two countries, this difference is natural and reasonable. However, the values that the employee carries may be different and this may even motivate him or her to work in a country with better monetary compensation (even though it may not mean anything). The solution for this is not to offer US salaries to people in India! Some of the ways to address this challenge are

1. Providing challenging job content;

2. Increasing career opportunities in testing, with models like competency centers;

3. Providing long-term retention incentives like stock options; and

4. Providing travel opportunities.

Ability to track effectively When teams are distributed, tracking their progress becomes more difficult. Opportunities for informal tracking such as hallway chats are completely lost. Hence, the tracking mechanism has to be more robust, less person dependent. Some of the ways to increase the effectiveness of tracking include

1. Having planned communication exchanges such as weekly conference calls;

2. Having a clear allocation of tasks;

3. Having a commonly understood and well-enforced reporting mechanism; and

4. Automating as much of the tracking function as possible.

Dependence on communication infrastructure Communication infrastructure through the Internet and Intranet form the lifeline of geographically distributed teams. This is especially true of the "round the clock" model of testing wherein the testers pick up the builds on a daily basis. Such a model mandates the availability of a high bandwidth and highly reliability communication infrastructure. While the communication technology has become fairly robust and this may not be a major issue, it is important to have alternative plans in case communication links snap for some reason. One way to mitigate this risk is to have a backup/mirror site at every location. This may be an expensive proposition. Another way could be to have a small "on site" team in different locations who can proxy for the "offsite" teams if the need arises.

Time difference In the various models of distribution of work and organizing teams, time difference is normally an advantage. However, time difference can also present some challenges. For example, in the round the clock model of testing, when a tester in India, say, encounters a show stopper, he or she may have to call a developer during the developer's night time (assuming that the developer is in USA). If the developer is not available, that workday for the tester in India may be lost completely. In addition, when the developer fixes the problem, the tester should be available or another twelve hours will be lost! Thus, time difference can end up eating up 36 hours for solving a problem that would get fixed within minutes in a single-site team. The key to making effective use of time difference is to have sound processes and proactive quality assurance (so that such show stoppers can be minimized) and also make people work in shifts in various locations so that there is someone to contact at any point of time and in any location.

14.5   TESTING SERVICES ORGANIZATIONS

14.5.1   Business Need for Testing Services

Most of the discussions we have had so far on testing functions have implicitly assumed testing activities as part of the same organization that is responsible for producing, marketing and supporting the product. However, today it is common to find testing activities outsourced to external companies who specialize is testing and provide testing services. There are several business drivers for this model of testing as a service.

1. As we have seen throughout this book, testing is becoming increasingly diverse and a very specialized function.

2. The variety and complexity of the test automation tools further increase the challenge in testing. A specialized testing service organization may be able to effectively fulfill such a niche need.

3. Testing as a process is becoming better defined. This makes testing (at least some phases and types of testing) more amenable to outsourcing.

4. A product development organization which has expertise in understanding the domain of software may not necessarily have expertise in setting up and running an effective testing function (especially if it involves the use of complex automation tools).

5. An outsourced organization can offer location advantages. As we saw in the multi-site teams, testing teams that exist in different time zones can provide a better round-the-clock coverage.

6. An outsourced organization can provide cost advantages. Certain locations can be more economical than others, thus, the overall costs can be reduced. This rationale applies to outsourcing any function (including development and testing).

Thus, testing as a service has gained significant acceptance in the industry. Coupled with the time zone and cost advantages, testing services are normally outsourced to geographically distributed teams.

14.5.2   Differences between Testing as a Service and Product— Testing Organizations

Organization structures and the associated people issues in a testing services organization are driven by certain fundamental factors.

Testing service organizations are generally held at arm's length from product developers   In a typical product development organization (where testing is one of the functions), there is a much closer binding between the development and testing teams, as people generally move from one group to another. Furthermore, there are no Intellectual Property Rights (IPR) issues in the testing team getting exposed to the product code. When testing is outsourced as a service to an external organization, the members of the outsourced organization may not have the same level of rapport with product developers as testers internal to the product organization. This is especially the case if the outsourced team works in a different location, wherein opportunities for rapport building are reduced. The IPR issues of product code ownership also play a role in distancing the testing team from the rest of the product organization.

Testing service organizations may not always provide full breadth of coverage for testing types　Most testing service organizations provide services like black box testing, domain testing, and certain specialized testing such as performance testing or test automation. White box testing is not one of the commonly outsourced types of tests. Other than the IPR issues mentioned in the previous paragraph, the sheer logistics of co-ordination between the development and testing teams, need for a shared configuration management system that should be kept current all the time, and in-depth knowledge of the code required make outsourcing of white box testing to a testing services organization somewhat difficult.

Testing service organizations tend to be more homogeneous in terms of job titles and roles than testing teams in product organizations　In a typical product organization, there is a variety of job functions—development, maintenance, testing, support, and so on. Since a testing services company focuses only on testing, the role definitions and job titles tend to be more homogeneous. This could be a double-edged sword. People who look for diversity in job experience (covering all aspects of a software life cycle) may find working in a testing services organization uninteresting in the long run. On the other hand, given the misconceptions of testing as an "uninteresting" job function if a testing services organization can staff its team with people who are passionate about testing, it may easier to offer a progressive career path to the employees. Table 14.2 summarizes these and other key differences between product testing and testing as a services.

14.5.3　Typical Roles and Responsibilities of Testing Services Organization

A testing services organization is made up of a number of *accounts*, with each account being responsible for a major customer. Each account is assigned an *account manager*, who is the single point of contact from the customer into the testing services organization. The account manager serves the following functions.

1. Is the single point of contact between the customer and the testing services organization for all matters and is also the point of escalation.

2. Develops rapport with the customer and is responsible for ensuring that current projects are delivered as promised and for getting new (repeat) business from the customer.

Table 14.2 Differences between product testing and testing as a service.

Attribute	Product testing	Testing as a service
Type of testing	Will have to address all types of testing as the entire product responsibility lies within the organization	An organization may be specializing in specific types of testing, for example, performance testing or internationalization testing
Exposure to code	There is likely to be a greater exposure to the product code for the product testing team. This is especially true for white box testing teams.	Generally, testing service organizations focus more on external functionality and hence work off some "product drops" on a SCM repository. In addition, the visibility to source code may be minimal or non-existent because of IPR or contractual reasons.
Accessibility to developers	Likely to be available as they are part of the same organization	Likely to be minimal
Career path issues	Since the organization has multiple roles and work functions, this may lead to people in the testing profession wanting to move on to other functions (for example, development) within the organization. Hence may be more difficult to provide testing-specific career paths.	Since the entire organization is fully focused on testing functions, it may be easier to provide career paths in testing for the employees. The expectations can be set and managed better.
Diversity of tools	It is likely that an entire organization (over time) will standardize on the same tools. Hence, there is usually no need for investing on acquisition and training on multiple tools.	A testing service organization may have to work with multiple clients who have different automation tools and hence may be forced to invest/train people on multiple tools.
Domain specialization	Since the product(s) is (are) usually focused on a specific domain, it may be more feasible to hire and develop domain expertise within the team.	Since a testing service organization may have to work with different customers who are in different domains, the organization may either have to hire people with different domain expertise or retrain people across multiple domains.

3. Participates in all strategic (and tactical, as needed) communication between the customer and the testing services organization.

4. Acts as a proxy for the customer within the testing services organization.

The account manager may be located close to the customer site or at the location of the testing services organization. To develop better rapport, this role would require frequent travel and face-to-face meetings with the customer. Usually this role has a single point of contact at the senior level from the customer organization to co-ordinate multiple projects from the account.

Since the testing services organization is a different entity from the customer, it is physically in a separate location. (Most often, these organizations are in countries with more competitive cost structures.)

The testing service team organizes its account team as a *near-site* team and a *remote* team. The near-site team is usually a small team. It is placed at or near the customer location. This team serves the following functions.

1. Be a point of direct first point of contact for the customer for tactical or urgent issues. For example, when a quick system study is required for understanding what needs to be tested for an incremental version, the near-site team, because of its proximity to the customer, can do this.

2. Act as a stop-gap to represent the remote team, in the event of emergencies like travel embargo infrastructure unavailability etc.

3. It also serves to increase the rapport between the customer's operational team and the testing services team.

This team is usually small and does not necessarily have a manager-engineer hierarchy.

The remote team is located on the site of the testing services organization. This team is usually large in number the team and does the bulk of the work. The organization of this team depends on the size and complexity of the testing project. The remote team manager manages the entire remote team and can have a peer-to-peer relationship with the near-site team or have the near-site team reporting to him or her. Depending on the need, there can

Figure 14.6

Typical organization structure for a testing service organization.

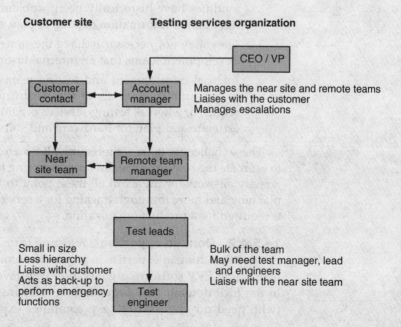

Customer site　　　**Testing services organization**

CEO / VP

Customer contact ←-→ Account manager

Manages the near site and remote teams
Liaises with the customer
Manages escalations

Near site team ←-→ Remote team manager

Test leads

Small in size
Less hierarchy
Liaise with customer
Acts as back-up to perform emergency functions

Bulk of the team
May need test manager, lead and engineers
Liaise with the near site team

Test engineer

be further hierarchies within the organization as test leads and test engineers much similar to the roles and responsibilities that we discussed in the last chapter.

The near-site and remote teams usually are rotated around. For example, some of the remote team members can be posted as a part of the near-site team. For testing services organizations that are in countries different from the customer location, this offers travel opportunities—a common employee-retention strategy. In addition, periodically, a remote team member may have to visit the customer site for any onsite testing and similar activities for which the near-site team may not be sufficient.

14.5.4   Challenges and Issues in Testing Services Organizations

All testing organizations face certain common challenges. In the case of a testing services organization to which testing is outsourced, some of these challenges are exacerbated, primarily because of the arm's length distance from the development team. We will now explore in detail these challenges and the ways to mitigate these challenges

14.5.4.1   The outsider effect and estimation of resources   The testing services organization is an "outsider" to the development organization. Some of the implications are as follows.

1. They do not necessarily have access to the product internals or code as much as a product testing team within the product organization would have.

2. They do not have access to product history in terms of which modules have historically been problem prone and thus may not have all the information needed to plan and prioritize test cases.

3. They may not necessarily have the same level of rapport with the development teams that an internal testing team may have.

4. Internal development and testing teams do not necessarily need to have information about the hardware and software resources required, whereas testing services organization would also have to estimate and plan for hardware and software resources.

These challenges make it more difficult for a testing services organization to estimate the resources needed for performing testing functions. There are no easy answers for these but all these point to the need for more upfront planning and more thorough tracking for a services organization than what is required for a product organization.

14.5.4.2   Domain expertise   A testing team in a product organization can develop domain expertise in a specific domain. For example, a testing team in an ERP software organization can develop specialized expertise in the ERP domain. The organization can hire a few domain specialists (who need not necessarily have computer expertise) who can augment the testing team. Such specialists will find it interesting to join a product organization because they can find a natural transition from their domain to the (apparently) more attractive IT arena. For example, for someone specialized in accounting, this can be a very natural transition to enter an IT product company.

However, a testing services organization may have to undertake projects from multiple customers. Since there is little product ownership in a testing service organization, it may be tougher to get domain experts to join a testing services company. (However, this disadvantage is fast disappearing as the size of the test services companies increases rapidly and the domain specialists see career growth opportunities.) Furthermore, the diversity of domains exacerbates the problem. Given that most testing service organizations perform functional testing (black box testing, integration testing, acceptance testing, and so on), having domain experts can go a long way in improving test quality. Product companies offer tough competition for these resources.

14.5.4.3 Privacy and customer isolation issues

For being viable, a testing services organization will have to work with multiple customers. As an organization works with customers in a given domain (for example, pharmaceutical or financial services), it develops not only general expertise but also domain expertise in a particular domain. As an organization develops domain expertise, it gains competitive advantage in offering testing services to other companies in the same domain. Similarly, when an organization develops expertise in a specific test automation tool, then it is placed in a position of strength to take on test automation projects for any organization that uses the same tool. However, with the strong linking of IT with organizational strategy in most businesses, a clear line of demarcation would have to be drawn between any two customers.

Two factors contribute to this being a major challenge. First, the testing service organization has a common infrastructure and hence physical isolation of the different teams may be difficult. Second, people move from one project (customer) to another. When this movement takes place, there should be full confidence and transparency in ensuring that the customer-specific knowledge acquired in one project is not taken to other projects. At the same time, for continuous improvement of the testing services organization, the learnings will have to be captured and abstracted at the right level, without compromising the privacy and confidentiality of customer-specific information.

The organization structure we discussed in the previous section addresses the above issues. First, each customer can be treated as a separate entity by associating an account manager working with a distinct and dedicated team for the customer. During the time the project is initiated, appropriate Non Disclosure Agreements (NDA) is draw up between the customer and the testing services organization. Such NDAs provide a framework ensuring that confidential information is not compromised. In certain cases, the teams are located in physically separate locations. Second, customer data for specific customers should also be isolated and secured. This leads us to the next issue of apportioning hardware and software resources and costs.

14.5.4.4   Apportioning hardware and software resources and costs

When a testing service organization bids for and works with multiple customers, it would have to use internal hardware and software resources. Some of these resources can be identified directly and specifically for a particular account. There are other resources that get multiplexed across multiple projects. For example, communication infrastructure such as satellite links; common infrastructure such email servers; and physical infrastructure costs.

These costs have to be apportioned across different projects while costing the project. The challenge is that it is difficult to know how much of these resources should be apportioned to each project.

14.5.4.5   Maintaining a "Bench"   A testing services organization should always have people ready to be deployed in any new project that may suddenly come from customers. In addition, some prospects may require some initial studies to be done or some demonstration of initial capability before they sign up fully. These would again need technical resources. There may also be cases where the customer would like to look at the resumes of specific individuals and have a say in handpicking people from the services organization to participate in the testing project. In all these cases, there may be a need to maintain "people on the bench," that is, people not allocated to any project but ready in the wings to take on new projects or to convince customers.

The bench resources are not billable and hence have to be subsidized by the projects. Further, the people on the bench usually get frustrated, develop insecurity, and are at a high risk of attrition. A part of the planning, looking at the business pipeline, is to estimate the bench size—that is, the number of people that can be on the bench at any point of time.

14.6   SUCCESS FACTORS FOR TESTING ORGANIZATIONS

Whether it is product testing organizations or testing services organizations, there are some common success factors between them. These are as follows.

Communication and teamwork   As have discussed in Chapter 1, Principles of Testing, and Chapter 13, People Issues in Testing, the testing teams and development teams should work in a co-operative spirit, without viewing each other as adversaries. However, since the testing team's job is to find defects in the development team's work, this spirit of camaraderie is not easy to achieve. Some of the ways that product companies can achieve this spirit of co-operation and teamwork is to have periodic job rotation. This may not always be possible for testing service organizations that remain at arm's length from the development team. There should also be frequent opportunities for communication between the teams and some of this should be in non-work related environments and scenarios. The problem of communication and teamwork becomes magnified when the team is geographically distributed, when there is little opportunity for face-to-face interactions.

Bringing in customer perspective The testing team should act as a proxy for the customer. This requires getting to know the customer perspective. How does a testing team get this perspective? One way could be to bring in domain experts or customer representatives into the testing team. Another way could be to rotate people from customer support into testing. In a product organization, customer support is the point of contact for the customers to report problems. They are usually familiar with the kind of problems customers face, what hurts the customers most, and what would be acceptable to customers. Having them participate in designing test cases or in performing ad hoc testing (see Chapter 10) can increase customer perspective. Another approach is to rotate the testing team members and even the development team members into product support, so that they get a first hand idea of the issues customers face.

Providing appropriate tools and environment To be effective, a test organization must have appropriate supporting tools. Two of the most important ones are the defect repository and configuration management tools. A defect repository provides a way to track defects to completion. As discussed earlier, configuration management tools provide a mechanism for the teams to share the software environment and make sure the entire team gets one consistent view of the product source and object code and other associated files. (We will go into the details of some of these tools in Chapter 15, Test Management.

Providing periodic skill upgrades Testing teams will need periodic skill upgrades to keep them current. These skill upgrades include.

1. Domain skills, to upgrade to new domains or new features in future versions;
2. Technology skills, for example, use of new languages;
3. Automation skills, to get acclimatized to new automation tools; and
4. Soft skills, including spoken communication, written communication, negotiation skills, and conflict resolution skills to be able to communicate better.

The challenge is to find the time for these skill upgrades amid the tight schedules and deadlines of the team. Career planning of individuals should budget time for these skill upgrades. Or else, the effectiveness of testing teams will reduce over time.

REFERENCES

As mentioned in the previous chapter, the topics of people issues and organizational structures are not discussed at great length in literature. The organizational and project models discussed in [RAME-2002] for any geographically distributed project can be adapted and applied to testing teams as well.

PROBLEMS AND EXERCISES

1. When a company moves from a single product to multiple products, how can it leverage its past experience?

2. Which type of work distribution between development and testing is suited for each of the following cases?

   a. A product that is using emerging technologies that require niche skill sets

   b. A product that is going through very short release cycles with frequent builds

   c. A product wherein work on multiple releases are going on at the same time

   d. A product to which incremental features are being added on top of already existing features that are stable

   e. A product being developed in an organization where there are clear cut processes and methods of hand over of work from development.

3. A group was initially established to provide testing services to internal "customers" (application developers) in a bank. Soon the group developed competence and spun off as an independent company providing testing services to other banks and financial institutions. Outline some of the organizational and business challenges that this new company should watch out for and how it can leverage its past experience.

4. In which of the cases in Problem 2, would a geographically distributed team be appropriate?

5. A company makes multiple products in the systems and applications arena. Discuss the pros and cons of having separate teams for testing versus having a common team for testing.

6. A product has a nine-month release cycle, followed by a ten-month maintenance period. When would you decide to set up geographically distributed testing teams? What activities would you distribute at what timeframe? Justify your answer.

7. Which of the following testing activities can be outsourced to a testing services organization? Why?

    a. Code coverage testing

    b. Performance testing

    c. Ad hoc testing

    d. Integrating several products from different companies

    e. Hardware/software integration

8. We discussed specific people issues in the previous chapter. Take each of the issues and see what are the additional challenges you need to face when we add the dimension of multiple teams.

FIVE

Test Management and Automation

This part of the book addresses the planning and management of testing projects. Chapter 15, *Test Planning, Management, and Execution*, addresses the common project management aspects of testing projects such as planning, risk management, estimation, tracking, and reporting, etc. This also provides checklists and templates to address the various aspects of planning and executing testing projects. Chapter 16, *Test Automation*, address the issues, challenges, and some solutions to automate testing functions. Well planned and executed automation is a key to address some of the perceptions discussed in People Issues and to achieve organizational efficiency. The final chapter of the book, Chapter 17, discusses the various metrics that are relevant to track and improve testing projects. These measurements augment the planning and automation to be the enabler for effective testing in the organization.

Test Planning, Management, Execution, and Reporting

CHAPTER 15

In this chapter—

- ✓ Introduction
- ✓ Test planning
- ✓ Test management
- ✓ Test process
- ✓ Test reporting
- ✓ Best practices

15.1   INTRODUCTION

In this chapter, we will look at some of the project management aspects of testing. The Project Management Institute [PMI–2004] defines a project formally as *a temporary endeavor to create a unique product or service*. This means that every project has a definite beginning and a definite end and that the product or service is different in some distinguishing way from all similar products or services.

Testing is integrated into the endeavor of creating a given product or service; each phase and each type of testing has different characteristics and what is tested in each version could be different. Hence, testing satisfies this definition of a project fully.

Given that testing can be considered as a project on its own, it has to be planned, executed, tracked, and periodically reported on. We will look at the test planning aspects in the next section. We will then look into the process that drives a testing project. Subsequently, we will look at the execution of tests and the various types of reporting that takes place during a testing project. We will conclude this chapter by sharing some of the best practices in test management and execution.

15.2   TEST PLANNING

15.2.1   Preparing a Test Plan

Failing to plan is planning to fail.

Testing—like any project—should be driven by a plan. The test plan acts as the anchor for the execution, tracking, and reporting of the entire testing project and covers

1. What needs to be tested—the scope of testing, including clear identification of what will be tested and what will not be tested.

2. How the testing is going to be performed—breaking down the testing into small and manageable tasks and identifying the strategies to be used for carrying out the tasks.

3. What resources are needed for testing—computer as well as human resources.

4. The time lines by which the testing activities will be performed.

5. Risks that may be faced in all of the above, with appropriate mitigation and contingency plans.

15.2.2   Scope Management: Deciding Features to be Tested/Not Tested

As was explained in the earlier chapters, various testing teams do testing for various phases of testing. One single test plan can be prepared to cover all phases and all teams or there can be separate plans for each phase or for each type of testing. For example, there needs to be plans for unit testing integration testing, performance testing, acceptance testing, and so on. They can all be part of a single plan or could be covered by multiple plans. In situations where there are multiple test plans, there should be one test plan, which covers the activities common for all plans. This is called the *master test plan*.

Scope management pertains to specifying the scope of a project. For testing, scope management entails

1. Understanding what constitutes a release of a product;
2. Breaking down the release into features;
3. Prioritizing the features for testing;
4. Deciding which features will be tested and which will not be; and
5. Gathering details to prepare for estimation of resources for testing.

It is always good to start from the end-goal or product-release perspective and get a holistic picture of the entire product to decide the scope and priority of testing. Usually, during the planning stages of a release, the *features* that constitute the release are identified. For example, a particular release of an inventory control system may introduce new features to automatically integrate with supply chain management and to provide the user with various options of costing. The testing teams should get involved early in the planning cycle and understand the features. Knowing the features and understanding them from the usage perspective will enable the testing team to prioritize the features for testing.

The following factors drive the choice and prioritization of features to be tested.

Features that are new and critical for the release   The new features of a release set the expectations of the customers and must perform properly. These new features result in new program code and thus have a higher susceptibility and exposure to defects. Furthermore, these are likely to be areas where both the development and testing teams will have to go through a learning curve. Hence, it makes sense to put these features on top of the priority list to be tested. This will ensure that these key features get enough planning and learning time for testing and do not go out with inadequate testing. In order to get this prioritization right, the product marketing team and some select customers participate in identification of the features to be tested.

Features whose failures can be catastrophic   Regardless of whether a feature is new or not, any feature the failure of which can be catastrophic or produce adverse business impact has to be high on the list of features to be tested. For example, recovery mechanisms in a database will always have to be among the most important features to be tested.

Features that are expected to be complex to test   Early participation by the testing team can help identify features that are difficult to test. This can help in starting the work on these features early and line up appropriate resources in time.

Features which are extensions of earlier features that have been defect prone   As we have seen in Chapter 8, Regression Testing, certain areas of a code tend to be defect prone and such areas need very thorough testing so that old defects do not creep in again. Such features that are defect prone should be included ahead of more stable features for testing.

A product is not just a heterogeneous mixture of these features. These features work together in various combinations and depend on several environmental factors and execution conditions. The test plan should clearly identify these combinations that will be tested.

Given the limitations on resources and time, it is likely that it will not be possible to test all the combinations exhaustively. During planning time, a test manager should also consciously identify the features or combinations that will *not* be tested. This choice should balance the requirements of time and resources while not exposing the customers to any serious defects. Thus, the test plan should contain clear justifications of why certain combinations will not be tested and what are the risks that may be faced by doing so.

15.2.3   Deciding Test Approach/Strategy

Once we have this prioritized feature list, the next step is to drill down into some more details of what needs to be tested, to enable estimation of size, effort, and schedule. This includes identifying

1. What type of testing would you use for testing the functionality?
2. What are the configurations or scenarios for testing the features?
3. What integration testing would you do to ensure these features work together?
4. What localization validations would be needed?
5. What "non-functional" tests would you need to do?

We have discussed various types of tests in earlier chapters of this book. Each of these types has applicability and usefulness under certain conditions. The test approach/strategy part of the test plan identifies the right type of testing to effectively test a given feature or combination.

The test strategy or approach should result in identifying the right type of test for each of the features or combinations. There should also be objective criteria for measuring the success of a test. This is covered in the next sub-section.

15.2.4   Setting up Criteria for Testing

As we have discussed in earlier chapters (especially chapters on system and acceptance testing) there must be clear entry and exit criteria for different phases of testing. The test strategies for the various features and combinations determined how these features and combinations would be tested. Ideally, tests must be run as early as possible so that the last-minute pressure of running tests after development delays (see the section on Risk Management below) is minimized. However, it is futile to run certain tests too early. The entry criteria for a test specify threshold criteria for each phase or type of test. There may also be entry criteria for the entire testing activity to start. The completion/exit criteria specify when a test cycle or a testing activity can be deemed complete. Without objective exit criteria, it is possible for testing to continue beyond the point of diminishing returns.

A test cycle or a test activity will not be an isolated, continuous activity that can be carried out at one go. It may have to be suspended at various points of time because it is not possible to proceed further. When it is possible to proceed further, it will have to be resumed. Suspension criteria specify when a test cycle or a test activity can be suspended. Resumption criteria specify when the suspended tests can be resumed. Some of the typical suspension criteria include

1. Encountering more than a certain number of defects, causing frequent stoppage of testing activity;

2. Hitting show stoppers that prevent further progress of testing (for example, if a database does not start, further tests of query, data manipulation, and so on are is simply not possible to execute); and

3. Developers releasing a new version which they advise should be used in lieu of the product under test (because of some critical defect fixes).

When such conditions are addressed, the tests can resume.

15.2.5   Identifying Responsibilities, Staffing, and Training Needs

Scope management identifies *what* needs to be tested. The test strategy outlines *how* to do it. The next aspect of planning is the *who* part of it. Identifying responsibilities, staffing, and training needs addresses this aspect.

A testing project requires different people to play different roles. As discussed in the previous two chapters, there are the roles of test engineers, test leads, and test managers. There is also role definition on the dimensions of the modules being tested or the type of testing. These different roles should complement each other. The different role definitions should

1. Ensure there is clear accountability for a given task, so that each person knows what he or she has to do;
2. Clearly list the responsibilities for various functions to various people, so that everyone knows how his or her work fits into the entire project;
3. Complement each other, ensuring no one steps on an others' toes; and
4. Supplement each other, so that no task is left unassigned.

Role definitions should not only address technical roles, but also list the management and reporting responsibilities. This includes frequency, format, and recipients of status reports and other project-tracking mechanisms. In addition, responsibilities in terms of SLAs for responding to queries should also be addressed during the planning stage.

Staffing is done based on estimation of effort involved and the availability of time for release. In order to ensure that the right tasks get executed, the features and tasks are prioritized the basis of on effort, time, and importance.

People are assigned to tasks that achieve the best possible fit between the requirements of the job and skills and experience levels needed to perform that function. It may not always be possible to find the perfect fit between the requirements and the skills available. In case there are gaps between the requirements and availability of skills, they should be addressed with appropriate training programs. It is important to plan for such training programs upfront as they are usually are de-prioritized under project pressures.

15.2.6　Identifying Resource Requirements

As a part of planning for a testing project, the project manager (or test manager) should provide estimates for the various hardware and software resources required. Some of the following factors need to be considered.

1. Machine configuration (RAM, processor, disk, and so on) needed to run the product under test
2. Overheads required by the test automation tool, if any
3. Supporting tools such as compilers, test data generators, configuration management tools, and so on
4. The different configurations of the supporting software (for example, OS) that must be present
5. Special requirements for running machine-intensive tests such as load tests and performance tests
6. Appropriate number of licenses of all the software

In addition to all of the above, there are also other implied environmental requirements that need to be satisfied. These include office space, support functions (like HR), and so on.

Underestimation of these resources can lead to considerable slowing down of the testing efforts and this can lead to delayed product release and to de-motivated testing teams. However, being overly conservative and "safe" in estimating these resources can prove to be unnecessarily expensive. Proper estimation of these resources requires co-operation and teamwork among different groups—product development team, testing team, system administration team, and senior management.

15.2.7   Identifying Test Deliverables

The test plan also identifies the deliverables that should come out of the test cycle/testing activity. The deliverables include the following, all reviewed and approved by the appropriate people.

1. The test plan itself (master test plan, and various other test plans for the project)
2. Test case design specifications
3. Test cases, including any automation that is specified in the plan
4. Test logs produced by running the tests
5. Test summary reports

As we will see in the next section, a defect repository gives the status of the defects reported in a product life cycle. Part of the deliverables of a test cycle is to ensure that the defect repository is kept current. This includes entering new defects in the repository and updating the status of defect fixes after verification. We will see the contents of some of these deliverables in the later parts of this chapter.

15.2.8   Testing Tasks: Size and Effort Estimation

The scope identified above gives a broad overview of what needs to be tested. This understanding is quantified in the estimation step. Estimation happens broadly in three phases.

1. Size estimation
2. Effort estimation
3. Schedule estimation

We will cover size estimation and effort estimation in this sub-section and address schedule estimation in the next sub-section.

Size estimate quantifies the actual amount of testing that needs to be done. Several factors contribute to the size estimate of a testing project.

Size of the product under test This obviously determines the amount of testing that needs to be done. The larger the product, in general, greater is the size of testing to be done. Some of the measures of the size of product under test are as follows.

1. Lines of code (LOC) is a somewhat controversial measure as it depends on the language, style of programming, compactness of programming, and so on. Furthermore, LOC represents size estimate only for the coding phase and not for the other phases such as requirements, design, and so on. Notwithstanding these limitations, LOC is still a popular measure for estimating size.

2. A function point (FP) is a popular method to estimate the size of an application. Function points provide a representation of application size, independent of programming language. The application features (also called functions) are classified as inputs, outputs, interfaces, external data files, and enquiries. These are increasingly complex and hence are assigned increasingly higher weights. The weighted average of functions (number of functions of each type multiplied by the weight for that function type) gives an initial estimate of size or complexity. In addition, the function point methodology of estimating size also provides for 14 environmental factors such as distributed processing, transaction rate, and so on.

   This methodology of estimating size or complexity of an application is comprehensive in terms of taking into account realistic factors. The major challenge in this method is that it requires formal training and is not easy to use. Furthermore, this method is not directly suited to systems software type of projects.

3. A somewhat simpler representation of application size is the number of screens, reports, or transactions. Each of these can be further classified as "simple," "medium," or "complex." This classification can be based on intuitive factors such as number of fields in the screen, number of validations to be done, and so on.

Extent of automation required When automation is involved, the size of work to be done for testing increases. This is because, for automation, we should first perform the basic test case design (identifying input data and expected results by techniques like condition coverage, boundary value analysis, equivalence partitioning, and so on.) and then scripting them into the programming language of the test automation tool.

Number of platforms and inter-operability environments to be tested If a particular product is to be tested under several different platforms or under several different configurations, then the size of the testing task increases. In fact, as the number of platforms or touch points across different environments increases, the amount of testing increases almost exponentially.

All the above size estimates pertain to "regular" test case development. Estimation of size for regression testing (as discussed in Chapter 8) involves considering the changes in the product and other similar factors.

In order to have a better handle on the size estimate, the work to be done is broken down into smaller and more manageable parts called work breakdown structure (WBS) units. For a testing project, WBS units are typically test cases for a given module, test cases for a given platform, and so on. This decomposition breaks down the problem domain or the product into simpler parts and is likely to reduce the uncertainty and unknown factors.

Size estimate is expressed in terms of any of the following.

1. Number of test cases
2. Number of test scenarios
3. Number of configurations to be tested

Size estimate provides an estimate of the actual ground to be covered for testing. This acts as a primary input for estimating effort. Estimating effort is important because often effort has a more direct influence on cost than size. The other factors that drive the effort estimate are as follows.

Productivity data   Productivity refers to the speed at which the various activities of testing can be carried out. This is based on historical data available in the organization. Productivity data can be further classified into the number of test cases that can be developed per day (or some unit time), the number of test cases that can be run per day, the number of pages of pages of documentation that can be tested per day, and so on. Having these fine-grained productivity data enables better planning and increases the confidence level and accuracy of the estimates.

Reuse opportunities   If the test architecture has been designed keeping reuse in mind, then the effort required to cover a given size of testing can come down. For example, if the tests are designed in such a way that some of the earlier tests can be reused, then the effort of test development decreases.

Robustness of processes   Reuse is a specific example of process maturity of an organization. Existence of well-defined processes will go a long way in reducing the effort involved in any activity. For example, in an organization with higher levels of process maturity, there are likely to be

1. Well-documented standards for writing test specifications, test scripts, and so on;
2. Proven processes for performing functions such as reviews and audits;
3. Consistent ways of training people; and
4. Objective ways of measuring the effectiveness of compliance to processes.

All these reduce the need to reinvent the wheel and thus enable reduction in the effort involved.

Effort estimate is derived from size estimate by taking the individual WBS units and classifying them as "reusable," "modifications," and "new development." For example, if parts of a test case can be reused from existing test cases, then the effort involved in developing these would be close to zero. If, on the other hand, a given test case is to be developed fully from scratch, it is reasonable to assume that the effort would be the size of the test case divided by productivity.

Effort estimate is given in person days, person months, or person years. The effort estimate is then translated to a schedule estimate. We will address scheduling in the next sub-section.

15.2.9 Activity Breakdown and Scheduling

Activity breakdown and schedule estimation entail translating the effort required into specific time frames. The following steps make up this translation.

1. Identifying external and internal dependencies among the activities
2. Sequencing the activities, based on the expected duration as well as on the dependencies
3. Identifying the time required for each of the WBS activities, taking into account the above two factors
4. Monitoring the progress in terms of time and effort
5. Rebalancing schedules and resources as necessary

During the effort estimation phase, we have identified the effort required for each of the WBS unit, factoring in the effect of reuse. This effort was expressed in terms of person months. If the effort for a particular WBS unit is estimated as, say, 40 person months, it is not possible to trade the "persons" for "months," that is, we cannot indefinitely increase the number of people working on it, expecting the duration to come down proportionally. As stated in [BROO-74], adding more people to an already delayed project is a sure way of delaying the project even further! This is because, when new people are added to a project, it increases the communication overheads and it takes some time for the new members to gel with the rest of the team. Furthermore, these WBS units cannot be executed in any random order because there will be dependencies among the activities. These dependencies can be external dependencies or internal dependencies. External dependencies of an activity are beyond the control and purview of the manager/person performing the activity. Some of the common external dependencies are

1. Availability of the product from developers;
2. Hiring;
3. Training;
4. Acquisition of hardware/software required for training; and
5. Availability of translated message files for testing.

Internal dependencies are fully within the control of the manager/person performing that activity. For example, some of the internal dependencies could be.

1. Completing the test specification
2. Coding/scripting the tests
3. Executing the tests

The testing activities will also face parallelism constraints that will further restrict the activities that can be done at a time. For example, certain tests cannot be run together because of conflicting conditions (for example, requiring different versions of a component for testing) or a high-end machine may have to be multiplexed across multiple tests.

Based on the dependencies and the parallelism possible, the test activities are scheduled in a sequence that helps accomplish the activities in the minimum possible time, while taking care of all the dependencies. This schedule is expressed in the form of a Gantt chart as shown in Figure 15.1. The coloured figure is available on page 472.

Figure 15.1

Gantt chart.

	Task Name	Duration	Start	Finish
1	☐ **Test schedule for release**	**33 days**	**Tue 2/22/00**	**Thu 4/6/00**
2	Test plan	2 days	Tue 2/22/00	Wed 2/23/00
3	Test strategy	2 days	Tue 2/22/00	Wed 2/23/00
4	Developing test cases	3 days	Thu 2/24/00	Mon 2/28/00
5	Review of test cases	1 day	Tue 2/29/00	Tue 2/29/00
6	Performance benchmark plan	2 days	Wed 3/1/00	Thu 3/2/00
7	Unit testing	4 days	Fri 3/3/00	Wed 3/8/00
8	Integration testing	3 days	Thu 3/9/00	Mon 3/13/00
9	Buddy testing	2 days	Tue 3/14/00	Wed 3/15/00
10	System testing	4 days	Thu 3/16/00	Tue 3/21/00
11	Regression testing	3 days	Wed 3/22/00	Fri 3/24/00
12	Performance test 1	3 days	Mon 3/27/00	Wed 3/29/00
13	Performance test 2	2 days	Thu 3/30/00	Fri 3/31/00
14	Documentation and reports	2 days	Mon 4/3/00	Tue 4/4/00
15	User acceptance test	1 day	Wed 4/5/00	Wed 4/5/00
16	**Release**	1 day	Thu 4/6/00	Thu 4/6/00

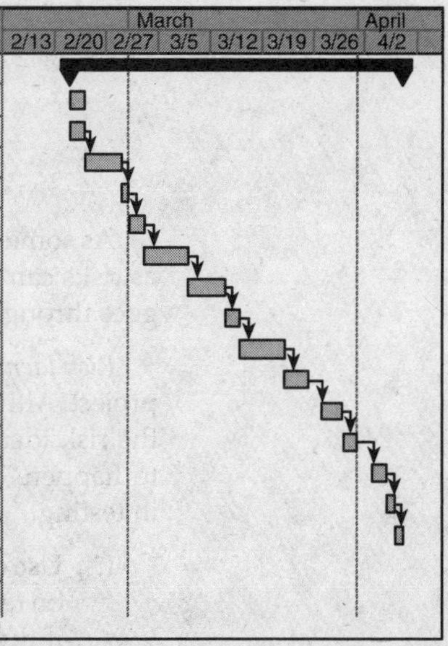

15.2.10 Communications Management

Communications management consists of evolving and following procedures for communication that ensure that everyone is kept in sync with the right level of detail. Since this is intimately connected with the test execution and progress of the testing project, we will take this up in more detail in Section 15.3 when we take up the various types of reports in a test cycle.

15.2.11   Risk Management

Just like every project, testing projects also face risks. Risks are events that could potentially affect a project's outcome. These events are normally beyond the control of the project manager. As shown in Figure 15.2, risk management entails

1. Identifying the possible risks;
2. Quantifying the risks;
3. Planning how to mitigate the risks; and
4. Responding to risks when they become a reality.

Figure 15.2

Aspects of risk management.

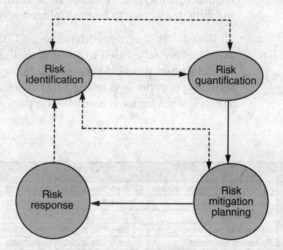

As some risks are identified and resolved, other risks may surface. Hence as risks can happen any time, risk management is essentially a cycle, which goes through the above four steps repeatedly.

Risk identification consists of identifying the possible risks that may hit a project. Although there could potentially be many risks that can hit a project, the risk identification step should focus on those risks that are more likely to happen. The following are some of the common ways to identify risks in testing.

1. **Use of checklists**   Over time, an organization may find new gleanings on testing that can be captured in the form of a checklist. For example, if during installation testing, it is found that a particular step of the installation has repeatedly given problems, then the checklist can have an explicit line item to check that particular problem. When checklists are used for risk identification, there is also a great risk of the checklist itself being out of date, thereby pointing to red herrings instead of risks!

2. **Use of organizational history and metrics**   When an organization collects and analyzes the various metrics (see Chapter 17), the information can provide valuable insights into what possible risks

can hit a project. For example, the past effort variance in testing can give pointers to how much contingency planning is required.

3. **Informal networking across the industry**   The informal networking across the industry can help in identifying risks that other organizations have encountered.

Risk quantification deals with expressing the risk in numerical terms. There are two components to the quantification of risk. One is the *probability* of the risk happening and the other is the *impact* of the risk, if the risk happens. For example, the occurrence of a low-priority defect may have a high probability, but a low impact. However, a show stopper may have (hopefully!) a low probability, but a very high impact (for both the customer and the vendor organization). To quantify both these into one number, *Risk exposure* is used. This is defined as the product of risk probability and risk impact. To make comparisons easy, risk impact is expressed in monetary terms (for example, in dollars).

Risk mitigation planning deals with identifying alternative strategies to combat a risk event, should that risk materialize. For example, a couple of mitigation strategies for the risk of attrition are to spread the knowledge to multiple people and to introduce organization-wide processes and standards. To be better prepared to handle the effects of a risk, it is advisable to have multiple mitigation strategies.

When the above three steps are carried out systematically and in a timely manner, the organization would be in a better position to respond to the risks, should the risks become a reality. When sufficient care is not given to these initial steps, a project may find itself under immense pressure to react to a risk. In such cases, the choices made may not be the most optimal or prudent, as the choices are made under pressure.

The following are some of the common risks encountered in testing projects and their characteristics.

Unclear requirements   The success of testing depends a lot on knowing what the correct expected behavior of the product under test is. When the requirements to be satisfied by a product are not clearly documented, there is ambiguity in how to interpret the results of a test. This could result in wrong defects being reported or in the real defects being missed out. This will, in turn, result in unnecessary and wasted cycles of communication between the development and testing teams and consequent loss of time. One way to minimize the impact of this risk is to ensure upfront participation of the testing team during the requirements phase itself.

Schedule dependence   The schedule of the testing team depends significantly on the schedules of the development team. Thus, it becomes difficult for the testing team to line up resources properly at the right time. The impact of this risk is especially severe in cases where a testing team is shared across multiple-product groups or in a testing services organization (see Chapter 14). A possible mitigation strategy against this risk is to identify a backup project for a testing resource. Such a backup project may be one of that could use an additional resource to speed up execution but would not be unduly affected if the resource were not available. An example of such a backup project is chipping in for speeding up test automation.

Insufficient time for testing Throughout the book, we have stressed the different types of testing and the different phases of testing. Though some of these types of testing—such as white box testing—can happen early in the cycle, most of the tests tend to happen closer to the product release. For example, system testing and performance testing can happen only after the entire product is ready and close to the release date. Usually these tests are resource intensive for the testing team and, in addition, the defects that these tests uncover are challenging for the developers to fix. As discussed in performance testing chapter, fixing some of these defects could lead to changes in architecture and design. Carrying out such changes into the cycle may be expensive or even impossible. Once the developers fix the defects, the testing team would have even lesser time to complete the testing and is under even greater pressure. The use of the V model to at least shift the test design part of the various test types to the earlier phases of the project can help in anticipating the risks of tests failing at each level in a better manner. This in turn could lead to a reduction in the last-minute crunch. The metric *days needed for release* (see Chapter 17) when captured and calculated properly, can help in planning the time required for testing better.

"Show stopper" defects When the testing team reports defects, the development team has to fix them. Certain defects which are show stoppers may prevent the testing team to proceed further with testing, until development fixes such show stopper defects. Encountering this type of defects will have a double impact on the testing team: Firstly, they will not be able to continue with the testing and hence end up with idle time. Secondly, when the defects do get fixed and the testing team restarts testing, they would have lost valuable time and will be under tremendous pressure with the deadline being nearer. This risk of show stopper defects can pose a big challenge to scheduling and resource utilization of the testing teams. The mitigation strategies for this risk are similar to those seen on account of dependence on development schedules.

Availability of skilled and motivated people for testing As we saw in Chapter 13, People Issues in Testing, hiring and motivating people in testing is a major challenge. Hiring, retaining, and constant skill upgrade of testers in an organization is vital. This is especially important for testing functions because of the tendency of people to look for development positions.

Inability to get a test automation tool Manual testing is error prone and labor intensive. Test automation, as discussed in Chapter 16, alleviates some of these problems. However, test automation tools are expensive. An organization may face the risk of not being able to afford a test automation tool. This risk can in turn lead to less effective and efficient testing as well as more attrition. One of the ways in which organizations may try to red... this risk is to develop in-house tools. However, this approach could lead t... an even greater risk of having a poorly written or inadequately documented in-house tool.

These risks are not only potentially dangerous individually, but even more dangerous when they occur in tandem. Unfortunately, often, these risks do happen in tandem! A testing group plans its schedules based on development schedules, development schedules slip, testing team resources get into an idle time, pressure builds, schedules slip, and the vicious cycle starts all over again. It is important that these risks be caught early or before they create serious impact on the testing teams. Hence, we need to identify the symptoms for each of these risks. These symptoms and their impacts need to be tracked closely throughout the project.

Table 15.1 gives typical risks, their symptoms, impacts and mitigation/contingency plans.

Table 15.1 Typical risks, symptoms, impact, and mitigation plans.

Risks	Symptoms	Impacts	Mitigation/contingency plans
Development delay	• Code drops from development going through constant slippage	• Less time becomes available for testing • Pushes product release date forward	• Constant involvement of the testing team in development plans • Periodic and timely communication • Staggering the testing activities by following the modified V model (Chapter 2)
Show stopper defects	• The test cycle gets suspended/resumed often	• Wasted/idle testing resources • Pressure on the testing teams when testing resumes after the defects are fixed • Possible pushing of the schedule forward	• Having clear exit criteria for development before a product can be accepted for testing • Making the testing team perform other functions during the wait time
Unclear requirements	• Defects getting uncovered by customers after the product has passed all the internal tests	• Rework that may extend all the way back to requirements gathering • Customer dissatisfaction because of product not meeting requirements	• Early user/product marketing involvement in development of prototypes to better elicit requirements • Clear definitions of acceptance criteria • Stringent approval cycles for the requirements

Table 15.1 Continued.

Risks	Symptoms	Impacts	Mitigation/contingency plans
Insufficient time for testing	• Constantly overworked test engineers • Time spent on testing is a small fraction of the overall product life cycle	• Defects seeping out to customers • Attrition in the testing team	• Distributing the testing activities throughout the life cycle of the product • Automating testing activities • Getting upfront consensus for time schedules from all stakeholders
Over cautiousness in testing	• Insignificant defects getting reported • Testing team becoming a bottleneck for release	• Resources on testing not producing a good "bang for the buck"	• Setting objective exit criteria for testing
Lack of skilled people for testing	• Trend of constant request for transfers out of testing function into other functions (for example, development) • Higher attrition in testing teams vis-à-vis other teams	• Poor quality of testing, resulting in more defects escaping the testing net to the customers • Reduced credibility for the testing team	• Periodic training and skill upgradation • Showing career paths and demonstrating role models for testing • Job rotation among development, testing, and support teams
Lack of automation tools	• Long hours spent on manual testing	• Wasted efforts in manual testing • Dissatisfaction among test engineers	• Demonstration of success stories of using automation

15.3 TEST MANAGEMENT

In the previous section, we considered testing as a project in its own right and addressed some of the typical project management issues in testing. In this section, we will look at some of the aspects that should be taken care of in planning such a project. These planning aspects are proactive measures that can have an across-the-board influence on all testing projects.

15.3.1 Choice of Standards

Standards comprise an important part of planning in any organization. Standards are of two types—external standards and internal standards. External standards are standards that a product should comply with, are externally visible, and are usually stipulated by external consortia. From a testing perspective, these standards include standard tests supplied by external consortia and acceptance tests supplied by customers. Compliance to external standards is usually mandated by external parties.

Internal standards are standards formulated by a testing organization to bring in consistency and predictability. They standardize the processes and methods of working within the organization. Some of the internal standards include

1. Naming and storage conventions for test artifacts;
2. Document standards;
3. Test coding standards; and
4. Test reporting standards.

Naming and storage conventions for test artifacts   Every test artifact (test specification, test case, test results, and so on) have to be named appropriately and meaningfully. Such naming conventions should enable

1. Easy identification of the product functionality that a set of tests are intended for; and
2. Reverse mapping to identify the functionality corresponding to a given set of tests.

As an example of using naming conventions, consider a product P, with modules `M01`, `M02`, and `M03`. The test suites can be named as `PM01nnnn.<file type>`. Here `nnnn` can be a running sequence number or any other string. For a given test, different files may be required. For example, a given test may use a test script (which provides details of the specific actions to be performed), a recorded keystroke capture file, an expected results file. In addition, it may require other supporting files (for example, an SQL script for a database). All these related files can have the same file name (for example, `PM01nnnn`) and different file types (for example, `.sh`, `.SQL`, `.KEY`, `.OUT`). By such a naming convention, one can find

* All files relating to a specific test (for example, by searching for all files with file name `PM01nnnn`), and
* All tests relating to a given module (for example, those files starting with name `PM01` will correspond to tests for module `M01`)

With this, when the functionality corresponding to module `M01` changes, it becomes easy to locate those tests that may have to be modified or deleted.

This two-way mapping between tests and product functionality through appropriate naming conventions will enable identification of appropriate tests to be modified and run when product functionality changes.

In addition to file-naming conventions, the standards may also stipulate the conventions for directory structures for tests. Such directory structures can group logically related tests together (along with the related product functionality). These directory structures are mapped into a configuration management repository (discussed later in the chapter).

Documentation standards   Most of the discussion on documentation and coding standards pertain to automated testing. In the case of manual testing, documentation standards correspond to specifying the user and system responses at the right level of detail that is consistent with the skill level of the tester.

While naming and directory standards specify how a test entity is represented externally, documentation standards specify how to capture information about the tests within the test scripts themselves. Internal documentation of test scripts are similar to internal documentation of program code and should include the following.

1. Appropriate header level comments at the beginning of a file that outlines the functions to be served by the test.

2. Sufficient in-line comments, spread throughout the file, explaining the functions served by the various parts of a test script. This is especially needed for those parts of a test script that are difficult to understand or have multiple levels of loops and iterations.

3. Up-to-date change history information, recording all the changes made to the test file.

Without such detailed documentation, a person maintaining the test scripts is forced to rely only on the actual test code or script to guess what the test is supposed to do or what changes happened to the test scripts. This may not give a true picture. Furthermore, it may place an undue dependence on the person who originally wrote the tests.

Test coding standards   Test coding standards go one level deeper into the tests and enforce standards on how the tests themselves are written. The standards may

1. Enforce the right type of initialization and clean-up that the test should do to make the results independent of other tests;

2. Stipulate ways of naming variables within the scripts to make sure that a reader understands consistently the purpose of a variable. (for example, instead of using generic names such as i, j, and so on, the names can be meaningful such as `network_init_flag`);

3. Encourage reusability of test artifacts (for example, all tests should call an initialization module `init_env` first, rather than use their own initialization routines); and

4. Provide standard interfaces to external entities like operating system, hardware, and so on. For example, if it is required for tests to spawn multiple OS processes, rather than have each of the tests directly spawn the processes, the coding standards may dictate that they should all call a standard function, say, `create_os_process`. By isolating the external interfaces separately, the tests can be reasonably insulated from changes to these lower-level layers.

Test reporting standards   Since testing is tightly interlinked with product quality, all the stakeholders must get a consistent and timely view of the progress of tests. Test reporting standards address this issue. They provide guidelines on the level of detail that should be present in the test reports, their standard formats and contents, recipients of the report, and so on. We will revisit this in more detail later in this chapter.

Internal standards provide a competitive edge to a testing organization and act as a first-level insurance against employee turnover and attrition. Internal standards help bring new test engineers up to speed rapidly. When such consistent processes and standards are followed across an organization, it brings about predictability and increases the confidence level one can have on the quality of the final product. In addition, any anomalies can be brought to light in a timely manner.

15.3.2   Test Infrastructure Management

Testing requires a robust infrastructure to be planned upfront. This infrastructure is made up of three essential elements.

1.   A test case database (TCDB)
2.   A defect repository
3.   Configuration management repository and tool

A test case database captures all the relevant information about the test cases in an organization. Some of the entities and the attributes in each of the entities in such a TCDB are given in Table 15.2.

Table 15.2   Content of a test case database.

Entity	Purpose	Attributes
Test case	Records all the "static" information about the tests	• Test case ID • Test case name (file name) • Test case owner • Associated files for the test case
Test case – Product cross-reference	Provides a mapping between the tests and the corresponding product features; enables identification of tests for a given feature	• Test case ID • Module ID
Test case run history	Gives the history of when a test was run and what was the result; provides inputs on selection of tests for regression runs (see Chapter 8)	• Test case ID • Run date • Time taken • Run status (success/failure)
Test case—Defect cross-reference	Gives details of test cases introduced to test certain specific defects detected in the product; provides inputs on the selection of tests for regression runs	• Test case ID • Defect reference # (points to a record in the defect repository)

A defect repository captures all the relevant details of defects reported for a product. The information that a defect repository includes is given in Table 15.3.

The defect repository is an important vehicle of communication that influences the work flow within a software organization. It also provides the base data in arriving at several of the metrics we will discuss in Chapter 17, Metrics and Measurements. In particular, most of the metrics classified as testing defect metrics and development defect metrics are derived out of the data in defect repository.

Yet another infrastructure that is required for a software product organization (and in particular for a testing team) is a software configuration management (SCM) repository. An SCM repository also known as (CM repository) keeps track of change control and version control of all the

Table 15.3 Information in a defect repository.

Entity	Purpose	Attributes
Defect details	Records all the "static" information about the tests	• Defect ID • Defect priority/severity • Defect description • Affected product(s) • Any relevant version information • Environmental information (for example, OS version) • Customers who encountered the problem (could be reported by the internal testing team also) • Date and time of defect occurrence
Defect test details	Provides details of test cases for a given defect. Cross-references the TCDB	• Defect ID • Test case ID
Fix details	Provides details of fixes for a given defect; cross-references the configuration management repository	• Defect ID • Fix details (file changed, fix release information)
Communication	Captures all the details of the communication that transpired for this defect among the various stakeholders. These could include communication between the testing team and development team, customer communication, and so on. Provides insights into effectiveness of communication	• Test case ID • Defect reference # • Details of communication

files/entities that make up a software product. A particular case of the files/entities is test files. Change control ensures that

1.   Changes to test files are made in a controlled fashion and only with proper approvals.

2.   Changes made by one test engineer are not accidentally lost or overwritten by other changes.

3.   Each change produces a distinct version of the file that is recreatable at any point of time.

4.   At any point of time, everyone gets access to only the most recent version of the test files (except in exceptional cases).

Version control ensures that the test scripts associated with a given release of a product are *baselined* along with the product files. Baselining is akin to taking a snapshot of the set of related files of a version, assigning a unique identifier to this set. In future, when anyone wants to recreate the environment for the given release, this label would enable him or her to do so.

TCDB, defect repository, and SCM repository should complement each other and work together in an integrated fashion as shown in Figure 15.3. For example, the defect repository links the defects, fixes, and tests. The files for all these will be in the SCM. The meta data about the modified test files will be in the TCDB. Thus, starting with a given defect, one can trace all the test cases that test the defect (from the TCDB) and then find the corresponding test case files and source files from the SCM repository.

Figure 15.3

Relationship SCM, AR, and TCDB.

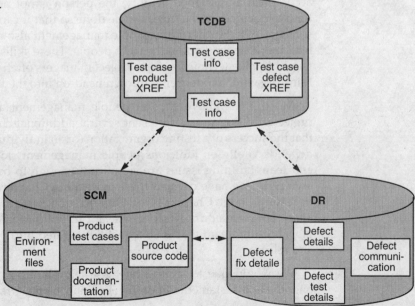

Similarly, in order to decide which tests to run for a given regression run,

1. The defects recently fixed can be obtained from the defect repository and tests for these can be obtained from the TCDB and included in the regression tests.
2. The list of files changed since the last regression run can be obtained from the SCM repository and the corresponding test files traced from the TCDB.
3. The set of tests not run recently can be obtained from the TCDB and these can become potential candidates to be run at certain frequencies

15.3.3　Test People Management

Developer: These testing folks... they are always nitpicking!

Tester: Why don't these developers do anything right?!

Sales person: When will I get a product out that I can sell?!

People management is an integral part of any project management. Often, it is a difficult chasm for engineers-turned-managers to cross. As an individual contributor, a person relies only on his or her own skills to accomplish an assigned activity; the person is not necessarily trained on how to document what needs to be done so that it can be accomplished by someone else. Furthermore, people management also requires the ability to hire, motivate, and retain the right people. These skills are seldom formally taught (unlike technical skills). Project managers often learn these skills in a "sink or swim" mode, being thrown head-on into the task.

Most of the above gaps in people management apply to all types of projects. Testing projects present several additional challenges. We believe that the success of a testing organization (or an individual in a testing career) depends vitally on judicious people management skills. Since the people and team-building issues are significant enough to be considered in their own right, we have covered these in detail in Chapter 13, on People Issues in Testing, and in Chapter 14, on Organization Structures for Testing Teams. These chapters address issues relevant to building and managing a good global testing team that is effectively integrated into product development and release.

We would like to stress that these team-building exercises should be ongoing and sustained, rather than be done in one burst. The effects of these exercises tend to wear out under the pressure of deadlines of delivery and quality. Hence, they need to be periodically recharged. The important point is that the common goals and the spirit of teamwork have to be internalized by all the stakeholders. Once this internalization is achieved, then they are unlikely to be swayed by operational hurdles that crop up during project execution. Such an internalization and upfront team building has to be part of the planning process for the team to succeed.

15.3.4   Integrating with Product Release

Ultimately, the success of a product depends on the effectiveness of integration of the development and testing activities. These job functions have to work in tight unison between themselves and with other groups such as product support, product management, and so on. The schedules of testing have to be linked directly to product release. Thus, project planning for the entire product should be done in a holistic way, encompassing the project plan for testing and development. The following are some of the points to be decided for this planning.

1. Sync points between development and testing as to when different types of testing can commence. For example, when integration testing could start, when system testing could start and so on. These are governed by objective entry criteria for each phase of testing (to be satisfied by development).

2. Service level agreements between development and testing as to how long it would take for the testing team to complete the testing. This will ensure that testing focuses on finding relevant and important defects only.

3. Consistent definitions of the various priorities and severities of the defects. This will bring in a shared vision between development and testing teams, on the nature of the defects to focus on.

4. Communication mechanisms to the documentation group to ensure that the documentation is kept in sync with the product in terms of known defects, workarounds, and so on.

The purpose of the testing team is to identify the defects in the product and the risks that could be faced by releasing the product with the existing defects. Ultimately, the decision to release or not is a management decision, dictated by market forces and weighing the business impact for the organization and the customers.

15.4   TEST PROCESS

15.4.1   Putting Together and Baselining a Test Plan

A test plan combines all the points discussed above into a single document that acts as an anchor point for the entire testing project. A template of a test plan is provided in Appendix B at the end of this chapter. Appendix A gives a check list of questions that are useful to arrive at a Test Plan.

An organization normally arrives at a template that is to be used across the board. Each testing project puts together a test plan based on the template. Should any changes be required in the template, then such a change is made only after careful deliberations (and with appropriate approvals). The test plan is reviewed by a designated set of competent people in the organization. It then is approved by a competent authority, who is independent of the project manager directly responsible for testing. After this, the test plan is baselined into the configuration management repository. From then on, the baselined test plan becomes the basis for running the testing project. Any significant changes in the testing project should thereafter be reflected in the test plan and the changed test plan baselined again in the configuration management repository. In addition, periodically, any change needed to the test plan templates are discussed among the different stake holders and this is kept current and applicable to the testing teams.

15.4.2   Test Case Specification

Using the test plan as the basis, the testing team designs *test case specifications*, which then becomes the basis for preparing individual *test cases*. We have been using the term test cases freely throughout this book. Formally, a test case is nothing but a series of steps executed on a product, using a pre-defined set of input data, expected to produce a pre-defined set of outputs, in a given environment. Hence, a test case specification should clearly identify

1. The purpose of the test: This lists what feature or part the test is intended for. The test case should follow the naming conventions (as discussed earlier) that are consistent with the feature/module being tested.

2. Items being tested, along with their version/release numbers as appropriate.

3. Environment that needs to be set up for running the test case: This can include the hardware environment setup, supporting software environment setup (for example, setup of the operating system, database, and so on), setup of the product under test (installation of the right version, configuration, data initialization, and so on).

4. Input data to be used for the test case: The choice of input data will be dependent on the test case itself and the technique followed

in the test case (for example, equivalence partitioning, boundary value analysis, and so on). The actual values to be used for the various fields should be specified unambiguously (for example, instead of saying "enter a three-digit positive integer," it is better to say "enter 789"). If automated testing is to be used, these values should be captured in a file and used, rather than having to enter the data manually every time.

5. Steps to be followed to execute the test: If automated testing is used, then, these steps are translated to the scripting language of the tool. If the testing is manual, then the steps are detailed instructions that can be used by a tester to execute the test. It is important to ensure that the level of detail in documenting the steps is consistent with the skill and expertise level of the person who will execute the tests.

6. The expected results that are considered to be "correct results." These expected results can be what the user may see in the form of a GUI, report, and so on and can be in the form of updates to persistent storage in a database or in files.

7. A step to compare the actual results produced with the expected results: This step should do an "intelligent" comparison of the expected and actual results to highlight any discrepancies. By "intelligent" comparison, we mean that the comparison should take care of "acceptable differences" between the expected results and the actual results, like terminal ID, user ID, system date, and so on.

8. Any relationship between this test and other tests: This can be in the form of dependencies among the tests or the possibility of reuse across the tests.

15.4.3 Update of Traceability Matrix

As we have discussed in Chapter 4, Black Box Testing, a requirements traceability matrix ensures that the requirements make it through the subsequent life cycle phases and do not get orphaned mid-course. In particular, the traceability matrix is a tool to validate that every requirement is tested. The traceability matrix is created during the requirements gathering phase itself by filling up the unique identifier for each requirement. Subsequently, as the project proceeds through the design and coding phases, the unique identifier for design features and the program file name is entered in the traceability matrix. When a test case specification is complete, the row corresponding to the requirement which is being tested by the test case is updated with the test case specification identifier. This ensures that there is a two-way mapping between requirements and test cases.

15.4.4 Identifying Possible Candidates for Automation

The test case design forms the basis for writing the test cases. Before writing the test cases, a decision should be taken as to which tests are to be automated and which should be run manually. We have described test automation in detail in Chapter 16. Suffice to say here, some of the criteria that will be used in deciding which scripts to automate include

1. Repetitive nature of the test;
2. Effort involved in automation;
3. Amount of manual intervention required for the test; and
4. Cost of automation tool.

15.4.5   Developing and Baselining Test Cases

Based on the test case specifications and the choice of candidates for automation, test cases have to be developed. The development of test cases entails translating the test specifications to a form from which the tests can be executed. If a test case is a candidate for automation, then, this step requires writing test scripts in the automation language. If the test case is a manual test case, then test case writing maps to writing detailed step-by-step instructions for executing the test and validating the results. In addition, the test case should also capture the documentation for the changes made to the test case since the original development. Hence, the test cases should also have change history documentation, which specifies

1. What was the change;
2. Why the change was necessitated;
3. Who made the change;
4. When was the change made;
5. A brief description of how the change has been implemented; and
6. Other files affected by the change.

All the artifacts of test cases—the test scripts, inputs, scripts, expected outputs, and so on—should be stored in the test case database and SCM, as described earlier. Since these artifacts enter the SCM, they have to be reviewed and approved by appropriate authorities before being baselined.

15.4.6   Executing Test Cases and Keeping Traceability Matrix Current

The prepared test cases have to be executed at the appropriate times during a project. For example, test cases corresponding to smoke tests may be run on a daily basis. System testing test cases will be run during system testing.

As the test cases are executed during a test cycle, the defect repository is updated with

1. Defects from the earlier test cycles that are fixed in the current build; and
2. New defects that get uncovered in the current run of the tests.

The defect repository should be the primary vehicle of communication between the test team and the development team. As mentioned earlier, the defect repository contains all the information about defects uncovered by testing (and defects reported by customers). All the stakeholders should be referring to the defect repository for knowing the current status of all the defects. This communication can be augmented by other means like emails, conference calls, and so on.

As discussed in the test plan, a test may have to be suspended during its run because of certain show stopper defects. In this case, the suspended test case should wait till the resumption criteria are satisfied. Likewise, a test should be run only when the entry criteria for the test are satisfied and should be deemed complete only when the exit criteria are satisfied.

During test design and execution, the traceability matrix should be kept current. As and when tests get designed and executed successfully, the traceability matrix should be updated. The traceability matrix itself should be subject to configuration management, that is, it should be subject to version control and change control.

15.4.7   Collecting and Analyzing Metrics

When tests are executed, information about test execution gets collected in test logs and other files. The basic measurements from running the tests are then converted to meaningful metrics by the use of appropriate transformations and formulae, as described in Chapter 17, Metrics and Measurements.

15.4.8   Preparing Test Summary Report

At the completion of a test cycle, a test summary report is produced. This report gives insights to the senior management about the fitness of the product for release. We will see details of this report later in the chapter.

15.4.9   Recommending Product Release Criteria

While "under testing," a product could be a risk "over testing" a product trying to remove "that last defect" could be as much of a risk!

One of the purposes of testing is to decide the fitness of a product for release. As we have seen in Chapter 1, testing can never conclusively prove the absence of defects in a software product. What it provides is an evidence of what defects exist in the product, their severity, and impact. As we discussed earlier, the job of the testing team is to articulate to the senior management and the product release team

1.   What defects the product has;

2.   What is the impact/severity of each of the defects; and

3.   What would be the risks of releasing the product with the existing defects.

The senior management can then take a meaningful business decision on whether to release a given version or not.

15.5   TEST REPORTING

Testing requires constant communication between the test team and other teams (like the development team). Test reporting is a means of achieving this communication. There are two types of reports or communication that are required: test incident reports and test summary reports (also called test completion reports).

15.5.1.1 Test incident report   A test incident report is a communication that happens through the testing cycle as and when defects are encountered. Earlier, we described the defect repository. A test incident report is nothing but an entry made in the defect repository. Each defect has a unique ID and this is used to identify the incident. The high impact test incidents (defects) are highlighted in the test summary report.

15.5.1.2 Test cycle report   As discussed, test projects take place in units of test cycles. A test cycle entails planning and running certain tests in cycles, each cycle using a different build of the product. As the product progresses through the various cycles, it is to be expected to stabilize. A test cycle report, at the end of each cycle, gives

1. A summary of the activities carried out during that cycle;
2. Defects that were uncovered during that cycle, based on their severity and impact;
3. Progress from the previous cycle to the current cycle in terms of defects fixed;
4. Outstanding defects that are yet to be fixed in this cycle; and
5. Any variations observed in effort or schedule (that can be used for future planning).

15.5.1.3 Test summary report   The final step in a test cycle is to recommend the suitability of a product for release. A report that summarizes the results of a test cycle is the test summary report.

There are two types of test summary reports.

1. Phase-wise test summary, which is produced at the end of every phase
2. Final test summary reports (which has all the details of all testing done by all phases and teams, also called as "release test report")

A summary report should present

1. A summary of the activities carried out during the test cycle or phase
2. Variance of the activities carried out from the activities planned. This includes

   ✠ the tests that were planned to be run but could not be run (with reasons);

   ✠ modifications to tests from what was in the original test specifications (in this case, the TCDB should be updated);

   ✠ additional tests that were run (that were not in the original test plan);

   ✠ differences in effort and time taken between what was planned and what was executed; and

   ✠ any other deviations from plan.

3. Summary of results should include

   ✠ tests that failed, with any root cause descriptions; and

   ✠ severity of impact of the defects uncovered by the tests.

4. Comprehensive assessment and recommendation for release should include

   ✠ "Fit for release" assessment; and

   ✠ Recommendation of release.

15.5.1   Recommending Product Release

Based on the test summary report, an organization can take a decision on whether to release the product or not.

Ideally, an organization would like to release a product with zero defects. However, market pressures may cause the product to be released with the defects provided that the senior management is convinced that there is no major risk of customer dissatisfaction. If the remnant defects are of low priority/impact, or if the conditions under which the defects are manifested are not realistic, an organization may choose to release the product with these defects. Such a decision should be taken by the senior manager only after consultation with the customer support team, development team, and testing team so that the overall workload for all parts of the organization can be evaluated.

15.6   BEST PRACTICES

Best practices in testing can be classified into three categories.

1. Process related
2. People related
3. Technology related

15.6.1   Process Related Best Practices

Ensuring people-friendly processes makes for process-friendly people.

A strong process infrastructure and process culture is required to achieve better predictability and consistency. Process models such as CMMI can provide a framework to build such an infrastructure. Implementing a formal process model that makes business sense can provide consistent training to all the employees, and ensure consistency in the way the tasks are executed.

Integrating processes with technology in an intelligent manner is a key to the success of an organization. A *process database*, a federation of information about the definition and execution of various processes can be a valuable addition to the repertoire of tools in an organization. When this process database is integrated with other tools such as defect repository, SCM tool, and TCDB, the organization can maximize the benefits.

15.6.2   People Related Best Practices

Best practices in testing related to people management have been covered in detail in Chapter 13, People Issues in Testing. We will summarize here those best practices that pertain to test management.

The key to successful management is to ensure that the testing and development teams gel well. This gelling can be enhanced by creating a sense of ownership in the overarching product goals. While individual goals are required for the development and testing teams, it is very important to get to a common understanding of the overall goals that define the success of the product as a whole. The participation of the testing teams in this goal-setting process and their early involvement in the overall product-planning process can help enhance the required gelling. This gelling can be strengthened by keeping the testing teams in the loop for decision-making on product-release decisions and criteria used for release.

As discussed earlier in this chapter, job rotation among support, development, and testing can also increase the gelling among the teams. Such job rotation can help the different teams develop better empathy and appreciation of the challenges faced in each other's roles and thus result in better teamwork.

15.6.3   Technology Related Best Practices

As we saw earlier, a fully integrated TCDB – SCM – defect repository can help in better automation of testing activities. This can help choose those tests that are likely to uncover defects. Even if a full-scale test automation tool is not available, a tight integration among these three tools can greatly enhance the effectiveness of testing. In Chapter 17, Metrics and Measurements, we shall look at metrics like defects per 100 hours of testing, defect density, defect removal rate, and so on. The calculation of these metrics will be greatly simplified by a tight integration among these three tools.

> Twenty-first century tools with nineteenth-century processes can only lead to nineteenth-century productivity!

As we will discuss in Chapter 16, Test Automation, automation tools take the boredom and routine out of testing functions and enhance the challenge and interest in the testing functions. Despite the high initial costs that may be incurred, test automation tends to pay significant direct long-term cost savings by reducing the manual labor required to run tests. There are also indirect benefits in terms of lower attrition of test engineers, since test automation not only reduces the routine, but also brings some "programming" into the job, that engineers usually like.

When test automation tools are used, it is useful to integrate the tool with TCDB, defect repository, and an SCM tool. In fact, most of the test automation tools provide the features of TCDB and defect repository, while integrating with commercial SCM tools.

A final remark on best practices. The three dimensions of best practices cannot be carried out in isolation. A good technology infrastructure should be aptly supported by effective process infrastructure and be executed by competent people. These best practices are inter-dependent, self-supporting, and mutually enhancing. Thus, the organization needs to take a holistic view of these practices and keep a fine balance among the three dimensions.

APPENDIX A: TEST PLANNING CHECKLIST

Scope Related

✠ Have you identified the features to be tested?

✠ Have you identified the features not to be tested?

✠ Have you justified the reasons for the choice of features not to be tested and ascertained the impact from product management/ senior management?

✠ Have you identified the new features in the release ?

✠ Have you included in the scope of testing areas which failures can be catastrophed ?

✠ Have you included for testing those area that are defect prove or complex to test ?

Environment Related

✠ Do you have a software configuration management tool in place?

✠ Do you have a defect repository in place?

✠ Do you have a test case data base in place?

✠ Have you set up institutionalized procedures to update any of these?

⌖ Have you identified the necessary hardware and software to design and run the tests?

⌖ Have you identified the costs and other resource requirements of any test automation tools that may be needed?

Criteria Definition Related

⌖ Have you defined the entry and exit criteria for the various test phases?

⌖ Have you defined the suspension and resumption criteria for the various tests?

Test Case Related

⌖ Have you published naming conventions and other internal standards for designing, writing, and executing test cases?

⌖ Are the test specifications documented adequately according to the above standards?

⌖ Are the test specifications reviewed and approved by appropriate people?

⌖ Are the test specifications baselined into the SCM repository?

⌖ Are the test cases written according to specifications?

⌖ Are the test cases reviewed and approved by appropriate people?

⌖ Are the test cases baselined into the SCM repository?

⌖ Is the traceability matrix updated once the test specifications/test cases are baselined?

Effort Estimation Related

⌖ Have you translated the scope to a size estimate (for example, number of test cases)

⌖ Have you arrived at an estimate of the effort required to design and construct the tests?

⌖ Have you arrived at an effort required for repeated execution of the tests?

⌖ Have the effort estimates been reviewed and approved by appropriate people?

Schedule Related

⌖ Have you put together a schedule that utilizes all the resources available?

⌖ Have you accounted for any parallelism constraints?

⌖ Have you factored in the availability of releases from the development team?

✠ Have you accounted for any show stopper defects?

✠ Have you prioritized the tests in the event of any schedule crunch?

✠ Has the schedule been reviewed and approved by appropriate people?

Risks Related

✠ Have you identified the possible risks in the testing project?

✠ Have you quantified the likelihood and impact of these risks?

✠ Have you identified possible symptoms to catch the risks before they happen?

✠ Have you identified possible mitigation strategies for the risks?

✠ Have you taken care not to squeeze in all the testing activities towards then end of the development cycle?

✠ What mechanisms have you tried to distribute the testing activities throughout the life cycle (for example, doing an early test design like in the V model)?

✠ Have you prepared for the risk of idle time because of tests being suspended?

People Related

✠ Have you identified the number and skill levels of people required?

✠ Have you identified the gaps and prepared for training and skill upgradation?

Execution Related

✠ Are you executing the tests as per plan? If there is any deviation, have you updated the plan?

✠ Did the test execution necessitate changing any test cases design? If so, is the TCDB kept current?

✠ Have you logged any defects that come up during testing in the defect repository?

✠ Have you updated the defect repository for any defects that are fixed in the current test cycle?

✠ Have you kept the traceability matrix current with the changes?

Completion Related

✠ Have you prepared a test summary report?

✠ Have you clearly documented the outstanding defects, along with their severity and impact?

✠ Have you put forth your recommendations for product release?

APPENDIX B: TEST PLAN TEMPLATE

1. Introduction
   1.1 Scope
   > *What features are to be tested and what features will not be tested; what combinations of environment are to be tested and what not.*

2. References
   > *(Gives references and links to documents such as requirement specifications, design specifications, program specifications, project plan, project estimates, test estimates, process documents, internal standards, external standards, and so on.)*

3. Test Methodology and Strategy/Approach

4. Test Criteria
   4.1 Entry Criteria
   4.2 Exit Criteria
   4.3 Suspension Criteria
   4.4 Resumption Criteria

5. Assumptions, Dependencies, and Risks
   5.1 Assumptions
   5.2 Dependencies
   5.3 Risks and Risk Management Plans

6. Estimations
   6.1 Size Estimate
   6.2 Effort Estimate
   6.3 Schedule Estimate

7. Test Deliverables and Milestones

8. Responsibilities

9. Resource Requirements
   9.1 Hardware Resources
   9.2 Software Resources
   9.3 People Resources (*Number of people, skills, duration, etc.*)
   9.4 Other Resources

10. Training Requirements
    10.1 Details of Training Required
    10.2 Possible Attendees
    10.3 Any Constraints

11. Defect Logging and Tracking Process

12. Metrics Plan

13. Product Release Criteria

REFERENCES

[PMI-2004] is a comprehensive guide that covers all aspects of project management. [RAME-2002] discusses the activities of managing a globally distributed project, including topics like risk management, configuration management, etc. [BURN-2004] provides inputs on test planning. [FAIR-97] discussed methods of work breakdown structure applicable in general to projects. [HUMP-86] is the initial work that introduced the concept of process models for software development that eventually led to the Capability Maturity Model (CMM). [CMMI-2002] covers the Capability Maturity Model Integrated, a popular process model. [ALBE-79] and [ALBE-83] discuss function points, a method of size estimation for applications. [IEEE-829] presents the various templates and documentation required for testing like test plans, test case specifications, test incident report, etc. [IEEE-1059], [IEEE-1012] also contain useful information for these topics.

PROBLEMS AND EXERCISES

1. Someone made the remark, "Testing heavily depends on development – so I cannot plan a testing project." How will you argue against this statement?

2. Consider a new version of an operating system. While deciding the scope of what needs to be tested in that version, which of these features would be essential to test?

   a. The OS introduces support for a new network protocol which is becoming a de facto standard

   b. The OS has been modified to work in an embedded system on a manned flight to Mars

   c. The OS feature for support for long file names has been stable and working for the past five versions and has not undergone any major change

   d. The caching part of the file system of the OS has often given performance problems and every slight change seems to upset the apple cart

   e. The features of OS are expected works on different chips and in a network, different machines may be running on different chips

3. Give some typical entry, exit, suspension, and resumption criteria for unit testing. Considering the classification of white box and black box testing for the case of unit testing, should there be such criteria for separating white box and black box testing parts of unit testing?

4. When we discussed identifying responsibilities and staffing needs, we were looking at the requirements of the testing team. What kind of SLAs or responsibilities of other involved teams (e.g., development teams) should a test plan document? How would one enforce or track such responsibilities?

5. For estimating the size of a testing project, give the pros and cons of using the lines of code of the product as a basis. Would this apply only to white box testing or also to black box testing?

6. What would be the base data required for estimating the size and effort of a testing project that involved automation?

7. Assuming you have historical productivity data for the various activities like test planning, design, execution and defect fixing, what factors would you consider before adapting/modifying the historical figures to more directly be applicable to your project?

8. In the text Risk Exposure was quantified as the product of probability of the risk happening and the impact of the risk, if the risk happens. How would you estimate each of these two parameters? When quantitative data is not available for these two parameters, how would you go about quantifying riak?

9. We discussed the various infrastructure components (TCDB, Defect Repository, Configuration Management Repository). How would you make these tools operate in unison to effectively:

   a. Choose tests for regression testing for a given release

   b. Predict the time required for releasing a product, after fixing the identified defects

   c. Maintain test cases based on their effectiveness of detecting defects

10. Adapt the test plan template given in this chapter to suit the needs of your organization

11. Can the Defect Repository be accessible by customers? If so, what security aspects would you have to take into account?

12. What should be the contents of a test incident report, keeping in mind the goal that the defects found in a test should eventually be fixed.

13. What factors would an organization take into account to decide the fitness of a product for release?

Software Test Automation

CHAPTER 16

In this chapter—

✓ What is test automation?

✓ Terms used in automation

✓ Skills needed for automation

✓ What to automate, scope of automation

✓ Design and architecture for automation

✓ Generic requirements for test tool/framework

✓ Process model for automation

✓ Selecting a test tool

✓ Automation for extreme programming model

✓ Challenges in automation

✓ Summary

16.1 WHAT IS TEST AUTOMATION?

In the previous chapters we have seen several types of testing and how test cases can be developed for those testing types. When these test cases are run and checked, the coverage and quality of testing (and the quality of the product) will definitely improve. However, this throws up a challenge that additional time is required to run those test cases. One way to overcome that challenge is to automate running of most of the test cases that are repetitive in nature.

Developing software to test the software is called test automation. Test automation can help address several problems.

Automation saves time as software can execute test cases faster than human do   This can help in running the tests overnight or unattended. The time thus saved can be used effectively for test engineers to

1.   Develop additional test cases to achieve better coverage;
2.   Perform some esoteric or specialized tests like ad hoc testing; or
3.   Perform some extra manual testing.

The time saved in automation can also be utilized to develop additional test cases, thereby improving the coverage of testing. Moreover, the automated tests can be run overnight, saving the elapsed time for testing, thereby enabling the product to be released frequently.

Test automation can free the test engineers from mundane tasks and make them focus on more creative tasks   We read about ad hoc testing in Chapter 10. This testing requires intuition and creativity to test the product for those perspectives that may have been missed out by planned test cases. If there are too many planned test cases that need to be run manually and adequate automation does not exist, then the test team may spend most of its time in test execution. This creates a situation where there is no scope for intuition and creativity in the test team. This also creates fatigue and boredom in the test team. Automating the more mundane tasks gives some time to the test engineers for creativity and challenging tasks. As we saw in Chapter 13, People Issues in Testing, motivating test engineers is a significant challenge and automation can go a long way in helping this cause.

Automated tests can be more reliable   When an engineer executes a particular test case many times manually, there is a chance for human error or a bias because of which some of the defects may get missed out. As with all machine-oriented activities, automation can be expected to produce more reliable results every time, and eliminates the factors of boredom and fatigue.

Automation helps in immediate testing   Automation reduces the time gap between development and testing as scripts can be executed as soon as the product build is ready. Automation can be designed in such a way that the tests can be kicked off automatically, after a successful build is over. Automated testing need not wait for the availability of test engineers.

Automation can protect an organization against attrition of test engineers   Automation can also be used as a knowledge transfer tool to train test engineers on the product as it has a repository of different tests for the product. With manual testing, any specialized knowledge or "undocumented ways" of running tests gets lost with the test engineer's leaving. On the other hand, automating tests makes the test execution less person dependent.

Test automation opens up opportunities for better utilization of global resources   Manual testing requires the presence of test engineers, but automated tests can be run round the clock, twenty-four hours a day and seven days a week. This will also enable teams in different parts of the world, in different time zones, to monitor and control the tests, thus providing round the-clock coverage.

> Automation makes the software to test the software and enables the human effort to be spent on creative testing.

Certain types of testing cannot be executed without automation   Test cases for certain types testing such as reliability testing, stress testing, load and performance testing, cannot be executed without automation. For example, if we want to study the behavior of a system with thousands of users logged in, there is no way one can perform these tests without using automated tools.

Automation means end-to-end, not test execution alone   Automation does not end with developing programs for the test cases. In fact, that is where it starts. Automation should consider all activities such as picking up the right product build, choosing the right configuration, performing installation, running the tests, generating the right test data, analyzing the results, and filing the defects in the defect repository. When talking about automation, this large picture should always be kept in mind.

Automation should have scripts that produce test data to maximize coverage of permutations and combinations of inputs and expected output for result comparison. They are called *test data generators*. It is not always easy to predict the output for all input conditions. Even if all input conditions are known and the expected results are met, the error produced by the software and the functioning of the product after such an error may not be predictable. The automation script should be able to map the error patterns dynamically to conclude the result. The error pattern mapping is done not only to conclude the result of a test, but also to point out the root cause. The definition of automation should encompass this aspect.

While it is mentioned in the above paragraphs, that automation should try to cover the entire spectrum of activities for testing, it is important for such automation to relinquish the control back to test engineers in situations where a further set of actions to be taken are not known or cannot be determined automatically (for example, if test results cannot be ascertained by test scripts for pass/fail). If automated scripts determine the results wrongly, such conclusions can delay the product release. If automated scripts are found to have even one or two such problems, irrespective of their quality, they will lose credibility and may not get used during later cycles of the release and the team will depend on manual testing. This may lead the organization to believe that the automation is the cause of all problems. This in turn will result in automation being completely ignored by the organization. Hence automation not only should try to cover the entire operation of activities but also should allow human intervention where required.

Once tests are automated keeping all the requirements in mind, it becomes easier to transfer or rotate the ownership for running the tests. As the objective of testing is to catch defects early, the automated tests can be given to developers so that they can execute them as part of unit testing. The automated tests can also be given to a CM engineer (build engineer) and the tests can be executed soon after the build is ready. As we discussed in Chapter 8, on regression tests, many companies have a practice of *Daily build and smoke test*, to ensure that the build is ready for further testing and that existing functionality is not broken due to changes.

16.2   TERMS USED IN AUTOMATION

We have been using the term "test case" freely in this book. As formally defined in Chapter 15, a *test case* is a set of sequential steps to execute a test operating on a set of predefined inputs to produce certain expected outputs. There are two types of test cases—automated and manual. As the names suggest, a manual test case is executed manually while an automated test case is executed using automation. Test cases in this chapter refer to automated test cases, unless otherwise specified. A test case should always have an expected result associated when executed.

A test case (manual or automated) can be represented in many forms. It can be documented as a set of simple steps, or it could be an assertion statement or a set of assertions. An example of an assertion is "Opening a file, which is already opened should fail." An assertion statement includes the expected result in the definition itself, as in the above example, and makes it easy for the automation engineer to write the code for the steps and to conclude the correctness of result of the test case.

As we have seen earlier, testing involves several phases and several types of testing..Some test cases are repeated several times during a product release because the product is built several times. Not only are the test cases repetitive in testing, some operations that are described as steps in the test cases too are repetitive. Some of the basic operations such as "log in to the system" are generally performed in a large number of test cases for a product. Even though these test cases (and the operations within them) are repeated, every time the intent or area of focus may keep changing. This presents an opportunity for the automation code to be reused for different purposes and scenarios.

Table 16.1 describes some test cases for the log in example, on how the log in can be tested for different types of testing.

Table 16.1 Same test case being used for different types of testing.

S.No.	Test cases for testing	Belongs to what type of testing
1	Check whether log in works	Functionality
2	Repeat log in operation *in a loop for 48 hours*	Reliability
3	Perform log in *from 10000 clients*	Load/stress testing
4	*Measure time taken* for log in operations in different conditions	Performance
5	Run log in operation from a *machine running Japanese language*	Internationalization

Table 16.1 can be further extended for other types of testing. From the above example, it is obvious that certain operations of a product (such as log in) get repeated when we try to test the product for different types of testing. If this is kept in mind, the code written for automating the log in operation can be reused in many places, thereby saving effort and time.

If we closely go through the above table, one can observe that there are two important dimensions: "*What operations have to be tested,*" and "*how the operations have to be tested.*" The how portion of the test case is called *scenarios* (shown in *Italics* in the above table). "What an operation has to do" is a product-specific feature and "how they are to be run" is a *framework*-specific requirement. The framework-/test tool-specific requirements are not just for test cases or products. They are generic requirements for all products that are being tested in an organization.

The automation belief is based on the fact that product operations (such as log in) are repetitive in nature and by automating the basic operations and leaving the different scenarios (how to test) to the framework/test tool, great progress can be made. This ensures code re-use for automation and draws a clear boundary between "what a test suite has to do" and "what a framework or a test tool should complement." When scenarios are combined by basic operations of the product, they become automated test cases.

When a set of test cases is combined and associated with a set of scenarios, they are called "test suite." A Test suite is nothing but a set of test cases that are automated and scenarios that are associated with the test cases.

Figure 16.1 depicts the terms discussed in the above paragraphs. The coloured figure is available on page 473.

Figure 16.1

Framework for test automation.

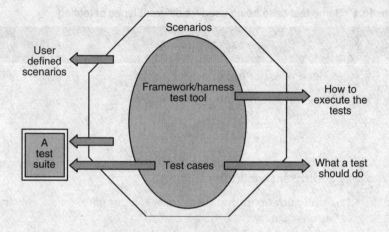

16.3 SKILLS NEEDED FOR AUTOMATION

There are different *"Generations of Automation."* The skills required for automation depends on what generation of automation the company is in or desires to be in the near future.

The automation of testing is broadly classified into three generations.

First generation—Record and Playback Record and playback avoids the repetitive nature of executing tests. Almost all the test tools available in the market have the record and playback feature. A test engineer *records* the sequence of actions by keyboard characters or mouse clicks and those recorded scripts are *played back* later, in the same order as they were recorded. Since a recorded script can be played back multiple times, it reduces the tedium of the testing function. Besides avoiding repetitive work, it is also simple to record and save the script. But this generation of tool has several disadvantages. The scripts may contain hard-coded values, thereby making it difficult to perform general types of tests. For example, when a report has to use the current date and time, it becomes difficult to use a recorded script. The handling error condition is left to the testers and thus, the played back scripts may require a lot of manual intervention to detect and correct error conditions. When the application changes, all the scripts have to be re-recorded, thereby increasing the test maintenance costs. Thus, when there is frequent change or when there is not much of opportunity to reuse or re-run the tests, the record and playback generation of test automation tools may not be very effective.

Second generation—Data-driven This method helps in developing test scripts that generates the set of input conditions and corresponding expected output. This enables the tests to be repeated for different input and output conditions. The approach takes as much time and effort as the product.

> Automation bridges the gap in skills requirement between testing and development; at times it demands more skills for test teams.

However, changes to application does not require the automated test cases to be changed as long as the input conditions and expected output are still valid. This generation of automation focuses on input and output conditions using the black box testing approach.

Third generation—Action-driven This technique enables a layman to create automated tests. There are no input and expected output conditions required for running the tests. All actions that appear on the application are automatically tested, based on a generic set of controls defined for automation. The set of actions are represented as objects and those objects are reused. The user needs to specify only the operations (such as log in, download, and so on) and everything else that is needed for those actions are automatically generated. The input and output conditions are automatically generated and used. The scenarios for test execution can be dynamically changed using the test framework that is available in this approach of automation. Hence, automation in the third generation involves two major aspects—"*test case automation*" and "*framework design*." We will see the details of framework design in the next section.

From the above approaches/generations of automation, it is clear that different levels of skills are needed based on the generation of automation selected. The skills needed for automation are classified into four levels for three generations as the third generation of automation introduces two levels of skills for development of test cases and framework, as shown in Table 16.2.

Table 16.2 Classification of skills for automation.

Automation—first generation	Automation—second generation	Automation—third generation	
Skills for test case automation	*Skills for test case automation*	*Skills for test case automation*	*Skills for framework*
Scripting languages	Scripting languages	Scripting languages	Programming languages
Record-playback tools usage	Programming languages	Programming languages	Design and architecture skills for framework creation
	Knowledge of data generation techniques	Design and architecture of the product under test	Generic test requirements for multiple products
	Usage of the product under test	Usage of the framework	

16.4   WHAT TO AUTOMATE, SCOPE OF AUTOMATION

The first phase involved in product development is requirements gathering; it is no different for test automation as the output of automation can also be considered as a product (the automated tests). The automation requirements define what needs to be automated looking into various aspects. The specific requirements can vary from product to product, from situation to situation, from time to time. We present below some generic tips for identifying the scope for automation.

16.4.1   Identifying the Types of Testing Amenable to Automation

Certain types of tests automatically lend themselves to automation.

Stress, reliability, scalability, and performance testing   These types of testing require the test cases to be run from a large number of different machines for an extended period of time, such as 24 hours, 48 hours, and so on. It is just not possible to have hundreds of users trying out the product day in and day out—they may neither be willing to perform the repetitive tasks, nor will it be possible to find that many people with the required skill sets. Test cases belonging to these testing types become the first candidates for automation.

Regression tests   Regression tests are repetitive in nature. These test cases are executed multiple times during the product development phases. Given the repetitive nature of the test cases, automation will save significant time and effort in the long run. Furthermore, as discussed earlier in this chapter, the time thus gained can be effectively utilized for ad hoc testing and other more creative avenues.

Functional tests   These kinds of tests may require a complex set up and thus require specialized skill, which may not be available on an ongoing basis. Automating these once, using the expert skill sets, can enable using less-skilled people to run these tests on an ongoing basis.

In the product development scenario, a lot of testing is repetitive as a good product can have a long lifetime if the periodic enhancements and maintenance releases are taken into account. This provides an opportunity to automate test cases and execute them multiple times during release cycles. As a thumb rule, if test cases need to be executed at least ten times in the near future, say, one year, and if the effort for automation does not exceed ten times of executing those test cases, then they become candidates for automation. Of course, this is just a thumb rule and the exact choice of what to automate will be determined by various factors such as availability of skill sets, availability of time for designing automated test scripts vis-à-vis release pressures, cost of the tool, availability of support, and so on.

The summary of arriving at the scope of what to automate is simply that we should choose to automate those functions (based on the above guidelines) that can amortize the investments in automation with minimum time delay.

16.4.2   Automating Areas Less Prone to Change

In a product scenario, the changes in requirements are quite common. In such a situation, what to automate is easy to answer. Automation should consider those areas where requirements go through lesser or no changes. Normally change in requirements cause scenarios and new features to be impacted, not the basic functionality of the product. As explained in the car manufacturing example in the extreme testing section of Chapter 10, the basic components of the car such as steering, brake, and accelerator have not changed over the years. While automating, such basic functionality of the product has to be considered first, so that they can be used for *"regression test bed"* and *"daily builds and smoke test."*

User interfaces normally go through significant changes during a project. To avoid rework on automated test cases, proper analysis has to be done to find out the areas of changes to user interfaces, and automate only those areas that will go through relatively less change. The non-user interface portions of the product can be automated first. While automating functions involving user interfaces-and non-user interface-oriented ("backend") elements, clear demarcation and "pluggability" have to be provided so that they can be executed together as well as executed independently. This enables the non-GUI portions of the automation to be reused even when GUI goes through changes.

16.4.3   Automate Tests that Pertain to Standards

One of the tests that products may have to undergo is compliance to standards. For example, a product providing a JDBC interface should satisfy the standard JDBC tests. These tests undergo relatively less change. Even if they do change, they provide backward compatibility by which automated scripts will continue to run.

Automating for standards provides a dual advantage. Test suites developed for standards are not only used for product testing but can also be sold as test tools for the market. A large number of tools available in the commercial market were internally developed for in-house usage. Hence, automating for standards creates new opportunities for them to be sold as commercial tools.

In case there are tools already available in the market for checking such standards, then there is no point in reinventing the wheel and rebuilding these tests. Rather, focus should be towards other areas for which tools are not available and in providing interfaces to other tools.

Testing for standards have certain legal and organization requirements. To certify the software or hardware, a test suite is developed and handed over to different companies. The certification suites are executed every time by the supporting organization before the release of software and hardware. This is called *"certification testing"* and requires perfectly compliant results every time the tests are executed. The companies that do certification testing may not know much about the product and standards but do the majority of this testing. Hence, automation in this area will go a long way. This is definitely an area of focus for automation. For example, some companies develop test suites for their software product and hardware manufacturers execute them before releasing a new hardware platform. This enables the customers to ascertain that the new hardware that is being released is compatible with software products that are popular in the market.

16.4.4   Management Aspects in Automation

> What to automate takes into account the technical and management aspects, as well as the long-term vision.

Prior to starting automation, adequate effort has to be spent to obtain *management commitment*. Automation generally is a phase involving a large amount of effort and is not necessarily a one-time activity. The automated test cases need to be maintained till the product reaches obsolesence. Since it involves significant effort to develop and maintain automated tools, obtaining management commitment is an important activity. Since automation involves effort over an extended period of time, management permissions are only given in phases and part by part. Hence, automation effort should focus on those areas for which management commitment exists already.

Return on investment is another aspect to be considered seriously. Effort estimates for automation should give a clear indication to the management on the expected return on investment. While starting automation, the effort should focus on areas where good permutations and combinations exist. This enables automation to cover more test cases with less code. Secondly, test cases which are easy to automate in less time should be considered first for automation. Some of the test cases do not have pre-associated expected results and such test cases take long to automate. Such test cases should be considered for the later phases of automation. This satisfies those amongst the management who look for quick returns from automation.

In line with Stephen Covey's principle of "First Things First," [COVE-89] it is important to automate the critical and basic functionalities of a product first. To achieve this, all test cases need to be prioritized as high, medium, and low, based on customer expectations, and automation should start from high priority and then cover medium and low-priority requirements.

16.5   DESIGN AND ARCHITECTURE FOR AUTOMATION

Design and architecture is an important aspect of automation. As in product development, the design has to represent all requirements in modules

Figure 16.2

Components of test
automation.

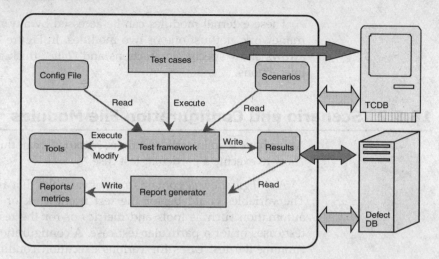

and in the interactions between modules. As we have seen in Chapter 5, Integration Testing, both internal interfaces and external interfaces have to be captured by design and architecture. In Figure 16.2, the thin arrows represent the internal interfaces and the direction of flow and thick arrows show the external interfaces. All the modules, their purpose, and interactions between them are described in the subsequent sections. The coloured figure is available on page 473.

Architecture for test automation involves two major heads: a test infrastructure that covers a test case database and a defect database or defect repository. These are shown as external modules in Figure 16.2. Using this infrastructure, the test framework provides a backbone that ties the selection and execution of test cases.

16.5.1   External Modules

There are two modules that are external modules to automation—TCDB and defect DB. We have described details of these in Chapter 15. To recall, all the test cases, the steps to execute them, and the history of their execution (such as when a particular test case was run and whether it passed/failed) are stored in the TCDB. The test cases in TCDB can be manual or automated. The interface shown by thick arrows represents the interaction between TCDB and the automation framework only for automated test cases. Please note that manual test cases do not need any interaction between the framework and TCDB.

Defect DB or *defect database* or *defect repository* contains details of all the defects that are found in various products that are tested in a particular organization. It contains defects and all the related information (when the defect was found, to whom it is assigned, what is the current status, the type of defect, its impact, and so on). Test engineers submit the defects for manual test cases. For automated test cases, the framework can automatically submit the defects to the defect DB during execution.

These external modules can be accessed by any module in automation framework, not just one or two modules. In Figure 16.2, the "*green*" thick arrows show specific interactions and "*blue*" thick arrows show multiple interactions.

16.5.2   Scenario and Configuration File Modules

As we have seen in earlier sections, *scenarios* are nothing but information on "how to execute a particular test case."

A *configuration file* contains a set of variables that are used in automation. The variables could be for the test framework or for other modules in automation such as tools and metrics or for the test suite or for a set of test cases or for a particular test case. A configuration file is important for running the test cases for various execution conditions and for running the tests for various input and output conditions and states. The values of variables in this configuration file can be changed dynamically to achieve different execution, input, output, and state conditions.

16.5.3   Test Cases and Test Framework Modules

A *test case* in Figure 16.2 means the automated test cases that are taken from TCDB and executed by the framework. Test case is an object for execution for other modules in the architecture and does not represent any interaction by itself.

A *test framework* is a module that combines "what to execute" and "how they have to be executed." It picks up the specific test cases that are automated from TCDB and picks up the scenarios and executes them. The variables and their defined values are picked up by the test framework and the test cases are executed for those values.

The test framework is considered the core of automation design. It subjects the test cases to different scenarios. For example, if there is a scenario that requests a particular test case be executed for 48 hours in a loop, then the test framework executes those test cases in the loop and times out when the duration is met. The framework monitors the results of every iteration and the results are stored. The test framework contains the main logic for interacting, initiating, and controlling all modules. The various requirements for the test framework are covered in the next section.

A test framework can be developed by the organization internally or can be bought from the vendor. Test framework and test tool are the two terms that are used interchangeably in this chapter. To differentiate between the usage of these two terms (wherever needed), in this chapter "framework" is used to mean an internal tool developed by the organization and "test tool" is used to mean a tool obtained from a tool vendor.

16.5.4   Tools and Results Modules

When a test framework performs its operations, there are a set of tools that may be required. For example, when test cases are stored as source code files in TCDB, they need to be extracted and compiled by build tools. In order to run the compiled code, certain runtime tools and utilities may be required. For example, IP Packet Simulators or User Login Simulators or Machine Simulators may be needed. In this case, the test framework invokes all these different tools and utilities.

When a test framework executes a set of test cases with a set of scenarios for the different values provided by the configuration file, the results for each of the test case along with scenarios and variable values have to be stored for future analysis and action. The results that come out of the tests run by the test framework should not overwrite the results from the previous test runs. The history of all the previous tests run should be recorded and kept as archives. The archive of results help in executing test cases based on previous test results. For example, a test engineer can request the test framework to "execute all test cases that are failed in previous test run." The audit of all tests that are run and the related information are stored in the module of automation. This can also help in selecting test cases for regression runs, as explained in Chapter 8, Regression Testing.

16.5.5   Report Generator and Reports/Metrics Modules

Once the results of a test run are available, the next step is to prepare the test reports and metrics. Preparing reports is a complex and time-consuming effort and hence it should be part of the automation design. There should be customized reports such as an executive report, which gives very high level status; technical reports, which give a moderate level of detail of the tests run; and detailed or debug reports which are generated for developers to debug the failed test cases and the product. The periodicity of the reports is different, such as daily, weekly, monthly, and milestone reports. Having reports of different levels of detail and different periodicities can address the needs of multiple constituents and thus provide significant returns.

The module that takes the necessary inputs and prepares a formatted report is called a *report generator*. Once the results are available, the report generator can generate *metrics*.

All the reports and metrics that are generated are stored in the reports/metrics module of automation for future use and analysis.

16.6   GENERIC REQUIREMENTS FOR TEST TOOL/FRAMEWORK

In the previous section, we described a generic framework for test automation. We will now present certain detailed criteria that such a framework and its usage should satisfy.

While illustrating the requirements, we have used examples in a hypothetical metalanguage to drive home the concept. The reader should verify the availability, syntax, and semantics of his or her chosen automation tool.

<table>
<tr><td>Requirement 1: No hard coding in the test suite</td></tr>
</table>

One of the important requirements for a test suite is to keep all variables separately in a file. By following this practice, the source code for the test suite need not be modified every time it is required to run the tests for different values of the variables. This enables a person who does not know the program to change the values and run the test suite. As we saw earlier, the variables for the test suite are called *configuration variables*. The file in which all variable names and their associated values are kept is called *configuration file*. It is quite possible that there could be several variables in the configuration file. Some of them could be for the test tool and some of them for the test suite. The variables belonging to the test tool and the test suite need to be separated so that the user of the test suite need not worry about test tool variables. Moreover, inadvertently changing test tool variables, without knowing their purpose, may impact the results of the tests. Providing inline comment for each of the variables will make the test suite more usable and may avoid improper usage of variables. An example of such a well-documented configuration file is provided below.

Test framework Configuration Parameters
WARNING: DO NOT MODIFY THIS SET WITHOUT CONSULTING YOUR SYADMIN

```
TOOL_PATH=/tools                  #   Path for test tool
COMMONLIB_PATH=/tools/crm/lib  #   Common Library
                                       Functions
SUITE_PATH=/tools/crm             #   Test suite path
```

Parameters common to all the test cases in the test suite

```
VERBOSE_LEVEL=3                   #   Messaging Level to
                                       screen
MAX_ERRORS=200                    #   Maximum allowable
                                       errors before the
                                  #   Test suite exits
USER_PASSWD=hello123              #   System administrator
                                       password
```

Test Case 1 parameters

```
TC1_USR_CREATE=0                  #   Whether users to be
                                       created, 1= yes, 0 = no
TC1_USR_PASSWD=hello1             #   User Password
TC1_USR_PREFIX=user               #   User Prefix
TC1_MAX_USRS=200                  #   Maximum users
```

In a product scenario involving several releases and several test cycles and defect fixes, the test cases go through large amount of changes and additionally there are situations for the new test cases to be added to the test suite. Test case modification and new test case insertion should not result in the existing test cases failing. If such modifications and new test cases result in the quality of the test suite being impacted, it defeats the purpose of automation, and maintenance requirements of the test suite become high. Similarly, test tools are not only used for one product having one test suite. They are used for various products that may have multiple test suites. In this case, it is important for the test suites be added to the framework without affecting other test suites. To summarize

✠ Adding a test case should not affect other test cases

✠ Adding a test case should not result in retesting the complete test suite

✠ Adding a new test suite to the framework should not affect existing test suites

Requirement 3: Reuse
of code for different
types of testing, test
cases

As we have seen in the "log in" example, the functionality of the product when subjected to different scenarios becomes test cases for different types of testing. This encourages the reuse of code in automation. By following the objectives of framework and test suite to take care of the "how" and "what" portions of automation respectively, reuse of test cases can be increased. The reuse of code is not only applicable to various types of testing; it is also applicable for modules within automation. All those functions that are needed by more than one test case can be separated and included in libraries. When writing code for automation, adequate care has to be taken to make them modular by providing functions, libraries and including files. To summarize

1. The test suite should only do what a test is expected to do. The test framework needs to take care of "how," and

2. The test programs need to be modular to encourage reuse of code.

For each test case there could be some prerequisite to be met before they are run. The test cases may expect some objects to be created or certain portions of the product to be configured in a particular way. If this portion is not met by automation, then it introduces some manual intervention before running the test cases. When test cases expect a particular setup to run the tests, it will be very difficult to remember each one of them and do the setup accordingly in the manual method. Hence, each test program should have a "setup" program that will create the necessary setup before executing the test cases. The test framework should have the intelligence to find out what test cases are executed and call the appropriate setup program.

A setup for one test case may work negatively for another test case. Hence, it is important not only to create the setup but also "undo" the setup soon after the test execution for the test case. Hence, a "cleanup" program becomes important and the test framework should have facilities to invoke this program after test execution for a test case is over.

Requirement 5: Independent test cases

We discussed test case expandability in requirement 2. The test cases need to be independent not only in the design phase, but also in the execution phase. To execute a particular test case, it should not expect any other test case to have been executed before nor should it implicitly assume that certain other test case will be run after it. Each test case should be executed alone; there should be no dependency between test cases such as test case-2 to be executed after test case-1 and so on. This requirement enables the test engineer to select and execute any test case at random without worrying about other dependencies.

Requirement 6: Test case dependency

Contrary to what was discussed in the previous requirement, sometimes there may be a need for test cases to depend on others. Making test cases independent enables any one case to be selected at random and executed. Making a test case dependent on an other makes it necessary for a particular test case to be executed before or after a dependent test case is selected for execution. A test tool or a framework should provide both features. The framework should help to specify the dynamic dependencies between test cases.

Requirement 7: Insulating test cases during execution

Insulating test cases from the environment is an important requirement for the framework or test tool. At the time of test case execution, there could be some events or interrupts or signals in the system that may affect the execution. Consider the example of automatic pop-up screens on web browsers. When such pop-up screens happen during execution, they affect test case execution as the test suite may be expecting some other screen based on an earlier step in the test case.

Hence, to avoid test cases failing due to some unforeseen events, the framework should provide an option for users to block some of the events. There has to be an option in the framework to specify what events can affect the test suite and what should not.

Requirement 8: Coding standards and directory structure

Coding standards and proper directory structures for a test suite may help the new engineers in understanding the test suite fast and help in maintaining the test suite. Incorporating the coding standards improves portability of the code. The test tool should have an option to specify (and sometimes to force) coding standards such as POSIX, XPG3, and so on. The test framework should provide an option or force the directory structure to enable multiple programmers to develop test suites/test cases in parallel, without duplicating the parts of the test case and by reusing the portion of the code.

Requirement 9: Selective execution of test cases

A framework may have multiple test suites; a test suite may have multiple test programs; and a test program may have multiple test cases. The test tool or a framework should have a facility for the test engineer to select a particular test case or a set of test cases and execute them. The selection of test cases need not be in any order and any combination should be allowed. Allowing test engineers to select test cases reduces the time and limits the focus to only those tests that are to be run and analyzed. These selections are normally done as part of the scenario file. The selection of test cases can be done dynamically just before running the test cases, by editing the scenario file.

Example:

test-program-name 2, 4, 1, 7-10

In the above scenario line, the test cases 2, 4, 1, 7, 8, 9, 10 are selected for execution in the same order mentioned. The hyphen (-) is used to mention the test cases in the chosen range—(7–10) have all to be executed. If the test case numbers are not mentioned in the above example, then the test tool should have the facility to execute all the test cases.

Requirement 10:
Random execution of test cases

While it is a requirement for a test engineer to select test cases from the available test cases as discussed in requirement 8 above, the same test engineer may sometimes need to select a test case randomly from a list of test cases. Giving a set of test cases and expecting the test tool to select the test case is called random execution of test cases. A test engineer selects a set of test cases from a test suite; selecting a random test case from the given list is done by the test tool. Given below are two examples to demonstrate random execution.

Example 1:
random
    test-program-name 2, 1, 5

Example 2:
random
    test-program1 (2, 1, 5)
    test-program2
    test-program3

In the first example, the test engineer wants the test tool to select one out of test cases 2, 1, 5 and executed. In the second example, the test engineer wants one out of test programs 1, 2, 3 to be randomly executed and if program 1 is selected, then one out of test cases 2, 1, 5 to be randomly executed. In this example if test programs 2 or 3 are selected, then all test cases in those programs are executed.

Requirement 11:
Parallel execution of test cases

There are certain defects which can be unearthed if some of the test cases are run at the same time. In a multi-tasking and multi processing operating systems it is possible to make several instances of the tests and make them run in parallel. Parallel execution simulates the behavior of several machines running the same test and hence is very useful for performance and load testing.

> **Example 1:**
> instances,5
>   Test-program1(3)
>
> **Example 2:**
> instances, 5
>   test-program1(2, 1, 5)
>   test-program2
>   test-program3

In the first example above, 5 instances of test case 3 from test program1, are created; in the second example, 5 instances of 3 test programs are created. Within each of the five instances that are created, the test programs 1, 2, 3 are executed in sequence.

Requirement 12: Looping the test cases

As discussed earlier, reliability testing requires the test cases to be executed in a loop. There are two types of loops that are available. One is the *iteration* loop which gives the number of iterations of a particular test case to be executed. The other is the *timed* loop, which keeps executing the test cases in a loop till the specified time duration is reached. These tests bring out reliability issues in the product.

> **Example 1:**
> Repeat_loop, 50
>   Test-program1(3)
>
> **Example 2:**
> Time_loop, 5 hours
>   test-program1(2, 1, 5)
>   test-program2
>   test-program3

In the first example, test case 3 from test program1 is repeated 50 times and in the second example, test cases 2, 1, 5 from test program1 and all test cases from test programs 2 and 3 are executed in order, in a loop for five hours.

Requirement 13: Grouping of test scenarios

We have seen many requirements and scenarios for test execution. Now let us discuss how we can combine those individual scenarios into a group so that they can run for a long time with a good mix of test cases. The group scenarios allow the selected test cases to be executed in order, random, in a loop all at the same time. The grouping of scenarios allows several tests to be executed in a predetermined combination of scenarios.

The following is an example of a group scenario.

Example:
```
group_scenario1
          parallel,2 AND repeat,10 @ scen1
scen1

          test_program1 (2, 1, 5)
          test_program2
          test_program3
```

In the above example, the group scenario was created to execute two instances of the individual scenario "scen1" in a loop for 10 times. The individual scenario is defined to execute test program1 (test cases 2, 1 and 5), test program2 and test program3. Hence, in the combined scenario, all test programs are executed by two instances simultaneously in an iteration loop for 10 times.

| Requirement 14: Test case execution based on previous results |

As we have seen in Chapter 8, regression test methodology requires that test cases be selected based on previous result and history. Hence, automation may not be of much help if the previous results of test execution are not considered for the choice of tests. Not only for regression testing, it is a requirement for various other types of testing also. One of the effective practices is to select the test cases that are not executed and test cases that failed in the past and focus more on them. Some of the common scenarios that require test cases to be executed based on the earlier results are

1. Rerun all test cases which were executed previously;
2. Resume the test cases from where they were stopped the previous time;
3. Rerun only failed/not run test cases; and
4. Execute all test cases that were executed on "Jan 26, 2005."

With automation, this task becomes very easy if the test tool or the framework can help make such choices.

| Requirement 15: Remote execution of test cases |

Most product testing requires more than one machine to be used. Hence there is a facility needed to start the testing on multiple machines at the same time from a central place. The central machine that allocates tests to multiple machines and co-ordinates the execution and result is called *test console or test monitor*. In the absence of a test console, not only does executing the results from multiple machines become difficult, collecting the results from all those machines also becomes difficult. In the absence of a test console, the results of tests need to be collected manually and consolidated. As it is against the objective of automation to introduce a manual step, this requirement is important for the framework to have. To summarize

✠   It should be possible to execute/stop the test suite on any machine/ set of machines from the test console.

✠   The test results and logs can be collected from the test console.

✠   The progress of testing can be found from the test console.

Figure 16.3 illustrates the role played be a test console and the multiple test machine. The coloured figure is available on page 474.

Figure 16.3

Role of test console and multiple execution machine.

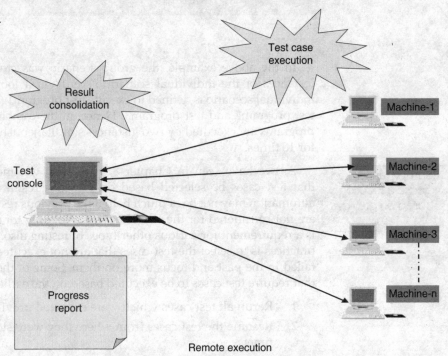

Requirement 16:
Automatic archival of test data

In requirement 13, we have seen that test cases are repeated on the basis of previous results. To confirm the results or to reproduce the problem, it is not enough repeat the test cases. The test cases have to be repeated the same way as before, with the same scenarios, same configuration variables and values, and so on. This requires that all the related information for the test cases have to be archived. Hence, this requirement becomes very important for repeating test cases and for analysis. Archival of test data must include

1.   What configuration variables were used;

2.   What scenario was used; and

3.   What programs were executed and from what path.

Requirement 17:
Reporting scheme

Every test suite needs to have a reporting scheme from where meaningful reports can be extracted. As we have seen in the design and architecture of framework, the report generator should have the capability to look at the results file and generate various reports. Hence, though the report generator is designed to develop dynamic reports, it is very difficult to say what information is needed and what not. Therefore, it is necessary to store all information related to test cases in the results file.

It is not only configuration variables that affect test cases and their results. The tunable parameters of the product and operating system also need to be archived to ensure repeatability or for analyzing defects.

Audit logs are very important to analyze the behavior of a test suite and a product. They store detailed information for each of the operations such as when the operation was invoked, the values for variables, and when the operation was completed, For performance tests, information such as when a framework was invoked, when a scenario was started, when a particular test case started and their corresponding completion time are important to calculate the performance of the product. Hence; a reporting scheme should include

1. When the framework, scenario, test suite, test program, and each test case were started/completed;
2. Result of each test case;
3. Log messages;
4. Category of events and log of events; and
5. Audit reports.

Requirement 18: Independent of languages

While coding for automation, there are some test cases which are easier coded using the scripting language provided by the tool, some in C and some in C++ and so on. Hence, a framework or test tool should provide a choice of languages and scripts that are popular in the software development area. Irrespective of the languages/scripts are used for automation, the framework should function the same way, meeting all requirements. Many test tools force the test scripts to be written in a particular language or force some proprietary scripts to be used. This needs to be avoided as it affects the momentum of automation because a new language has to be learned. To summarize

❊ A framework should be independent of programming languages and scripts.

❊ A framework should provide choice of programming languages, scripts, and their combinations.

❊ A framework or test suite should not force a language/script.

❊ A framework or test suite should work with different test programs written using different languages and scripts.

❊ A framework should have exported interfaces to support all popular, standard languages, and scripts.

❊ The internal scripts and options used by the framework should allow the developers of a test suite to migrate to better framework.

Requirement 19: Portability to different platforms

With the advent of platform-independent languages and technologies, there are many products in the market that are supported in multiple OS and language platforms. Products being cross-platform and test framework not working on some of those platforms are not good for automation. Hence, it is important for the test tools and framework to be cross-platform and be able to run on the same diversity of platforms and environments under which the product under test runs.

Having said that the test tools need to be cross-platform, it is important for the test suite developed for the product also be cross-platform or portable to other platforms with minimum amount of effort.

With a checklist for cross-platform capabilities of the test tools, it is important to look at platform architectures also. For example, 64-bit operating systems and products that work in 64-bit architecture are available in the market. The product being 64-bit and test suite functioning as a 32-bit application may not be a big issue, since all platforms support compatibility with legacy applications running 32 bits. However, this prevents some of the defects that are in the product from being unearthed. In a pure 64-bit environment which does not provide backward compatibility (for example, Digital Tru64), these 32-bit test suite cannot be run at all. To summarize

- ✠ The framework and its interfaces should be supported on various platforms.

- ✠ Portability to different platforms is a basic requirement for test tool/test suite.

- ✠ The language/script used in the test suite should be selected carefully so that it run on different platforms.

- ✠ The language/script written for the test suite should not contain platform-specific calls.

16.7 PROCESS MODEL FOR AUTOMATION

There is no hard and fast rule on when automation should start and when it should end. The work on automation can go simultaneously with product development and can overlap with multiple releases of the product. Like multiple-product releases, automation also has several releases. One specific requirement for automation is that the *delivery of the automated tests should be done before the test execution phase so that the deliverables from automation effort can be utilized for the current release* of the product. The requirements for automation span multiple phases for multiple releases, like product requirements. Test execution may stop soon after releasing the product but automation effort continues after a product release.

Given the above similarities between the product development and automation development, the process and life cycle model followed for automation and product development can also be very similar. In the majority

Figure 16.4

Similarities between product development and automation.

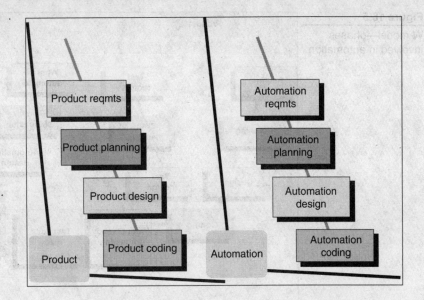

of cases, the software development life cycle (SDLC) model followed for the product is followed for automation also. This section focuses on the V model and its extensions to explain the process of test automation. Let us look at the phases involved in product development and phases in automation in Figure 16.4 to understand the similarities.

As we have seen in this chapter, test automation life cycle activities bear a strong similarity to product development activities. Just as product requirements need to be gathered on the product side, automation requirements too need to be gathered. Similarly, just as product planning, design, and coding are done, so also during test automation are automation planning, design, and coding.

It is important to test the test suite as we test the product. If there are defects in the test suite, much effort is involved in debugging to find out whether the defect is from the product or from the test suite. As mentioned in Chapter 1, "Test the test first"—an automated test suite has to be tested first before it can be used to test the product. If test suites report wrong defects, it will severely impact the credibility of test automation and will hamper further automation efforts. Hence, it is important to deliver trustworthy quality to the automated test suite. To produce test suites of trustworthy quality, some test phases become important as in product development. Figure 16.5, extends Figure 16.4 to introduce testing phases for the product and automated test suite. The coloured figure is available on page 474.

A set of four activities can be performed at each phase of product and automation development. While collecting development requirements for the product in the requirements phase, test requirements to test the product, requirements for development of automation, and test requirements for automation can be done simultaneously in the same phase. Similarly, the

Figure 16.5

W model—phases involved in automation.

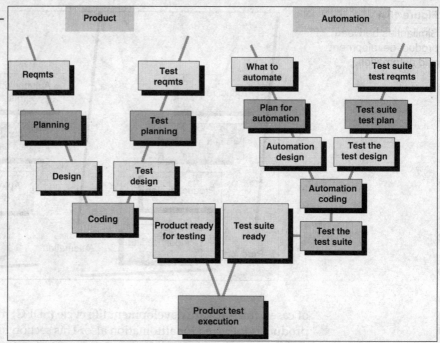

set of four activities can be performed at the planning and design phases. The coding for product and automation forms the coding phase in this W model where product and test suite get delivered. The coloured figure is available on page 475.

> Product and automation are like the two lines in a railway track; they go parallel in the same direction with similar expectations.

Test suites form one of the the deliverables from automation. In addition, the test framework itself can be considered as a deliverable from automation, the testing phases discussed in the above paragraph are only for the test suite, as the latter needs to be tested thoroughly for use in the product testing.

After introducing testing activities for both the product and automation, now the picture includes two parallel sets of activities for development and two parallel sets of activities for testing. When they are put together, it becomes a "W" model. Hence, for a product development involving automation, it will be a good choice to follow the W model to ensure that the quality of the product as well as the test suite developed meet the expected quality norms.

When talking about the W model it should not be interpreted that all activities that appear in a particular phase should start and finish at the same time. For example, in Figure 16.5, "design," "test design," "automation design," and "test design for test suite" appear in same phase (appearing side by side in the figure). The start and end date for the product and automation can be different for these activities. The model is only to ensure the flow of activities; there is no binding on the start and end date. Product development and automation can have independent schedules and can be handled as two different projects.

Another reason why there cannot be the same start and end date is because in many organizations the same test team is involved in testing the product and in developing the test suite. Obviously then the schedule in such case will be different. The start and end dates for activities are determined by project schedules based on resource availability and other dependencies.

Where a dedicated team exists for automation in an organization, the schedule for automation can be independent of product releases, with some (tested) deliverables marked for each product release. This enables the recently developed test suite to be used for testing the current release of the product.

16.8 SELECTING A TEST TOOL

Having identified the requirements of what to automate, a related question is the choice of an appropriate tool for automation. Even though we have listed these as two sequential steps, oftentimes, they are tightly interlinked.

Selecting the test tool is an important aspect of test automation for several reasons as given below.

1. Free tools are *not well supported and get phased out* soon. It will be extremely dangerous to see a release stalled because of a problem in a test tool.

2. Developing in-house tools *takes time*. Even though in-house tools can be less expensive and can meet needs better, they are often developed by the personal interest shown by a few engineers. They tend to have poor documentation and thus, once the person who developed the tools leaves the organization, the tools become unusable. Furthermore, such tool development takes a back seat if the pressure of actual product testing and delivery dates comes into play. Hence, this cannot be a sustained effort.

3. Test tools sold by vendors are *expensive*. In absolute dollar terms, the standard test automation tools in the market are expensive. Most organizations, especially small and medium enterprises, will have to carefully evaluate the economic impact of making such a significant investment.

4. Test tools require strong *training*. Test automation cannot be successful unless the people using the tools are properly trained. Such training usually involves getting familiar with the scripting languages that come with the tool, customizing the tool for use, and adding extensions or plug-ins for the tool. The effort involved in using the tools even after such training is quite high.

5. Test tools generally *do not meet all the requirements* for automation. Since tools are meant to be generic, they may not fully satisfy the needs of a particular customer. That is why customization and extensibility become key issues.

6. Not all test tools run on all platforms. To amortize the costs of automation, the tools and the automated tests should be reusable on all the platforms on which the product under test runs. Portability of the tool and the scripts to multiple platforms is therefore a key factor in deciding the test automation tool.

For all the above strong reasons, adequate focus needs to be provided for selecting the right tool for automation. As mentioned earlier, it is very important to ensure that we understand the requirements of automation while choosing the tools. The requirements should cover both the short-term and the long-term requirements. These requirements form the basis for tool selection.

16.8.1   Criteria for Selecting Test Tools

In the previous section, we looked at some reasons for evaluating the test tools and how requirements gathering will help. These change according to context and are different for different companies and products. We will now look into the broad categories for classifying the criteria. The categories are

1. Meeting requirements;
2. Technology expectations;
3. Training/skills; and
4. Management aspects.

16.8.1.1   Meeting requirements   Firstly, there are plenty of tools available in the market but rarely do they meet *all* the requirements of a given product or a given organization. Evaluating different tools for different requirements involves significant effort, money, and time. Given of the plethora of choice available (with each choice meeting some part of the requirement), huge delay is involved in selecting and implanting test tools.

Secondly, test tools are usually one generation behind and may not provide backward or forward compatibility (for example, JAVA SDK support) with the product under test. For example, if a product uses the latest version of SDK, say, version 2, the supported version of SDK in test tool could be 1.2. In this case some of the features that are coded in the product using version 2.0 new features, cannot be tested using the test tool. The time lag required for the test tool to catch up with the technology change in the product is something that a product organization may not be able to afford.

Thirdly, test tools may not go through the same amount of evaluation for new requirements. For example during Year 2000 testing, some of the tools could not be used for testing as they had similar problems (of not handling the date properly) as that of the products. Like the products, the test tools were not adequately tested for these new requirements. True to the dictum of "test the tests first" discussed in Chapter 1, the test tool must be tested and found fit for testing a product.

Finally, a number of test tools cannot differentiate between a product failure and a test failure. This causes increased analysis time and manual testing. The test tools may not provide the required amount of trouble-shooting/debug/error messages to help in analysis. This can result in increased log messages and auditing in the test suite or may result in going through the test manually. In the case of testing a GUI application, the test tools may determine the results based on messages and screen co-ordinates at run-time. Therefore, if the screen elements of the product are changed, it requires the test suite to be changed. The test tool must have some intelligence to proactively find out the changes that happened in the product and accordingly analyze the results.

16.8.1.2 Technology expectations

Firstly, test tools in general may not allow test developers to extend/modify the functionality of the framework. So extending the functionality requires going back to the tool vendor and involves additional cost and effort. Test tools may not provide the same amount of SDK or exported interfaces as provided by the products. Very few tools available in the market provide source code for extending functionality or fixing some problems. Extensibility and customization are important expectations of a test tool.

Secondly, a good number of test tools require their libraries to be linked with product binaries. When these libraries are linked with the source code of the product, it is called *"instrumented code."* This causes portions of the testing be repeated after those libraries are removed, as the results of certain types of testing will be different and better when those libraries are removed. For example, instrumented code has a major impact on performance testing since the test tools introduce an additional code and there could be a delay in executing the additional code.

Finally, test tools are not 100% cross-platform. They are supported only on some operating system platforms and the scripts generated from these tools may not be compatible on other platforms. Moreover, many of the test tools are capable of testing only the product, not the impact of the product/test tool to the system or network. When there is an impact analysis of the product on the network or system, the first suspect is the test tool and it is uninstalled when such analysis starts.

16.8.1.3 Training skills

While test tools require plenty of training, very few vendors provide the training to the required level. Organization-level training is needed to deploy the test tools, as the users of the test suite are not only the test team but also the development team and other areas like configuration management. Test tools expect the users to learn new language/scripts and may not use standard languages/scripts. This increases skill requirements for automation and increases the need for a learning curve inside the organization.

16.8.1.4 Management aspects

A test tool increases the system requirement and requires the hardware and software to be upgraded. This increases the cost of the already-expensive test tool. When selecting the test tool, it is important to note the system requirements, and the cost involved in upgrading the software and hardware needs to be included with the cost of the tool. Migrating from one test tool to another may be difficult and requires a lot of effort. Not only is this difficult as the test suite that is written cannot be used with other test tools, but also because of the cost involved. As the tools are expensive and unless the management feels that the returns on the investment are justified, changing tools are generally not permitted.

Deploying a test tool requires as much effort as deploying a product in a company. However, due to project pressures, test tools the effort at deploying gets diluted, not spent. Later, thus becomes one of the reasons for delay or for automation not meeting expectations. The support available on the tool is another important point to be considered while selecting and deploying the test tool.

Table 16.3 summarizes the above discussion.

Table 16.3 Issues in selecting a testing tool.

Meeting requirements	Technology expectations	Training/skills	Management aspects
Checking whether the tools meet requirements, involves effort and money	Extending the test tool is difficult	Lack of trainers for test tools	Test tools requires system upgrades
Test tools are not fully compatible with products	Requires instrumented code to be removed for certain tests	Test tools requires people to learn new language/scripts	Migration to other test tools difficult
Test tools are not tested with the same seriousness as products for new requirements	Test tools are not cross-platform		Deploying tool requires huge planning and effort
Difficult to isolate problems of product and test suite; change in product causes test suite to be changed			

16.8.2 Steps for Tool Selection and Deployment

> Tools have very high entry, maintenance, and exit costs and hence careful selection is required.

The objective of this section is to put seven simple steps to select and deploy a test tool in an organization based on aspects discussed in the earlier sections of this chapter. The steps are

1. Identify your test suite requirements among the generic requirements discussed. Add other requirements (if any).
2. Make sure experiences discussed in previous sections are taken care of.
3. Collect the experiences of other organizations which used similar test tools.
4. Keep a checklist of questions to be asked to the vendors on cost/ effort/support.
5. Identify list of tools that meet the above requirements (give priority for the tool which is available with source code).
6. Evaluate and shortlist one/set of tools and train all test developers on the tool.
7. Deploy the tool across test teams after training all potential users of the tool.

16.9 AUTOMATION FOR EXTREME PROGRAMMING MODEL

As we have seen in Chapter 10, the extreme programming model is based on basic concepts such as

1. Unit test cases are developed before coding phase starts;
2. Code is written for test cases and are written to ensure test cases pass;
3. All unit tests must run 100% all the time; and
4. Everyone owns the product; they often cross boundaries.

The above concepts in the extreme programming model makes automation an integral part of product development. For this reason, the model gets a special mention in this chapter. Automation in extreme programming is not considered as an additional activity. The requirements for automation are available at the same time as product requirements are. This enables the automation to be started from the first day of product development.

The test cases are written before the coding phase starts in extreme programming. The developers write code to ensure the test cases pass. This keeps the code and the test cases in sync all the time. It also enables the code written for the product to be reused for automation. Moreover, since the objective of the code is to ensure that the test cases pass, automated test cases are developed automatically by the developer while coding.

All unit test cases should be run with 100% pass rate in extreme programming all the time. This goal gives additional importance to automation because without automation the goal cannot be met every time the code is touched.

The gap between development skills and coding skills for automation is not an issue in a team that follows extreme programming. Hence people cross boundaries to perform various roles as developers, testers, and so on. In the extreme programming model. Development, testing, and automation skills are not put in separate water-tight compartments.

The above concepts make automation an integral part of the product development cycle for the extreme programming model.

16.10   CHALLENGES IN AUTOMATION

As can be inferred from the above sections, test automation presents some very unique challenges. The most important of these challenges is management commitment.

As discussed in Chapter 1, automation should not be viewed as a panacea for all problems nor should it be perceived as a quick-fix solution for all the quality problems in a product. Automation takes time and effort and pays off in the long run. However, automation requires significant initial outlay of money as well as a steep learning curve for the test engineers before it can start paying off. Management should have patience and persist with automation. The main challenge here is because of the heavy front-loading of costs of test automation, management starts to look for an early payback. Successful test automation endeavors are characterized by unflinching management commitment, a clear vision of the goals, and the ability to set realistic short-term goals that track progress with respect to the long-term vision. When any of these attributes are found lacking in the management team, it is likely that the automation initiative will fail. Worse, it may even wrongly start a negative mindset about automation, much as it did for the farmer in Chapter 1.

16.11   SUMMARY

In Chapter 1, we discussed the importance of testing the test suite in "Test the tests first." Testing the test suite properly and ensuring it meets the required expectations on quality needs to be done before the test suite is used for testing the product. As discussed earlier, there is an effort and a debate involved in finding out whether a defect happened due to a test suite or product, if there is a suspicion on the quality of the test suite. To ensure that such doubts do not arise and to ensure a smooth running of tests, all quality requirements and process steps need to be followed as in product development.

There is a perception that automation means automating the process of test execution. The scope of automation should get extended to *all* the phases involved in product development involving several people and several roles in the organization. Test execution is where automation starts as this is a phase where good repetition exists and manual effort involved is more. Automation does not stop with automating the execution of test cases alone. The test suite needs to be linked with other tools and activities for increased effectiveness (for example, test case database, defect filing, sending automatic mails on test and build status, preparing automatic reports, and so on). Having said that about automation, not everything can be automated and 100% automation is not always possible. A combination of test suite with a number of test cases automated with creative manual testing will make testing more effective. Automation does not stop with recording and playing back the user commands. An automated test suite should be intelligent enough to say what was expected, why a test case failed, and give manual steps to reproduce the problem. Automation should not be done for saving effort alone; it should be an effort to increase the coverage and improve repeatability. Sometimes, manual test cases that are documented need to be modified to suit automation requirements. Where automation exists, the documentation need not be elaborate, as the steps for test cases can at any point of time be derived by looking at automation scripts.

> The quality requirements for the test suite are equal to or more stringent than that of the product.

> A good automation can help in 24 × 7 test execution, saving effort and time.

The progress in automation is not only hampered because of technical complexities but also because of lack of people resources allocated. Even when people resources are allocated, they are pulled out when the product is close to release or when it reaches a critical state. This urgency is understandable, as releasing the product on time, meeting the commitments given to the customer, should receive relatively higher priority than automation. However, a frequent repeat of this situation is not good for automation. A separate team in the organization looking at automation requirements, tool evaluation, and developing generic test suites would add more value. An independent team for automation can realize the long-term goals of the organization on automation.

There is a career in tool usage and administration and expertise. There are certification courses available on test tool usage and there are many career options available in automation. Hence it is important to consider automation as an important area and a role where developers and testers can grow.

> At times automation is more complex than product development. Plan to have your best development and test engineers in the automation team.

Automation should not be considered as a stopgap arrangement to engage test engineers ("when there is no test execution work, do automation!") when they are have free time. A broad vision is needed to make automation more useful. A plan should exist to maintain the test suites as is done for product maintenance. *Automation should be considered as a product, not as a project*. Like a product road map, automation should also have a road map (denoted as "space map" in the adjacent box).

Selecting test tools without proper analysis will result in expensive test tools gathering dust on the shelf. This is termed as shelf ware.

Selecting the proper test tool represents only one part of the success for automation. Timeliness and the test suite meeting the testing requirements with required quality are other factors to be considered. The test suite thus developed should be delivered before test execution starts and automation objectives for the product should be delivered before the product reaches the end of its life. Else, success in automation alone will be like the proverbial *Operation successful but patient dead*. A successful automation is one where the product requirements are met *along* with automation requirements.

Having talked about factors for successful automation, it is time to discuss certain observations on failures. Generally, there is lack of ownership on failures for automation that are brought out by certain surveys and testing books. This view is supported by the fact that 30% of test tools remain as shelf ware. We have discussed "automation syndrome" in Chapter 1, where the farmer blames the failure of the crop on automation. Automation does not fail by itself, and perceptions that are around automation need to be taken care of. For example, there is a perception that automation will reduce the staffing level in the organization. Automation does not reduce staffing levels. It makes test engineers focus on more creative tasks that have a direct bearing on product quality.

> Keeping a road map does not help while flying; both "space map" and "road map" are needed to fly and to reach your place.

Automation makes life easier for testers for better reproduction of test results, coverage and, of course, reduction in effort as a side product. Automation should be considered as a part of life in product development and should be maintained as a basic habit for the success of products and organizations. Finally, with automation, one can produce better and more effective metrics that can help in understanding the state of health of a product in a quantifiable way, thus taking us to the next change.

REFERENCES

Automation in testing is covered by several books and in the articles that are available in the web. However, this chapter tries to unify all concepts and methods in a simple way. [KANE-2001] is a good place to look at some of the experiences that are faced in automation and how they can be resolved. [TET] is a tool that can explored further to understand the requirements of a generic framework or a test tool.

PROBLEMS AND EXERCISES

1. We talked of end-to-end automation of testing both in this chapter as well as in earlier chapters. Consider the automation requirements and evaluate the options of tools available for each:

    a. Designing test cases from requirements/design/program specifications

    b. Generation of test data

    c. Choice of test cases for a given release, based on the changes made to code

    d. Tools for automatic analysis of correctness of tests

    e. Tools for automatic assignment of right people to work on defects uncovered by tests

    f. Tools for performance testing

    g. Tools for test reporting

2. Design a simple schema that enables mapping between test case database, configuration management tool, and test history to perform some of the automation listed in Problem 1.

3. What aspects of white box testing lend themselves to automation? What tools would be required?

4. What are some of the challenges in automating the testing of GUI portions of an application? How do these compare with the automation of back-end testing?

5. We have discussed metrics in the final chapter. Look at the various metrics that are presented and present how the schema in Problem 2 could be useful in generating these metrics. List the queries in a language like SQL that can be used to generate the above metrics.

6. Consider writing automated test cases for testing out the various query options of a database. What type of initialization and cleanup would be required for test scripts?

7. While using automated scripts, derive standards that can enhance and promote reuse.

8. We had mentioned about not hard coding any values in tests. We also gave an example of where there are different configuration parameters for different layers of software. Outline of some of the challenges in maintaining such configuration files that contain parameters for different levels. How will you overcome some of these challenges?

9. One of the common problems in testing web-based applications is the appearance of pop-ups, advertisements, etc. Explore the features available in test automation tools to insulate an application from the effect of these interruptions

10. We have illustrated the test automation requirements using a meta language. What other features would be required in such a meta language to aid practical testing of software?

Test Metrics and Measurements

CHAPTER 17

In this chapter—

17.1   WHAT ARE METRICS AND MEASUREMENTS?

This is the period we noticed excellent profits in the organization...and...Boss, you were on vacation that time!

What cannot be measured cannot be managed.

All significant activities in a project need to be tracked to ensure that the project is going as per plan and to decide on any corrective actions. The measurement of key parameters is an integral part of tracking. Measurements first entail collecting a set of data. But, raw data by itself may not throw light on why a particular event has happened. The collected data have to be analyzed in totality to draw the appropriate conclusions. In the above cartoon, the two data points were that the boss had gone on vacation and the profits zoomed in the previous quarter. However (hopefully!) the two events are not directly linked to each other! So the conclusion from the raw data was not useful for decision making.

Metrics derive information from raw data with a view to help in decision making. Some of the areas that such information would shed light on are

1.   Relationship between the data points;
2.   Any cause and effect correlation between the observed data points; and
3.   Any pointers to how the data can be used for future planning and continuous improvements.

Metrics are thus derived from measurements using appropriate formulae or calculations. Obviously, the same set of measurements can help product different set of metrics, of interest to different people.

From the above discussion, it is obvious that in order that a project performance be tracked and its progress monitored effectively,

1.   The right parameters must be measured; the parameters may pertain to product or to process.
2.   The right analysis must be done on the data measured, to draw correct conclusions about the health of the product or process within a project or organization.

3. The results of the analysis must be presented in an appropriate form to the stakeholders to enable them to make the right decisions on improving product or process quality (or any other relevant business drivers).

Since the focus of this book is on testing and products under test, only metrics related to testing and product are discussed in this chapter and not those meant for process improvements.

The metrics and analysis of metrics may convey the reason when data points are combined. Relating several data points and consolidating the result in terms of charts and pictures simplifies the analysis and facilitates the use of metrics for decision making. A *metrics program* is intended to achieve precisely the above objectives and is the intended focus of this chapter. We will first baseline certain terminology we will be using in this chapter.

Effort is the actual time that is spent on a particular activity or a phase. *Elapsed days* is the difference between the start of an activity and the completion of the activity. For example, ordering a product through the web may involve five minutes of effort and three elapsed days. It is the packaging and shipping that takes that much duration, not the time spent by the person in ordering. However, in the schedule, this latency or delay needs to be entered as three days. Of course, during these three days, the person who ordered the product can get on to some other activity and do it in simultaneously. In general, effort is derived from productivity numbers, and elapsed days is the number of days required to complete the set of activities. Elapsed days for a complete set of activities becomes the *schedule* for the project.

Collecting and analyzing metrics involves effort and several steps. This is depicted in Figure 17.1. The coloured figure is available on page 476. The

Figure 17.1

Steps in a metrics program.

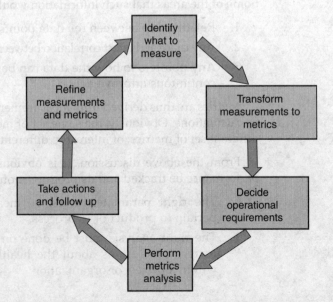

first step involved in a metrics program is to decide *what measurements are important* and collect data accordingly. The effort spent on testing, number of defects, and number of test cases, are some examples of measurements. Depending on what the data is used for, the granularity of measurement will vary.

While deciding what to measure, the following aspects need to be kept in mind.

1. What is measured should be of relevance to what we are trying to achieve. For testing functions, we would obviously be interested in the effort spent on testing, number of test cases, number of defects reported from test cases, and so on.

2. The entities measured should be natural and should not involve too many overheads for measurements. If there are too many overheads in making the measurements or if the measurements do not follow naturally from the actual work being done, then the people who supply the data may resist giving the measurement data (or even give wrong data).

3. What is measured should be at the right level of granularity to satisfy the objective for which the measurement is being made.

Let us look at the last point on granularity of data in more detail. The different people who use the measurements may want to make inferences on different dimensions. The level of granularity of data obtained depends on the level of detail required by a specific audience. Hence the measurements—and the metrics derived from them—will have to be at different levels for different people. An approach involved in getting the granular detail is called *data drilling*. Given in the next page is an example of a data drilling exercise. This is what typically happens in many organizations when metrics/test reports are presented and shows how different granularity of data is relevant for decision making at different levels.

The conversation in the example continues till all questions are answered or till the defects in focus becomes small in number and can be traced to certain root causes. The depth to which data drilling happens depends on the focus area of the discussion or need. Hence, it is important to provide as much granularity in measurements as possible. In the above example, the measurement was "number of defects."

Not all conversations involve just one measurement as in the example. A *set* of measurements can be combined to generate metrics that will be explained in further sections of this chapter. An example question involving multiple measurements is "How many *test cases* produced the 40 *defects* in data migration involving different schema?" There are two measurements involved in this question: the number of test cases and the number of defects. Hence, the second step involved in metrics collection is defining how to *combine* data points or measurements to provide meaningful metrics. A particular metric can use one or more measurements.

> **Tester:** We found 100 more defects in this test cycle compared to the previous one.
>
> **Manager:** What aspect of the product testing produced more defects?
>
> **Tester:** Usability produced 60 defects out of 100.
>
> **Manager:** Ok! What are the components in the product that produced more defects?
>
> **Tester:** "Data migration" component produced 40 out of those 60.
>
> **Manager:** What particular feature produced that many defects?
>
> **Tester:** Data migration involving different schema produced 35 out of those 40 defects.

Knowing the ways in which a measurement is going to be used and knowing the granularity of measurements leads us to the third step in the metrics program—deciding the operational requirement for measurements. The operational requirement for a metrics plan should lay down not only the periodicity but also other operational issues such as who should collect measurements, who should receive the analysis, and so on. This step helps to decide on the appropriate periodicity for the measurements as well as assign operational responsibility for collecting, recording, and reporting the measurements and dissemination of the metrics information. Some measurements need to be made on a daily basis (for example, how many test cases were executed, how many defects found, defects fixed, and so on). But the metrics involving a question like the one above ("how many test cases produced 40 defects") is a type of metric that needs to be monitored at extended periods of time, say, once in a week or at the end of a test cycle. Hence, planning metrics generation also needs to consider the periodicity of the metrics.

The fourth step involved in a metrics program is to analyze the metrics to identify both positive areas and improvement areas on product quality. Often, only the improvement aspects pointed to by the metrics are analyzed and focused; it is important to also highlight and sustain the positive areas of the product. This will ensure that the best practices get institutionalized and also motivate the team better.

The final step involved in a metrics plan is to take necessary action and follow up on the action. The purpose of a metrics program will be defeated if the action items are not followed through to completion. This is especially true of testing, which is the penultimate phase before release. Any delay in analysis and following through with action items to completion can result in undue delays in product release.

Any metrics program, as described above, is a continuous and ongoing process. As we make measurements, transform the measurements into metrics, analyze the metrics, and take corrective action, the issues for which the measurements were made in the first place will become resolved. Then, we would have to continue the next iteration of metrics programs, measuring (possibly) a different set of measurements, leading to more refined metrics addressing (possibly) different issues. As shown in Figure 17.1, metrics programs continually go through the steps described above with different measurements or metrics.

17.2 WHY METRICS IN TESTING?

Since testing is the penultimate phase before product release, it is essential to measure the progress of testing and product quality. Tracking test progress and product quality can give a good idea about the release—whether it will be met on time with known quality. Measuring and producing metrics to determine the progress of testing is thus very important.

> Days needed to complete testing = Total test cases yet to be executed/ Test case execution productivity

Knowing only how much testing got completed does not answer the question on when the testing will get completed and when the product will be ready for release. To answer these questions, one needs to know how much more time is needed for testing. To judge the remaining days needed for testing, two data points are needed—remaining test cases yet to be executed and how many test cases can be executed per elapsed day. The test cases that can be executed per person day are calculated based on a measure called *test case execution productivity*. This productivity number is derived from the previous test cycles. It is represented by the formula, given alongside in the margin.

Thus, metrics are needed to know *test case execution productivity* and to estimate *test completion date*.

It is not testing alone that determines the date at which the product can be released. The number of days needed to fix all outstanding defects is another crucial data point. The number of days needed for defects fixes needs to take into account the "outstanding defects waiting to be fixed" and a projection of "how many more defects that will be unearthed from testing in future cycles." The *defect trend* collected over a period of time gives a rough estimate of the defects that will come through future test cycles. Hence, metrics helps in predicting the number of defects that can be found in future test cycles.

Total days needed for defect fixes = (Outstanding defects yet to fixed + Defects that can be found in future test cycles)/Defect-fixing capability

The *defect-fixing trend* collected over a period of time gives another estimate of the *defect-fixing capability* of the team. This measure gives the number of defects that can be fixed in a particular duration by the development team. Combining defect prediction with defect-fixing capability produces an estimate of the days needed for the release. The formula given alongside in the margin can help arrive at a rough estimate of the total days needed for defect fixes.

Hence, metrics helps in estimating the total days needed for fixing defects. Once the time needed for testing and the time for defects fixing are known, the release date can be estimated. Testing and defect fixing are activities that can be executed simultaneously, as long as there is a regression testing planned to verify the outstanding defects fixes and their side-effects. If a product team follows the model of separate development and testing teams, the release date is arrived at on the basis of which one (days needed for testing or days needed for defect fixes) is on the critical path. The formula given alongside in the margin helps in arriving at the release date.

Days needed for release = Max (Days needed for testing, days needed for defect fixes)

Days needed for release = Max [Days needed for testing, (Days needed for defect fixes + Days needed for regressing outstanding defect fixes)]

The defect fixes may arrive after the regular test cycles are completed. These defect fixes will have to be verified by regression testing before the product can be released. Hence, the formula for days needed for release is to be modified as alongside in the margin.

The above formula can be further tuned to provide more accuracy to estimates as the current formula does not include various other activities such as documentation, meetings, and so on. The idea of discussing the formula here is to explain that metrics are important and help in *arriving at the release date* for the product.

The measurements collected during the development and test cycle are not only used for release but also used for post-release activities. Looking at the defect trend for a period helps in arriving at approximate estimates for the number of *defects that may get reported post release*. This defect trend is used as one of the parameters to increase the size of the maintenance/sustenance team to take care of defects that may be reported post release. Knowing the type of defects that are found during a release cycle and having an idea of all outstanding defects and their impact helps in training the support staff, thereby ensuring they are well equipped and prepared for the defects that may get reported by the customers.

Metrics are not only used for reactive activities. Metrics and their analysis help in *preventing the defects* proactively, thereby saving cost and effort. For example, if there is a type of defect (say, coding defects) that is reported in large numbers, it is advisable to perform a code review and prevent those defects, rather than finding them one by one and fixing them in the code. Metrics help in identifying these opportunities.

Metrics are used in resource management to identify the right size of product development teams. Since resource management is an important aspect of product development and maintenance, metrics go a long way in helping in this area.

There are various other areas where metrics can help; *ability of test cases in finding defects* is one such area. We discussed test case result history in Chapter 8, Regression Testing. When this history is combined with the metrics of the project, it provides detailed information on what test cases have the capabilities to produce more/less defects in the current cycle.

To summarize, metrics in testing help in identifying

✠ *When to make the release.*

✠ *What to release* – Based on defect density (formally defined later) across modules, their importance to customers, and impact analysis of those defects, the scope of the product can be decided to release the product on time. Metrics help in making this decision.

✠ *Whether the product is being released with known quality* – The idea of metrics is not only for meeting the release date but also to know the quality of the product and ascertaining the decision on whether we are releasing the product with the known quality and whether it will function in a predictable way in the field.

17.3   TYPES OF METRICS

Metrics can be classified into different types based on what they measure and what area they focus on. At a very high level, metrics can be classified as *product metrics* and *process metrics*. As explained earlier, process metrics are not discussed in this chapter.

Product metrics can be further classified as

1. **Project metrics**   A set of metrics that indicates how the project is planned and executed.

2. **Progress metrics**   A set of metrics that tracks how the different activities of the project are progressing. The activities include both development activities and testing activities. Since the focus of this book is testing, only metrics applicable to testing activities are discussed in this book (and in this chapter). Progress metrics is monitored during testing phases. Progress metrics helps in finding out the status of test activities and they are also good indicators of product quality. The defects that emerge from testing provide a wealth of information that help both development team and test team to analyze and improve. For this reason, progress metrics in this chapter focus only on defects. Progress metrics, for convenience, is further classified into *test defect metrics* and *development defect metrics*.

3. **Productivity metrics** A set of metrics that takes into account various productivity numbers that can be collected and used for planning and tracking testing activities. These metrics help in planning and estimating of testing activities.

All the types of metrics just discussed and specific metrics that will be discussed in this chapter are depicted in Figure 17.2. The coloured figure is available on page 476.

Figure 17.2

Types of metrics.

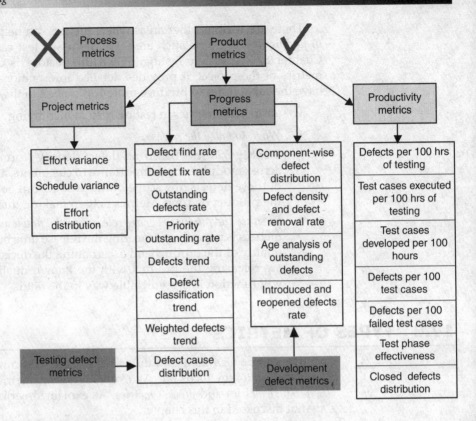

17.4　PROJECT METRICS

A typical project starts with requirements gathering and ends with product release. All the phases that fall in between these points need to be planned and tracked. In the planning cycle, the scope of the project is finalized. The project scope gets translated to size estimates, which specify the quantum of work to be done. This size estimate gets translated to effort estimate for each of the phases and activities by using the available productivity data available. This initial effort is called *baselined effort*.

As the project progresses and if the scope of the project changes or if the available productivity numbers are not correct, then the effort estimates are re-evaluated again and this re-evaluated effort estimate is called *revised effort*. The estimates can change based on the frequency of changing requirements and other parameters that impact the effort.

Over or under estimating the effort are normal experiences faced by many organizations. Perils of such wrong estimates are financial losses, delay in release, and wrong brand image among the customers. Right estimation comes by experience and by having the right productivity numbers from the team.

Effort and schedule are two factors to be tracked for any phase or activity. Tracking the activities in the SDLC phase is done by two means, that is, effort and schedule. In an ideal situation, if the effort is tracked closely and met, then the schedule can be met. The schedule can also be met by adding more effort to the project (additional resources or asking the engineers to work late). If the release date (that is, schedule) is met by putting more effort, then the project planning and execution cannot be considered successful. In fact, such an idea of adding effort may not be possible always as the resources may not be available in the organization every time and engineers working late may not be productive beyond a certain point.

At the same time, if planned effort and actual effort are the same but if the schedule is not met then too the project cannot be considered successful. Hence, it is a good idea to track both effort and schedule in project metrics.

The basic measurements that are very natural, simple to capture, and form the inputs to the metrics in this section are

1. The different activities and the initial baselined effort and schedule for each of the activities; this is input at the beginning of the project/phase.
2. The actual effort and time taken for the various activities; this is entered as and when the activities take place.
3. The revised estimate of effort and schedule; these are re-calculated at appropriate times in the project life.

17.4.1 Effort Variance (Planned vs Actual)

When the baselined effort estimates, revised effort estimates, and actual effort are plotted together for all the phases of SDLC, it provides many insights about the estimation process. As different set of people may get involved in different phases, it is a good idea to plot these effort numbers phase-wise. Normally, this variation chart is plotted as the point revised estimates are being made or at the end of a release. A sample data for each of the phase is plotted in the chart in Figure 17.3. The coloured figure is available on page 477.

If there is a substantial difference between the baselined and revised effort, it points to incorrect initial estimation. Calculating *effort variance* for each of the phases (as calculated by the formula below) provides a quantitative measure of the relative difference between the revised and actual efforts.

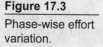

Figure 17.3

Phase-wise effort variation.

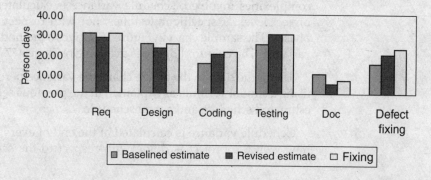

Table 17.1   Sample variance percentage by phase.

Effort	Req	Design	Coding	Testing	Doc	Defect fixing
Variance %	7.1	8.7	5	0	40	15

Variance % = [(Actual effort – Revised estimate)/Revised estimate] * 100

If variance takes into account only revised estimate and actual effort, then a question arises, what is the use of baselined estimate? As mentioned earlier, the effort variation chart provides input to estimation process. When estimates are going wrong (or right), it is important to find out where we are going wrong (or right). Many times the revised estimates are done in a hurry, to respond fast enough to the changing requirements or unclear requirements. If this is the case, the right parameter for variance calculation is the baselined estimate. In this case analysis should point out the problems in the revised estimation process. Similarly, there could be a problem in the baseline estimation process that can be brought out by variance calculation. Hence, all the baselined estimates, revised estimates, and actual effort are plotted together for each of the phases. The variance can be consolidated into as shown in Table 17.1.

A variance of more than 5% in any of the SDLC phase indicates the scope for improvement in the estimation. In Table 17.1, the variance is acceptable only for the coding and testing phases.

The variance can be negative also. A negative variance is an indication of an over estimate. These variance numbers along with analysis can help in better estimation for the next release or the next revised estimation cycle.

17.4.2   Schedule Variance (Planned vs Actual)

Most software projects are not only concerned about the variance in effort, but are also concerned about meeting schedules. This leads us to the schedule variance metric. Schedule variance, like effort variance, is the deviation of the actual schedule from the estimated schedule. There is one difference, though. Depending on the SDLC model used by the project, several phases could be active at the same time. Further, the different phases in SDLC are interrelated and could share the same set of individuals. Because of all these complexities involved, schedule variance is calculated only at the overall project level, at specific milestones, not with respect to each of the SDLC phases. The sample chart in Figure 17.4 gives a method for plotting schedule variance. The coloured figure is available on page 477.

Using the data in the above chart, the variance percent can be calculated using a similar formula as explained in the previous section, considering the estimated schedule and actual schedule.

Schedule variance is calculated at the end of every milestone to find out how well the project is doing with respect to the schedule. To get a real

Figure 17.4
Schedule variance.

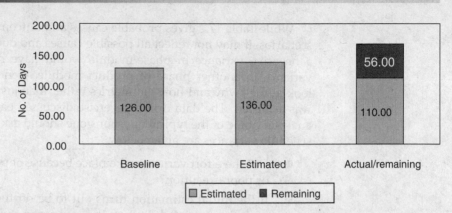

Table 17.2 Interpretation of ranges of effort and schedule variation.

Effort variance	Schedule variance	Probable causes/result
Zero or acceptable variance	Zero variance	A well-executed project
Zero or acceptable variance	Acceptable variance	Need slight improvement in effort/schedule estimation
Unacceptable variance	Zero or acceptable variance	Underestimation; needs further analysis
Unacceptable variance	Unacceptable variance	Underestimation of both effort and schedule
Negative variance	Zero or acceptable variance	Overestimation and schedule; both effort and schedule estimation need improvement
Negative variance	Negative variance	Overestimation and over schedule; both effort and schedule estimation need improvement

picture on schedule in the middle of project execution, it is important to calculate "remaining days yet to be spent" on the project and plot it along with the "actual schedule spent" as in the above chart. "Remaining days yet to be spent" can be calculated by adding up all remaining activities. If the remaining days yet to be spent on project is not calculated and plotted, it does not give any value to the chart in the middle of the project, because the deviation cannot be inferred visually from the chart. The remaining days in the schedule becomes zero when the release is met.

Effort and schedule variance have to be analyzed in totality, not in isolation. This is because while effort is a major driver of the cost, schedule determines how best a product can exploit market opportunities. Variance can be classified into negative variance, zero variance, acceptable variance, and unacceptable variance. Generally 0–5% is considered as acceptable variance. Table 17.2 gives certain scenarios, probable causes, and conclusions.

While Table 17.2 gives probable causes and outcomes under the various scenarios, it may not reflect all possible causes and outcomes. For example, a negative variance in phase/module would have nullified the positive variance in another phase of product module. Hence, it is important to look at the "why and how" in metrics rather than just focusing on "what" was achieved. The data drilling exercise discussed earlier will help in this analysis. Some of the typical questions one should ask to analyze effort and schedule variances are given below.

✠ Did the effort variance take place because of poor initial estimation or poor execution?

✠ If the initial estimation turns out to be off the mark, is it because of lack of availability of the supporting data to enable good estimation?

✠ If the effort or schedule in some cases is not in line with what was estimated, what changes caused the variation? Was there a change in technology of what was tested? Was there a new tool introduced for testing? Did some key people leave the team?

✠ If the effort was on target, but the schedule was not, did the plan take into account appropriate parallelism? Did it explore the right multiplexing of the resources?

✠ Can any process or tool be enhanced to improve parallelism and thereby speed up the schedules?

✠ Whenever we get negative variance in effort or schedule (that is, we are completing the project with lesser effort and/or faster than what was planned), do we know what contributed to the efficiency and if so, can we institutionalize the efficiencies to achieve continuous improvement?

17.4.3   Effort Distribution Across Phases

> Adequate and appropriate effort needs to be spent in each of the SDLC phase for a quality product release.

Variance calculation helps in finding out whether commitments are met on time and whether the estimation method works well. In addition, some indications on product quality can be obtained if the effort distribution across the various phases are captured and analyzed. For example,

✠ Spending very little effort on requirements may lead to frequent changes but one should also leave sufficient time for development and testing phases.

✠ Spending less effort in testing may cause defects to crop up in the customer place but spending more time in testing than what is needed may make the product lose the market window.

The distribution percentage across the different phases can be estimated at the time of planning and these can be compared with the actuals at the time of release for getting a comfort feeling on the release and estimation methods. A sample distribution of effort across phases is given in Figure 17.5. The coloured figure is avilable on page 478.

Figure 17.5

Actual effort distribution.

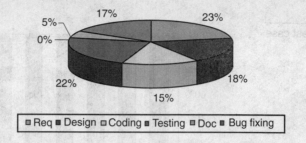

Mature organizations spend at least 10–15% of the total effort in requirements and approximately the same effort in the design phase. The effort percentage for testing depends on the type of release and amount of change to the existing code base and functionality. Typically, organizations spend about 20–50% of their total effort in testing.

17.5 PROGRESS METRICS

Any project needs to be tracked from two angles. One, how well the project is doing with respect to effort and schedule. This is the angle we have been looking at so far in this chapter. The other equally important angle is to find out how well the product is meeting the quality requirements for the release. There is no point in producing a release on time and within the effort estimate but with a lot of defects, causing the product to be unusable. One of the main objectives of testing is to find as many defects as possible before any customer finds them. The number of defects that are found in the product is one of the main indicators of quality. Hence in this section, we will look at progress metrics that reflect the defects (and hence the quality) of a product.

Defects get detected by the testing team and get fixed by the development team. In line with this thought, defect metrics are further classified in to *test defect metrics* (which help the testing team in analysis of product quality and testing) and *development defect metrics* (which help the development team in analysis of development activities).

How many defects have already been found and how many more defects *may* get unearthed are two parameters that determine product quality and its assessment. For this assessment, the progress of testing has to be understood. If only 50% of testing is complete and if 100 defects are found, then, assuming that the defects are uniformly distributed over the product (and keeping all other parameters same), another 80–100 defects can be estimated as residual defects. Figure 17.6 shows testing progress by plotting the test execution status and the outcome.

The progress chart gives the pass rate and fail rate of executed test cases, pending test cases, and test cases that are waiting for defects to be fixed. Representing testing progress in this manner will make it is easy to

Figure 17.6

Progress of test case execution.

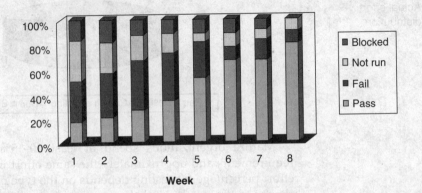

understand the status and for further analysis. In Figure 17.6, (coloured figure is available on page 478) the "not run" cases reduce in number as the weeks progress, meaning that more tests are being run. Another perspective from the chart is that the pass percentage increases and fail percentage decreases, showing the positive progress of testing and product quality. The defects that are blocking the execution of certain test cases also get reduced in number as weeks progress in the above chart. Hence, a scenario represented by such a progress chart shows that not only is testing progressing well, but also that the product quality is improving (which in turn means that the testing is effective). If, on the other hand, the chart had shown a trend that as the weeks progress, the "not run" cases are not reducing in number, or "blocked" cases are increasing in number, or "pass" cases are not increasing, then it would clearly point to quality problems in the product that prevent the product from being ready for release.

17.5.1 Test Defect Metrics

The test progress metrics discussed in the previous section capture the progress of defects found with time. The next set of metrics help us understand how the defects that are found can be used to improve testing and product quality. Not all defects are equal in impact or importance. Some organizations classify defects by assigning a *defect priority* (for example, P1, P2, P3, and so on). The priority of a defect provides a management perspective for the order of defect fixes. For example, a defect with priority P1 indicates that it should be fixed before another defect with priority P2. Some organizations use *defect severity* levels (for example, S1, S2, S3, and so on). The severity of defects provides the test team a perspective of the impact of that defect in product functionality. For example, a defect with severity level S1 means that either the major functionality is not working or the software is crashing. S2 may mean a failure or functionality not working. A sample of what different priorities and severities mean is given in Table 17.3. From the above example it is clear that priority is a management perspective and priority levels are relative. This means that the priority of a defect can change dynamically once assigned. Severity is absolute and does not change often as they reflect the state and quality of the product. Some organizations use a combination of priority and severity to classify the defects.

Since different organization use different methods of defining priorities and severities, a common set of defect definitions and classification are provided in Table 17.4 to take care of both priority and severity levels. We will adhere to this classification consistently in this chapter.

Table 17.3 Defect priority and defect severity—sample interpretation.

Priority	What it means
1	Fix the defect on highest priority; fix it before the next build
2	Fix the defect on high priority before next test cycle
3	Fix the defect on moderate priority when time permits, before the release
4	Postpone this defect for next release or live with this defect

Severity	What it means
1	The basic product functionality failing or product crashes
2	Unexpected error condition or a functionality not working
3	A minor functionality is failing or behaves differently than expected
4	Cosmetic issue and no impact on the users

Table 17.4 A common defect definition and classification.

Defect classification	What it means
Extreme	• Product crashes or unusable • Needs to be fixed immediately
Critical	• Basic functionality of the product not working • Needs to be fixed before next test cycle starts
Important	• Extended functionality of the product not working • Does not affect the progress of testing • Fix it before the release
Minor	• Product behaves differently • No impact on the test team or customers • Fix it when time permits
Cosmetic	• Minor irritant • Need not be fixed for this release

17.5.1.1   Defect find rate

When tracking and plotting the total number of defects found in the product at regular intervals (say, daily or weekly) from beginning to end of a product development cycle, it may show a pattern for defect arrival. The idea of testing is to find as many defects as possible early in the cycle. However, this may not be possible for two reasons. First, not all features of a product may become available early; because of scheduling of resources, the features of a product arrive in a particular sequence. Second, as seen earlier in the chapter, some of the test cases may be blocked because of some show stopper defects. If there are defects in the product features that arrive later or if the tests that are supposed to detect certain defects are blocked, then the goal to uncover defects early may not be achieved. Once a majority of the modules become available and the defects that are blocking the tests are fixed, the defect arrival rate increases. After a certain period of defect fixing and testing, the arrival of defects tends to slow down and a continuation of that trend enables product release. This results in a *"bell curve"* as shown in Figure 17.7.

For a product to be fit for release, not only is such a pattern of defect arrival important but also the defect arrival in a particular duration should be kept at a bare minimum number. A bell curve along with minimum number of defects found in the last few days indicate that the release quality of the product is likely to be good.

17.5.1.2   Defect fix rate

If the goal of testing is to find defects as early as possible, it is natural to expect that the goal of development should be to fix defects as soon as they arrive. If the defect fixing curve is in line with defect arrival a *"bell curve"* as shown in Figure 17.7 will be the result again. The coloured figure is available on page 479. There is a reason why defect fixing rate should be same as defect arrival rate. If more defects are fixed later in the cycle, they may not get tested properly for all possible side-effects. As discussed in regression testing, when defects are fixed in the product, it opens the doors for the introduction of new defects. Hence, it is a good idea to fix the defects early and test those defect fixes thoroughly to find out all introduced defects. If this principle is not followed, defects introduced by the defect fixes may come up for testing just before the release and end up in surfacing of new defects or resurfacing of old defects. This may delay

Figure 17.7

Typical pattern for finding defects in a product.

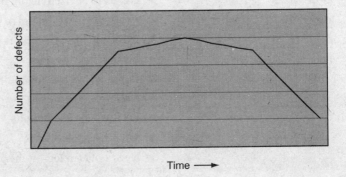

the product release. Such last-minute fixes generally not only cause slips in deadlines or product quality but also put the development and testing teams under tremendous pressure, further aggravating the product quality.

> In a well-executed project, the number of outstanding defects is very close to zero all the time during the test cycle.

17.5.1.3 Outstanding defects rate The number of defects outstanding in the product is calculated by subtracting the total defects fixed from the total defects found in the product. As discussed before, the defects need to be fixed as soon as they arrive and defects arrive in the pattern of bell curve. If the defect-fixing pattern is constant like a straight line, the outstanding defects will result in a bell curve again as shown in Figure 17.7. If the defect-fixing pattern matches the arrival rate, then the outstanding defects curve will look like a straight line. However, it is not possible to fix all defects when the arrival rate is at the top end of the bell curve. Hence, the outstanding defect rate results in a bell curve in many projects. When testing is in progress, the outstanding defects should be kept very close to zero so that the development team's bandwidth is available to analyze and fix the issues soon after they arrive.

17.5.1.4 Priority outstanding rate Having an eye on the find rate, fix rate, and outstanding defects are not enough to give an idea of the sheer quantity of defects. As we saw earlier, not all defects are equal in impact or severity. Sometimes the defects that are coming out of testing may be very critical and may take enormous effort to fix and to test. Hence, it is important to look at how many *serious* issues are being uncovered in the product. The modification to the outstanding defects rate curve by plotting only the high-priority defects and filtering out the low-priority defects is called *priority outstanding defects*. This is an important method because closer to product release, the product team would not want to fix the low-priority defects lest the fixes should cause undesirable side-effects. Normally only high-priority defects are tracked during the period closer to release.

The priority outstanding defects correspond to *extreme* and *critical* classification of defects. Some organizations include *important* defects also in priority outstanding defects. (See Table 17.3 for defect classification terminology.)

Some high-priority defects may require a change in design or architecture. If they are found late in the cycle, the release may get delayed to address the defect. But if a low-priority defect found is close to the release date and it requires a design change, a likely decision of the management would be not to fix that defect. If possible, a short-term workaround is proposed and the design change can be considered for a future release.

Some defect fixes may require relatively little time but substantial effort to test. The fix may be fairly straightforward, but retesting may be a time-consuming affair. If the product is close to release, then a conscious choice has to be made about such defect fixes. This is especially true of high-priority defects. The effort needed for testing needs to be estimated before proceeding to fix such defects. Some of the developers may go ahead and fix the defects if the effort involved in fixing is less. If the defect fix requires enormous amount of effort in testing to verify, then careful analysis needs to done and a decision taken on the basis of this analysis. In this case, trying to provide a workaround is more important than fixing the defect because of the large amount of test effort involved. Hence, the priority outstanding defects have to be monitored separately.

> Provide additional focus for those defects that matter to the release.

When priority outstanding defects are plotted, the objective is to see the curve going towards zero all the time during the test cycle. This means priority defects need to be fixed almost immediately.

> The effectiveness of analysis increases when several perspectives of find rate, fix rate, outstanding, and priority outstanding defects are combined.

17.5.1.5 Defect trend   Having discussed individual measures of defects, it is time for the trend chart to consolidate all of the above into one chart. Figure 17.8 shows a chart with sample data containing all the charts discussed in this section.

From Figure 17.8, (coloured figure available on page 479) the following observations can be made.

1. The find rate, fix rate, outstanding defects, and priority outstanding follow a bell curve pattern, indicating readiness for release at the end of the 19th week.

2. A sudden downward movement as well as upward spike in defect fixes rate needs analysis (13th to 17th week in the chart above).

3. There are close to 75 outstanding defects at the end of the 19th week. By looking at the priority outstanding which shows close to zero defects in the 19th week, it can be concluded that all outstanding defects belong to low priority, indicating release readiness. The outstanding defects need analysis before the release.

4. Defect fix rate is not in line with outstanding defects rate. If defect fix rate had been improved, it would have enabled a quicker release cycle (could have reduced the schedule by four to five weeks) as incoming defects from the 14th week were in control.

Figure 17.8

Defect trend.

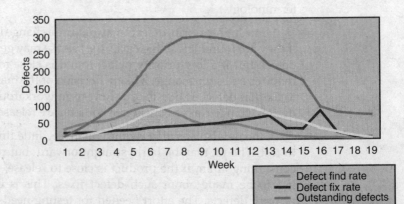

5. Defect fix rate was not at the same degree of defect find rate. Find rate was more than the fix rate till the 10th week. Making find rate and fix rate equal to each other would have avoided the outstanding defects peaking from the 4th to 16th week.

6. A smooth priority outstanding rate suggests that priority defects were closely tracked and fixed.

Further points can be arrived at by analyzing the above data and by relating each data point and the series. The outcome of such an analysis will help the current as well as the future releases.

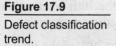

Providing the perspective of defect classification in the chart helps in finding out release readiness of the product.

17.5.1.6   Defect classification trend

In Figure 17.8, the classifications of defects are only at two levels (high-priority and low-priority defects). Some of the data drilling or chart analysis needs further information on defects with respect to each classification of defects—extreme, critical, important, minor, and cosmetic. When talking about the total number of outstanding defects, some of the questions that can be asked are

✠   How many of them are extreme defects?

✠   How many are critical?

✠   How many are important?

These questions require the charts to be plotted separately based on defect classification. The sum of extreme, critical, important, minor, and cosmetic defects is equal to the total number of defects. A graph in which each type of defects is plotted separately on top of each other to get the total defects is called *"Stacked area charts."* This type of graph helps in identifying each type of defect and also presents a perspective of how they add up to or contribute to the total defects. In Figure 17.9, the sample data explains the stacked area chart concept.

Figure 17.9

Defect classification trend.

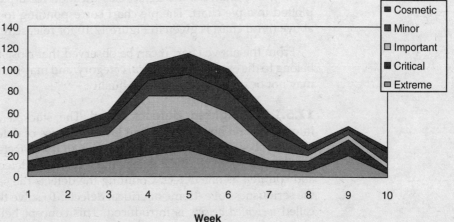

Figure 17.10

A pie chart of defect distribution.

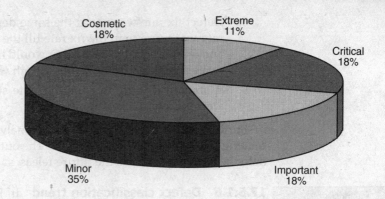

From the above chart, the following observations can be made

1. The peak in defect count in the 5th week is due to all types of defects contributing to it, with extreme and critical defects contributing significantly.

2. The peak defect count in the 9th week is due to extreme and critical defects.

3. Due to peak in the 9th week, the product needs to be observed for another two weeks to study release readiness.

The priority distribution trend (Figure 17.9) can be plotted for both arrival rate and outstanding rate. However, if the analysis for incoming defects is needed separately, then the defect classification trend can be plotted for arrival rate.

For analysis of release readiness, it is important to consider what percentage of incoming or outstanding defects is made up of extreme and critical defects. A high percentage of minor and cosmetic defects and low percentage of extreme and critical defects indicate release readiness. For making this analysis, the defect classification for a particular week can be plotted in a pie chart. The pie chart corresponding to the 10th week of the above trend chart is given in Figure 17.10 for release readiness analysis.

From the above chart it can be observed that close to 29% of the defects belong to the extreme and critical category, and may indicate that the product may not be of acceptable release quality.

17.5.1.7 Weighted defects trend The stacked area chart provides information on how the different levels or types of defects contribute to the total number of defects. In this approach all the defects are counted on par, for example, both a critical defect and a cosmetic defect are treated equally and counted as one defect. Counting the defects the same way takes away the seriousness of extreme or critical defects. To solve this problem, a metric called *weighted defects* is introduced. This concept helps in quick analysis of defects, instead of worrying about the classification of defects. In this

Figure 17.11

Weighted defects trend.

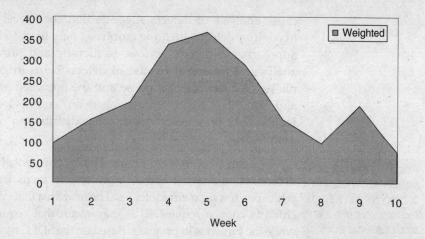

approach, not all the defects are counted the same way. More serious defects are given a higher weightage than less serious ones. For example, the total *weighted defect count* can be arrived at using a formula like the one given below. The numbers by which each defect gets weighted or multiplied can be organization specific, based on the priority and severity of defects.

> Weighted defects =
> (Extreme* 5 + Critical *
> 4 + Important
> *3 + Minor *2+
> Cosmetic)

When analyzing the above formula, it can be noted that each extreme defect is counted as five defects and cosmetic defect as one. This formula removes the need for a stacked area and the pie chart for analysis while incorporating both perspectives needed. The weighted defects trend corresponding to Figure 17.10 is given in Figure 17.11.

From Figure 17.11 it can be noted that

1. The ninth week has more weighted defects, which means existence of "large number of small defects" or "significant numbers of large defects" or a combination of the two. This is consistent with our interpretation of the same data using the stacked area chart.

2. The tenth week has a significant (more than 50) number of weighted defects indicating the product is not ready for release.

> Both "large defects" and "large number of small defects" affect product release.

Hence, weighted defects provide a combined perspective of defects without needing to go into the details. This saves time for analysis of defects.

17.5.1.8 Defect cause distribution   All the metrics discussed above help in analyzing defects and their impact. The next logical questions that would arise are

1. Why are those defects occurring and what are the root causes?
2. What areas must be focused for getting more defects out of testing?

Finding the root causes of the defects help in identifying more defects and sometimes help in even preventing the defects. For example, if root cause analysis of defects suggests that code level issues are causing the maximum defects, then the emphasis may have to be on white box testing approaches and code reviews to identify and prevent more defects. This analysis of finding the cause of defects helps in going back to the SDLC phases and redoing that phase and the impacted areas, rather than finding and fixing the defects that may mean an "endless loop" in certain scenarios. Figure 17.12 presents a "defect cause distribution" chart drawn with some sample data.

> Knowing the causes of defects helps in finding more defects and also in preventing such defects early in the cycle.

As it can be seen from Figure 17.12, code contributes to 37% of the total defects. As discussed above, more testing focus would have to be put on white box testing methodologies. The next area that contributes most to defects (20%) is change request. This may mean that requirements keep changing while the project is in progress. Based on the SDLC model followed (Chapter 2), appropriate actions can be taken here. For example, the 20% of change request in a project following spiral or agile methodologies is acceptable but not in a project that is following the V model or waterfall model, as these changes may impact the quality and time of release.

This root cause analysis can be repeated at periodic intervals and the trend of the root causes can be observed. At the start of the project, there may be only requirement defects. As we move to subsequent phases, other defects will start coming in. Knowing this will help in analyzing what defects are found in which phase of the SDLC cycle. For example, finding a requirement defect at the time of the final regression test cycle involves great effort and cost compared to defects found in the requirement phase itself. This kind of analysis helps in identifying problem areas in specific phases of SDLC model and in preventing such problems for current and future releases.

Figure 17.12

Defect cause distribution chart.

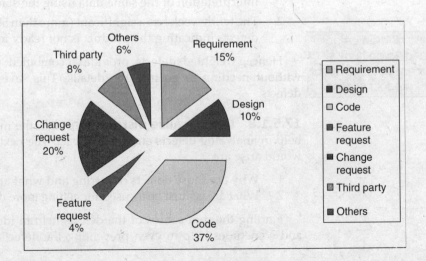

17.5.2 Development Defect Metrics

So far, our focus has been on defects and their analysis to help in knowing product quality and in improving the effectiveness of testing. We will now take a different perspective and see how metrics can be used to improve development activities. The defect metrics that directly help in improving development activities are discussed in this section and are termed as development *defect metrics*. While defect metrics focus on the number of defects, development defect metrics try to map those defects to different components of the product and to some of the parameters of development such as lines of code.

17.5.2.1 Component-wise defect distribution

While it is important to count the number of defects in the product, for development it is important to map them to different components of the product so that they can be assigned to the appropriate developer to fix those defects. The project manager in charge of development maintains a module ownership list where all product modules and owners are listed. Based on the number of defects existing in each of the modules, the effort needed to fix them, and the availability of skill sets for each of the modules, the project manager assigns resources accordingly. As an example, the distribution of defects across the various components may look like the chart in Figure 17.13.

It can be noted from the chart that there are four components (install, reports, client, and database) with over 20 defects, indicating that more focus and resources are needed for these components. The number of defects and their classification are denoted in different colors and shading as

Figure 17.13

Module-wise defect distribution.

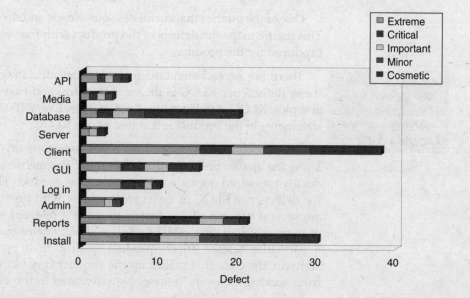

mentioned in the legend. The defect classification as well as the total defects corresponding to each component in the product helps the project manager in assigning and resolving those defects.

There is another aspect of release, that is, what to release. If there is an independent component which is producing a large number of defects, and if all other components are stable, then the scope of the release can be reduced to remove the component producing the defects and release other stable components thereby meeting the release date and release quality, provided the functionality provided by that component is not critical to the release. The above classification of defects into components helps in making such decisions.

> **Knowing the components producing more defects helps in defect fix plan and in deciding what to release.**

17.5.2.2 Defect density and defect removal rate

A good quality product can have a long lifetime before becoming obsolete. The lifetime of the product depends on its quality, over the different releases it goes through. For a given release, reasonable measures of the quality of the product are the number of defects found in testing and the number of defects found after the product is released. When the trend of these metrics is traced over different releases, it gives an idea of how well the product is improving (or not) with the releases. The objective of collecting and analyzing this kind of data is to improve the product quality release by release. The expectations of customers only go up with time and this metric is thus very important.

However it is not appropriate to just compare the number of defects across releases. Normally, as a software product goes through releases (and later through versions), the size of the product—in terms of lines of code or other similar measures—also increases. Customers expect the quality of the product to improve, notwithstanding the increase in product size.

One of the metrics that correlates source code and defects is *defect density*. This metric maps the defects in the product with the volume of code that is produced for the product.

> **Defects per KLOC = (Total defects found in the product)/ (Total executable lines of code in KLOC)**

There are several standard formulae for calculating defect density. Of these, defects per KLOC is the most practical and easy metric to calculate and plot. KLOC stands for kilo lines of code. Every 1000 lines of executable statements in the product is counted as one KLOC.

This information is plotted on a per milestone or per release basis to know the quality of the product over time. The metric is related to product quality measured over several releases of the product. The metric compares the defects per KLOC of the current release with previous releases. There are several variants of this metric to make it relevant to releases, and one of them is calculating *AMD* (*added, modified, deleted code*) to find out how a particular release affects product quality. In a product development scenario, the code that makes up the product is not developed completely from scratch for every release. New features to the existing product are added, the product is modified to fix the existing defects, and some features that are no longer being used are deleted from the product for each release. Hence, calculating the complete lines of code may not be appropriate in that situation to analyze why product quality went up or came down. For such reasons, the denominator used in the above formula is modified to include "total executable AMD lines of code in KLOC." The modified formula now reads

Defects per KLOC = (Total defects found in the product)/(Total executable AMD lines of code in KLOC)

Defect per KLOC can be used as a release criteria as well as a product quality indicator with respect to code and defects. Defects found by the testing team have to be fixed by the development team. The ultimate quality of the product depends both on development and testing activities and there is a need for a metric to analyze both the development and the testing phases together and map them to releases. The *defect removal rate (or percentage)* is used for the purpose.

The formula for calculating the defect removal rate is

(Defects found by verification activities + Defects found in unit testing)/(Defects found by test teams)* 100

The above formula helps in finding the efficiency of verification activities and unit testing which are normally responsibilities of the development team and compare them to the defects found by the testing teams. These metrics are tracked over various releases to study in-release-on-release trends in the verification/quality assurance activities. As an example, the two metrics discussed above—defects/KLOC and defect removal rate/percentage—are plotted together in the chart in Figure 17.14.

Figure 17.14

Defects/KLOC and defect removal %.

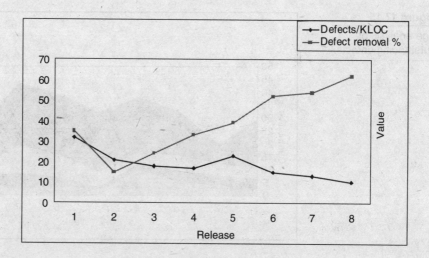

In this chart, it can be noticed that the defect removal percentage is going up and defects per KLOC is coming down, indicating improvement in product quality over releases. The drop in the defect removal percentage during the second release compared to the first release and the like in the defects per KLOC during the fifth release compared to the fourth release indicate some problems that need more analysis to find out the root causes and to rectify them.

> The time needed to fix a defect may be proportional to its age.

17.5.2.3 Age analysis of outstanding defects
Most of the charts and metrics discussed above—outstanding defect trend, their classification, and their fix rate—just indicate the *number* of defects and do not reflect the information on the *age* of the defects. Age here means those defects that have been waiting to be fixed for a long time. Some defects that are difficult to be fixed or require significant effort may get postponed for a longer duration. Hence, the age of a defect in a way represents the complexity of the defect fix needed. Given the complexity and time involved in fixing those defects, they need to be tracked closely else they may get postponed close to release which may even delay the release. A method to track such defects is called *age analysis of outstanding defects*.

To perform this analysis, the time duration from the filing of outstanding defects to the current period is calculated and plotted every week for each criticality of defects in stacked area graph. See Figure 17.15. This graph is useful in finding out whether the defects are fixed as soon as they arrive and to ensure that long pending defects are given adequate priority. The defect fixing rate discussed earlier talks only about numbers, but age analysis talks about their age. The purpose of this metric and the corresponding chart is to identify those defects—especially the high-priority ones—that are waiting for a long time to be fixed.

Figure 17.15

Age analysis of outstanding defects.

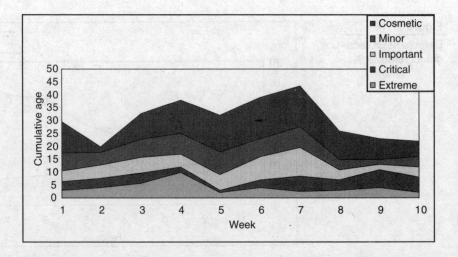

From the above chart, the following few observations can be made.

1. The age of extreme defects were increasing in week 4.

2. The age of cosmetic defects were not in control from week 3 to week 7.

3. The cumulative age of defects were in control starting from week 8 and in week 2.

17.5.2.4 Introduced and reopened defects trend When adding new code or modifying the code to provide a defect fix, something that was working earlier may stop working. This is called an *introduced* defect. These defects are those injected in to the code while fixing the defects or while trying to provide an enhancement to the product. This means that those defects were not in the code before and functionalities corresponding to those were working fine.

Sometimes, a fix that is provided in the code may not have fixed the problem completely or some other modification may have reproduced a defect that was fixed earlier. This is called a *reopened* defect. Hence, reopened defects are defects for which defects fixes provided do not work properly or a particular defect that was fixed that reappears. A reopened defect can also occur if the defect fix was provided without understanding all the reasons that produced the defect in the first place. This is called a *partial fix* of a defect.

All the situations mentioned above call for code discipline and proper review mechanisms when adding and modifying any code for the purpose of proving additional functionality or for providing defect fixes. Such a discipline optimizes the testing effort and helps in arriving at regression test methodology discussed in Chapter 8. Too many introduced and reopened defects may mean additional defect fixing and testing cycles. Therefore, these metrics need to be collected and analyzed periodically. The introduced and reopened defects trend with sample data is plotted in Figure 17.16.

Figure 17.16

Introduced and reopened defects.

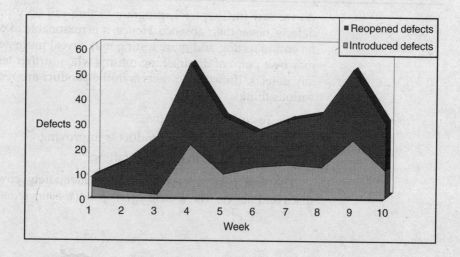

Testing is not meant to find the same defects again; release readiness should consider the quality of defect fixes.

From the above chart, the following observations can be made.

1. Reopened defects were at a high level from week 4. (Thickness of area graph corresponding to reopened defects suggests this in the above chart.)

2. After week 3, introduced defects were at a high level, with more defects observed in week 4 and week 9.

3. The combined data of reopened and introduced defects from week 9 and week 10 suggests the product is not ready for release and also suggests the code is not stable because there is no declining trend. In such a case, the development team should examine the code changes made during the week and get to the root causes of the trend. Doing such an analysis at more frequent intervals enables easier identification of the problem areas.

17.6   PRODUCTIVITY METRICS

Productivity metrics combine several measurements and parameters with effort spent on the product. They help in finding out the capability of the team as well as for other purposes, such as

1. Estimating for the new release.
2. Finding out how well the team is progressing, understanding the reasons for (both positive and negative) variations in results.
3. Estimating the number of defects that can be found.
4. Estimating release date and quality.
5. Estimating the cost involved in the release.

17.6.1   Defects per 100 Hours of Testing

As we saw in Chapter 1, program testing can only prove the presence of defects, never their absence. Hence, it is reasonable to conclude that there is no end to testing and more testing may reveal more new defects. But there may be a point of diminishing returns when further testing may not reveal any defects. If incoming defects in the product are reducing, it may mean various things.

1. Testing is not effective.
2. The quality of the product is improving.
3. Effort spent in testing is falling.

The first two aspects have been adequately covered in the metrics discussed above. The metric *defects per 100 hours of testing* covers the third point and normalizes the number of defects found in the product with respect to the effort spent. It is calculated as given below:

Defects per 100 hours of testing = (Total defects found in the product for a period/Total hours spent to get those defects) * 100

Effort plays an important role in judging quality. The charts in Figure 17.17 explain this role with sample data plotted using the above formula.

Both the charts use the same defect data as that of defect classification trend in Figure 17.17 with only difference in effort spent. In (i), it is assumed that constant effort is spent in all the weeks. The chart produced a bell curve, indicating readiness for the release.

However, in real life, the above assumption may not be true and effort is not spent equally on testing week by week. Sometimes, the charts and analysis can be misleading if the effort spent towards the end of the release reduces and may mean that the downward trend in defect arrival is because of less focus on testing, not because of improved quality. In (ii), it is assumed that 15 hours are spent in weeks 9 and 10 and 120 hours in all other weeks. This assumption, which could mean reality too, actually suggests that the quality of the product has fallen and more defects were found by investing less effort in testing for weeks 9 and 10. This example in (ii) clearly shows that the product is not ready for release at all.

It may be misleading to judge the quality of a product without looking at effort because a downward trend shown in (i) assumes that effort spent is equal across all weeks. This chart provides the insight—where people were pulled out of testing or less number of people were available for testing and that is making the defect count come down. Defects per 100 hours of testing provides this important perspective, to make the right decision for the release.

> Normalizing the defects with effort spent indicates another perspective for release quality.

Figure 17.17

Defect classification trend.

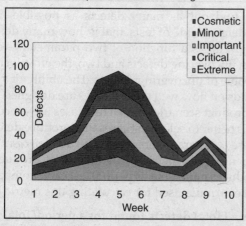

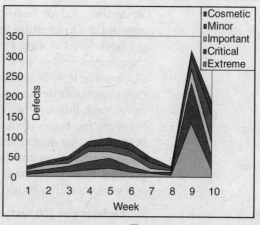

(i)   (ii)

17.6.2   Test Cases Executed per 100 Hours of Testing

The number of test cases executed by the test team for a particular duration depends on team productivity and quality of product. The team productivity has to be calculated accurately so that it can be tracked for the current release and be used to estimate the next release of the product. If the quality of the product is good, more test cases can be executed, as there may not be defects blocking the tests. Also, there may be few defects and the effort required in filing, reproducing, and analyzing defects could be minimized. Hence, test cases executed per 100 hours of testing helps in tracking productivity and also in judging the product quality. It is calculated using the formula

Test cases executed per 100 hours of testing = (Total test cases executed for a period/Total hours spent in test execution) * 100

17.6.3   Test Cases Developed per 100 Hours of Testing

Both manual execution of test cases and automating test cases require estimating and tracking of productivity numbers. In a product scenario, not all test cases are written afresh for every release. New test cases are added to address new functionality and for testing features that were not tested earlier. Existing test cases are modified to reflect changes in the product. Some test cases are deleted if they are no longer useful or if corresponding features are removed from the product. Hence the formula for test cases developed uses the count corresponding to added/modified and deleted test cases.

Test cases developed per 100 hours of testing = (Total test cases developed for a period/Total hours spent in test case development) * 100

17.6.4   Defects per 100 Test Cases

Since the goal of testing is find out as many defects as possible, it is appropriate to measure the "defect yield" of tests, that is, how many defects get uncovered during testing. This is a function of two parameters—one, the effectiveness of the tests in uncovering defects and two, the effectiveness of choosing tests that are capable of uncovering defects. The ability of a test case to uncover defects depends on how well the test cases are designed and developed. But, in a typical product scenario, not all test cases are executed for every test cycle. Hence, it is better to select test cases that produce defects. A measure that quantifies these two parameters is *defect per 100 test cases*. Yet another parameter that influences this metric is the quality of product. If product quality is poor, it produces more defects per 100 test cases compared to a good quality product. The formula used for calculating this metric is

Defects per 100 test cases = (Total defects found for a period/Total test cases executed for the same period) * 100

17.6.5 Defects per 100 Failed Test Cases

Defects per 100 failed test cases is a good measure to find out how granular the test cases are. It indicates

1. How many test cases need to be executed when a defect is fixed;
2. What defects need to be fixed so that an acceptable number of test cases reach the pass state; and
3. How the fail rate of test cases and defects affect each other for release readiness analysis.

Defects per 100 failed test cases = (Total defects found for a period/ Total test cases failed due to those defects) * 100

All the productivity metrics discussed in this section except defect per 100 hours of testing are plotted together with sample data in Figure 17.18.

The following observations can be made by looking at the above chart.

1. Defects per 100 test cases showing a downward trend suggests product readiness for release.
2. Test cases executed per 100 hours on upward trend suggests improved productivity and product quality (Week 3 data needs analysis).
3. Test cases developed per 100 hours showing a slight upward movement suggests improved productivity (Week 3 needs analysis).
4. Defects per 100 failed test cases in a band of 80–90 suggests equal number of test cases to be verified when defects are fixed. It also suggests that the test case pass rate will improve when defects are fixed.

Figure 17.18

Productivity metrics.

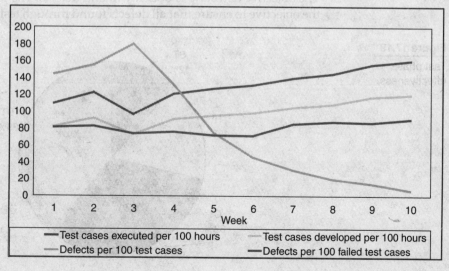

Test cases executed per 100 hours ——
Test cases developed per 100 hours
—— Defects per 100 test cases
—— Defects per 100 failed test cases

17.6.6   Test Phase Effectiveness

In Chapter 1, Principles of Testing, we saw that testing is not the job of testers alone. Developers perform unit testing and there could be multiple testing teams performing component, integration, and system testing phases. The idea of testing is to find defects early in the cycle and in the early phases of testing. As testing is performed by various teams with the objective of finding defects early at various phases, a metric is needed to compare the defects filed by each of the phases in testing. The defects found in various phases such as unit testing (UT), component testing (CT), integration testing (IT), and system testing (ST) are plotted and analyzed. See Figure 17.19.

In the above chart, the total defects found by each test phase is plotted. The following few observations can be made.

1. A good proportion of defects were found in the early phases of testing (UT and CT).

2. Product quality improved from phase to phase (shown by less percent of defects found in the later test phases—IT and ST).

Extending this data, some projections on post-release defects can be arrived at. CT found 32% of defects and IT found 17% of defects. This is approximately a 45% reduction in the number of defects. Similarly, approximately 35% reduction in the number of defects was found going from IT to ST. A post release can now assume 35% reduction in the number of defects which amounts to 7.5% of the total defects. A conservative estimate thus indicates that close to 7.5% of total defects will be found by customers. This may not be an accurate estimate but can be used for staffing and planning of support activities.

17.6.7   Closed Defect Distribution

The objective of testing is not only to find defects. The testing team also has the objective to ensure that all defects found through testing are fixed so that

Figure 17.19
Test phase
effectiveness.

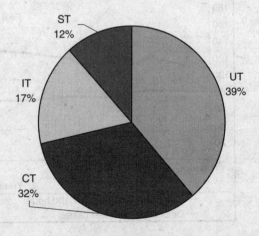

Figure 17.20

Closed defect distribution.

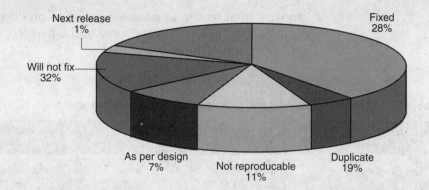

the customer gets the benefit of testing and the product quality improves. To ensure that most of the defects are fixed, the testing team has to track the defects and analyze how they are closed. The *closed defect distribution* helps in this analysis. See Figure 17.20.

From the above chart, the following observations can be made.

1. Only 28% of the defects found by test team were fixed in the product. This suggests that product quality needs improvement before release.

2. Of the defects filed 19% were duplicates. It suggests that the test team needs to update itself on existing defects before new defects are filed.

3. Non-reproducible defects amounted to 11%. This means that the product has some random defects or the defects are not provided with reproducible test cases. This area needs further analysis.

4. Close to 40% of defects were not fixed for reasons "as per design," "will not fix," and "next release." These defects may impact the customers. They need further discussion and defect fixes need to be provided to improve release quality.

17.7 RELEASE METRICS

We discussed several metrics and how they can be used to determine whether the product is ready for release. The decision to release a product would need to consider several perspectives and several metrics. All the metrics that were discussed in the previous sections need to be considered in totality for making the release decision. The purpose of this section is to provide certain guidelines that will assist in making this decision. These are only set of guidelines and the exact number and nature of criteria can vary from release to release, product to product, and organization to organization. Table 17.5 gives some of the perspectives and some sample guidelines needed for release analysis.

Table 17.5   Some perspectives and sample guidelines for release analysis.

Metric	Perspectives to be considered	Guidelines
Test cases executed	Execution % Pass %	• All 100% of test cases to be executed • Test cases passed should be minimum 98%
Effort distribution	Adequate effort has been spent on all phases	• 15–20% effort spent each on requirements, design, and testing phases
Defect find rate	Defect trend	• Defect arrival trend showing bell curve • Incoming defects close to zero in the last week
Defect fix rate	Defect fix trend	• Defect fixing trend matching arrival trend
Outstanding defects trend	Outstanding defects	• Outstanding defects trend showing "downward" trend • Close to zero outstanding defects in the last few weeks prior to release
Priority outstanding defects trend	High-priority defects	• Close to zero high-priority defects in the last few weeks prior to release
Weighted defects trend	High-priority defects as well as high number of low-priority defects	• Weighted defects trend showing "bell curve" • Close to zero weighted defects in the last few weeks prior to release
Defect density and defect removal rate	Defects/KLOC Defect removal %	• Defects/KLOC less than 7 • Defects/KLOC less than last release • Defect removal percentage is 50% more • Defect removal percentage better than last release
Age analysis of outstanding defects	Age of defects	• Age of defects showing downward trend
Introduced and reopened defects	Quality of defect fix Same defects reappearing again	• Combined number of outstanding and reopened defects showing downward trend • Introduced and reopened defects are less than 5% of defect arrival rate
Defects per 100 hours of testing	Whether defect arrival is proportional to effort spent	• Defects per 100 hours of testing should be less than 5 • Defects per 100 hours of testing trend showing downward trend

Metric	Perspectives to be considered	Guidelines
Test cases executed per 100 hours of testing	Whether improved quality in product allowing more test cases being executed Whether test cases executed is proportional to effort spent	• Test cases executed showing an upward trend
Test phase effectiveness	Defects found in each of the test phases	• Very low percentage of defects found in system and acceptance test phase (say less than 12%) • A distribution of defects and reduction in defects % compared to next test phase • A distribution of UT = 50%, CT = 30%, IT = 15% and ST = 5% would be ideal
Closed defects distribution	Whether good proportion of defects found by testing are fixed	• At least 70% of closed defects are fixed • Non-reproducible defects are less than 5% • Defects moved to next release should be less than 10%

17.8   SUMMARY

The metrics defined in this chapter provide different perspectives and are complementary to each other. Hence, all these metrics have to be analyzed in totality, not any of them in isolation. Also, not all metrics may be equally significant in all situations.

Management commitment and a culture for promoting the capture and analysis of metrics are important aspects for the success of the metrics program in an organization. There is a perception that if project management experience is available in an organization, then metrics are not needed. One may hear statements like "I trust my gut feeling, why do I need metrics?" The point is that in addition to validating the gut feeling, metrics provide several new perspectives that may be very difficult even for experienced project managers to visualize. There are several other perceptions on metrics that can be addressed only if metrics are part of the habit and culture in an organization.

Metrics are meant only for process improvement, project management, and to assess and improve product quality. The metrics and productivity numbers generated for the purpose of metrics should never be used to evaluate the performance of the team and individuals in the team. This will defeat the purpose of metrics and the intention behind it.

If the people in an organization do not consistently understand the intention and purpose of metrics, then they may not supply actual, accurate, and realistic data. The analysis of such a wrong data will be misleading.

Even if the data is correct, it can be twisted by the people to suit their own perspectives and needs.

Generating metrics and producing charts are only part of the effort involved in a metrics program. The analysis of metrics and tracking the action items to closure are time-consuming and difficult activities. When metrics are generated but if there is a tendency of ignoring the results and if the team goes by the so-called gut feeling to release the product, then it is as good as not having any metrics at all.

Automating data collection and producing the charts automatically can reduce the effort involved in metrics. However, analysis of metrics and taking actions still remains manual activities since analysis needs human intelligence and effort. Assigning the right people in the organization to analyze the metrics results and ensuring that the right follow through actions take place in a timely fashion will help build the credibility of a metrics program and increase the effectiveness of the metrics in an organization.

REFERENCES

Metrics & Measurements are discussed in several books and articles. [KARL-E] is a place to go to understand the basics of metrics and to create the culture of metrics creation. This place has several metrics that are defined for people performing various roles.

PROBLEMS AND EXERCISES

1. What is the difference between effort and schedule?
2. What are the steps involved in a metrics program. Briefly explain each step.
3. What are the key benefits in using metrics in product development and testing?
4. If there is a negative variance in effort and schedule, what does it signify?
5. What is the additional value of plotting weighted defects? In what way does it provide an additional perspective than the defect classification trend?
6. List and discuss the metrics that can be used for defect prevention and how?
7. How do you calculate defect density and defect removal rate? Discuss ways to improve these rates for a better quality product?
8. What are the insights and quality factors that are to be considered for a product release? Please explain few guidelines on how those quality factors can be plotted and analyzed in the form of metrics.

Illustrations

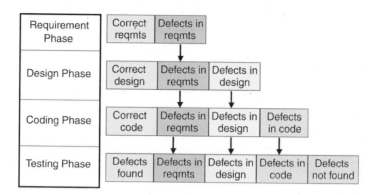

Figure 1.2

How defects from early phases add to the costs. (The black and white figure is available on page 10.)

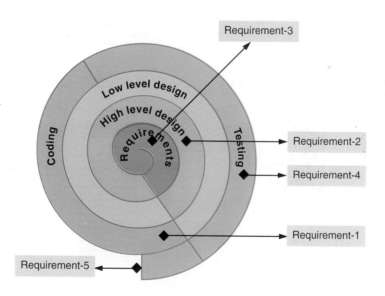

Figure 2.3

Spiral model. (The black and white figure is available on page 37.)

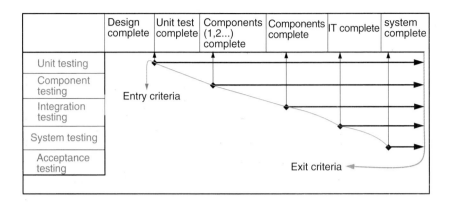

Figure 2.6

Modified V model. (The black and white figure is available on page 41.)

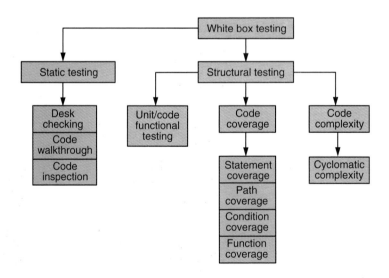

Figure 3.1

Classification of white box testing. (The black and white figure is available on page 48.)

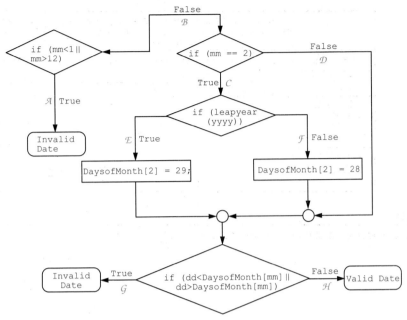

Figure 3.2

Flowchart for a date validation routine. (The black and white figure is available on page 60.)

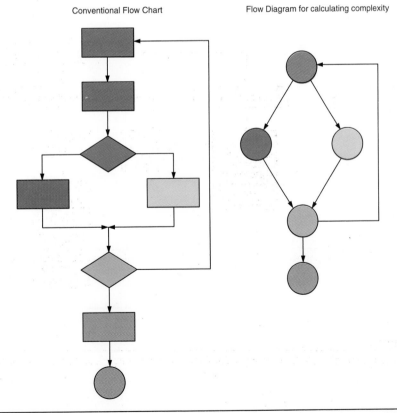

Conventional Flow Chart   Flow Diagram for calculating complexity

Figure 3.4

Converting a conventional flowchart to a flow graph. (The black and white figure is available on page 65.)

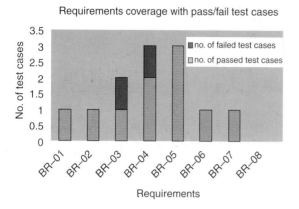
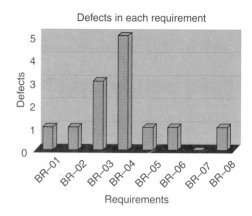

Figure 4.1

Graphical representation of test case results. (The black and white figure is available on page 82.)

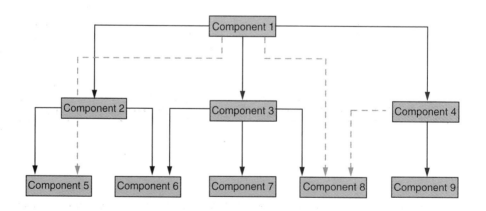

Figure 5.1

A set of modules and interfaces. (The black and white figure is available on page 110.)

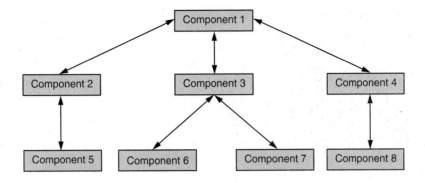

Figure 5.2

Example of top down integrations. (The black and white figure is available on page 111.)

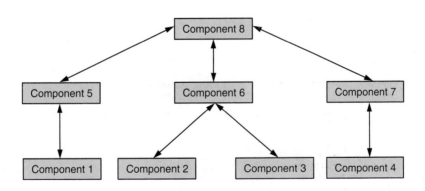

Note: *Double arrow in the above picture denotes both the logical flow of components and integration approach. Logic flow is from top to bottom, and integration path is from bottom to up.*

Figure 5.3

Example of bottom up integration. Arrows pointing down depict logic flow; arrows pointing up indicate integration paths. (The black and white figure is available on page 113.)

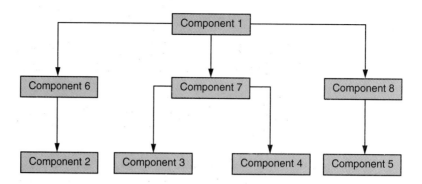

Figure 5.4

Bi-directional integration. (The black and white figure is available on page 115.)

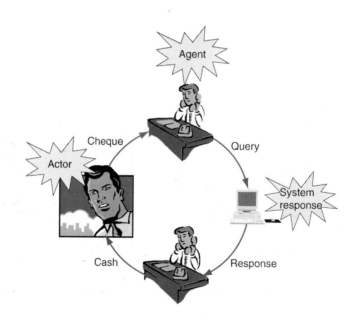

Figure 5.5

Example of use case scenario in a bank. (The black and white figure is available on page 120.)

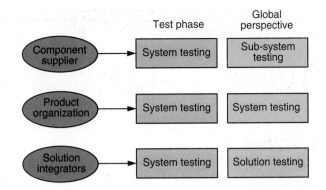

Figure 6.1

Different perspectives of system testing. (The black and white figure is available on page 129.)

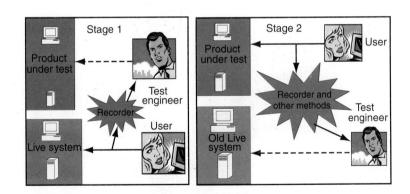

Figure 6.2

Stages of deployment testing. (The black and white figure is available on page 137.)

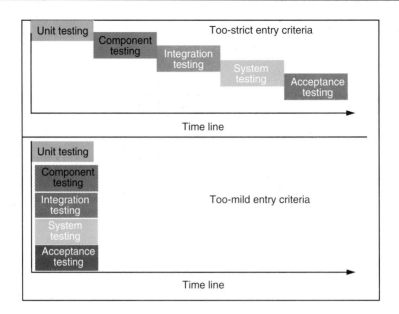

Figure 6.9

Relationship of entry criteria to time lines. (The black and white figure is available on page 163.)

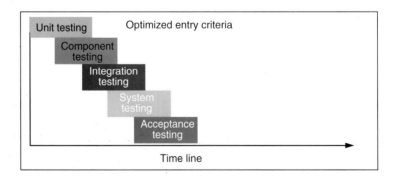

Figure 6.10

Entry criteria to balance parallelism with quality. (The black and white figure is available on page 163.)

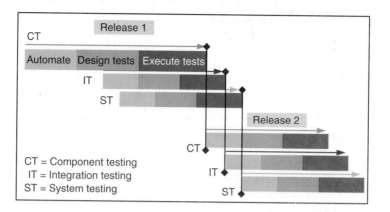

Figure 6.11

Exploiting parallelism across test phases to work on multiple releases simultaneously. (The black and white figure is available on page 165.)

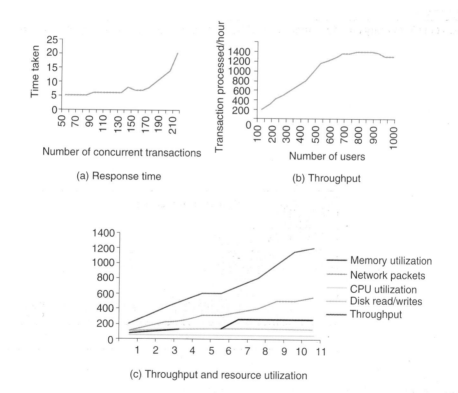

(c) Throughput and resource utilization

Figure 7.3

(a) Response time; (b) throughput; (c) throughput and resource utilization. (The black and white figure is available on page 179.)

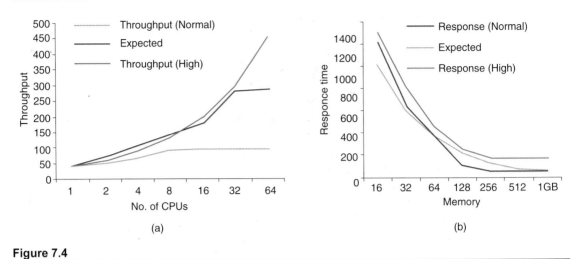

Figure 7.4

(a) Throughput; (b) response time. (The black and white figure is available on page 184.)

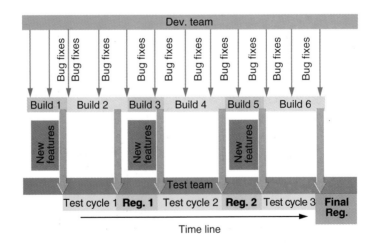

Figure 8.1

Regression testing—types. (The black and white figure is available on page 196.)

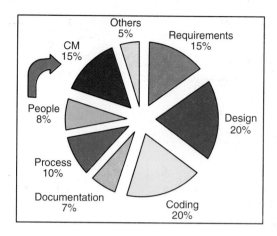

Figure 8.3

CM defects. (The black and white figure is available on page 199.)

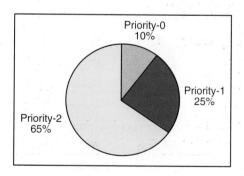

Figure 8.4

Classification of test cases—An example. (The black and white figure is available on page 201.)

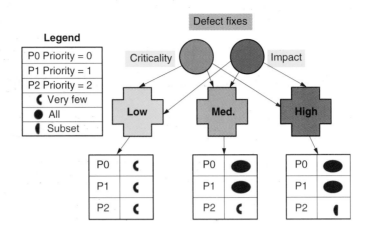

Figure 8.5

Methodology for selection of test cases. (The black and white figure is available on page 202.)

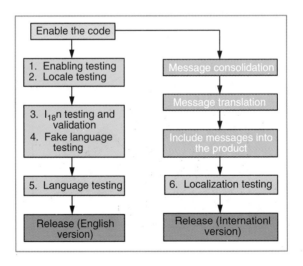

Figure 9.1

Major activities in internationalization testing. (The black and white figure is available on page 215.)

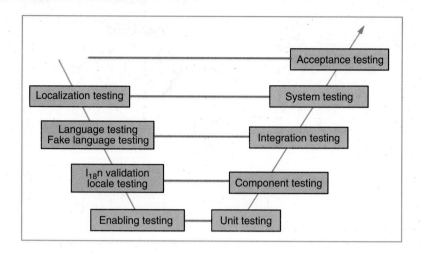

Figure 9.2

Phases of SDLC V model related to internationalization activities. (The black and white figure is available on page 216.)

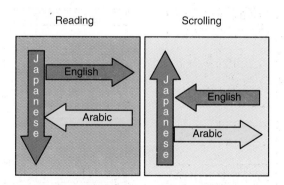

Figure 9.3

Reading and scrolling direction. (The black and white figure is available on page 218.)

Figure 9.4

IME soft keyboard for Japanese. (The black and white figure is available on page 220.)

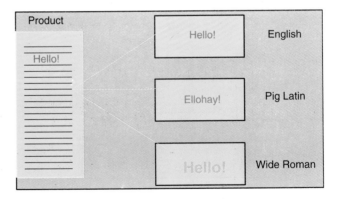

Figure 9.5

Fake language testing. (The black and white figure is available on page 221.)

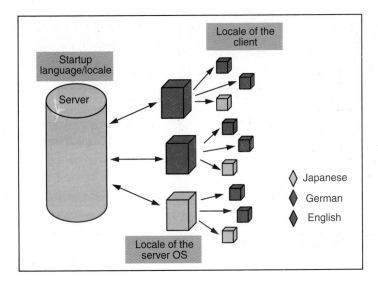

Figure 9.6

Language testing and locale combinations that have to be tested in a client-server architecture. (The black and white figure is available on page 223.)

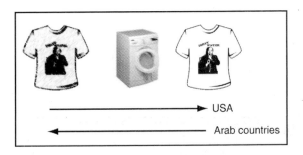

Figure 9.7

Difference in read directions. (The black and white figure is available on page 224.)

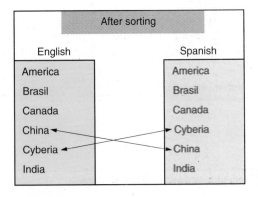

Figure 9.8

Sort order in English and Spanish. (The black and white figure is available on page 225.)

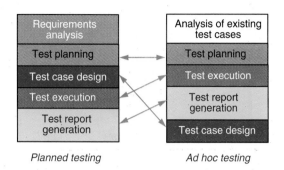

Planned testing   *Ad hoc testing*

Figure 10.1

Ad hoc testing versus planned testing. (The black and white figure is available on page 230.)

	Task Name	Duration	Start	Finish	2/13	2/20	2/27	3/5	3/12	3/19	3/26	4/2
1	⊟ **Test schedule for release**	**33 days**	**Tue 2/22/00**	**Thu 4/6/00**								
2	Test plan	2 days	Tue 2/22/00	Wed 2/23/00								
3	Test strategy	2 days	Tue 2/22/00	Wed 2/23/00								
4	Developing test cases	3 days	Thu 2/24/00	Mon 2/28/00								
5	Review of test cases	1 day	Tue 2/29/00	Tue 2/29/00								
6	Performance benchmark plan	2 days	Wed 3/1/00	Thu 3/2/00								
7	Unit testing	4 days	Fri 3/3/00	Wed 3/8/00								
8	Integration testing	3 days	Thu 3/9/00	Mon 3/13/00								
9	Buddy testing	2 days	Tue 3/14/00	Wed 3/15/00								
10	System testing	4 days	Thu 3/16/00	Tue 3/21/00								
11	Regression testing	3 days	Wed 3/22/00	Fri 3/24/00								
12	Performance Test 1	3 days	Mon 3/27/00	Wed 3/29/00								
13	Performance Test 2	2 days	Thu 3/30/00	Fri 3/31/00								
14	Documentation and Reports	2 days	Mon 4/3/00	Tue 4/4/00								
15	User acceptance test	1 day	Wed 4/5/00	Wed 4/5/00								
16	**Release**	1 day	Thu 4/6/00	Thu 4/6/00								

(March column spans 2/27–3/26; April column covers 4/2)

Figure 15.1

Gantt chart. (The black and white figure is available on page 361.)

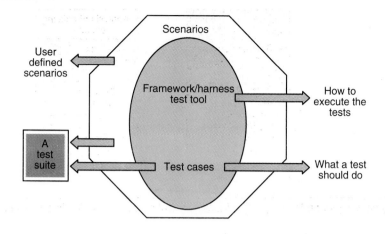

Figure 16.1

Framework for test automation. (The black and white figure is available on page 392.)

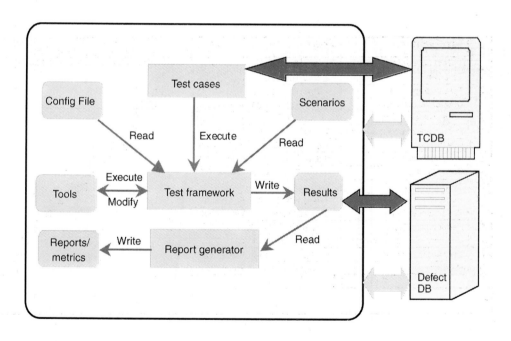

Figure 16.2

Components of test automation. (The black and white figure is available on page 397.)

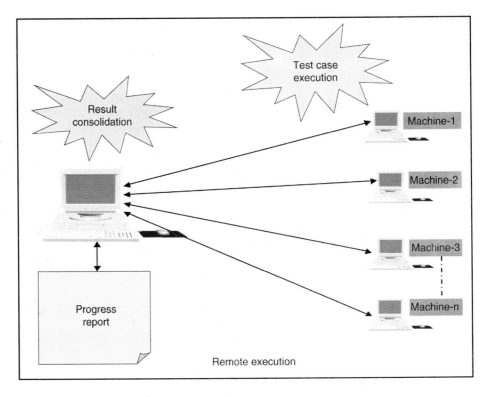

Figure 16.3

Role of test console and multiple execution module. (The black and white figure is available on page 406.)

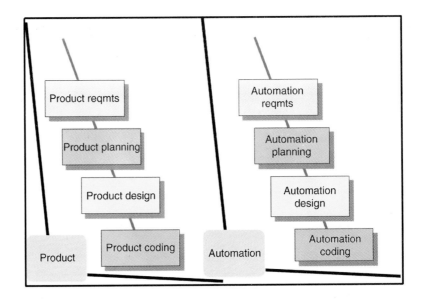

Figure 16.4

Similiarities between product development and automation. (The black and white figure is available on page 409.)

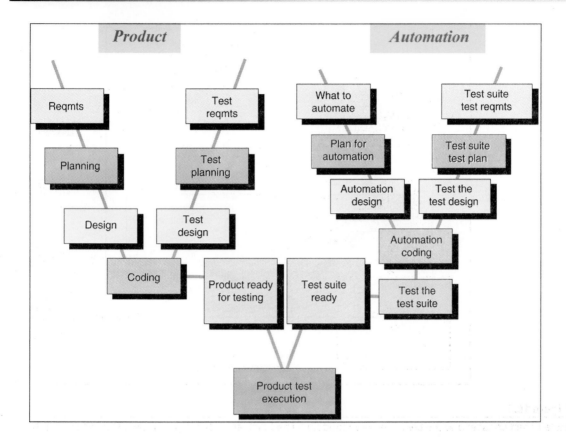

Figure 16.5

W model: Phases involved in automation. (The black and white figure is available on page 410.)

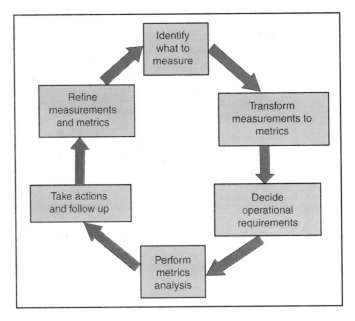

Figure 17.1

Setps in a metrics program. (The black and white figure is available on page 422.)

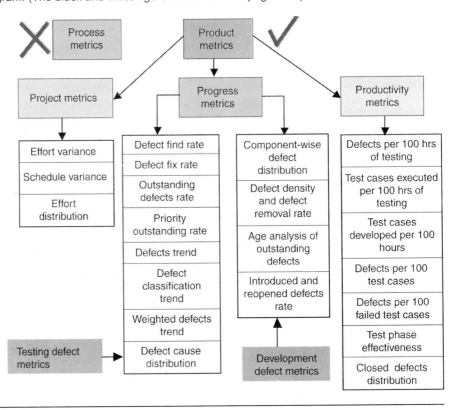

Figure 17.2

Types of metrics. (The black and white figure is available on page 428.)

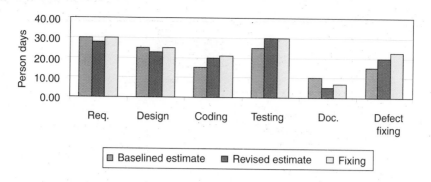

Figure 17.3

Phase-wire effort variation. (The black and white figure is available on page 429.)

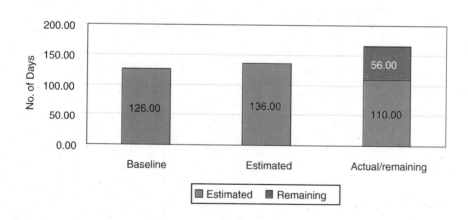

Figure 17.4

Schedule variance. (The black and white figure is available on page 431.)

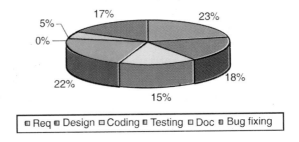

Figure 17.5

Actual effort distribution. (The black and white figure is available on page 433.)

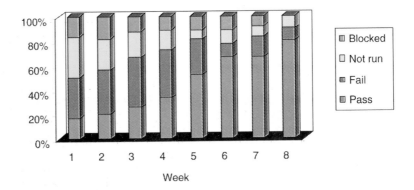

Figure 17.6

Progress of test case execution. (The black and white figure is available on page 434.)

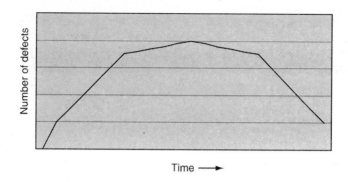

Figure 17.7

Typical pattern for finding defects in a product. (The black and white figure is available on page 436.)

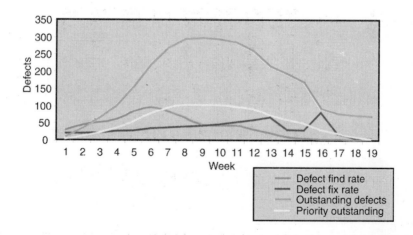

Figure 17.8

Defect trend. (The black and white figure is available on page 438.)

Table 5.1　Order of testing interfaces for the example in Figure 5.2. (The black and white format is available on page 111.)

Step	Interfaces tested
1	1–2
2	1–3
3	1–4
4	1–2–5
5	1–3–6
6	1–3–6–(3–7)
7	(1–2–5)–(1–3–6–(3–7))
8	1–4–8
9	(1–2–5)–(1–3–6–(3–7))–(1–4–8)

Table 5.2　Order of interfaces tested using bottom up integration for Figure 5.3. (The black and white format is available on page 113.)

Step	Interfaces tested
1	1–5
2	2–6, 3–6
3	2–6–(3–6)
4	4–7
5	1–5–8
6	2–6–(3–6)–8
7	4–7–8
8	(1–5–8)–(2–6–(3–6)–8)–(4–7–8)

Table 5.3　Steps for integration using sandwich testing. (The black and white format is available on page 115.)

Step	Interfaces tested
1	6–2
2	7–3–4
3	8–5
4	(1–6–2)–(1–7–3–4)–(1–8–5)

REFERENCES AND BIBLIOGRAPHY

ALBE-79	Albrecht A.J., *Measuring Application Development Productivity*, Proc IBM Application Development Symposium, October 1979, pp. 83–92.
ALBE-83	Albrecht A.J., and Gaffney J.E. Jr., *Software Function, Source Lines of Code and Development Effort Prediction: A Software Science Validation*, IEEE Transactions on Software Engineering, SE-9, pp. 639–648 (1983).
BACH-2003	James Bach, *Exploratory Testing Explained*, http://satisfice.com (2003).
BCS-2001	British Computer Society, *BCS SIGIST Standard for Software Component Testing*, Draft 3.4, April (2001).
BEIZ-90	Boris Beizer, *Software Testing Technique, 2nd edition*, International Thomson Press, New York (1990).
BIND-2000	Robert Binder, *Testing Object-Oriented Systems: Models Patterns and Tools*, Addison Wesley (2000).
BOEH-81	B. Boehm, *Software Engineering Economics*, Prentice Hall (1981).
BOEH-88	B. Boehm, *A spiral model of software development and enhancement*, IEEE Computer, 1988, Vol. 21, No. 5, pp. 61–72.
BOOC-94	Grady Booch, *Object Oriented Analysis and Design With Applications*, Addison Wesley (1994).
BOOC-99	Grady Booch, Ivar Jacobson and James Rumbaugh, *The Unified Development Process*, Pearson Education (1999).
BROO-75	F.P. Brooks, *The Mythical Man Month*, Addison Wesley (1975).
BURN-2004	Ilene Burnstein, *Practical Software Testing*, Springer (2004).
CMMI-2002	Capability Maturity Model Integration (CMMI), Version 1.1, CMU/SEI-2002-TR-012.
COVE-89	Stephen Covey, *The Seven Habits of Highly Effecive People*, Fine cide, 1989.
CROS-80	Philip. B. Crosby., *Quality is Free: The Art of Making Quality Certain*, Mentor Book (1980).
DEMA-87	Tom DeMarco and Timothy Lister, *Peopleware—Productive Projects and Teams*, Dorset House Publishing Company, New York (1987).
DEMI-86	W.E. Deming., *Out of the Crisis*, MIT Center for Advanced Engineering Study (1986).
DIJK-72	Edsger W. Dijkstra: *The Humble Programmer*, ACM Turing Lecture, 1972.
FAGA-76	Fagan., M.E., Design and *Code Inspections to Reduce Errors in Program Development*, IBM Systems Journal. Vol 15, No 3 (1976).
FAIR-97	Richard. E. Fairley and Richard. H. Thayer, *Work breakdown structure, In: Software Engineering Project Management*, IEEE Computer Society (1997).
GOOD-75	Goodenough, J.B., Gerhart, S.L., *Towards a Theory for Test Data Selection*, IEEE Transactions on Software Engineering, pp. 156–173 (1975).
GRAD-97	Robert Grady, *Successful Software Process Improvement*, Prentice Hall, 1997.
GRAH-94	Ian Graham, *Object Oriented Methods, 2nd Ed.*, Addison Wesley (1994).
HUMP-86	Watts Humphrey, *Managing the Software Process*, Addison Wesley (1990).
IEEE-1012	*IEEE Standard for Software Verification and Validation*, IEEE Std 1012–1998.
IEEE-1059	*IEEE Guide for Software Verification and Validation Plans*, IEEE Std 1059–1993.

IEEE-1994	*IEEE standards collection, Software Engineering* (1994).
IEEE-2001	*IEEE Software March/April* 2001—*Special Issue on Global Software Development.*
IEEE-829	*IEEE Standard for Software Test Document IEEE Std* 829–1998.
IFPU-94	*Function Point Counting Practices Manual*, Release 4.0., IFPUG., 1994.
KANE-2001	Cem Kaner, James Bach and Bret Pettichord, *Lessons Learned in Software Testing*, Wiley (2001).
KARL-E	Karl E. Wiegers, *Software Metrics Primer*, www.processimpact.com.
MARI-2001	Brian Marics, *Pair Testing*, http://www.testing.com, (2001).
MCCA-76	Thomas J. MCabe, *A Complexity Measure*, IEEE Transactions on Software Engineering, pp. 101–111 December, (1976).
MYER-79	Glenford Myers., *The Art of Software Testing*, Wiley (1979).
NIST-1	NIST Special publication 500–235, *Structured Testing (A Testing Methodology Using Cyclomatic Complexity Metric).*
PMI-2004	*Guide to Project Management Book of Knowledge, 3rd Ed.*, Project Management Institute (2004).
PRES-97	Roger Pressman: *Software Engineering—A Practitioner's Approach*, 4th Ed., McGraw Hill (1997).
RAME-2002	Gopalaswamy Ramesh, *Managing Global Software Projects*, Tata McGraw Hill (2002).
ROYC-70	W. W. Royce, *"Managing the Development of Large Software Systems"*, Proceedings of IEEE WESCON, August 1970.
SHNE-97	Ben Shneiderman, *Designing the User Interface—Strategies for Effective Human-Computer Interaction*, Addison Wesley (1997).
SRINI-2003	Srinivasan Desikan, *Building an Effective Test Organization*, S|E|A Software Journal, June (2003).
SRINI-2003A	Srinivasan Desikan, *A Test Methodology for Effective Regression Testing*, www.stickyminds.com (2003).
TET	*Test Environment Toolkit*, http://tetworks.opengroup.org.
UMES-2002	Umesh M.S. and Srinivasan Desikan, *Validating Mission Critical Server Software for Reliability*, February (2002).
UNI-2005	www.unicode.org *What is Unicode?* (2005).
UNI-2005A	www.Unicde.org/glossary, *Glossary of Terms* (2005).
YEWU-2001	Ye Wu, *A Presentation on Integration Testing*, George Mason University (2001).
YOGI-2002	Yogita Sahoo, *Looks Do Matter*, ASIASTAR-2002 conference proceedings (2002).

Web references for Standards

MSXP	Microsoft XP Accessibility Help Document XXX Needs a Full Reference
508	www.access-board.gov/sec508/508standards.htm
W3C	www.w3.org/

Web references for Testing Tools

Mercury	www.mercury.com
Compuware	www.compuware.com
Segue	www.segue.com

Index